The European Casebook Series on Management

Series Editor: Paul Stonham, EAP European School of Management, Oxford

Competing Through Services: Strategy and Implementation, Vandermerwe / Lovelock with Taishoff

European Casebook on Business Alliances, Greenwood

European Casebook on Business Ethics, Harvey / Van Luijk / Steinmann

European Casebook on Human Resource and Change Management, Hiltrop / Sparrow

European Casebook on Industrial and Trade Policy, Cadot / Gabel / Story / Webber

European Casebook on Competing through Information Technology, Jelassi

European Casebook on Cooperative Strategies, Roos

European Casebook on Finance, Stonham / Redhead

European Casebook on Managing Industrial and Business-to-Business Marketing, Jenster IMD

European Casebook on

Industrial and
Trade Policy

European Casebook on

Industrial and Trade Policy

Edited by

Olivier Cadot, H. Landis Gabel, Jonathan Story & Douglas Webber

Prentice Hall

London   New York   Toronto   Sydney   Tokyo   Singapore
Madrid   Mexico City   Munich

First published 1996 by
Prentice Hall Europe
Campus 400, Maylands Avenue
Hemel Hempstead
Hertfordshire, HP2 7EZ
A division of
Simon & Schuster International Group

© Prentice Hall Europe, 1996;
case studies copyright © INSEAD or INSEAD-CEDEP,
Fontainebleau, France, dates as given

Typeset in 10½/12pt Palatino and 10/12pt Times
by Hands Fotoset, Leicester

Printed and bound in Great Britain by
Redwood Books Ltd, Trowbridge, Wiltshire

Library of Congress Cataloging-in-Publication Data

European casebook on industrial and trade policy / edited by Olivier
  . . . [et al.].
      p.   cm.—(The European casebook series on management)
    Includes bibliographical references.   1000732023
    ISBN 0-13-353574-6
    1. Industrial policy—European Union countries—Case studies.
    2. European Union countries—Commercial policy—Case studies.
    I. Cadot, Olivier.   II. Series.
    HD3616.E8E87   1996
    338.94—dc20   95-34219
                                                              CIP

British Library Cataloguing in Publication Data

A catalogue record for this book is available from
The British Library

ISBN 0-13-353574-6

---

1 2 3 4 5   00 99 98 97 96

To our wives: Dominique, Elisa and Heidi,
and children: Alexander, Christina, Etienne, Henry, Josiane,
Mahdiya, Nicholas and Selma

Contents

Series Editorial

The idea of a Series of European Casebooks on Management arose from discussions during the annual case writing competition organized by the European Foundation for Management Development (EFMD) in Brussels. The case writing competition itself was set up to encourage the production of more case studies in management with a specifically European content, to meet the growing demand in European business schools and training programmes of corporations. Begun in 1989, the competition has now established itself as a major focus of interest for case study writers.

However, knowing that many European cases were being produced outside the context of the competition, it was decided to extend the search for cases more widely. The project was taken up by Prentice Hall in 1991, who undertook to publish the Series, and appointed a Series Editor to manage the academic aspects of the collection of volumes.

From the inception of the project, the EAP European School of Management, a *grande école* of the Paris Chamber of Commerce and Industry, agreed to finance the costs of the Series Editor, and Prentice Hall funded secretarial assistance. As well as its financial support, EAP is well positioned to supply an appropriate academic infrastructure to the editorial management of the Series. From its headquarters in Paris, it maintains establishments in Berlin, Madrid and Oxford, and its masters' level students train in three countries. EAP is one of the leaders in European multicultural management education and, of course, a major user of case studies with a European focus in its courses.

Early market research showed a strong and largely unsatisfied demand for case studies in European management at a time when interest in the completion of the Single European Market was at its height. Calls for case study writers and for volume editors met with a good response, and the major fields of management were quickly covered as well as several important specialized areas not originally considered.

There is an increasing number of titles available in this Series of European Casebooks on Management on a wide range of topics including Business Alliances, Business Ethics, Competing Through Services, Cooperative Strategies, Entrepreneurship and New Ventures, Environmental Issues, Finance, Human Resource Management, Managing Industrial and Business-to-Business Marketing, Industrial and Trade Policy, Information Technology, International Business, Leadership, Management in Eastern Europe, Production and Operations Management, Research and Technology Management and Strategy. A full list of current titles is available from the publisher's UK address shown on page iv.

The case studies are intended to draw on the main developments and changes in their respective fields of management in recent years, focusing on managerial issues in corporations trading in or with the European Union. Although the principal concentration is on the non-governmental sector, the experience of governments and governmental agencies is included in some of the volumes to the extent that they affect the corporate sector. In the light of the title of the Series, cases dealing with European cross-border involvements have been given priority in inclusion, but material that relates to national experience or is conceptual or global in nature has been considered relevant if it satisfies the criteria for good cases.

A driving motive for developing the Series of European Casebooks on Management has been the wish to encourage the production of cases with a specifically European dimension. Not only have the regulatory background, institutional framework and behavioural traits of cases developed in the American business schools like Harvard always been barriers to their use in European management education, but the developing European Union has emphasized aspects of corporate development and strategy completely ignored in most American cases. With the build-up of cross-border business activity in Europe have come difficulties in cultural adjustment. The growing legislation of the European Commission in its '1992 programme' has imposed constraints and given freedoms not known in an American context, in such fields as technology, patents, competition, take-overs and mergers, freedom of establishment and workers' rights. There was clearly a need for case studies which took account of the rapid changes occurring in the European Union and which analysed corporations' responses to them. It is recognized in the kind of terminology which is now much more current in management thinking: 'European management', 'Euromanagers' and 'Pan-Europeanization' no longer raise eyebrows even if not everyone believes these are totally valid terms.

In selecting cases for their volumes, the Editors and the Series Editor asked the leading question again and again – what is a good case? It was not sufficient to take the accepted Harvard view. Cases are critically important to teaching at the Harvard Business School, and have been since they were first produced in 1910. For example, in 1986 Benson Shapiro said that 'one must understand the fundamentals of course design, because each case must fit into the rubric of the course' (Benson Shapiro, 1986). Shapiro also said the case writer should 'Ensure the case includes a balanced conflict'. Robert Davies, also of Harvard, wrote (1955) that 'there are two kinds of cases . . . the *issue case* in which the writer poses a particular problem and the reader prepares a recommendation designed to overcome the problem, and an *appraisal case* in which the writer describes a management decision already made and the reader evaluates this decision'. Generally, cases now being written in Europe are less rigid and constrained. They reflect the multifunctional and multicultural aspects of modern European business. They are pedagogical, but less tied to functional disciplines than the Harvard cases described by Shapiro, and this again is probably because the boundaries of the functional disciplines themselves, like marketing and finance, are becoming less distinct. Many of the 'good' points of Harvard case study teaching are nonetheless incorporated into European case writing: the emphasis on complex, real-life situations, the degree of interest aroused, the use of 'springboard cases', and the need for good reporting (Paul Lawrence, 1953).

The essentials of 'good' case writing in European management have been discussed extensively by the judges of the annual case writing competition organized by EFMD. They can be summarized as follows from the main points of a presentation by Robert Collins of IMD Lausanne at the annual conference workshop and prize-giving in Jouy-en-Josas, Paris, in September 1993.

Although writing case studies in management involves an element of opportunistic, investigative journalism, the pedagogical needs of students should be paramount. The case writer should be objective; there is no place for personal opinion or advocacy – the case writer or teacher is neither judge nor jury.

As far as the audience for cases is concerned, the case must be interesting. The setting or topic should be attractive and the case raise compelling issues. A decision-forcing case is more likely to turn students on than a descriptive or expository one – but the snag is that students do not generally like open-ended and vague cases. The case should be transferable – across faculty members, programmes and institutions.

In terms of product quality, the case should exceed audience expectations of both performance and conformance. The length of a case is important – it should give optimal time for reading and analysis, and the quality and quantity of data should be right. Assimilation is made easier when the case focuses on characters or issues, is structured, has internally consistent data, avoids jargon and is written in high-quality prose. It should be remembered that inexperienced students have a low tolerance of ambiguity and of data/information.

Writing a good case involves creating a favourable climate among all the stakeholders in a company. They will not assist if there is not confidence, discretion and cooperation. In a company there are archetypal executives who must all be managed, for example, the 'champion' may steer the casewriter through the company (but only when he or she is on hand); the 'guerilla' will appear to help, but snipe from out of sight; the 'security guard' will consider everything classified and not for discussion. The reality for a casewriter on site in a company is that not everyone will love you.

The teacher can maximize the benefits of a good case. Opportunities for customization and experimentation should always be sought – among different sets of participants, programmes and in-team teaching. A good teacher can exploit the richness of a case and the acuity of the participants.

Clearly, the case method is not the only pedagogical method of teaching management. Charles Croué of the École Supérieure de Commerce de Tours believes it is the most revolutionary, because unlike teacher-centred or self-tutoring methods, it is an active and interactive method.

The method encourages students to organize their work, to exchange different points of view in complex discussions, to find compromise by negotiating, and to improve their skills at oral presentation. They learn to compare different solutions and to synthesize information and decisions. They can observe the relationships between different disciplines of management – like marketing and strategy, and understand the difference between theory and practice. In the case study method they do all this in a situation of reality, solving a real management problem. All of these skills prepare students well for manager status.

The case method has three main distinguishing characteristics which set it aside from other teaching methods. It is *cooperative* – students work in groups, they exchange information, and it improves their communicative abilities. It is *dynamic* – students are stimulated from passivity to effort. It is *democratic* – teachers and students have equal roles; there are no preset solutions, and ideas are freely exchanged.

Finally, the case method is well suited to the changing nature of management and business at the present time. The current environment is moving very quickly, case studies can 'catch' new events and issues as they happen (likewise, they may quickly date). They lend themselves well to performance measurement, as the managerial qualities of the students improve. The current wish for 'action-learning' is satisfied, and cases can be delivered using multiple media like videos and computers.

This volume, *European Casebook on Industrial and Trade Policy*, is edited by four members of the faculty of INSEAD, France, Olivier Cadot, H. Landis Gabel, Jonathan Story and Douglas Webber, and all of the cases are 'classroom-tested' in INSEAD MBA courses.

In line with the European focus of the Casebook Series, the editors have collected (and authored) case studies which have a setting inside the European Union, its industrial sectors and corporations, and its triad partners, Japan and the United States.

The Editors are keen to make the point that, unusually, they are dealing with those conventional concerns of economics, trade and industrial policy, on a case-by-case basis. This means that the two dominant models of economic thought about international trade – classical (Ricardo) and intra-industry trade (Krugman) – are not so much ignored as illustrated in one aspect or another by corporate-, sectoral-, issue-, or policy-based case studies. To some extent, this releases the authors from normative judgements on the events or issues under discussion since we are not measuring any situation against a standard of model value. Instead, the editors urge that, whilst the case studies *may* be of relevance in supporting one or other theoretically based policy, they are much more useful in showing how governmental manipulation of international trade can often be powerless in the face of concerted private business interests. This is the essence of the case study approach to management learning, the building up of a core of practice which itself provides the major lessons to be learned by managers. Policy-makers frequently take a macroeconomic approach to international business issues; it is refreshing to have light thrown on them at the corporate or industry level.

The case studies in this volume are grouped into the major post-War trade concerns of Europe and the international community – the first group deals with international competition, restructuring and protectionism (and inevitably includes the European auto market and steel-making in Europe); the second group deals with trade, industrial policy and technological change (and brings in European aircraft construction, television and telecommunications); and the third group covers privatization, competition policy and social policy (and includes cases dealing with the privatizing of British Airways, as well as the EC's merger and acquisition directive and social policy in Europe).

Since issues of international trade and industry policy are (like the poor) always with us, some of the case studies included in this volume are vintage 1980s. For instance, the Nissan Corporation case written in 1985, is a case study supporting a set of five cases involving Ford of Europe and its early responses to the rapid growth threat of Japanese competition in the European auto market. This story is essential background to any further analysis of Nissan's current (mid-1990s) policy of localizing production in Europe in preference to setting up 'screwdriver' plants. Another case study concerns the evolution of business relationships between Alcatel, the French telecommunications, energy and transport equipment firm, and France-Télécom and the French Government. This case was written in 1994, but concerns two periods in Alcatel's development, one in the 1980s and the other in the 1990s, the first involving acquisition and the second involving internationalization and EC deregulation. Just these two case studies illustrate the long-term nature of industrial and trade policy issues.

This present volume is a welcome addition to the European Casebook on Management Series since it places the case studies in the context of broad and wide-ranging policies and issues. Its particular contribution is to allow policy-makers to focus down on the microeconomic aspects of their concerns, and managers to see the issues which are generated at inter-governmental and international agency level by their actions and operations as they affect market trade and industry. The contribution of the case studies to management learning cannot be overstated.

Paul Stonham, Series Editor
EAP, European School of Management, Oxford

About the Contributors

Olivier Cadot. Assistant Professor of Economics at INSEAD, Olivier Cadot received his PhD in Economics from Princeton University, after a Masters in Economic History from McGill University (Canada). Before joining INSEAD, he was visiting faculty at McGill University and worked for the OECD and the International Monetary Fund. He has been consulting or doing research on industrial policy and international trade issues for the French Government, the European Commission and a think-tank in New Delhi.

Professor Cadot's research, published in European and American journals, currently focuses on international trade issues (such as the liberalization of EU trade with Eastern Europe), on technology policy, and on environmental policy. He has also written on economic-development issues for Third-World countries, such as the international debt crisis of the 1980s.

Landis Gabel. Professor of Economics and Management, Landis Gabel holds a BSc (Engineering), MBA and PhD (Economics) from the University of Pennsylvania and a MSc (Economics) from the London School of Economics. Before coming to INSEAD in 1982, he was on the faculty of the University of Virginia and previously was a manufacturing manager for Honeywell Inc.'s industrial products division. Professor Gabel's research interests are in the area of economics and public policy, and he has published papers in economics, environment, business and legal journals. Professor Gabel is the Otto Fellow of Environment Resource Management and co-directs INSEAD's Centre for the Management of Environmental Resources.

Damien Neven. Damien Neven is Professor of Economics at the Ecoles des Hautes Etudes Commerciales, University of Lausanne. He holds a doctorate in Economics from Nuffield College, Oxford. Before joining the faculty at Lausanne, he taught at INSEAD and the University of Brussels. He is an advisor to the industry directorate (DG III) of the European Commission. His research focuses on the economics of trade and industry. He has recently completed a book (with Paul Seabright) on the economics and politics of merger control in the European Community. His current work deals with the evaluation and control of cartels as well as the evaluation of the consequences for Western Europe of trade liberalization with Eastern Europe.

Jonathan Story. Jonathan Story writes and teaches on European and world politics. Over the past few years, he has focused on the European Union in the world political economy, European monetary union, European diplomacy with respect to Spain, European Monetary Union, 'Social Europe', EC Competition Policy, as well as German unity and investment in Central and Eastern Europe, including Russia. His most recent publications include a book on *European Financial Services* (co-authored with Professor Ingo Walter, forthcoming, Manchester University Press); and *Democratic Spain in the International Context*, of which Professor Story is editor and contributing author (forthcoming, Routledge).

Douglas Webber. Associate Professor of Political Science at INSEAD, Douglas Webber's principal research interests lie in the analysis of German politics, government–business relations in Western Europe and the process of European integration. He is the co-author of two books (including *Hostile Brothers*, Oxford, Clarendon Press, 1990) and has published numerous articles on German and West European politics in social science journals in Germany and Britain. Prior to joining INSEAD he was a research fellow at the universities of Strathclyde and Sussex in Britain and at the Max Planck Institute for Social Research at Cologne in Germany.

Introduction

Industrial and trade policy:
a case-by-case approach

Few areas of economics raise passions as much as international trade. For some, any infringement on *laissez-faire* (and more relevantly *laissez-passer*) is inherently dangerous. For others, international trade is a permanent threat to jobs and national welfare and should be severely restricted to areas where it can do no harm[1]. Yet there are also few areas of economic theory where consensus is so strong among economists. Why is this? Two broad paradigms dominate economic thinking about international trade. The first one is the 'classical' model, in its Ricardian or Heckscher–Ohlin avatar. The second one is the 'intra-industry trade' model, developed to a large extent under the impetus of Paul Krugman. These two models or rather families of models emphasize different aspects of the determinants and effects of international trade; yet they are by no means incompatible. In economic parlance, one would say that they are complements rather than substitutes, as they apply the same reasoning to different contexts rather than offer conflicting explanations for the same thing. The cases presented in this book illustrate a wide range of trading situations; as the relevance of one or the other model of thinking is a matter of context rather than of ideological preferences, it is important to give here a brief summary of the two models.

The classical model is based on a view of the world where countries differ by their endowments of fundamental factors of production – labour, physical

---

[1] A recent French Senate report, for instance, wrote: 'Quality goods produced in cheap-labour countries come back on our markets at prices which defy any competition. But when prices defy any competition, there is no competition left any more! Our enterprises are condemned either to shutting down or relocating production abroad in order to survive. This phenomenon is prevalent throughout the economy and progresses slowly but surely, like an – industrial – fabric that would little by little tear away.' Jean Arthuis, rapp., *Rapport d'information sur l'incidence économique et fiscale des délocalisations hors du territoire national des activités industrielles et de services*, Sénat, rapport # 337, 1993, p. 14. Quote freely translated by the authors.

capital, human capital and natural resources. These differences in factor endowments drive differences in comparative advantage: a country has a comparative advantage in industries which use intensively the factors it has plenty of. This has two major implications. First, every country has a comparative advantage in something, and so will be a natural exporter of that something. Second, and consequently, international trade ensures that goods are produced where they are cheapest to produce, which generates gains from trade to all trading countries. But the 'neo-classical' version of the model, due to Swedish economists Eli Heckscher and Bertil Ohlin, also yields a third result, which is equally important but rather unfortunate: within each country, not everyone will gain from the opening of international trade. For instance, owners of factors of production that are less abundant at home than elsewhere, say, unskilled labour in European countries, will lose to competition from those same factors in partner countries (for instance, unskilled labour in Sri Lanka). As a result, not everyone will favour free trade.

But the basic lesson of the classical model is clear enough: in its purest form, the model suggests that there is no such thing as 'unfair trade practices' (except for the type of anticompetitive behaviour that would be illegal under national legislations): any form of government meddling in international trade hurts the country that is doing it. Therefore, *unilateral* free trade is always best (except only for large countries which can influence world prices to their advantage). In a milder form, the model suggests that the best policies to alter the pattern of international specialization are *supply-side* policies, i.e. policies capable of generating a comparative advantage, such as investment in R&D and education, in infrastructure, and so on. What does this imply in real-life situations? Consider steel, for instance. The countries of the European Union have over the years spent large amounts of taxpayer money to sustain steelmaking. But is steelmaking Europe's comparative advantage? Is smokestack industry the comparative advantage of countries having increasingly stiff environmental regulations? If not, what should yield: the regulations or the activities that prove incompatible with the regulations? What is the cost of sustaining Europe's steelmakers in spite of negative market signals? These are some of the questions that can be raised about steel but also about virtually every declining sector in rich countries. What may perhaps come as a surprise, *Television without Frontiers* is also a case that lends itself to a fascinating discussion about comparative advantage, more precisely about whether the United States is a 'natural exporter' in the cinematographic industry. Did all the talented Europeans who emigrated to Hollywood in the 1930s and '40s shift comparative advantage in favour of the United States? Is an inherently 'exportable' culture the valid basis of a comparative advantage? These are not-so-obvious questions that never fail to fuel a heated class debate about EU policy in the audio-visual industry. But we have also included in Part 1 cases about sectors such as automobiles, where few people would argue that Europeans have a comparative *dis*advantage. Competition in automobiles is mainly between rich countries having roughly the same relative endowments of physical and human capital and labour. Clearly the classical model is going to be of little use here. So what forces are at play?

The nature of competition in industries such as automobiles is best analyzed using the alternative class of models alluded to above: models of intra-industry trade, which explain trade in similar products between countries that are themselves similar in terms of their relative factor endowments. One can broadly distinguish two sub-families of models within this broad class. First, 'reciprocal-dumping' models explain two-way trade in identical products (such as detergents and the like) by oligopolistic competition between firms. The gains from trade then take the form of increased competition, that is to say, lower prices for the consumer. That a major source of gains from international trade derives from the fact that open markets impose competitive discipline on domestic firms is certainly a very intuitive idea, and an idea which one suspects might well turn out to be *the* critical reason why trade is so beneficial. A second family of models stresses two-way trade in roughly similar but differentiated manufactures, such as automobiles. Here the gains from international trade come from economies of scale inducing firms to rationalize production at a transnational level, and from increased product diversity within each category.

Both families of intra-industry trade models, as opposed to the classical model, focus on the effects of imperfect competition. Now whenever competition is imperfect, super-normal profits (or 'rents') appear, and a critical question is who is going to appropriate those rents. We are now in a paradigm that is markedly different from the classical one, as governments may well want to intervene to increase the share of global profits appropriated by domestic firms. Governments may also be convinced that some industries are 'strategic' in the sense that they have technological spillovers to other industries which are not fully reflected in the stock market value of the firms originating those spillovers – machine tools may be a case in point. Furthermore, since trade in these models is between countries that are roughly similar, the pattern of specialization is indeterminate and can be affected permanently by targeted government intervention. Clearly, European thinking about Airbus has been influenced by this line of thought. In fact, the civil aeronautics industry seems to fit all the assumptions of the intra-industry trade models. Yet, is Airbus a model of successful industrial policy? How should success be measured? Answering this question requires a thorough discussion of what the initial objectives were – maximizing technological spillovers or simply selling airplanes at a profit, for instance. The same question applies to European attempts at creating their own high-definition TV technology, except that targeting new and unknown technologies ('picking winners') turns out to be even more difficult than targeting existing American technologies for imitation or marginal improvement.

If imperfect competition is prevalent, certainly competition policy must be a major instrument of government intervention in the economy. But while the broad principles may be clear enough (preventing abuses of dominant positions as well as cartels and price-fixing are propositions that have a general appeal), implementation may be far from simple, especially when privatization gets intermingled with competition policy, as illustrated by the case of British Airways. Even the distinction between a dominant position acquired by merger and its abuse raises interesting questions.

Is economic theory any guide for trade and industrial policy-making? It might look like one can find good theoretical reasons for almost any prescription, depending on one's ideological tastes. There is a little truth in this, and in fact we believe that this is fortunate. No dogma can pretend to be supported by 'The Theory'. What the theory says is a lot more subtle than just 'free trade is always optimal' or 'government intervention can always do better than the market'. It essentially says that in particular circumstances policies exist that could do, on paper at least, better than the market. But those policies when they exist are usually very demanding on information (information on technological spillovers, on the extent of super-normal profits, etc.) and can be easily perverted by private interests or government bureaucracies. So whether or not those policies can be safely followed by public officials with their own interests and rationale is a tricky question that must be solved *case by case*. This is indeed the rationale for approaching trade and industrial policy from a case-based rather than a model-based approach. We have therefore two hopes about what the cases collected in this volume can contribute. On the one hand, we hope that they will clearly illustrate how difficult it is to improve on the market in modern economies. The point here is certainly not to dash any hope on the potential benefits of enlightened trade policy, but rather to suggest some modesty in this regard. On the other hand, we also hope that exposure to these eleven INSEAD cases will encourage managers as well as business school students to think about government action beyond just assuming that all bureaucrats are stupid. Government action has a logic of its own, and businesses that ignore it do so at their own risk.

The cases collected in this volume have been taught over many years in two core courses at INSEAD, International Political Analysis (IPA) and Industrial Policy and International Competitiveness (IPIC). Our thanks go to the many generations of participants in our MBA program whose constant enthusiasm and constructive comments have encouraged us to put this volume together. We also thank the many dedicated and talented research associates who have contributed to the cases: Anthony E. Hall, Pamela Denby, Kathy Burton, John F. Thomas, Mohamed Razeen Sally, Robert Levy, Ethan Schwartz, and Valérie Milhavy who helped in the book's preparation. Finally, we gratefully acknowledge the financial support of INSEAD and CEDEP.

PART 1

International Competition, Restructuring and Protectionism

Cases: Ford of Europe and Local Content Regulations, General Motors Corporation, The Nissan Company, United Kingdom: Industrial Policy toward the Automobile Industry, The European Economic Community

This is a set of five cases in which a principal case about Ford is accompanied by four satellite cases intended for role playing by other actors in the evolving story of protectionism, restructuring, and competition in the European automobile industry. At the time of the case, Ford is contemplating its political response to the rapidly growing threat of Japanese competition in a European market that is unprepared for it. The greatest threat is from a new greenfield Nissan plant in Ford's 'backyard' – the UK. The different cases look at the prospective Japanese foreign direct investment from different perspectives, requiring the reader to map out objectives, strategies, and tactics for each. Local content regulations feature in each, but exactly how they feature is left for the reader to work out.

As with many cases in this volume, the interests of companies, member states in the European Community, and the Community itself as embodied by the Commission, must all be reconciled to develop a clear picture of the industry's future. In analyzing the case, the reader must come to grips with questions of comparative *vs* competitive advantage, the role of international trade compared with that of foreign direct investment, and the role of multinational companies in an integrating world.

Case: The EC–Japan Elements of Consensus

The case provides one example of the formulation of European trade policy. The reader may appreciate that the political process takes place at a number of levels of analysis: the automobile producers, governments, the European Community and markets. At first sight, there was little to suggest that the European governments and manufacturers would ever be able to agree on a common policy different from that agreed on in 1972, dividing the EC national markets between those open to competition from Japanese suppliers and those which imposed quotas on imports, in reference to Article 115 of the Rome Treaty. Yet the EC's '1992' strategy was launched to complete the internal market, but also to strengthen the EC in negotiations on trade and investment with the United States and Japan. This entailed a simultaneous campaign by the Commission to reach an agreement with the Japanese government and corporations, while fostering changes in intra-EC arrangements. In a formal sense, too, the Commission's functions, together with the member states, are to set the EC's agenda, and advance proposals that take into account the different interests at play but that may also be presented in the broader interest of the EC; to act as guardian of the Treaties; to mediate between the varied parties, and then to implement the policy agreed on in the Council of Ministers and with the member states. What were the varied interests at stake? What were the problems involved in negotiating this 'grey area' agreement with the Japanese government? What were the forces at work allowing for a realignment of arrangements among the automobile producers in the EC, and around which formulas were they able to reconcile their differences? And what are the implications for the varied parties of the formal as well as informal agreements and disagreements embodied in 'the element of consensus'?

Case: The European Steel Industry in crisis

This is a 'pure policy' case, in which the problem is to identify, from the perspective of the Commission of the European Communities, the causes of European steel's decline and the proper policy remedies. The reader must first understand the background to the present crisis, namely another crisis that took place in the late 1970s. At that time, European steelmakers suffered from chronic overcapacity and high costs. Ten years and more than thirty billion dollars later, they seem to suffer from the same illnesses all over again. What went wrong with EC policy intervention to help the steel industry? Is all policy intervention in declining sectors doomed to failure? Or are there finer lessons to be learnt from the steel industry's debacle about what governments should do or should not do? The reader must form an opinion about policy intervention in such sectors that goes beyond the mere statement 'let the bureaucrats stay out'.

Cases: Television without Frontiers, (A) and (B)

The two cases are designed to prompt discussion on the markets, business and politics of cultural goods as provided and consumed through television. The case focuses on the directive which was agreed on under the French Presidency in late 1989, and was immediately pounced upon by the US Congress and administration as contravening GATT principles. The economics of the industry have been undergoing rapid changes, undermining the older national television monopolies' hold on markets. There is also a charged political agenda, which different producer or consumer interests seek to fashion at regional, national, European or worldwide levels. The reader has to grapple with the content as well as the process of policy in the complex institutional environment of Europe, as exemplified in the case by the number of private and public organizations involved. Not least, the subject matter touches on central questions of national culture and European identity.

As in the case on the EC–Japan automobile trade agreement where the EC policy process yielded significant *implicit* incentives to participants, the reader is invited to consider what the directive means for the future of producers in the EC. What is at stake for the EC's TV market? Should or could European producers and governments lean to more or less freer trade policies? What is the politics of Television without Frontiers in the light of the procedures under the internal market legislation? What should the US administration, Congress or suppliers do in the light of what is happening in the EC?

Ford of Europe and Local Content Regulations

H. Landis Gabel

In mid-1983, the Management Committee of Ford of Europe (the company's senior decision-making committee) was once again examining the trends, opportunities and threats offered by the European market. The principal threat perceived by management was the growing Japanese presence in Europe. Japanese manufacturers had increased their car sales in Western Europe from 750,000 units in 1979 to almost one million in 1983 and were beginning to establish a manufacturing foothold in Europe. Nissan, for example, was just beginning to produce automobiles in Italy, it would soon increase its production of vehicles for Europe from a Spanish plant, and, most worrisome, the company was expected to announce imminently a decision to proceed with a previously shelved plan to construct a new and very large assembly plant in the United Kingdom. Although Ford competed very successfully against the other European producers – and for the first time had captured the number one European market share position in the second quarter of 1983 – Japanese producers' plants in Europe would constitute a new and severe challenge. What especially worried Ford was the possibility that Nissan's new UK plant would import major automobile components into Europe from Japan, assemble them into finished vehicles, and then claim that the vehicles were European in origin and thus not subject to any existing European–Japanese trade agreements or understandings.

This worry had led Ford executives back in 1981 to consider seriously local content regulations as a way of reducing this risk and helping to stem the growth of the Japanese producers' share of the European market. Local content regulations, most commonly employed by developing countries against multinational firms based

This case was prepared by Anthony E. Hall, Research Associate, under the supervision of H. Landis Gabel, Associate Professor at INSEAD. It is intended to be used as a basis for class discussion rather than to illustrate either effective or ineffective handling of an administrative situation. This case study was developed after discussions with certain Ford personnel but does not necessarily reflect the actual scope or manner of deliberations undertaken by Ford management or the conclusions of Ford management. The case study was not formulated by Ford and is solely the responsibility of INSEAD.
Copyright© 1984 INSEAD Fontainebleau, France.

in developed countries, define the percentage of a product that must be produced in a specified geographical region as a precondition of sale in that region.

Although local content regulations had been discussed occasionally in the Management Committee for the past two years with no conclusions reached, pressure was building to push the discussion through to a definitive policy stance. If the Committee were to decide to favour local content regulations, it would then have to decide on strategy and tactics. Regulations could take various forms, some of which might be more advantageous to Ford than others. And, of course, Ford would have to decide how to represent its position to the governmental bodies which would have to introduce, monitor and enforce the regulations.

Ford of Europe

Ford's European headquarters are based at Warley near Brentwood in south-east England. The sixth floor of its 2500-person office building houses Ford of Europe's executive suites, where trade policy is a frequent – and often emotional – topic of conversation. The Ford Motor Company had a long tradition of favouring unrestricted international trade. Henry Ford declared in 1928 that, 'I don't believe in anything else than free trade all 'round'. Indeed, he exported the sixth car he made (to Canada). But the international trade environment of the 1920s was not that of the 1970s and 1980s, and although Henry Ford II was a strong free-trader like his grandfather, Ford US had altered its official policy position in 1980 away from free trade toward fair trade with an element of protectionism. The management of Ford of Europe could follow this lead by lobbying for local content regulations, but they did not feel obliged to do so. They were sufficiently independent of their American parent that the decision was theirs to make.

Ford of Europe was a product of the Ford Motor Company's traditional internationalism. It was created in 1967 when the managing director of Ford of Germany, John Andrews, convinced Henry Ford II of the need to coordinate the design, development, production and marketing operations of the Ford European national operating companies within the framework of the European Economic Community (EEC).

Ford now has 25 manufacturing sites in six European countries, and it is the most geographically integrated car producer in Europe. In the last five years the company spent more than $5 billion on automation and common design of its European cars, with the objective of making at least half the parts used in its European line interchangeable. Ford's European integration and focus and its image as a national producer in each national market is an important advantage with growing nationalistic car buying. The company proudly claims that 90 percent of the content of its European cars is European in origin.

Ford of Europe had sales of $9.9 billion in 1981 and would have ranked 34th on the *Fortune* 500 listing. From 1980 through 1982 – one of the worst periods for the auto industry since the 1950s – Ford of Europe earned $1 billion in profit.

Exhibit 1.1   *Automobile production by producer 1975, 1980, 1982 (in thousands of units)*

	Producer	1975	1980	1982
1.	General Motors (USA)	4,649	4,753	4,069
2.	Toyota (Japan)	2,336	3,293	3,144
3.	Gr. Nissan (Nissan-Fuji)	2,280	3,177	2,958
4.	Volkswagen-Audi	1,940	2,529	2,108
5.	Renault-RVI (F)	1,427	2,132	1,965
6.	Ford Motor (USA)	2,500	1,888	1,817
7.	Peugeot-Talbot-Citroën (F)	659	1,408	1,574
8.	Ford Europe	1,099	1,395	1,450
9.	Fiat-Autobianchi-Lancia-OM	1,231	1,554	1,170
10.	Toyo-Kogyo (Mazda)	642	1,121	1,110
11.	Honda	413	956	1,020
12.	Mitsubishi	520	1,104	969
13.	Chrysler Co (USA-Canada)	1,508	882	967
14.	Opel (General Motors)	675	833	961
15.	Lada (Fiat-USSR)	690	825	800
16.	Daimler-Benz	556	717	700
17.	Suzuki	184	468	603
18.	General Motors (Canada)	598	763	560
	Talbot (F, GB, E)	719	642	–
19.	British Leyland	738	525	494
20.	Isuzu	244	472	404
21.	BMW	221	341	378
22.	Ford Canada	481	434	374
23.	Volvo (Sweden-Netherlands)	331	285	335
24.	Seat (Fiat)	332	297	246
25.	Polski Fiat	135	330	240
26.	Moskvitch	300	230	205
27.	American Motors	463	252	194
28.	Alfa Romeo	191	221	189
29.	Vauxhall	190	151	164
30.	Saporoskje (USSR)	130	150	150

Source: L'Argus de l'Automobile

The Growing Japanese Presence in Europe

Ford of Europe had identified Japanese automotive products as the principal threat in the 1980s. To respond to that threat, Ford's European companies launched a major education and development program in the late 1970s called 'After Japan'. The program had started with trips by management to Japan to tour Japanese automobile assembly plants. By 1983, 'After Japan' was well established with emphasis on robotics, quality circles, 'just-in-time' inventory controls, and other work practices imported from Japan. Already, over 700 robots were at work in Ford's European plants with 1500 planned by 1986.

Ford's top management believed, however, that it would still take at least 5 to 10 years for their European plants to establish the cost and productivity levels necessary to match the landed price of Japanese imports. The Japanese cost advantage has been estimated to be about $1,500 ex-works per automobile.

A series of bilateral trade agreements between individual European countries and Japan currently capped Japanese automobile imports into Europe.

A reciprocal trade treaty between Italy and Japan (ironically initiated by the Japanese in the 1950s) restricted exports to each other's market to 2,200 units annually. Japan's shares of the French and UK markets were informally limited to 3 and 11 percent respectively. The French quota was imposed by President Valéry Giscard d'Estaing in 1976 after an abrupt increase in Japan's share of the French market. The UK quota was negotiated with the Japanese Ministry of International Trade and Industry (MITI) in 1978 after a previous, less formal agreement on export restraint failed. The Benelux countries and West Germany were technically open to the Japanese after the lapse of a 1981 informal one-year agreement in those countries establishing a maximum share of 10 percent of each market for the Japanese. Although there was no evidence that the Japanese were moving quickly to exploit this opening into Europe, Ford executives feared that the whole structure of trade understandings could be very fragile.[1]

It was not only by exporting vehicles that the Japanese were making their presence felt in Europe, threatening European producers, and prompting European government concern. In 1981, British Leyland launched its Triumph 'Acclaim'. The Acclaim was a Honda 'Ballade' assembled under licence from Honda. Mechanical components were imported from Japan, and a royalty was paid to Honda on each car. The Acclaim was introduced to plug a gap in British Leyland's model range, and it precipitated a considerable outcry by some European governments. For example, although British Leyland argued that 70 percent of the car was British in origin, the Italian government refused to allow the first consignment of Acclaims to enter their country from Britain in 1982. The Italians classified the car as Japanese and thus subject to the strict quota agreement between Italy and Japan. British Leyland successfully mobilized support from the UK government and the EEC, and the Italians eventually backed down. Nonetheless, the nature of the future battle was becoming clear.

In August 1983, the French government announced that starting in 1984 the Acclaim would be subject to the French 'voluntary' agreement with Japan. Or rather 40 percent of it would be. That was the percentage that the French government deemed to be of Japanese origin. Again the threat to the Acclaim was withdrawn after a visit to Paris by the UK Trade Minister, Cecil Parkinson, in August 1983.

The UK also experienced a similar situation on the import side. In 1983 a Mitsubishi automobile named the 'Lonsdale' was imported for the first time into the UK from Australia, where it was assembled from Japanese components. Strong industry concern was again expressed about hidden loopholes in the network of orderly marketing agreements, but no action was taken.

Exhibit 1.2 *Automobile industry in leading countries (data in thousands of units)*

	1973	1980	1982[a]
Worldwide production	29,793	29,244	27,197
Federal Republic of Germany			
New car registrations	2,031	2,426	2,156
Imports	763	1,013	824
Exports	2,173	1,873	2,194
of which: to Europe	1,150	1,381	1,785
to US	786	335	257
Production	3,650	3,521	3,761
France			
New car registrations	1,746	1,873	2,056
Imports	461	675	972
Exports	1,446	1,530	1,464
of which: to Europe	1,222	1,203	1,095
Production	2,867	2,939	2,777
Great Britain			
New car registrations	1,664	1,516	1,557
Imports	505	863	934
Exports	599	359	313
of which: to Europe	296	143	140
Production	1,747	959	888
Italy			
New car registrations	1,449	1,530	1,900
Imports	419	908	868
Exports	656	511	437
of which: to Europe	505	385	383
Production	1,823	1,445	1,297
Spain			
Exports	158	492	495
Production	706	1,029	928
USSR			
Production	917	1,327	1,307
Japan[b]			
New car registrations	2,919	2,854	3,038
Imports	37	46	35
Exports	1,451	3,947	3,770
of which: to Europe	357	1,003	896
to US	601	1,887	1,741
Production	4,471	7,038	6,882
US			
New car registrations	11,351	8,761	7,754
Imports	2,437	3,248	3,091
Exports[c]	579	560	353
of which: to Europe	15	24	6
Production	9,667	6,376	5,073

[a] Figures are partly estimated
[b] From 1978 on, actual figures excluding major components
[c] Including exports to Canada

Source: Daimler-Benz

Japanese components were also beginning to appear on the European market in the 1980s in what had been until then strictly European automobiles. In Milan, Innocenti replaced the old British Leyland mini engine in its small car with a Japanese Daihatsu engine. And in 1981 General Motors started to purchase gearboxes from Japan for its 'Cavalier' (UK) and 'Rekord' (Germany) models. GM was thought by many industry observers to be pursuing a policy of increasing the percentage of Japanese components in its European and US models.

In addition to their direct exports of vehicles, and their indirect exports through cooperative agreements with some European producers, the Japanese were beginning to explore direct foreign investment in Europe. Nissan (Datsun) had for some time been actively looking at sites for overseas automobile assembly plants. In 1981, Nissan commissioned the consulting firm of McKinsey & Co. to undertake a feasibility study for the location of an assembly plant in the United Kingdom. It was to produce up to 200,000 units annually by 1986, rising possibly to 500,000 by 1990. Employment on a greenfield site was to be 4,000–5,000, rising to perhaps 12,000 workers. The scheme would be eligible for government grants of £50–£100 million.

Included in the negotiations between Nissan and the UK government was a discussion of the degree of voluntary local content. It was widely rumoured at the time that Nissan was prepared to accept an EEC content level of 60 percent by value from the outset, rising to 80 percent later. The UK Department of Industry was rumoured to want these percentages to apply to the ex-works price, after classifying Nissan's profit after tax on the operation as an import. British Leyland and Ford lobbied hard for an immediate 80 percent local content. Further uncertainty revolved around the impact of the new plant on an understanding between the UK Society of Motor Manufacturers and Traders and the Japanese Association of Motor Assemblers. That understanding restrained the Japanese share of the UK market to 11 percent. The project had been temporarily shelved in 1982 due to uncertainty about future car sales, possible hostility from European governments (notably Italy and France), and fears of poor labour relations. It now threatened to come off the shelf.

Although the UK project was at least temporarily stalled, the first cars had just begun to roll off the line from a factory in southern Italy that Nissan built jointly with Alfa Romeo[2] The production rate planned was 60,000 units annually. The Italian government was said to be satisfied that no more than 20 percent of the value of the cars was being imported into Italy.

Finally, Nissan was sending 4-wheel drive vehicles into the EEC from a Spanish plant in which it held a two-thirds share. Next year, panel vans would follow.[3]

The US Situation

Much of what might be envisioned in Europe's future was already taking place in the United States. Japanese imports had been taking a progressively larger and

Exhibit 1.3 *European motor industry, net profits in m (unless otherwise stated)*

	1977	1978	1979	1980	1981	1982
Peugeot	226	526	1,800	−150	−184	−336
Renault	31[b]	19[b]	133[b]	−55	−112	
Ford UK	116	144	347	204	165	192
Ford Werke	143	143	124	11	32	76
Ford Europe[a]	1,045	1,271	1,219	323	289	451
Vauxhall	−2	−2	−31	−183	−57	−29
Opel	84	128	65	−97	−130	22
GM Europe[a]	277	376	338	−359	−427	6
BL	−52	−28	−145	−536	−497	−293
VAG	103	149	172z	76	20	−11
Daimler-Benz	145	154	164	261	181	217
BMW	31	39	45	28	32	47
MAN	−	17	18	13	12	7
Alfa-Romeo	−98	−77	−52	−28	−51	−29
Fiat	41	46	22	26	39	58
Seat	n/a	n/a	n/a	−106.6	−104.7	−122.6
Motor Iberica	5.8	6.6	4.2	−2.3	−13.4	−17.2
Volvo	25	36	46	74	45	45
SAAB	23	23	26	36	39	43

[a] US$m
[b] Unconsolidated
n/a Not available

Source: Company accounts and University of East Anglia, finance and accountancy department

Source: Krish Bhaskar

larger share of the market until a voluntary limit of 1.68 million vehicles was negotiated between Washington and Tokyo in 1981. That agreement was due to expire in March 1984, and there was widespread speculation that the Japanese wanted at least a substantially higher ceiling in the future. In the meantime, Ford's share of the US market had dropped alarmingly from 26 percent in 1976 to 16 percent in 1982. Analysts blamed much of this on a 1975 decision by Henry Ford II to postpone a major US-based small car program. (A US-based 'Fiesta' had been planned.) Ford re-engineered and re-styled its existing Pinto line instead and relied on that for the small car market.

Regardless of the question of fault, Ford's deteriorating position in the late 1970s led the company in 1980 to reverse its historic free trade policy, arguing for what was called 'fair trade' instead. 'Fair trade' was defined by its proponents as trade between countries with similar social and industrial infrastructures and similar national trade policies. (For example, similar wage rates, indirect tax burdens and export incentives.)

In November 1980 Ford and the United Auto Workers Union lost a petition they had filed in June with the US International Trade Commission[4] seeking protection from imports. A three-to-two majority of the commissioners ruled that imports were not the major cause of the industry's problems. The causes, according to the majority, were the recession and Detroit's own mistakes.

Ford had requested in its statement to the International Trade Commission that imports from Japan be limited to 1.7 million cars – the 1976 import level. Ford's setback by the Commission was short-lived, however. In April 1981, President Reagan announced the voluntary export restraint agreement with MITI. Automobile imports would not exceed 1.68 million units for the next three years.

In spite of the voluntary export restraint, Ford continued lobbying for legislative relief from the pressure of Japanese imports. Ford favoured a policy which combined a continuing cap on Japanese imports, a better yen/dollar exchange rate, and tax incentives. The United Auto Workers Union, fearful of the threat to American jobs, was also active lobbying hard for domestic content legislation.

In February 1983, a bill was introduced in Congress entitled 'Fair Practices in Automotive Products Act'. If passed, the bill would impose a graduated minimum domestic content percentage for automobile importers which depended on the total volume of the importer's sales. The percentages ranged from zero for foreign producers with US sales of less than 100,000 units per year to an upper limit of 90 percent for those with annual sales of more than 500,000 units.

The conflicting positions on trade policy of GM on one hand and Ford, Chrysler, and AMC on the other were brought into the open by the proposed bill. GM lobbied against the bill, arguing that any moves toward protectionism could cause a cascade of restrictive measures that would threaten global traders such as itself. Said Thomas R. Atkinson, GM's Director of International Economic Policy:

> Local content and other performance regulations decrease our flexibility as a corporation, and force us to do things we otherwise might not be doing. We wish these laws had never been invented, and would not like to see them increased or created in countries where they don't exist now.[5]

General Motors' position was particularly suspect in the eyes of the other major US manufacturers given the 1982 announcement by GM and Toyota of a cooperative plan to produce 450,000 small cars annually by 1985 from a mothballed GM plant in Freemont, California. GM and Toyota would have equal shares in the venture, and half of the output would be sold under the Toyota name, half under the GM name (to replace GM's 'Chevette'). Ford and other US manufacturers were strongly opposed to the deal, fearing that it was a precedent that could end up threatening the native US industry. The implications of a joint venture by the world's first and third largest automobile manufacturers were plain to see by all their competitors.

Of course, there were other risks involved in the proposed US domestic content law that went beyond those cited by GM. The more restrictive the import regulations in the United States, for example, the greater the pressure on Europe from Japanese exports diverted away from US shores. And some analysts within

Ford felt that the bill would stimulate Japanese direct investment in the United States, perhaps constituting a greater threat to the US manufacturers than some limited degree of imports. On this point the interest of the US labor unions and manufacturers could conflict. Finally, there was the general realization that the government could exact a 'price' in return for protectionist favors granted the industry.

The bill was currently being debated in Congress where it was felt to have a reasonable chance of passage. It was not expected to pass the Senate, however, and would almost certainly be vetoed by the President even if it did.

Local Content Regulations

Local content regulations have long been a device used by developing countries to force multinational companies to increase the rate at which they transfer technology and employment to their local operations. With respect to automobiles, these regulations typically require that a certain percentage of a vehicle's content be produced in the country of sale. This percentage may be defined by value or by weight. Weight is generally thought to be a stricter criterion since it is not susceptible to manipulation by transfer pricing. Yet it can lead to only low technology, high weight items being produced locally (e.g. steel castings and chassis components).

Although simple in concept, local content regulations can often be quite complicated in practice. The treatment of overhead and profit is often a problem. Some countries apply the regulations on the basis of fleet averaging, others to specific

Exhibit 1.4　*Share of Japanese exports in registrations by importing country in Europe*

Country	1966	1970	1975	1979	1981
Belgium	0.3	4.9	16.5	18.0	28%
France	0	0.2	1.6	2.2	2%
Germany	0	0.1	1.7	5.6	10%
Italy	0	0	0.1	0.1	–
Netherlands	0.6	3.2	15.5	19.5	26%
UK	0.1	0.4	9.0	10.8	10%
Denmark	0.5	3.4	14.7	18.1	28%
Ireland	0	0	8.9	25.2	30%
Austria	0	0.9	5.4	12.4	23%
Switzerland	0.1	5.6	8.4	16.0	26%
Portugal	0	10.7	11.8	7.8	11%
Finland	14.4	18.3	20.8	23.9	26%
Norway	1.9	11.4	28.4	24.2	36%
Sweden	0.2	0.7	6.5	10.0	14%

Source: G. Sinclair, *The World Car*

models. Mexico, where at least 50 percent of the value of all cars sold must be produced locally, strengthened its regulations by also requiring that the value of all component imports must be matched by component exports for each assembler. This led to a flurry of investments by Chrysler and Ford in engine facilities in Mexico.

Until recently, Spain had a 95 percent domestic content rule. All component imports were assessed a 30 percent customs duty, and 50 percent of all local manufacturing operations had to be Spanish-owned. All this was changed in the 1975 negotiations between the Spanish government and Ford over Ford's 'Bobcat' (or 'Fiesta') project in Valencia. Contemplating the attractive prospect of a plant producing 225,000 cars annually, the Spanish government settled for 100 percent Ford ownership, 75 percent Spanish content, and 5 percent import duty on component parts. Concessions on import duty were also granted for machine tools and equipment unavailable in Spain. But two-thirds of automobile production had to be exported from Spain, and Ford's sales in Spain could not exceed 10 percent of the previous year's total Spanish market size. General Motors arranged a similar deal for a plant in Zaragoza, Spain, producing 280,000 small 'S-cars' ('Corsas') annually. Spanish accession to the EEC would phase out much of its protective legislation.

Local content regulations did not exist in any EEC or European Free Trade Association (EFTA) country except Portugal and Ireland. (The European Community's trade regime did have a scheme for defining local assembly with the EFTA countries for the purpose of trade classification – 60 percent of value added had to be locally produced.) Nevertheless, there was a variety of statutory powers in the EEC and the General Agreement on Tariffs and Trade (GATT) which could protect specific industries. For example, Regulation No. 926 of the EEC allowed for the protection of specific industries and could be triggered by the Commission of the EEC after advice from the Council of Ministers.

At the GATT level, any member country could ask for temporary protection from imports from another member (under Articles 19–23) if those imports severely endangered national industry. These 'escape clause' articles were difficult for EEC countries to use, however, since each country delegated responsibility for all trade negotiations to the EEC Commission in Brussels. Thus, the European automobile industry would have to coordinate campaigns in a number of EEC member countries before it could approach the EEC Commission. Even then, there was no guarantee that the Commission would agree to take a case to the GATT. Not surprisingly, existing import restrictions were essentially bilateral diplomatic agreements – varying widely from country to country – rather than statutory enactments.

Ford's Deliberations

At least on the surface, informal local content regulations in Europe looked very attractive to Ford's executives. The Japanese threat was surely very real. Production levels in Europe in 1980 were about the same as they had been in 1970, and in the last decade, while European exports to non-European markets fell 42 percent, Japanese worldwide exports rose 426 percent. Ford's market analysts forecast slow growth for the European market in the future, indicating that higher Japanese sales in Europe would come directly from those of the established European producers. The existing structure of voluntary agreements to limit Japanese imports into individual European countries was fragile. Although 'voluntary' was clearly a euphemism, any cracks in the agreements could quickly lead to more Japanese imports before new and possibly more lenient agreements were negotiated. West Germany and Belgium were clearly the weak spots.

If a European local content rule were to be established on the basis of local sales (i.e. if a specified percentage of each manufacturer's European sales had to be produced in Europe), then the existing system of individual national voluntary trade agreements would become redundant. Alternatively, if a local content rule were to be applied to local production (i.e. if a specified percentage of the content of each manufacturer's cars assembled in Europe had to be sourced in Europe), then some controls on automobile imports would still be needed. A local content rule of this type would prevent the Japanese from circumventing the intent of import controls by importing the bulk of their components from Japan while establishing only token assembly operations in Europe.

Yet there were many potential negative consequences for European producers if local content regulations spread across Europe. It was not obvious that European producers should object to Japanese imports, even at a substantially higher level than at present, if the alternative was to be new Japanese greenfield plants in Europe. Even if they complied scrupulously with local content rules, these new plants, employing the most advanced production technology and work methods, could be tough competitors, unshackled from any form on constraint. At the very least, they would add production capacity to a market already suffering from 20 percent excess capacity. A price war was certainly not impossible to imagine. And Ford, among others, was worried about the impact that these plants could have on fleet sales, particularly in the high-margin UK market, if nationalistic customers began to think of Nissan, for example, as a 'national' producer.

Another problem was that local content rules could limit Ford's own manufacturing flexibility. The key new concept in the automobile industry in the 1970s was that of a 'world car'. A world car is assembled in local markets (tailored to local consumers' tastes) from a common set of components. Each component is produced in very high volume at one site, where it can be done cheapest, and then shipped around the world to the scattered assembly plants. Local content rules and world cars were seemingly incompatible.

Ford's 'Erika' project (the 1981 'Escort') was the first of the world cars. In actual practice, the world car concept was of questionable success. The Escort that was marketed in the US differed so much in style and design from its European sibling that there was little parts commonality, and transportation costs ate away at the efficiency gains from large scale production of the parts that were common. The result was that although there was some international trade in components within Ford, most movement of parts was either within Europe or within the United States.

General Motors had similar problems with its 'J-car' (the Vauxhall 'Cavalier' in the UK and Opel 'Rekord' in West Germany) and 'X-car' (the Vauxhall 'Royale' in the UK and Opel 'Senator' in Germany). GM seemed to have been more successful than Ford, however, in standardizing components, and whereas Ford had primarily maintained an approach of European sourcing for European markets, GM had already moved to exploit its global reach.

To make matters even more complex, Ford had a 25 percent share in Toyo Kogyo (Mazda) and thus an option of working with Mazda to import inexpensive Japanese vehicles. Indeed, a Mazda pickup truck was sold in the United States and Greece as a Ford truck, and the very successful Ford 'Laser' in the Far East was a version of the Mazda 626 made in Japan. (In July 1983, Ford was threatening such a policy to counteract the proposed GM–Toyota production plant in California.)

Technical Aspects of Local Content Regulations

If the management of Ford of Europe were to support local content regulations, they felt they would have to answer four technical questions.

1. How should 'local' be defined geographically?
2. How was local content to be measured?
3. To what should local content regulations be applied – individual cars, models, or a producer's entire fleet?
4. What should the minimum percentage of local content be?

The company had already done some thinking about each question.

Of all the producers, Ford was the most geographically integrated in Europe. It would therefore be important to encompass most or all of Europe in the term 'local'. A definition restricted to the EEC would exclude Ford's big Valencia plant in Spain and a 200,000 unit per year plant contemplated for Portugal. These plants represented critical low cost sources for small cars for the other European markets. (Both Spain and Portugal had applied for admission to the EEC however.) Ford regarded a nation-state definition as impractical and intolerable.

The question of how to define local content was a very difficult one to answer. One proposal was to define content by weight. This had the advantage of being difficult to manipulate by transfer pricing, but it might allow the importation of high value, high technology components that were light in weight.

The other common definition of local content was by value. Essentially, the percentage of local content was established by subtracting the value of the imported components as declared on customs documentation from (a) the distributor's price, (b) the ex-works price or (c) the ex-works price minus the labour and overhead content of the car. Then the local content residue was divided by the corresponding denominator.

Clearly the percentage of the imported components gets larger from (a) to (c) as the value of the domestic content gets smaller. Ford had not decided its position with regard to this issue, except that it did not want specific components identified for mandatory local production. It was also possible to devise other hybrid methods of valuing local content, but they were generally not under discussion.

Regarding the question of to what should the local content rules be applied, Ford favored applying them to the average of a producer's entire line of cars, rather than to each individual car or model. The former would jeopardize Ford's current importation from South Africa of small quantities of their P100 pickup truck (based on the 'Cortina').

There was also a related question of whether automobile production or regional sales should form the basis of measurement. Ford preferred that a specified

Exhibit 1.5 *Restrictions on Japanese car sales in developed countries, 1981/2*

United Kingdom	10–11% market share ceiling, dating from 1975 package to nationalize BL
Federal Republic of Germany	Growth limit of 10% per annum on 1980 sales (252,000 units)
Netherlands	No increase on 1980 level
Luxembourg	No increase on 1980 level
Italy	Quota of 2,200 units
France	3% market share ceiling
Belgium	Reduction of 7% on 1980 sales
EEC as a whole	Common External Tariff is 10.9%
Canada	Shipments of 'around 174,000' units as against 158,000 in in 1980
Australia	All imports restricted to 20% of market. Tariff of 57%. Local content must be 85% to count as home-produced
USA	Shipments of 1.68m for 1981 (Japanese fiscal year). Subsequent shipment limits to be calculated taking account of US market conditions. Tariff is 2.9%
Denmark Greece Ireland	No restrictions
Japan	No quotas or tariffs on assembled cars, but internal taxes, depending on engine size. Distribution and administrative checking systems alleged to operate as non-tariff barriers.

Note: The Benelux and Canadian restrictions are supposed to last only for 1981. The others appear to be more permanent.
Source: G. Sinclair, *The World Car*

percentage of a producer's European sales be made in Europe, since such a rule was insurance against circumvention of the current import quotas. A production-based local content rule would only prevent circumvention of the intent of import quotas by token local final assembly.

Finally, there was the question of what the appropriate percentage should be. Figures currently under discussion ranged from 60 to 80 percent, although the percentage clearly depended on the format of the specific proposals. Of particular significance in terms of these percentages was the fact that a 60 percent rule might allow importation of engines and major parts of the drive train which would all be excluded by an 80 percent rule. Also, it might be very difficult for the Japanese to start up a new plant with an immediate 80 percent local content (even if that percentage were to be achieved with more time). Startup at 60 percent would be substantially easier.

The Political Options

Should Ford decide to support local content regulations and then find answers to the technical questions, it would still have to determine the best way to carry its case to the appropriate government body. And here again, the way was not clear.

Ford definitely did not want to act on its own. It would be much better to act in concert with the other European producers. (Despite the all-American image of the founder and his name, Ford of Europe unquestionably considered itself 'European'.) Not only was this desirable on general principles, but for one quite specific reason Ford preferred not to lobby the EEC directly. It had recently fought and was currently fighting other battles with the European Commission. In 1982, the Commission had issued an interim order to Ford under Article 85 of the Treaty of Rome (an antitrust statute) requiring the company to offer right-hand-drive cars to the West German market. The background to this directive consisted of repeated complaints by British consumers that most major automobile producers charged significantly higher prices in the United Kingdom than on the Continent.

In June of 1983 the Commission issued a draft regulation applicable to the distribution systems of all motor manufacturers operating in Europe. The regulation aimed at harmonizing vehicle availability and prices across Europe. Any model of vehicle sold in any EEC member state would have to be made available in all other member states. And if price differences exceeded 12 percent (net of taxes) between any EEC markets, new importers (not authorized by the manufacturer) could enter the market. Ford, along with all other European motor manufacturers, was opposing this proposal vigorously.

Although Ford preferred to have a common industry position to press on the governmental authorities, there was little likelihood of unanimity among the European producers even on the most basic question of whether local content rules were desirable. General Motors was an almost certain opponent to local content rules despite the fact that it too might welcome relief from Japanese competition.

Exhibit 1.6 *Foreign sourcing – recently announced commitments by US automobile manufacturers to purchase foreign-made components for use in domestic vehicles production*

Automobile manufac-turers	Description of component	Intended use	Manufacturing source	Approximate number of components	Period
GM	2.8 lit V-6	Cars	GM Mexico	<400,000/year	1982–
	2.0 lit L-4 with transmission	Mini trucks	Isuzu (Japan)	100,000/year	1981–
	1.8 lit diesel L-4	Chevette	Isuzu (Japan)	small numbers	1982–
	1.8 lit L-4	J-car	GM Brazil	250,000/year	1979
	THM 180 automatic transmission	Chevette	GM Strasbourg (France)	−250,000/year	1979–
Ford	2.2 lit L-4	Cars	Ford Mexico	<400,000/year	1983–
	Diesel L-4	Cars	Toyo Kogyo	150,000/year	1983–
	2.0 lit L-4	Mini trucks	Toyo Kogyo	<100,000/year	1982–
	2.3 lit L-4	Cars	Ford Brazil	−50,000/year	1979–
	Diesel 6 cyl.	Cars	BMW/Steyr	100,000/year	1983–
	Turbo-diesel/4 cyl.	Cars	BMW/Steyr	–	1985–
	Manual transaxles	Front disc cars	Toyo Kogyo	100 000/year	1980–
	Aluminum cylinder heads	1.6 lit L-4	Europe, Mexico	–	1980–
	Electronic engine control devices	Cars	Toshiba	100,000+/year	1978–
	Ball joints	Cars	Musashi Seimibu	1,000,000/year	1980–84
Chrysler	L-6 and V-8 engines	Cars	Chrysler Mexico	<100,000/year	early 1970
	2.2 lit L-4	K-body	Chrysler Mexico	<270,000/year	1981
	2.6 lit L-4	K-body	Mitsubishi	1 million	1981–85
	1.7 lit L-4	L-body (Omni)	Volkswagen	1.2 million	1978–82
	1.6 lit L-4	L-body	Talbot (Peugeot)	400,000 total	1982–84
	2.0 lit Diesel V6	K-body	Peugeot	100,000/year	1982–
	1.4 lit L-4	A-body (Omni re-placement)	Mitsubishi	300,000/year	1984–
	Aluminum cylinder heads	2.2 lit L-4	Fiat		
AMC	Car components and power train	AMC Renault	Renault in France and Mexico	300,000/year	1982–
VW of America	Radiators, stampings	Rabbit	VW Mexico	250,000/year	1979–
	L-4 diesel and gas	Cars	VW Mexico	300,000/year	1982–

Source: Bulletin of the European Communities, The European Automobile Industry: Commission Statement

Fiat, Renault, and British Leyland, on the other hand, might be strong allies who could perhaps rally the support of their respective governments. They appeared to have much to gain from local content rules since they had most of their operations in Europe and they purchased most of their components locally.

There were a number of sourcing arrangements, however, which could undermine the support of some of these firms. Japanese cars assembled in Australia were entering the UK with a certificate of origin from Australia. British Leyland's Acclaim was of questionable origin. Fiat was bringing in 'Pandas' from Brazil, and VW 'Beetles' came into Europe from Mexico. Renault had extensive operations in the US which could alter the company's outlook. And on July 27, 1983, *The Wall Street Journal* reported that Fiat was being indicted by the Italian authorities for selling cars made in Spain and Brazil under the guise of Italian manufacture. Fiat denied the charge. Ford executives believed, nonetheless, that with the exception of GM, Ford was likely to find general support within the industry. In fact, in a 1981 draft paper, the CLCA,[6] stated that: 'The establishment of Japanese motor vehicle manufacturing plants should be subject to the following durable conditions:

(a) The CIF value of the components not originating from the EEC should not exceed 20 percent of the price ex-works of the vehicle.

(b) The manufacturing and assembly of mechanical components (engines, gearboxes and drivetrain) should be performed within the EEC.'

The European Commission

Ford executives believed that the European Commission was prepared to take some action on the automobile imports issue. In January 1983 the Commission had held discussions with the Japanese in Tokyo and had obtained a non-binding commitment to moderate vehicle exports to the EEC. The Commission was currently monitoring the agreement. Beyond this it was unclear what action the European Commission was considering. In principle, the EEC should be expected to favor relatively free trade between its member countries and the rest of the world. The history of international trade since the Second World War – a history in which the EEC featured prominently – was one of declining tariffs (from an average of 20 percent on manufactured goods in the 1950s to 8 percent in the mid-1970s), dramatically growing trade volumes, and greater interdependence of national economies. Two other principles dear to the EEC were that all member countries maintain a *common* trade policy vis-à-vis non-EEC countries, and that there be no barriers to trade between member countries. Clearly, the existing set of non-uniform bilateral trade agreements with the Japanese offended these principles.

Although the principles underlying the EEC were relatively unambiguous, the EEC often resorted to protective policies, and it was not immune to pressures to maintain jobs in the automotive sector. But granted this observation, it was still not evident just how job preservation might best be achieved. Formal local content rules

Exhibit 1.7   *Analysis of automobile construction cost*

		Percentage of ex-works price
Freight		2
Administration, selling cost, warranty and profit		7
Production and assembly overheads		22
Variable manufacturing costs:		69
Engine	10.4	
Gearbox	4.8	
Axles	6.9	
Other mechanical parts	8.3	
Body stamping	5.5	
Body assembly	6.9	
Accessories and seating	7.6	
Final assembly and painting	18.6	
	———	
	69.0	
		———
		100%

Notes

1. The labour content of variable manufacturing costs accounts for 14 percent of the total ex-works price.
2. For a typical medium-size saloon at a production level of 200,000 annually.
3. Final Retail Price is usually 22 percent higher than the ex-works price.

Sources: Yves Doz: *Internationalization of Manufacturing in the Automobile Industry*, unpublished paper, and Ford of Europe estimates

would be inconsistent with EEC law and would violate the GATT. Thus any local content measures would have to be informal such as those which currently existed between the Japanese and the British. Would the EEC prefer to see a uniform (albeit informal) external quota and internal production-based local content rule? Or would it rather see a uniform internal sales-based content rule and no quota? Would its preference in either case be less restrictive than the status quo, shaky though it might be? And was it realistic to expect that an informal negotiating process could create a common position among the different EEC member states? A weak, contentious and non-uniform set of local content rules established and enforced by each EEC member country could be the worst of all the imaginable alternatives.

The Japanese, of course, would have some influence on EEC thinking on this matter. Any EEC action would probably come in the context of trade negotiations – not simply unilaterally-imposed trade sanctions. And what position might the Japanese take? It is conceivable that they might agree to some reasonable export restraints into the EEC in return for open markets within the EEC. That would give them access to the two big markets from which they were currently virtually excluded – France and Italy. But would those two countries agree? Each would face greater Japanese competition in its home market but less in its export markets in other EEC countries.

The executives on the Management Committee considered their alternatives. If they were to have any role in determining the public policies that would undoubtedly have a significant impact on their company, they would have to act quickly.

Notes

1.   Ford also perceived an import threat from the emerging automobile industries of Eastern Europe. Many of the countries of Eastern Europe had established their industries with the help of Western European producers (e.g. Fiat in Russia and Poland, and Renault in Romania). The cars now produced in Eastern Europe were of outdated design, however, and with rapidly growing domestic demand, Eastern European countries were not expected to be a challenge in Western European markets on a scale close to that of the Japanese.
2.   This plant was a 50/50 joint venture in which Alfa Romeo mechanical components were installed in a Nissan 'Cherry' body coming from Japan, Alfa Romeo ran the assembly operation. Half of the finished vehicles went to Alfa Romeo and half to Nissan.
3.   In 1980 Nissan bought 36 percent of Motor Iberica and later increased that share to 66 percent.
4.   The International Trade Commission is an advisory commission with the role of determining whether a given industry was substantially injured by foreign imports, and if so, making recommendations to the President. Traditionally, the Commission has been viewed as a valuable ally of beleaguered US industries in the Executive branch of the government. Thus, its decision in this case was a surprise to everyone.
5.   *New York Herald Tribune*, June 27, 1983.
6.   Comité de Liaison des Constructeurs Associations. The CLCA was basically a political liaison committee of the national automative trade associations of France, the United Kingdom, Germany, Belgium, Holland and Italy.

General Motors Corporation

H. Landis Gabel

In late 1982, General Motors Corporation launched a long-awaited offensive to establish itself as a leading European automobile producer. Although it had been a resident of Europe ever since 1928, when it acquired control of Vauxhall in the UK, GM had never succeeded in building a dominant position. In contrast, its main US rival, Ford, had been remarkably successful over the years in Europe. This was especially true since the 1960s, when Ford began to implement a strategy of expanding and geographically integrating its European operations. GM currently ranked sixth in European market share behind (in declining order) Ford, Renault, Fiat, Volkswagen, and Peugeot.

GM planned to use its German company, Adam Opel, to spearhead the expansion program. At the center of the program was the 'Corsa' – the first of GM's 'world cars' designed and initially launched outside the US and the first GM entry in the critical subcompact market in Europe. The 'Corsa' went on sale at the end of 1982 in Spain, Italy, and France, and in 1983 in West Germany and the UK. Preliminary sales figures seemed to indicate that GM would exceed its target for the car of capturing 2 percent of the European market. This would be a significant contribution to what analysts thought was GM's goal of lifting its current 9 percent share of the European car market to at least 15 percent by 1988, a market forecast to be 10 million vehicles.

GM's US History

General Motors Corporation was created in 1908 by William Durrant through the consolidation of three separate companies: Oldsmobile, Buick, and Chevrolet. From the very beginning, GM started buying component producers – companies like

This case was prepared by Anthony E. Hall, Research Associate, under the supervision of H. Landis Gabel, Associate Professor at INSEAD. It is intended to be used as a basis for class discussion rather than to illustrate either effective or ineffective handling of an administrative situation. This is a satellite case to Ford of Europe and Local Content Regulations. *Copyright © 1985 INSEAD Fontainebleau, France.*

Harrison Radiators and Saginaw Steering that still exist today as separate divisions. However, GM failed to match the success of Ford, and by the early 1920s Ford was ten times the size of GM (which had about 5 percent of the US market). In the 1920s Ford was also outdistanceing its rival by rapidly expanding its overseas operations. In 1923, Alfred P. Sloan took over GM from Durrant and began to reorganize the company.

GM achieved its prominent position by the 1930s through the efforts of Sloan and the mistaken decision of Henry Ford I not to replace his Model T until 1927. In the 1930s both Chrysler and GM managed to pull ahead of Ford in the US market. (William P. Chrysler had left GM to set up his own company after a row with Durrant.)

After the hiatus of the Second World War, the major US producers scrambled to re-establish production and dominant position. US market shares stabilized at approximately 50 percent for GM, 25–27 percent for Ford, and 16–18 percent for Chrysler. This prevailed until the turbulence of the 1970s in which both Ford and Chrysler lost ground to GM and all three lost ground to Japanese imports.

GM's European Operations

GM entered the European market shortly after Ford when it acquired Vauxhall in 1928. The next acquisition was the German firm Adam Opel in 1929. But GM's US management gave little direction to the European operations until the mid-1970s. By then, the parent company's management had become increasingly concerned about the poor productivity and profit performance of Vauxhall and the lack of any collaboration between the two European subsidiaries – Vauxhall in the UK and Opel in West Germany. Ford, although weaker than GM in the US, was markedly stronger in Europe and had made greater progress in its efforts to integrate its UK and West German operations.

In 1975, GM made two key organizational decisions. The first was to give responsibility for the car operations of Vauxhall to Opel while all truck operations were to be based in the UK using the successful Bedford trademark. The second decision was to set up a separate world headquarters in New York to emphasize the commitment of GM to its global operations.

General Motors had other operations in Europe in addition to those in the UK and West Germany. In Grennevilliers, France, GM's subsidiary AC Delco employed 2,000 people making fuel pumps, brake systems, and distributors for GM and all the French automobile firms. In Strasbourg, France, a similar-size facility made automatic transmissions and carburettors. In 1978, two large projects were started. Harrison/GM France built a radiator and heater plant at Donchery, near Sedan, and a battery plant was set up at Sarreguemines, in Lorraine.

In Antwerp, Belgium, Opel had a major assembly plant building the J-car, which was sold as the 'Rekord' and 'Cavalier' models for West Germany and the UK, respectively. Then in early 1979, investments in Spain and Austria were announced to build GM's small car, the 'Corsa'. The Corsa had its origins in 1977 when GM was first contemplating an integrated European strategy. Ford by that time had demonstrated success in its international operations. It had a strong production base in Brazil, it had displaced GM's dominance in Australia, and Ford of Europe was resoundingly successful. (Indeed, it was the profitability of its European operations that would sustain the company through its US depression of 1982–1983.)

GM's strategic thinking was centred on the world car concept, but Europe had not yet been satisfactorily integrated into that concept. The Corsa (originally the 'S-car') was to remedy that failing. It was to be a small car, designed by Opel, and first marketed in Europe. It would subsequently be transferred to the US with a minimum of changes.

GM management expected to find a huge market for the Corsa in southern Europe, where it had only a 4 percent share but where small cars in the same category as the Corsa constituted 40 percent of automobile sales. It estimated that the Corsa would give it an added two percentage points of the European market and 100,000 more unit sales in the fast-growing Spanish market if the Corsa assembly plant were located there.

After preliminary study, three countries were selected for final site evaluation – France, Austria, and Spain. This led to a widely publicized lobbying effort by all three countries to win the jobs. After further study, GM decided in 1978 to place the engine plant at Aspern, Austria, the components plant at Cadiz, Spain, and the $1.5 billion assembly operation for 270,000 units annually at Zaragoza, Spain. The package that GM negotiated with the Spanish government was similar to one previously worked out between Ford and the government for Ford's plant in Valencia. (In fact, GM's negotiating time was considerably shortened by having the Ford plant as a precedent.) The cars went on sale at the end of 1982 in Spain, Italy, and France, and were available in Germany and the UK in 1983.

GM's Global Operations

Prior to 1970, GM's major area of operation outside Europe and the US was Australia. GM Holden was established there in 1947 as an integrated car manufacturing operation with major investments made in what had been until then just an assembly operation. This enabled GM Holden to establish a dominant position in the marketplace that lasted until 1975. That year Ford, using the 626 model of Toyo Kogyo (Mazda) called the Ford 'Laser', took over the number one position.[1]

In the early 1970s, GM took positions in two Japanese companies – Isuzu, in which it held a 34.5 percent equity stake, and Suzuki, in which it held 5 percent of the equity. These investments were thought to be necessary to the developing GM policy of global sourcing and assembly. In 1981, Bedford announced that it would assemble an Isuzu light van/truck in England. Isuzu also started supplying the gearbox for GM's first world car, the 'J-car'.

In South Korea, GM announced in 1983 that new models were planned for the 50 percent-owned Daewoo Motor Company that was assembling a version of the Opel 'Kadette' called the 'Maepsy'.

In February 1983, GM and Toyota announced agreement to collaborate in the production of a new small car to replace the aging GM Chevette in the US market. Manufacturing was to be shared between the two companies. Production was initially set at 400,000 units annually but this was later reduced to 200,000 units. The car was to be designed by Toyota, and Toyota was to be responsible for running the previously mothballed GM plant in Freemont, California. Toyota would thus gain a manufacturing base in the US market.

The advantages of the deal to GM were that it could develop a new small car for the US market quickly and cheaply and get first-hand experience with Japanese automotive design concepts and management techniques. It would also re-employ some of the nearly 100,000 GM workers previously laid off. GM's hope was that by the end of the decade it would have learned enough to build small cars successfully on its own.

The GM–Toyota joint venture provoked a bitterly hostile response from both Chrysler and Ford, and intense scrutiny by the US Federal Trade Commission. (Toyota and Ford had held negotiations over a similar joint venture earlier, but the negotiations had broken down.) The Federal Trade Commission had the power to block the project, but recent policy changes in the US antitrust enforcement agencies made approval a likely prospect.

The Developing European Competition

General Motors had always been a strong proponent of free trade. Indeed, its global strategy now depended on the free flow of components internationally and on the ability of GM to execute the various cooperative ventures on which it had embarked. GM's world cars, code named the J, X, and T, were now well established in most of GM's markets and were increasingly using components sourced from around the world. As an example, the Vauxhall Cavalier built in Luton, England, had an engine from Australia, a gearbox from Japan, a radiator from France, and lights from West Germany. These components were not exclusively dedicated to the Cavalier. The Corsa, designed by Opel, had just been launched in Europe and would soon be transferred to the US and Australia, again with parts sourced from outside these areas. GM's joint venture with Toyota in California was critical to the company's success in the US small-car market. Suzuki, in which GM had a share, was starting work on another small car for the US.

Organizational changes had recently been made to support the evolving global manufacturing strategy. GM was not pleased with its New York worldwide headquarters experience, so in the late 1970s all domestic and international operations were consolidated in Detroit. International operations such as Opel, Bedford Truck, and GM Holden were given divisional status like Chevrolet and Fisher Body.

Some analysts thought that GM's strategy was to identify the optimum level of output for each constituent part, and to make sourcing and output decisions for components and vehicles from Detroit for the world markets. With close links to Japanese and South Korean producers, GM was well prepared to exploit its strategy.

GM in Europe had made no public statement about local content regulations or about the prospective Nissan plant in the UK. Industry analysts felt that GM had relatively little to fear from Nissan. In 1983, GM was very successful in its two traditional European markets – the UK and West Germany – and its new Corsa had made a big impact in Spain and Italy. In short, GM was well prepared for battle in Europe as long as relatively free trade was allowed.

Other principals in the European automobile theater agreed. Jean-Paul Parayre, president of Peugeot SA, was widely quoted as saying that the major threat to the native European producers came not from the Japanese, but from a war between the two American giants fought across Europe. Already skirmishes had taken place: in 1983, a fierce discounting battle started in the UK and spread across Europe. Ford was generally thought to have started it in a desire to keep the Sierra number one in European sales. The company cut prices to fleet buyers up to 25 percent to match GM's marketing push.

The worry for the Europeans, as well as perhaps for Ford, was that GM – a company that lost nearly $1 billion in Europe in 1980 and 1981 – was no longer an also-ran. It looked as though GM finally had the automobile models, the organization, the strategy, and (after its remarkable 1982–83 recovery in the US) the financial resources to build a position in Europe as strong as that it had long held in the US.

Note

1.   Foreign direct investment in the Australian automobile industry was subject to an 85 percent domestic content rule. This percentage could be offset, however, by exports of components and built-up units from Australia. Thus, for example, Mitsubishi exported its 'Lonsdale' to the UK and Nissan exported aluminium castings to Japan.

The Nissan Corporation

H. Landis Gabel

The Nissan Corporation was born in 1911 as a collaborative venture of three financiers, Mr Don, Mr Aoyama, and Mr Takemake. The first letter of each of their names was the basis of the name of their first automobile, a two-seat 'Datsun', which was built in 1933. On its fiftieth anniversary, the Nissan Corporation consolidated its corporate and automobile images by changing the name of its automobile products from 'Datsun' to 'Nissan', Nissan meaning Japanese Industrial Corporation.

In mid-1983, Nissan faced a decision on whether to go ahead with a previously shelved $735 million investment in an automobile assembly plant in the United Kingdom. The project, if undertaken, would have been Nissan's largest foreign investment. Although the investment plan was first announced in 1981, it had stalled because of the collapse of the European market in the recession of 1981–83, the resistance of both the company chairman, Katsuji Kawamata, and the head of the company union, Ichiro Shioji, and the possibility that the plant would be subject to very restrictive local content regulations.

The Japanese Automobile Industry

In the early 1930s, the Japanese automobile industry was dominated by Ford and General Motors, which had started Japanese operations in 1925 and 1927, respectively. In 1936, however, the Japanese government wrested control of its domestic automobile industry from the two American firms with the passage of the Automobile Manufacturing Law. Under this law, automobile companies required a license to operate in Japan. Only two companies were granted licenses – Toyota and Nissan.

Even after the Second World War, foreign automobile companies were excluded from Japan. However, the Ministry of International Trade and Industry (MITI) allowed licensing arrangements between Japanese and foreign manufacturers

This case was prepared by Anthony E. Hall, Research Associate, under the supervision of H. Landis Gabel, Associate Professor at INSEAD. It is intended to be used as a basis for class discussion rather than to illustrate either effective or ineffective handling of an administrative situation. This is a satellite case to Ford of Europe and Local Content Regulations. *Copyright© 1985 INSEAD Fontainebleau, France.*

if they would bring technology to the country. Nissan signed an agreement with Austin Motor Company of England under which Nissan would produce the Austin A-40 model and would receive automatic transfer machines required for fast and efficient engine machining. The agreement ran from 1952 to 1959, but by 1956 Nissan was building its own automatic transfer machines. Other companies signed similar agreements; for example, Rootes of Britain with Isuzu for the production of the Hillman Minx, and Renault with Hino for the Renault R-4 cv. Toyota, by contrast, embarked on a strategy of independence.

In 1966, MITI persuaded Nissan to acquire the faltering auto producer, Prince Motor Company. With the acquisition came the technical expertise that Prince had built up as an aircraft producer in the war. This was MITI's only success in its efforts to rationalize the Japanese automobile industry. MITI long felt that there were too many producers and had tried unsuccessfully to force mergers within the industry and to discourage the entry of new producers such as Honda and Suzuki. MITI felt that struggling domestic producers would provide a vehicle for the American firms to re-enter the Japanese market. Its fears were realized when Chrysler took a 15 percent equity participation in Mitsubishi in 1970, General Motors 34.1 percent of Isuzu in 1971, and Ford 25 percent of Toyo Kogyo in 1976. More recently, GM bought 5.3 percent of Suzuki.

The Japanese domestic industry is still dominated by the two pre-war firms – Toyota and Nissan. Toyota is the leader with 29 percent of the Japanese automobile market, while Nissan has 21 percent. Export shares are very similar – 29 percent compared to 24 percent. The industry is unusual in that it sustains far more independent producers than any other major market. There are nine significant producers in the industry – Toyota, Nissan, Toyo Kogyo, Honda, Mitsubishi, Daihatsu, Subaru and Isuzu. (Toyota own 6 percent of Daihatsu and 6 percent of Hino, a truck maker, and both companies make models for Toyota.)

Japanese producers are heavily reliant on their component suppliers. This reliance stems in part from the well-known 'just-in-time' inventory system (the 'Kaban' system) but more generally it results from overall synchronization of capacity planning which, in turn, involves component suppliers in the formulation of the assemblers' basic strategies. The component suppliers are equally dependent on the assemblers since in most cases a supplier serves only one assembler. Nissan even finances its suppliers. Because they are not vertically integrated, the Japanese automobile firms are really only designers, final assemblers and marketers.

Domestic production in 1982 was 11.5 million units, according to the Japanese Association of Motor Assemblers (JAMA). This figure includes light trucks, 4-wheel drive vehicles, and mini cars with engines of less than 500 cc. The level of domestic sales was 5.3 million units in 1982, compared to 4.1 million in 1970. Most of the industry growth had come from exports where volumes had grown from 1.1 million units in 1970 to 6.2 million by 1982. This figure includes knock-down kits where there had been especially rapid market growth. Over 600,000 kits were exported in 1982. Of all Japanese automobile and kit exports, 34 percent went to North America and 14 percent to Europe.

Nissan's Strategy

Nissan built its first overseas plant in 1961 in Aguascalientes, Mexico, 300 miles north of Mexico City. The plant assembled 60,000 trucks and cars yearly for Central and Latin America. Recently a new press shop, an aluminum and casting shop, and an engineering plant had been added to give a capacity of 360,000 engines annually.

By 1980, Nissan had 26 plants in 23 countries, but apart from the Mexican operation, they were very small. Typically they were financed by local capital, used a high degree of locally sourced components (as a government precondition for local sales), and assembled cars under a Nissan license. Nissan's objective for the 1980s was to change this situation dramatically.

Nissan's commitment to a policy of internationalization – a policy to be implemented in the 1980s – was born of fear of growing Western trade barriers and the acknowledgement of Toyota's supremacy in Eastern markets. The company's internationalization strategy, well publicized by the company's president, Takashi Ishihara, was to alter fundamentally its locus of production. The strategy became known as the '4/3/3 Strategy' – 40 percent of sales going to the Japanese market, 30 percent of sales exported from Japan, and 30 percent of sales manufactured and sold abroad. The ultimate objective was to win a 10 percent share of the 40 million-unit world market forecast for 1990.

The overseas investment program got underway in January 1980 when Nissan bought 36 percent of Spain's Motor Iberica for $43 million. This was later increased to 66 percent for an additional $22 million. The plant was producing 15,000 Nissan Patrols yearly by 1983 in addition to heavy trucks, which bear the name 'EBRO'. Should Spain enter the European Economic Community (EEC), this plant would be a base for Community-wide exports.

In April 1980, Nissan announced that it would invest $500 million in a light truck plant at Smyrna, Tennessee. Output was planned at 160,000 units annually, and the first pickup trucks began to roll off the assembly line in June 1983. The plant could be expanded to produce cars later.

In October 1980, Nissan invested $14 million in an Italian joint venture with Alfa Romeo to construct 60,000 cars yearly in a new plant near Naples. Most of the mechanical components were to come from the Alfa-Sud model. The body pressings and some trim would come from Japan (from the Nissan 'Cherry'). After fierce opposition from Fiat and the Italian government, the deal was allowed to proceed only if the Japanese content were less than 20 percent. Some of the cars were to be sold as Nissan 'Cherrys' through the Nissan dealer network in Europe, and some as Alfa-Romeo 'Arnas' through the Alfa network. Finally, in January 1981 Nissan announced its biggest foreign direct investment – a proposed car plant in Great Britain.

In 1982, Nissan produced 2.84 million units, about 8 percent of the global market of 35–36 million. The status of the company's operations was closer to 4/5/1 than 4/3/3, however, and its rival Toyota had begun to pressure Nissan harder both at home and overseas. Furthermore, Nissan's UK plans, announced in 1981, were delayed.

The UK Investment Proposal

The UK Labour government of 1974–79 had begun a strategy of encouraging increased industrial investment from abroad. The television industry was a spectacular policy success when five Japanese companies, led by Sony, set up manufacturing operations in the United Kingdom. Mrs Thatcher, as leader of the opposition in 1977, visited Nissan's Sama plant near Tokyo and was very impressed. On the basis of that impression and the television industry experience, Mrs Thatcher put a new Japanese automobile plant in the United Kingdom high on her list of priorities when she became Prime Minister in 1979. Nissan was a natural candidate for the investment.

To Nissan, which had just commenced an international investment program, a part of which was naturally aimed at access to the European market, the United Kingdom had much to offer and a few potential drawbacks as well. The political environment looked stable and Mrs Thatcher seemed determined to turn the economy around. Skilled labor was available and relatively inexpensive, and Japanese management had experienced good industrial relations in other instances. London was the European center of many Japanese companies in service sectors like banking, insurance and shipping. The language was English. Less openly stated was a fear that protectionist measures might foreclose Nissan's access to one of its most profitable markets. Britain took more than a third of Nissan's 260,000 cars exported to Europe in 1982, and auto prices were very high there.

On the other hand, British component suppliers worried Nissan. It would be unlikely that the close association between supplier and assembler that was customary in Japan could be anticipated in England. Component prices were also worrisome. Finally, the plant was estimated to take more than three years to build – twice what it would take in Japan.

The Nissan plan was originally conceived as a $450 million investment to produce 200,000 cars annually. Nissan would not consider taking over an existing plant, e.g. the Peugeut–Talbot plant at Linwood in Scotland which was closed in 1979, or the British Leyland Rover plant at Solihull, closed in 1980 only four years after it had opened.

Further study indicated that to achieve productivity and quality levels comparable to its Japanese plants, Nissan would have to raise its planned investment. The final estimate was $735 million. The consulting firm of McKinsey & Co. was retained to advise on the location of the greenfield plant. It was widely rumored that a site in the East Riding of Yorkshire had been chosen.

The project ran into problems almost from the start. It quickly became clear that the European market for cars was not growing as rapidly as had been forecast. Also the French and Italian governments were hostile towards UK-assembled cars with a partial Japanese content. BL had trouble sending its Triumph 'Acclaim' into either country. The 'Acclaim' was a Honda 'Ballade' produced by BL license, but it was acclaimed to have a 70 percent European content.

Local content was also an important issue for the UK government and entailed protracted negotiations with Nissan. It was believed that the UK government wanted a 60 percent start-up local content, measured on ex-works price, and counting parts, labor and direct overheads, but excluding profit remitted overseas. This would rise to 80 percent within two years. 'Local' was defined as 'European', partly because of the EEC, but also because the component industry was integrated across Europe. It was widely believed that Nissan found these conditions unacceptable and had negotiated a lower start-up percentage and a longer transition period.

UK automobile producers, including BL and Ford of Europe, opposed these arrangements. If satisfactorily concluded, the UK government would grant between £50 and £100 million to a Japanese producer to build a plant that would compete with the 'native' producers in the UK and Western European markets where there was already excess capacity! The UK component manufacturers were opponents of anything less than an immediate 80 percent local content.

Another problem for Nissan's management was the apparently implacable opposition of the Nissan union leader, Mr Tchira Shioji. It would be difficult to mount the UK operation without the support of the union since many foreman-level personnel would need the permission of the union to cooperate with the project.

In addition to problems specific to the UK investment plan, Nissan faced a renewed threat at home and abroad from Toyota. Since 1980, Nissan had invested $4 billion, with 75 percent of that going to the company's Japanese production and distribution system. Yet in the first half of 1983, Nissan lost two percentage points of the Japanese market to Toyota and fell to its lowest share of the Japanese market in 18 years. Pre-tax profits fell from $391 million to $260 million. Toyota has also announced its joint-venture with GM in California to produce up to 400,000 Toyota-designed cars annually. Toyota and GM would split output. This was a major policy reversal for Toyota which previously had shunned direct foreign investment.

Industry analysts, looking at Nissan's situation, were uncertain about whether the company would go ahead with the very expensive UK investment. Management was stretched thin, and the company's bankers were becoming increasingly worried about its $4.6 billion debt (63 percent of it short term). Said Sohei Nakayama, former President of the International Bank of Japan and in 1983 an advisor to it, 'Nissan will go bankrupt if it insists in Britain'[1]. The remark was not taken literally, but it did suggest the seriousness of the financial situation that Nissan faced as seen in influential financial circles.

Note

1.   Quoted in *Fortune*, September 19, 1983, p. 10.

CASE 4

United Kingdom: Industrial Policy Toward the Automobile Industry

H. Landis Gabel

In many ways, the decline of the UK automobile industry since 1945 mirrors the decline of the global strength of the United Kingdom's manufacturing base and overall economic performance. This decline has occurred despite (or because of) a wide variety of policies that directly or indirectly affected the fortunes of the automobile sector.

The UK automobile industry emerged from the Second World War with many modern plants and equipment. With the end of rationing of essential raw materials in the early 1950s, the industry rapidly became the world's leading car exporter and its second largest producer (after the United States). In 1953 the United Kingdom exported nearly 400,000 units, and exports peaked at 617,000 units in 1963. Domestic automobile registrations reached 300,000 in 1953, then 500,000 in 1955, and topped 1,000,000 in 1963. Import penetration was low. Even by the early 1970s, imports had not exceeded about 10 percent of the UK market.

After 1964, domestic demand stagnated as the country suffered the consequences of a series of balance of payments crises. Then in 1971, the Conservative government of Edward Heath introduced a number of policies (e.g. the easing of hire-purchase conditions and the reduction of indirect taxes on automobiles) that led to a boom in automobile sales. Domestic producers were unfortunately unable to satisfy demand, and in 1973 imports jumped to 31 percent of the market.

By the end of the 1970s, the import penetration rate approached 65 percent of the UK market, principally as a consequence of two factors. One factor was a series of problems at British Leyland and Chrysler UK, about which more will be said below. The other factor was Ford's and General Motors' gradual rationalization of automobile assembly on the Continent.

This case was prepared by Anthony E. Hall, Research Associate, under the supervision of H. Landis Gabel, Associate Professor at INSEAD. It is intended to be used as a basis for class discussion rather than to illustrate either effective or ineffective handling of an administrative situation. This is a satellite case to Ford of Europe and Local Content Regulations. *Copyright© 1985 INSEAD Fontainebleau, France.*

The Structure of the UK Automobile Industry

There were dramatic changes in the structure of the UK automobile industry from 1950 to 1980. In 1952, Morris and Austin combined to fight the growing influence of Ford. This established the 'big five' producers – British Motor Company, Ford, Rootes, Vauxhall (owned by General Motors since 1925), and Standard–Triumph.

Again, to counter the growth of Ford in the United Kingdom, Leyland (a relatively small specialist truck producer) bought Standard–Triumph in 1957. With the sponsorship of the Industrial Reorganization Commission (IRC), Leyland acquired British Motor Company in 1968 to become British Leyland, which was nationalized in 1975. Finally, Chrysler acquired 30 percent of Rootes in 1964, acquired control of the company in 1967, and then sold it and all other European operations to Peugeot–Citroën in 1978.

In the 1970s, Ford steadily increased its share of UK production from 27 to 37 percent. By this measure it was second to British Leyland, which held a stable 45–50 percent share throughout the decade. But by importing cars from Belgium, Spain, and Germany, Ford attained the leading sales share (rising to 30 percent by the end of the 1970s). British Leyland was second in sales share (which fell through the decade to 18 percent). Chrysler (Rootes) and Vauxhall both had shares of production below 10 percent, and had habitually lost money.

General Motors' fortunes improved in the 1980s with its Vauxhall Cavalier (especially popular in the important fleet market), the Corsa (produced in Spain), and its Opel imports. These cars, coupled with acceptance problems that troubled the 'wedge' shape of the Ford Sierra, boosted General Motors' share of UK sales to 14 percent in 1982.

Tools of Policy

Import tariffs were a key factor in the postwar development of the European industry. In the United Kingdom in the 1950s, the level for finished cars was 33.3 percent. This contrasted with a level in France at the same time of almost 70 percent and in Germany of only 13 percent. After the establishment of the European Economic Community (EEC) and the General Agreement on Tariffs and Trade (GATT), tariffs fell quite rapidly, and for the United Kingdom reached 18 percent by 1970. Japan was the first country completely to eliminate tariffs on imports (in 1978), and all tariffs on trade within the EEC were scheduled to be eliminated by January 1984.

The United Kingdom had three main forms of taxation on cars. Prior to 1973 a purchase tax was levied on the wholesale price. This purchase tax was replaced by a value added tax in 1973 (as an entry requirement of joining the EEC). The value added tax was supplemented by a special car tax on the wholesale price designed partly to keep the tax burden on cars at its original level and thus prevent a stimulation of demand. There was also a tax on fuel and a road tax levied at a fixed rate on each vehicle.

Major factors affecting car sales in the United Kingdom included the terms and conditions of hire-purchase agreements. Government policy traditionally set the minimum down payment percentage and the maximum repayment period, but this was abolished in 1971. After this policy change, there was a major shift of auto sales from the household market to the corporate market. A company car became an accepted part of an employee's remuneration. The percentage of car sales made to companies rose to 67 percent by 1978.

Demand-management policies employed by the government repeatedly disrupted the automobile industry in the United Kingdom in the 1960s and 1970s. Between 1960 and 1975 the tax rates on cars changed 25 times, resulting in abrupt and substantial swings in consumer demand.

Plant-location strategy was also heavily influenced by the government. The traditional center for car production was the Midlands of England around Birmingham, although Ford and General Motors had established plants near London (Ford at Dagenham, 20 miles east of London, and General Motors at Luton, 30 miles north of London). In the early 1950s, the government started to try to disperse the industry. Merseyside, Liverpool and Scotland were favored locations. Policy was enacted by means of Industrial Relocation Certificates. In essence, permission to relocate was refused unless a company chose a location favored by the government. Additional incentives offered after 1965 were investment grants and tax incentives for investments in the underdeveloped regions of the North and West. These incentives could be supplemented by discretionary grants. For example, Ford received direct aid totaling £180 million to locate the Erika (Escort) engine facility at Bridgend in South Wales, and the Welsh Development Authority provided all of the infrastructure, roads, and rail links free of cost. (The United Kingdom had to bid against Berlin for the facility.) The ill-fated DeLorean plant in West Belfast, Northern Ireland, is another example. An amount of £52 million was granted out of a total investment of £65 million to produce an aluminium-bodied sports car for the American market; the company collapsed in 1982 in scandal. These incentives were directly comparable to those offered by the West German government to locate industry in Berlin, by the Italians to locate in southern Italy, and by the French to locate in Alsace and Lorraine.

Two final areas of public policy that had significant impacts on the automobile industry were incomes policies and industrial relations policies. Until the Thatcher government in 1979, various pay policies had been in force for most of the time since 1961 when the Chancellor of the Exchequer mapped out pay norms for the public sector. Wage freezes and percentage limits on wage increases became a feature of government policy under both Labour and Conservative administrations. These limits were coupled with two attempts to curb trade union power. The first attempt came under the Tories in 1971, with their Industrial Relations Act, and the second came under Labour in 1978, with their 'in place of strife' policy. Both policies resulted in widespread disruption, especially in the automobile industry.

Margaret Thatcher swept away nearly all specific policy tools for controlling the automobile industry after her election in 1979. The National Enterprise Board was abolished, as were wage and price controls. Taxes were abandoned as a device to manage automobile demand. The Tories also reduced the scale of regional grants and incentives and narrowed their geographic scope.

Chrysler UK

Three times in the 1960s and 1970s, Labour administrations faced policy crises over the Rootes' operations. In 1963, Rootes launched a new car model called the Hillman Imp to counter the very successful British Motor Company Mini. Although Rootes had long been located in Coventry in the Midlands, the government's redevelopment policy forced it to locate its new Imp plant at Linwood, near Glasgow, Scotland. The project was a failure and by 1966 Rootes was in deep financial trouble. Chrysler was then undertaking a massive global expansion program to try belatedly to match the international operations of its rivals in the United States. The Labour administration initially rejected a Chrysler takeover of Rootes, but after the British Motor Company and Leyland refused help, the government agreed to Chrysler expanding its 30 percent minority stake in the company to 85 percent in 1964. The government, through the Industrial Relations Council, bought 15 percent of the shares. Chrysler agreed to preserve the Rootes operations and to expand employment, especially at Linwood.

Late in 1975 (only six months after the nationalization of British Leyland) Chrysler UK appealed to the UK government for financial assistance. Before the Department of Industry could reply, John Riccardo, Chairman of Chrysler US, demanded and got an appointment with the Prime Minister, Harold Wilson. Riccardo offered three alternatives: (1) liquidation of the UK operation in three months, (2) donation of Chrysler UK to the government, or (3) donation of 80 percent to the government, with Chrysler US keeping a minority stake. After frantic negotiations, the government agreed to bail out Chrysler. This decision went against the advice of the Industry Minister, Eric Varley, and a Central Policy Review Staff report urging further rationalization of the industry. A loan of £162.5 million was made to Chrysler UK in return for a Chrysler US investment of £64 million and a declaration of intent to introduce new models and to integrate the UK operation with its European operations in Spain and France.

In 1978, Chrysler went back to the Labour government and announced its intention to sell its entire European and UK operation to Peugeot–Citroën. Despite union opposition, the cabinet under James Callaghan agreed to the sale in September 1978, after Peugeot reached agreement similar to Chrysler's with the government. However, after the election of the Conservative administration in 1979, Peugeot closed the Talbot Linwood operation in Scotland and concentrated assembly at Ryton, near Coventry.

British Leyland

The problems that confronted British Leyland in the 1970s arose from its inability to rationalize the proliferation of models and assembly plants it inherited from its various mergers since the 1950s. By 1974 it was clear that British Leyland was bankrupt. In December 1974, the Labour government's Industry Minister, Tony Benn, declared that because of 'the company's position in the economy as a leading exporter and its importance to employment directly and indirectly', the government would assist British Leyland.

A formal investigation of British Leyland's problems culminated in the Ryder Report, which blamed British Leyland's difficulties on inappropriate organization, low investment, excessive dividends, incompetent management, and poor productivity from outdated plants. The report recommended an immediate investment of £265 million to buy out the equity, and then subsequent investments of £1.4 billion over eight years to be paid on a tranche system subject to satisfactory performance. The National Enterprise Board (a government holding authority set up in 1974) was to supervise British Leyland.

By 1977, it was clear that British Leyland was still in trouble. Little progress had been made with new model introductions, losses approached £500 million each year, and public confidence was at an all-time low following repeated disputes and strikes at the company. A new head of the National Enterprise Board, Leslie Murphy, was appointed to replace Ryder, and he quickly appointed Michael Edwardes as British Leyland Chairman. Edwardes insisted on a free hand, and he got it.

Edwardes' plan was a radical departure from Ryder's. Within a month most of the previous senior management had left the company. The plan called for 12,500 redundancies, decentralization of decision making, and an end to the tranche system of funding. Four hundred and fifty million pounds was immediately injected as further equity capital. After almost five years of tough – almost confrontational – management, Edwardes succeeded in reducing the number of assembly plants from nine to two, launched the successful Metro and Maestro, and established strong links with Honda. British Leyland began making the Triumph Acclaim (Honda Ballade) under licence, and jointly developed a new executive-class car with Honda for production in Japan, the United States and the United Kingdom. The company was expected to return a profit (albeit an insignificant one) in 1983.

Japanese Penetration of the UK Market

Import penetration stayed at very low levels in the United Kingdom until 1971. The sudden upsurge in demand that year surprised the domestic suppliers and was satisfied by imports. Nissan in particular launched a major marketing effort at this time, and both the Japanese and Continental European suppliers succeeded in acquiring discontented British Leyland and Chrysler dealers.

The leaders of British Leyland, Chrysler, and the trade unions repeatedly called for controls on imports in the 1973–75 period. Although most of the import pressure originated from the Continent, it was unrealistic to hope to control those imports because the United Kingdom has just joined the EEC in 1973. Rather, an attack on imports had to be an attack on the Japanese.

During a House of Commons inquiry into the automobile industry in 1975, Sir Peter Carey, the head of the Department of Industry, described the Japanese competition as 'not unfair'. He attributed the problems of the UK industry to underinvestment and too many strikes. However, he recognized an imbalance in trade, and asked for Japanese 'self-restraint'. The Japanese accepted the suggestion, and the Japanese Association of Motor Assemblers (JAMA) agreed to limit 1976 sales to 1975 levels. The Japanese had been shocked in Australia in 1975 when unheeded Australian government calls for restraint resulted in a unilaterally imposed quota on Japanese imports. This rapidly led to direct investments by Nissan and Toyota in Australia.

The self-restraint that the Japanese practiced was unsatisfactory to the British because the Japanese share of the UK market continued to rise. Part of the increase was due to two new Japanese entrants to the UK market (Subaru and Suzuki), but part resulted from continued domestic UK production problems. The British Ambassador to Japan argued with the Ministry of International Trade and Industry (MITI) that further 'forms of words' would be 'unsatisfactory' and that it was time for 'effective restraint'. The Ministry of International Trade and Industry undertook to establish administrative controls for the UK market, 'recognizing the special circumstances of British industry'. Japan was thus effectively limited to 11 percent of the UK market – its approximate market share at the time.

Nissan announced its intention to build an automobile assembly plant in the United Kingdom in 1981. The project was still under consideration in 1983, and negotiations were underway with the Department of Industry over financing arrangements and the level of local content. Nissan had problems with its own union in Japan, which was opposed to any further overseas investment. Concern about 'back-door' Japanese imports was also expressed by the French and Italian governments. The objections of both governments to British Leyland's Triumph Acclaim were only mollified by high-level UK diplomatic representations in Paris and Rome.

The Political Appraisal

In UK political circles there were two competing views of the prospective Nissan plant. The British government was obviously very keen to see the Nissan plant built in the United Kingdom. The government was developing a strategy of supporting British Leyland in its new slimmer form while at the same time hoping that Nissan would show how (and that) a state-of-the-art facility could be run in Britain. The government's hope (and its economic ideology) was that vigorous competition would revitalize not only the assembly industry but the component-supplying industries as well, where there were severe problems of excess capacity.

The opposition believed that in the long run neither British Leyland nor Ford, with their older plants and traditional union agreements and work practices, would be able to compete with a new Japanese greenfield operation. Were Nissan to go ahead with the investment, the two models it would be most likely to make would compete directly with British Leyland's forthcoming LM 10 range and Ford's Escorts and Cortinas. Although the new plant might employ 4,000–5,000 workers, a Ford-produced scenario suggested that under some admittedly pessimistic assumptions there could be a net loss of 50,000 jobs in the industry.

The health of the component industry was also worrisome to critics of Nissan's investment. Jeffrey Wilkinson, Chairman of the Independent Original Equipment Manufacturers' section of the Society of Motor Manufacturers and Traders, claimed that unless Nissan produced cars with 80 percent European content (at ex-works value) the component producers would face a net job loss. Going farther than that, there was a widely held theory that the next target of 'Japan Inc.' was the worldwide automobile component industry. The issue of required local content was clearly central to all this.

There was some speculation in the UK press that Nissan and the government would strike a deal whereby Nissan would substantially reduce its auto exports to the United Kingdom (running at about 100,000 units yearly) in return for lower local content requirements. This plan would mean slower build-up of Nissan's British plant (which would please those on Nissan's board who were cautious about rapid expansion at a time of stagnant world demand). Of course, to the British component industry, such a deal would be seen as a sellout of their interests.

In late 1983 it was not at all clear whether the government's strategy would work. Nissan had still not announced the go-ahead on the British plant. British Leyland had stopped its cash haemorrhage but was hardly a success yet. It had less than 20 percent of its domestic market and had made little headway on the Continent. Ford and General Motors continued to move assembly from the United Kingdom to the Continent while expanding their British market shares by exporting the assembled cars back to Britain. Meanwhile, in 1983 a fierce price-cutting war had broken out in the market as companies fought for market share. British Leyland's viability was still threatened.

CASE 5

The European Economic Community

H. Landis Gabel

The European Economic Community was founded in 1957 with the signing of the Treaty of Rome. The original signatories of the treaty were France, West Germany, Italy, Belgium, Holland, and Luxembourg. The hope of the founders was expressed in Article 2 of the Treaty, which read:

> The Community shall have as its task, by establishing a common market and progressively approximating the economic policies of Member States, to promote throughout the Community a harmonious development of economic activities, a continuous and balanced expansion, an increase in stability, an accelerated raising of the standard of living and closer relations between the States belonging to it.

But in 1983, there was virtually universal abandonment of any such hope. Indeed, some observers were questioning whether the EEC would survive another year. National self-interest had, since the various crises of the 1970s, become a progressively greater impediment to Community-wide cooperation, agricultural programs had grown to consume 80 percent of the EEC budget, and Britain refused to agree to the 1984 budget without a major restructuring of the Community's finances. The state of the automobile industry exemplified many of the EEC's problems.

European Industrial Policy

The European Economic Community was governed by the Treaty of Rome, and the European Commission was the official custodian of the articles of the treaty. The work of the commission was divided into 19 directorates, which were allocated to

---

This case was prepared by Anthony E. Hall, Research Associate, under the supervision of H. Landis Gabel, Associate Professor at INSEAD. It is intended to be used as a basis for class discussion rather than to illustrate either effective or ineffective handling of an administrative situation. This is a satellite case to Ford of Europe and Local Content Regulations. *Copyright© 1985 INSEAD Fontainebleau, France.*

14 commissioners who came from the 10 member states (Denmark, Ireland, and the United Kingdom joined in 1973, and Greece was admitted to membership after its return to democracy in 1979).

European industrial policy was the responsibility of the Industry Directorate of the EEC Commission. The head of the directorate – known as DG III – was Viscount Etienne Davignon, who was also a vice-president of the Commission. Davignon, a Belgian national, was widely regarded as the most able politician in Brussels and would be a contender for the presidency of the Commission when Gaston Thorn left that office in 1984.

Since the late 1970s, DG III had been moving toward a sectoral approach, as one major industrial sector after another experienced crises brought on, at least in part, by the worldwide recession. Steel, shipbuilding, and textiles were prominent cases of structural adjustment programs. In essence, these programs were attempts to sustain price levels while excess capacity was eliminated by multinationally negotiated agreements.

Japanese imports were a frequent target of EEC sectoral industrial policy, and by 1983, Viscount Davignon had led three major deputations to Japan. The result was that slightly less than 40 percent of all Japanese imports into the EEC were subject to some form of restriction (often a 'voluntary' one). Product categories with import restrictions included automobiles and vans, motorcycles, fork-lift-trucks, color televisions and picture tubes, machine tools, hi-fi equipment, quartz watches, and video tape recorders.

The European Automobile Industry and the State

There are major state-owned producers in each of the EEC's major markets – BL in the UK, Renault in France, Alfa-Romeo in Italy (through the holding company of IRI), and Volkswagen in West Germany (40 percent of which was owned by the federal government and the Länder of Saxony). This has given EEC member state governments a special interest in their own national producer that goes beyond each government's concern for the contribution that any company's automobile production could make to its domestic economy.

Each country has looked to the automobile industry for regional job creation. Chrysler (later to become Talbot) was persuaded to invest in a plant at Linwood, Scotland; both Peugeut and Renault had been encouraged to invest in new component plants in Alsace and Lorraine; an Alfa-Sud plant was built in depressed southern Italy; and even the German government offered attractive incentives to locate in high-priority areas such as West Berlin. These national efforts to attract automobile investments as part of regional development schemes led to intense competition among countries for producers' investments. Since 1971, the EEC Commission has tried, with limited success, to coordinate the incentives that member countries have offered and in particular to limit competitive bidding for industry. Looking back at some of the controversial cases of heavy government investment subsidies, the picture is not one of success. Chrysler's Linwood plant closed in 1982, the DeLorean plant in Northern Ireland was closed with the company's bankruptcy, Ford's Halewood facility continues to experience productivity problems, and GM has significantly reduced the output from its UK operations.

Many industry observers believe there is an inherent conflict between an employment objective and an objective of establishing a successful plant. Efficient new plants are very capital-intensive with CAD/CAM and robotic techniques used widely. Already enormous progress with these techniques had been made in Europe. For instance, Ford had installed 450 robots in Europe by 1982, and Fiat had made huge strides in automating production lines with consequent gains in productivity and quality.

EEC Competition Policy and the Automobile Industry

One of the most basic principles of the EEC was that goods and resources should move freely within the Common Market. The Directorate of Competition – DG IV – was responsible for ensuring that anticompetitive business conduct did not block such free movement. In October 1983, the directorate issued two draft proposals intended to ensure first that any type of car available in one country would be made available in all, and second that price differences across member countries would not exceed 12 percent, net of taxes.

Prior to these draft proposals, automobile manufacturers could establish exclusive distribution agreements with selected dealers in national markets.[1] The exclusivity of the agreements gave manufacturers the power to maintain price differences between different countries by withholding cars from anyone trying commercial arbitrage. But DG IV's new proposals included provision for 'parallel' imports from non-authorized dealers if pretax price differences exceeded 12 percent for more than six months.

The reaction of European producers and dealers was immediate and hostile. Both the CCMC and CLCA[2] filed objections to the proposals. Victor Dial, Marketing Director of Peugeot SA, said at a Data Resources International conference in November 1983 that the proposals jeopardized the whole distribution system and that if they were carried out they would cause poor levels of servicing and safety.

Regarding the issue of model availability, Ford was ordered in 1983 to supply 4,800 right-hand-drive cars to the Common Market[3]. Ford had stopped supplying right-hand-drive cars to Germany in 1981. At that time there was a 30 percent price difference between the German and UK markets, prompting significant private purchase of right-hand-drive Fords in Germany for export to the United Kingdom. Ford claimed that the cut-off was done to protect its UK dealers.

Another significant barrier to international trade in automobiles within the EEC was the difference in technical standards from country to country. Although the EEC had been working on technical standardization (homologation), by 1982 it had achieved it only in tires, windshields, and safety belts.

EEC Industrial Policy Toward the Automobile Industry

In 1983, the state of the European automobile industry could be described as a crisis. Umberto Agnelli, president of Fiat, made a widely reported prophecy in the late 1970s that by 1985 there would be only five major manufacturers in Europe. (He presumably included Fiat.) The shakeout was still to come. Some industry experts thought that there were as many as 2 million units of excess capacity in Europe. A price war was underway and only Ford of Europe and Mercedes made significant profits in 1982.

Yet huge sums were required to finance the development of the industry in the 1980s. Data Resources International estimated the requirement to be $80 billion. Ed Blanch, Chairman of Ford of Europe, said in the *Financial Times* in October 1983, 'If profit is not there, the industry will not be able to support its long-term investment program. Then the problem will become a jobs problem.'

The threat was not only to the EEC manufacturers (who employed about 2 million, compared with 2.2 million in the United States and 250,000 in Japan). Component suppliers such as Robert Bosch (West Germany), Lucas (UK), and Ferodo (France) had also suffered with the downturn in the industry.

In January 1981, the European Parliament passed a resolution criticizing the American producers and Japanese importers in Europe and urging action from the Commission. In June 1981, the Commission presented a report to the Council of Ministers that attempted to analyze the industry, especially in the context of its global competition. The report called for an evolutionary change in the structure of the industry controlled by a dialogue with the world's two other major producing nations. In its tone, the report was more supportive of the British approach of collaborative agreements with Japanese producers than it was supportive of protectionism and isolation. Many observers felt the report lacked specific proposals, however.

One problem that the report did foresee was the entry of Spain and Portugal into the community. Negotiations were underway by 1983 and were proceeding slowly. The two countries hoped to be full members by 1987. Both countries had significant car assembly operations. Seat was Spain's nationalized producer and was linked to Fiat. Ford and GM had major plants in Spain building small cars. The Ford plant was built in 1976 and GM's in 1982. Spain had relaxed its local content rules to attract these investments, but the plants were still subject to export performance requirements. Portugal, a member of EFTA, had penal tax rates on imported cars allowed as a transitional concession to protect its industrial base. Thus most manufacturers had assembly plants in Portugal building cars for the local market. Renault, however, had a plant building Renault 5s for export.

The EEC's Policy Discretion

The EEC wanted to present a unified trade policy to the outside world rather than to confront it with a set of disparate national policies. But despite the fact that under the Treaty of Rome all member states had surrendered their sovereignty over trade matters to the EEC, there was in fact little the EEC could do to impose its objective on uncooperative member states.

In the case of Italy, the 2,200-unit annual Japanese import limit was a bilateral treaty signed in 1956 by both countries before the Treaty of Rome and the GATT were established. Thus the EEC had no jurisdiction in Italy, and the Italian government showed no willingness to abolish the treaty. In the other countries, the Japanese car import limits were either agreements between national vehicle manufacturers' associations and JAMA or negotiated voluntary agreements between countries' governments.

Were the EEC to unify these disparate quantitative restrictions, it would need the unanimous agreement of all member countries. And then any single EEC trade position would have to be agreed to voluntarily by Japan to avoid a clear violation of the GATT. Yet unanimity within Europe seemed an unlikely prospect in the light of conflicting national objectives. The Germans generally preferred relatively open markets, the British wanted to export cars of questionable origin to the Continent, and the French and Italians wanted tight controls.

While all these problems loomed ahead of the EEC, a new problem surfaced. The German government announced that it would introduce US-style antipollution measures for all cars sold in the German market. This involved the use of lead-free gasoline and catalytic converters. It said that it was taking the action because of increasing atmospheric pollution and acid rainfall that threatened the German forests. The Germans took unilateral action because agreement could not be reached in Brussels for a common policy. However, the French and Italian producers announced that they would not comply with the regulations.

Notes

1.   From 1967 to 1983, exclusive distribution and exclusive purchasing agreements qualified for block exemption from prosecution under the EEC antitrust laws.
2.   The 'Committee of Common Market Automobile Constructors' and the 'Liaison Committee for the Motor Industry' in the EEC.
3.   The order was made under Article 85(1) of the Treaty of Rome, an antitrust article.

CASE 6

The EC–Japan Elements of Consensus

Jonathan Story

On July 31, 1991, The European Commission and the Japanese Ministry of International Trade (MITI) finally completed their three-year negotiations on limiting Japanese car exports to the European Community. The accords stipulated that Japanese exports to the EC would be controlled until December 31, 1999, with specific limits also set for five EC countries. Beginning on January 1, 2000 the market would be completely open.

The negotiations surrounding the quotas for the sale of Japanese cars in the European community were difficult for all concerned.

Although the EC and MITI had drawn up a draft accord as early as August 1990, the final agreement between the parties was delayed for a year, mainly over questions concerning the production of cars in Japanese factories situated within the European Community, known as transplants. The Japanese were adamant that no restrictions for transplants be allowed, while the EC wanted such cars included in the quotas.

The negotiations came at a time when automobile sales of the big six producers in Europe – VAG (Volkswagen, Seat and Audi), PSA, Renault, Ford, General Motors and Fiat – were starting to slide as a global recession took hold. Without an agreement, the Commission knew that the Japanese could legally sell as many cars as they wanted once the single market went into effect on January 1, 1993.

At the time of the negotiations, the car markets in five European countries were protected by bilateral agreements, limiting Japanese market share to 1 percent in Spain, 3 percent in France, 2,550 cars and 5,000 trucks (or less than 2 percent) in Italy, 11 percent in the UK and 14 percent in Portugal. Benelux, Holland, Ireland, Denmark and Greece had no limits on exports, and in those countries, Japanese car makers had already captured between 20 percent and 40 percent of the market.[1] A number of experts claimed that a secret German/Japanese accord finalized in 1986 set Japanese exports to Germany to 15 percent of the market in exchange for eliminating barriers for luxury German cars to enter Japan. The Germans denied the existence of such an accord.[2]

Despite these bilateral agreements, once the single market became a reality there was nothing to stop Japanese firms from exporting cars to these protected countries via EC member states that had no quotas for Japanese automobiles. Nor would there be any restriction on Japanese firms manufacturing cars in other EC countries for export to the protected EC markets.

The negotiations were especially crucial given the importance of the automobile industry to the European economy: it directly and indirectly employed 10 million people – in jobs ranging from auto factory worker to driving school instructor – although the importance to various countries varied widely. Germany for example accounted for 49 percent of the added value of the EC's automobile sector. France accounted for 18 percent, the UK 13 percent, Italy 11 percent and Spain 5 percent.

The Automobile Industry under Study

During the 1980s, the automobile industry was scrutinized by various consultants and organizations who were trying to understand the Japanese auto makers' success and to quantify the differences between US, European and Japanese manufacturing processes.

In 1990, a team of researchers at the Massachusetts Institute of Technology (MIT) published a study, *The Machine that Changed the World*, that suggested that American automobile makers lagged behind their Japanese rivals. In every aspect, from the quality of cars, the speed of production, the length of time from inception to showroom, and technological advancement, the Japanese won hands down. The MIT researchers called the Japanese approach 'lean production' (Eiji Toyoda – now chairman of Toyota – who first developed the system liked to call it 'the last fart of the ferret'), a new manufacturing philosophy that, he said, would make Henry Ford's 75-year old process of mass production obsolete. The tenets of the Japanese manufacturing philosophy were just-in-time production, less bureaucracy and less waste than in US firms. And the MIT study suggested that European manufacturers were even farther behind than their American counterparts, who had already made some moves, including massive layoffs, toward lean production (see Exhibits 6.1 and 6.2, MIT Study of Automobile Manufacturing).

Another study, this one conducted by the consulting group Booz Allen & Hamilton and published in January 1991 by The Economist Intelligence Unit, came to the same conclusions. The Japanese, it said, were more productive, although not to the extent that the MIT report suggested. Booz Allen researchers also attributed Japanese manufacturers' success to being market leaders in terms of new models and technology. The report suggested that the only way European manufacturers could compete would be to innovate sufficiently so they could drive, rather than be driven by, the market.

Exhibit 6.1 *Results of MIT study comparing Japanese and US factories*

	Japanese factories*	US factories
Productivity (hours/car)	16.8	25.1
Quality (defects/100 cars)	60.0	82.3
Stocks (by day for a sample of eight parts)	0.2	2.9
% of workers working in teams	69.3	17.3
Rotation of employee jobs (0 = never, 4 = frequent)	3.0	0.9
Suggestions/employee	61.6	0.4
Number of employee classifications	11.9	67.1
Training (in hours)	380.3	46.4
Absenteeism (days/year)	5.0	11.7
Automation: % soldering	86.2	76.2
Automation: % painting	54.6	33.6
Automation: % assembly	1.7	1.2
Hours for conception of new model (in millions)	1.7	3.1
Months of development of new mode	46.2	60.4
Number of works responsible for development	485	90.3
Body variations per model	2.3	1.7
% of spare parts in common	18	38
% of work done by subcontractors	51	14
Costs of modifying the conception as a % of total tool cost	10 to 20	30 to 50
Ratio of late projects	1 in 6	1 in 2
Time to develop tools (in months)	13.8	25
Time to realize prototype (in months)	6.2	12.4
Delay between first production and	1	4
Return to normal production after a launch (in months)	4	5
Return to normal quality after a launch (in months)	1.4	11

* in Japan
Source: Massachusetts Institute of Technology

The Boston Consulting Group, in its 1991 study of the European Automotive component industry, also found European and American component manufacturers lagging behind the Japanese in terms of quality and productivity. Part of the problem, it said, was that European car companies had between 800 and 2,000 suppliers, while Japanese firms had between 160 and 300 suppliers. Thus the relationship between Japanese car makers and their suppliers was more efficient than the partnership between European manufacturers and their suppliers.

The McKinsey consulting group also conducted a study that found the Japanese to be ahead in the automotive game. 'On the eve of the automobile industry's entrance into its globalization phase, European manufacturers are still largely national, or at best pan-European.' The report said that in comparison, the American and Japanese automobile makers already had a global structure of distribution and production in place.

Finally, a study published in *Asian Motor Vehicle Business Review* in 1992,

Exhibit 6.2 *Results of MIT study comparing Japanese and European factories*

	Japanese factories*	European factories
Productivity (hours/car)	16.8	35.5
Stocks (in hours)	5.0	48
Months of development of new model	46.2	57.3
Number of works responsible for development	485.0	904.0
Time to develop tools (in months)	13.8	28
Time to realize prototype (in months)	6.2	12.4
Ratio of late projects	1 in 6	1 in 3
Delay between first production and first sales (in months)	1	4
Return to normal production after a launch (in months)	4	5
Return to normal quality after a launch (in months)	1.4	11

* in Japan
Source: Massachusetts Institute of Technology

compared slightly different aspects of the global automobile industry. It took into account production per employee, how much of production was integrated, and the number of hours worked per employee. The Asian study found that although the Japanese were ahead of the bunch, some European manufacturers were as productive as their American counterparts (see Exhibit 6.3, Asian Motor Review Study).

Jean-Jacques Chanaron, a researcher at the French National Center of Scientific Research, argued that all these studies were slanted in favor of the Japanese thanks to the strong Japanese automobile lobby. He pointed out that

Exhibit 6.3 *Productivity study* – Asian Motor Vehicle Business Review

	# of Cars Produced/ yr (in min)	# of Employees (in thous.)	# of Cars by Employees	Rate of Integration	Cars/ Employee year	Hours Worked/ 1000 hrs	Cars/ Head/
Toyota	4.199	73	57.52	30	17.3	2,280	7.57
Nissan	2.380	55	43.27	30	13.0	2,281	5.69
Honda	1.369	25	54.76	27	14.8	1,955	7.56
GM	7.451	616	12.10	70	8.5	1,986	4.26
Ford	5.805	370	15.69	50	7.8	1,986	3.95
VW	3.058	261	11.72	50	5.9	1,576	3.72
PSA	2.220	159	13.96	50	7.7	1,646	4.24
Fiat	2.163	141	15.34	50	7.7	n.a.	n.a.

* Taking into account rate of integration
Source: Asian Motor Vehicle Business Review (based on 1990 data)

the MIT study had far more Japanese researchers and American researchers than European, and that since the study did not receive financial support from any French, German or Italian auto makers, that it was biased against them. Also most of the documents cited in the bibliography of the study were in English and much information also came from Japanese sources, which some automobile experts said were unreliable. He also argued that the study compared apples to oranges, given that the financial structure, the level of integration, the degree of internationalization and the type and range of models were all very different for US, European and Japanese automobile manufacturers.

Mr Chanaron argued that the Japanese had not abandoned mass production, but had simply transferred all activities that were not directly productive onto suppliers. Thus the suppliers were the ones to absorb the costs for just-in-time delivery, as well as the extra expense that resulted from the rise in the yen. Since the Japanese car makers made only about 20 percent to 25 percent of each vehicle themselves, compared to 50 percent to 60 percent for European car makers, they just appeared to be more efficient. He added that the Japanese work ethic, in which workers tie themselves to one company for a lifetime, was another factor contributing to the differences in productivity figures, as was the fact that the Japanese market was dictated by the car makers and not vice versa (see Exhibit 6.4, Chanaron Study).

Other critics also believed that MIT had overstated their case for the end of mass production. In an editorial in the *Wall Street Journal* (May 30, 1991), Vic Heylen, a journalist specializing in the automotive industry, said '. . . an assembly line in Japan is, technologically, no different from an assembly line in the West. The only difference is that Japanese manufacturers make much better use of their workforce, allowing them to use fewer workers to do the same job.' More specifically, he said that workers were given more responsibility, and therefore were more motivated.

Whether or not the studies painted an accurate picture of production efficiency and productivity, no one argued that the European manufacturers had improved their productivity between 1986 (when the MIT study was conducted) and the end of the 1980s. Between 1984 and 1989, according to a study done by *Autocar and Motor*: PSA's production had become 76 percent more efficient; Renault's, 55 percent; General Motors', 40 percent; Ford's, 30 percent; Fiat's, 29 percent; and Volkswagen's, 27 percent.

Changes in the World Automobile Industry and Markets

Nineteen eighty-nine proved to be a record sales year for many European automobile companies, but the 1990s brought trouble to the industry.

In 1990, European car sales rose by just 20,000 units, although the total of 13.42 billion passenger cars for the 17 western European countries was a record. Much of the growth, however, came from Germany, where reunification helped

Exhibit 6.4 *Divergence of competitive study results – J. J. Chanaron*

Number of hours per car in 1989 (MIT Study)	Worst	Average	Best
Japanese in Japan	25.9	16.8	13.2
Japanese in US	25.5	20.9	18.8
American in US	30.7	24.9	18.6
American and Japan in Europe	57.6	35.3	22.8
European in Europe	55.7	35.5	22.8
Production per worker (*Asian Motor Vehicle Business Review*)			
Toyota			7.57
Honda			7.56
Nissan			5.69
GM			4.25
Ford			3.95
PSA			4.24
VW			3.72
Fiat			4.64
Production per worker (Jean-Jaques Chanaron)			
Toyota			3.98
Honda			2.81
Nissan			2.02
GM			2.67
Ford			2.41
PSA			2.66
VW			3.09
Renault			1.58
Fiat			4.00

Source: La Dernière Bataille de l'Automobile Européenne, Thierry Gandillot, Fayard © 1992

push sales up 7.4 percent. Excluding Germany, sales in the rest of Europe fell 4.1 percent.[4] Philip Ayton, an analyst at Barclays de Zoete Wedd Securities in London, estimated that the combined European income of the Big Six European car makers fell by 27 percent in 1990, to $6.07 billion.

The next year proved no better. The general global economic slowdown coupled with the Gulf War hit car markers on every continent. In the US, General Motors lost $4.45 billion, Ford $2.3 billion, and Chrysler $795 million. Even the Japanese saw a decline in sales. Nissan's sales edged down 6.3 percent, Honda's dropped 6 percent and Toyota's dipped 4 percent.[5] In Europe total car sales grew only 1.9 percent to 13.46 million, and as in the previous year, that increase was thanks to German sales, which jumped 36.8 percent. But despite the somber economic environment, the Japanese were still holding their own in the US. While US car makers were obliged to give discounts of $1,896 to move cars off the lots, Japanese consumer discounts were only $917. The US trade deficit for automobiles reached $30 billion, which represented three-quarters of the US's trade deficit with Japan.[6]

It was at this time that US government officials and the US car manufacturers began accusing Japanese firms of dumping their products on the US market. One study, conducted by the US Commerce Department and MITI showed that Japanese spare parts for automobiles were much more expensive in Japan than in the United States. Other studies showed that Japanese companies were selling certain vehicles between 0.95 percent and 7.19 percent cheaper in the US than in Japan. Based on these studies the US Commerce Department announced that it would slap anti-dumping duties on offending Japanese manufacturers. This trade friction with Japan led to President George Bush's infamous visit to Tokyo in January 1992, accompanied by automobile executives, including the heads of Detroit's Big Three.

This embarrassing sojourn – which ended with President Bush, hit by intestinal flu, vomiting on the leg of the Japanese Prime Minister during a luncheon – yielded minimal results. The Japanese agreed to double their US car imports to 32,000 cars and to raise their purchases of spare parts by 20 percent to $19.1 billion annually by 1994. The Japanese government indicated it would also increase pressure on dealers to carry American cars. Japanese dealerships, although independent, had very strong relationships with Japanese car manufacturers, and thus foreign manufacturers had little luck in breaking into the established distribution network.

It was obvious to all car makers that their future lay in becoming global players. Unfortunately, none of the European car makers had made any significant inroads in the US or Japanese markets. In 1989, the EC imported ten times more passenger vehicles from Japan than they exported to that country. Nor had any American firm managed to penetrate the Japanese market. Imports sales in Japan equalled a measly 221,832 cars in 1990, with Volkswagen capturing 1.1 percent of Japanese market share, and the US Big Three holding 1.9 percent.

The Japanese, through exports and transplants, held almost 30 percent of the US market in 1990 (and 33.5 percent if one included Japanese cars made in Japan or the US but distributed by GM, Chrysler or Ford). Of the 3 million cars the Japanese sold in the US in 1990, 1.390 million were produced on US soil, although only ten years earlier, no Japanese cars had been made there. For some Japanese manufacturers, more than half the cars they sold in the US now came from transplant factories. Thus Japanese imports fell below their voluntary quota of 2.3 million units in 1990 to 1.7 million units.

The Japanese had, however, barely made inroads into the European Community, exporting only 1.143 million cars in 1990 and selling another 76,000 transplant vehicles. Together these represented roughly 10 percent of the EC car market of 12.1 million cars. But official Japanese government estimates said Japanese factories in Europe would be producing between 600,000 and 700,000 cars by 1992.[7] Indeed, Honda, Nissan and Toyota, the three biggest Japanese auto firms, all had ambitions to conquer the global car market, with goals of 5, 8 and 10 percent respectively for global market share. The Japanese also forecast that Europe offered the highest growth rates in the 90s for the auto market, mushrooming to 15 million cars by 1998. Europe also offered the highest profit margins. Even troubled General Motors made 60 percent of its profits in Europe.[8]

The head of Nissan, Yutaka Kume, summed up the Japanese ambitions best, 'Yes, Europe is now my primary target. In the world automobile market, the next three to five years will be difficult. At the end of the 1990s, there will be only four or five automobile makers: three Japanese, and without a doubt two Europeans, Fiat and Volkswagen, that's all.'[9]

The big three Japanese auto companies had, as early as the 1960s, begun to pave the way for their European expansion by opening marketing organizations, and beginning in the 1970s, assembly plants in Europe. Most were located in lower-cost labor countries like Ireland and Greece. Japanese full-scale manufacturing and foreign direct investment came to Europe in the 1980s. The Japanese set up transplants as part of their strategy to be close to their final markets, as well as to avoid export duties on cars sold in Europe (tariffs on cars exported to the EC were around 10 percent). Also, by 1990, labor costs in Spain, France and the UK were cheaper than in Japan, where total wage costs per hour in the automobile sector were 28.64 DM, according to the German Automobile Industry Federation (VDA).

The United Kingdom was particularly welcoming to Japanese firms, offering financial inducements to bring manufacturers to the island. In 1984, Nissan agreed to open a plant in England and Honda later set up a joint operation with British firm Rover (see Exhibit 6.5 for more information on European car markets and manufacturers).

Exhibit 6.5 *Automobile manufacturers*

Toyota

In 1990, Toyota was the world's third largest auto maker, producing 4.231 million cars. It had 2.2 percent of the EC's market share and 2.7 percent market share in Western Europe.

Toyota was a family-run business (Toyoda family), considered to be fairly conservative and very rich, with $15 billion in reserves. Toyota was the creator of just-in-time manufacturing, which allowed for greater diversity in its product line and reduced staffing and equipment costs.

In 1990, Toyota made 26,000 cars in Europe: 11,000 in Portugal and 15,000 in Germany, and it planned to increase production to 500,000 in Europe by 2000, with the addition of a UK plant in Burnaston, slated to open in 1992. The company also planned to open a motor manufacturing plant there in mid-1992 that would make 200,000 engines.

Toyota was committed to 80 percent local content in all its cars manufactured in the EC, a goal it said it would reach by 1995.

Nissan

In 1990, Nissan, the world's fourth largest automobile manufacturer (producing 2.416 passenger cars) sold 400,000 cars in Western Europe to capture 2.9 percent of the market (2.6 percent of the market in the EC). Its goal for 1995 was to sell 700,000 cars in Europe, half of which would be produced on the Continent, mostly in the UK.

Nissan opened its first wholly-owned factory in Europe in 1986 in Sunderland in northeast England (although the company had a 67.6 percent stake in a motor factory in Spain which opened in January 1985). Nissan made about 138,500 cars in Europe in 1990: 8,500 in Spain, 120,000 in the UK and 10,000 in Greece.[1]

Exhibit 6.5 *Continued*

Nissan was one of the first Japanese firms to use computer-aided design (CAD), which it introduced in 1967. CAD is one reason that Japanese car makers were able to bring a car to market in four years, while European manufacturers took five or six years.

In October 1991, Nissan acquired its French distributor, Richard Nissan.

Honda

Honda, the world's eighth largest automobile maker in 1990, held 1.1 percent of the EC market and 1.2 percent of the European market (160,000 cars).

Honda made 40,000 cars in Rover's factories in England and planned to increase that to 200,000 by 2000.[2] Honda bought a 20 percent stake in Rover in 1989.

Honda was considered the most innovative of the Japanese Big Three. Although it was number three in Japan, it had the biggest market share in the US among Japanese firms. It was the first Japanese firm to set up a factory in US and in 1987, it sold 833,300 cars in North America, and topped 1 million cars in 1991. About 25 percent of its production capacity was in North America.

Honda also sought to have the highest local content of any manufacturer in the US (Japanese and US car makers included), with a goal of 75 percent by 1991.

In September 1991, Honda announced it would expand its European dealership to about 2,000 dealers by the mid-1990s, from 1,500 in 1991. It said it needed the added dealers to cope with sales it expected would reach 250,000 cars per year.

General Motors

General Motors, in 1990, was the largest manufacturer of passenger cars in the world, selling 5.5 million cars.

In 1979, the company had 46 percent of the US market, but by 1990, that percentage had dropped to 35 percent. At the end of 1991, the company's Chairman, Bob Stempel, announced the closing of 21 of its 38 North American factories, and the lay-off of 74,000 employees. But despite problems in the US, GM Europe, maker of Vauxhalls in the UK and Opels on the Continent, was the third largest car manufacturer in Europe, accounting in 1990 for 11.8 percent of all new car registrations in Western Europe – up from 10.7 percent in 1987.

GM Europe posted sales of 18.65 billion Ecus in 1990, making it the most profitable European car company, with net profits equally 8.3 percent of sales.

GM's principal market was Germany, where it made 34 percent of its sales, and held 17.9 percent of the market, second only to Volkswagen.

Profits were held back slightly by Saab-Scania, the Swedish car company in which GM, in 1989, bought a 50 percent stake. The struggling company cost GM $430 million in earnings in 1990.

GM Europe was also moving aggressively into Eastern Europe, building state-of-the-art factories in Hungary and in former East Germany.

Ford

Ford, in 1990, was the number two auto maker worldwide, making 3.7 million passenger cars in 1990. Ford of Europe accounted for 11.6 percent of all car registrations in Western Europe.

Exhibit 6.5 *Continued*

The year 1990 did not prove to be a successful year for Ford in Europe because 38 percent of its sales were concentrated in Britain which was going through a deep recession. Nor did it have a particularly strong presence in Germany, which was fueling most of the growth in European car sales. The company also suffered from strikes and a rough introduction of its new model, the Escort. Its acquisition of Jaguar in 1989 for $2.5 billion also came just when the luxury-car market in Europe and the US was going into a skid, and that unit lost $86.8 million in 1990.

Despite these setbacks, Ford was considered to be one of the most productive manufacturers after the Japanese.

Volkswagen (VAG)

Volkswagen, which was created by Adolf Hitler and remained partially state-owned until the 1980s, was the fifth largest car maker in the world, with 2.9 million passenger vehicles in 1990.

VAG was considered by most analysts to be Europe's strongest automobile manufacturer, with 15.4 percent of the European market through its sale of Audis, Seats and Volkswagen brands. It absorbed Spain's Seat in the 1980s in order to get into the small car market, and took a controlling share in Skoda, the Czechoslovakian car manufacturer, a move which was expected to place VW at the head of the Eastern European car market. VW had the least dependence of the Big Six on its home market, making 28.3 percent of its sales in Germany, and 26.6 percent of its sales outside of Europe.

A French business magazine, *Capital*, in an analysis of which of the Big Six were best placed to compete against the Japanese, placed VW at the top, ranking it first in quality of management, industrial organization, model lineup, commercial strength, marketing efficiency, innovation and product quality.

VW's weaknesses were considered high production costs, due especially to high German labor costs. The company's 1990 profits equalled only 1.6 percent of its 33.1 billion Ecus in sales, one of the lowest profitability ratios among the Big Six European producers.

Fiat SpA

Fiat was the lead company in the largest investor-owned industrial group in Italy, run by the Agnelli family.

In 1990, Fiat, maker of Fiats, Lancias and Alfa Romeos, accounted for 14.2 percent of all car registrations in Western Europe, making it the second largest European car maker, and the sixth largest in the world, producing 2.4 million passenger vehicles. Its 1990 net profit equalled 2.27 percent of its 20.36 billion Ecus in sales.

Of all the European car makers, Fiat was the most dependent on its home market. In 1990, Italy accounted for almost 60 percent of its European sales, and was the home of 90 percent of its production. In addition, another 10 percent of sales came from the protected markets of France, Spain and Portugal, and only 9 percent of its sales were made outside of Europe. At the beginning of 1991, its Italian market share had fallen to 47.4 percent from 54.6 percent a year earlier, and 58.9 percent two years before, thanks to an invasion of the Italian market by other European competitors, notably Ford.

Fiat was aggressive in Eastern Europe, with joint-ventures in Russia and Poland, and the company claimed that more than half of the 2 million cars produced in Eastern Europe and the Soviet Union were Fiat derivatives.

Exhibit 6.5 *Continued*

Renault

In 1990, Renault accounted for 9.9 percent of all car registrations in Western Europe, and was the tenth larger car maker, producing 1.5 million passenger cars.

Renault, France's fifth largest exporter, had tried to beef up its business by joining forces with AB Volvo in 1989 (Renault owned 25 percent of Volvo's car operations and Volvo owned 20 percent of Renault's car operations), but analysts were not certain that such a partnership would be as effective in cutting development costs as the two companies hoped. Renault had the lowest profitability of the Big Six European car makers, with net profits equalling 0.7 percent of sales, which reached 18.75 billion Ecus in 1990. Its 1991 profits plunged 87 percent from 1989, a record sales year.

Renault made 45.5 percent of its sales in France and 11.9 percent of its sales outside Europe.

PSA Peugeot Citroën

In 1990, PSA, the maker of Peugeot, Talbot and Citroën brands, accounted for 12.9 percent of all car registrations in Western Europe, and was the seventh largest auto maker in the world producing almost 2 million cars.

Peugeot, despite being France's fourth largest exporter, was fairly dependent on its domestic market, selling 40.8 percent of its cars in France, and 8.46 percent outside of Europe. Its net profit to sales ratio was fairly high in 1990, at 5.8 percent, with sales reaching 22.18 billion Ecus.

Jacques Calvet, the company's chairman, was considered too protectionist by most other car makers, who claimed that Calvet was trying to blame the Japanese for all his company's ills.

Notes

1. *Tribune de l'Expansion*, August 9, 1991 (Graph).
2. *Tribune de l'Expansion*, August 9, 1991 (Graph).

The First Elements of Consensus: August 1990

The EC and MITI hammered out their first draft agreement, called 'Elements of Consensus', on August 8 and 9, 1990.

The draft outlined a number of essential elements. The parties agreed on a transition period of five to seven years after the opening of the single market in January 1993, during which time a quota on Japanese exports would continue to be maintained. It allowed for a rise in exports to 1.230 million vehicles by the end of the transition period, based on an EC estimate that 15.1 million cars would be sold in the Community in 1999. Adding in transplant sales, the Japanese would increase their market share in the EC from 10 percent in 1989 to 18.7 percent. The draft also fixed new quotas for the five EC countries that already had limits on Japanese exports. It also forbade 'targeting', concentrating the sale of Japanese transplants into the protected countries. Finally it set out guidelines for a system to monitor Japanese car sales every six months.

Intra EC Negotiations

The EC Commissioners charged with the dossier were the Commissioner for Competition – Sir Leon Brittan, Commissioner of Industry – Martin Bangemann, and Commissioner of External Affairs – Frans Andriessen. All were well known as liberal, free-market supporters, but behind their apparently unified stance was a number of warring factions made up of government officials from EC member states and European car makers.

On the Japanese side of the negotiations, MITI was the main negotiator with the EC Commission, although the Ministry of Foreign Affairs (MoFA) and the Japanese Automobile Manufacturers Associations (JAMA) also gave input to government negotiators. Unlike the European players, their stand was basically united.

The Japanese were putting pressure on the EC to come to an end of the negotiations by the end of 1990. MoFA threatened that if an agreement was not reached soon, they would take the question of quotas to GATT, which in principle forbids all restrictions on international trade (although to date had not banned such bilateral, gentlemen's agreements between countries). According to Martin Bangemann, who was considered the most pragmatic of the three EC commissioners heading the car negotiations, 'There are some Japanese who are waiting to put the EEC in infraction of free-trade laws to attack us in GATT. We are therefore condemned to "grey area" agreements.'[10] Grey area agreements are not treaties, but rather self-limiting accords between trade partners.

The biggest opponent of the liberal EC negotiators was Edith Cresson, the French Minister of European Affairs. In September 1990, she held a press conference with the support of the Spanish, Italian and Portuguese governments, at which she denounced the Commission's negotiations with Japan. She said the Commission was 'underestimating' the danger of Japanese manufacturers for the European automobile industry, which supported 5 million households.[11]

She supported a transition period of at least seven years, a limit on exports of Japanese cars made in the United States, monitoring of Japanese exports on a country by country basis, a non-targeting clause and a clause that would limit Japanese exports in case of a downturn in the market. The Portuguese, Spanish and Italian governments did not press for a longer transition period because they felt that increased competition would help European firms restructure more quickly. In addition Cresson asked for a reciprocity agreement to open the Japanese market to European exports. Cresson and the other hardliners also wanted an 80 percent local content clause – a stipulation that Ford and General Motors had followed for their European-produced cars since 1980.

The Japanese car makers argued that such a clause would be counter to GATT rules. However, a year earlier, the UK government, negotiating on behalf of Nissan, had struck such a deal with the French. In exchange for promising that Nissan's UK-produced Bluebirds would reach 80 percent local content by 1990, the French had agreed to consider these cars 'European', and not count them as part of Japan's 3 percent export limit.

European Car Makers Respond

Peugeot Chairman Jacques Calvet was one of the most outspoken proponents of protectionism for the European car market. He believed that strict quotas for Japanese car sales were necessary, especially since the Japanese were reluctant to open their markets to foreigners. Fiat chairman Giovanni Agnelli and Renault head, Raymond Levy also backed protectionist measures.

At the start of the EC/Japanese negotiations, the German manufacturers had a much more liberal stance than the Italian and French car makers. VAG chairman Carl Hahn stated that the challenge of borderless Europe would make the European car makers more efficient. Likewise, the German luxury car makers, Mercedes, BMW and Porsche believed in the late 1980s that they could compete against the Japanese in Europe, and were loath to put up strict barriers for fear of hurting their sales in Japan.

By 1990, however, when the Japanese car makers had introduced luxury cars like the Infiniti, Acura and Lexus to the European market, even the Germans began to worry. In April of 1990, for example, Albert Schneider, head of BMW Europe complained of the 'abnormally low prices' of Japanese cars.[12]

In October 1990, the heads of the four biggest European auto makers, Fiat, Peugeot, Renault and VW, met to create a counter proposition for the EC to present to Japan. The number two at Fiat, Umberto Agnelli, and Raymond Levy and Carl Hahn, heads of Renault and VW respectively, had composed a letter to the EC which they wanted Calvet to sign as a way of showing the Japanese that there was a unified stance among European car manufacturers. The basic tenets of the letter were:

1. A transition period of ten years, to cover both exports and transplant production, and 15 billion ECUS per year to help the industry modernize and slim down to face Japanese competition.

2. The understanding that cars imported from Japan, as well as cars manufactured in Japanese plants in the US and Europe, be considered Japanese.

3. Japanese market share would vary with the growth of the market. If market growth was slow, say 3 percent annually over 1989 levels, the Europeans would be given 90 percent of the growth. If market growth was mediocre, say 8 percent, they would get 75 percent, and if market growth

took off, above 8 percent, the Europeans would keep only 60 percent of the growth to themselves.

4. No targeting of protected markets.
5. Cars built in Europe must be made with 80 percent local content.
6. The Japanese must open their market to the Europeans.

Peugeot Chairman, Jacques Calvet, refused to sign the letter, wanting to go even farther and stop the creation of Japanese factories in the EC.

The three other car makers wanted to bring the proposal to the other major auto makers in the Community. Unfortunately they could not work directly through the established trade association, the Comité des Constructeurs du Marché Commun (CCMC) because the CCMC's charter demanded decision by unanimous vote, so Calvet, who was a member, would be able to veto the CCMC's approval of the letter.

The CCMC was formed in 1972, and included 12 members: German car makers BMW, DAF, Daimler-Benz, Porsche, MAN and VAG; British car makers Rolls-Royce and Rover; Volvo Car (subsidiary of Sweden-based AB Volvo headquartered in Holland); Fiat; Renault and PSA (Peugeot and Citroën). The association was dominated by the French manufacturers, who had a strong alliance with Fiat, and this Mediterranean faction was often at odds with the Germans. Of all the Germans, VAG was considered to be the most sympathetic to the Mediterranean group, since its cars were less expensive than other German automobiles, and thus depended more on volume than the likes of Daimler Benz and BMW.

To get around Calvet, a new trade organization was formed in February 1991, and opened in BMW's headquarters in Munich – the Association des Constructeurs Européens d'Automobiles (ACEA). The group had 15 members: all the former CCMC members, minus PSA, and four new members, Ford-Europe and General Motors Europe, and Swedish firms AB Volvo and Saab. Voting was no longer unanimous, but demanded only 75 percent approval of the members. The new organization was considered much more Germanic, since 7 out of 15 members were German (counting Ford and GM, which did most of their business there).

The formal stance of the ACEA called for a transition period of ten years, a division of market growth of 40 percent for the Japanese and 60 percent for the Europeans. In the case of a market slowdown or weak growth, Japanese imports would remain at their current level of 10 percent of the market. They also wanted an upper limit of 15 percent market share, including transplants, by the end of the transition period. The trade association demanded a non-targeting clause, a monitoring of the market, and the opening of the Japanese market. Finally, the ACEA pressed for financial help from the EC for R&D and training.

The basically unified stance of the European manufacturers did not persuade the northern European governments to take their side. Neither Germany, UK, Ireland, nor the other non-car producing countries, wanted to place formal limits on Japanese transplants. The MITI, as expected, was not happy with the tougher stance taken by Mediterranean governments and the ACEA. It accepted the seven-year transition period, but did not want any formal limits on Japanese transplants for fear that such a deal would influence future negotiations with the US concerning transplant production.

The EC Agrees to a Common Mandate

Everyone thought the seven EC ministers had finally adopted a common position on April 9, 1991, agreeing among other things, on a transition period of six years, and a limit of 17 percent of the market, including transplants, for the Japanese by the end of that period. Yet ten days later, the EC Commissioner for the Environment, Carlo Ripa di Meana, denounced the EC mandate as being too favorable to the Japanese, arguing in a letter to the Commission that the trade deficit between Japan and the EC was on the rise. He pointed out that the ratio between EC investments in Japan and Japanese investments in the EC was 1 to 17, and that between 1987 and 1990 these investments grew by a factor of four. He said that the Japanese continued to shut off their market from the rest of the world and that caution was demanded.[13] Ripa di Meana said that a clause should be added to the agreement, to allow for a possible extension of the transition period if economic, political and industrial conditions were not conducive to opening the European market completely. He also said that the opening of the market should be dependent on a reciprocal opening of the Japanese market.

Despite these complaints, the EC Commission ministers passed the mandate on April 30, 1991.

The Final Accord – a New Element of Consensus

Over the next few months, the final negotiations with the Japanese took place, and at the end of July, a final accord was reached between the Japanese and the EC.

The new Elements of Consensus included the following:

- A seven-year transition period through December 1999, after which the market would be completely opened.

- A cap on Japanese exports for 1999 of 1.23 million cars, or about 8 percent of the estimated 1999 EC market of 15.1 million cars.

- A clause stipulating that the Japanese limit exports to protected markets in the following manner (based on forecast for 1999):

	Est. Japanese exports 1999	Est. total sales 1999	Japanese exports 1990
France	150,000	2,850,000	76,000
Italy	138,000	2,608,000	45,000
Spain	79,000	1,475,000	45,000
UK	190,000	2,700,000	236,000
Portugal	23,000	275,000	16,000

In addition, the growth of exports would be more or less even over the course of the transition period.

- Bi-annual meetings (Spring and Fall) to begin in 1993 to evaluate the market and monitor Japanese exports, both to the EC as a whole and to each of the protected markets. Both sides agreed that changes in Japanese exports would be made depending on actual market conditions.

- The EC agreed not to impose restrictions on Japanese investments nor any controls on the free circulation of its products in the Community.

- The Japanese government said it would communicate to Japanese automobile manufacturers that excessive concentration of sales of their vehicles made in the Community on certain (i.e. protected) national markets would cause disruption in that market.

- The EC agreed it would not ask to prolong the transition period beyond December 31, 1999.

In addition, the EC issued a unilateral statement, an 'Internal Declaration', saying that throughout the transition period, EC auto makers should have at least one-third of any market growth, based on 1990 sales. But in the case of a market slowdown, three-quarters of any sales reductions would be absorbed by the Japanese.

Finally, the head negotiators, Frans Andriessen, Commissioner of External Affairs for the EC, and Eiichi Nakao, head of MITI, attached to the accords transcripts of oral 'conclusive declarations'.

Andriessen's statement included the following comment: 'During these negotiations, the Commission has based itself on various working assumptions concerning the automobile market's development in the future, including an estimate of 1.2 million vehicles for the annual sales by 1999 – the end of the transition period – of European-built Japanese vehicles in the EC.'[14] Therefore with exports and transplants, the Japanese would have 16.1 percent of the market by 1999.

The EC had also estimated the following level of transplant sales for each of the five protected markets, although these estimates were not specifically listed in the conclusive declarations.[15]

	Est. market share via exports	Est. market share via transplants
France	5.3%	1.7–5.7%
Italy	5.3%	1.7–5.7%
Spain	5.3%	6.8–10.8%
UK	7.0%	13.9–19.9%
Portugal	8.4%	8.1–13.1%

Although Nakao, responding in his own statement, did not directly challenge the transport limits, he made the following comment: 'During these negotiations, the Japanese side based itself on the working assumption that the export figure at the end of the transition period is forecast taking into account total demand and the EC manufacturers' supply capacity as a whole. Let me call your attention to your commitment in the Elements of Consensus that Japanese investment or sales of its products in the Community shall not be restricted.'[16]

Notes

1.   *International Herald Tribune*, April 5, 1991.
2.   *Le Monde*, March 15, 1991.
3.   Gandillot, Thierry, *La Dernière Bataille de l'Automobile Européenne* (Paris: Fayard, 1992) p. 18.
4.   *Wall Street Journal*, May 14, 1991.
5.   *La Dernière Bataille*, p. 196.
6.   Ibid, pp. 195–6.
7.   *Le Figaro*, July 26, 1990.
8.   *La Dernière Bataille*, pp. 19–20.
9.   *Le Figaro-Magazine*, April 7, 1990.
10.   *La Dernière Bataille*, p. 101.
11.   *Le Monde*, September 21, 1990.
12.   *Le Nouvel Observateur*, June 8, 1990.
13.   *La Dernière Bataille*, p. 132.
14.   Ibid, pp. 179–80.
15.   From internal EC documents.
16.   *La Dernière Bataille*, p. 180.

CASE 7

The European Steel Industry in Crisis

H. Landis Gabel and Olivier Cadot

Decision Point

Faced with a decline in demand and a rapid drop in prices that began in 1991, the European steel industry is posting record losses with no recovery in sight. Today, in February 1993, plant closures have already begun and massive layoffs are predicted. This is taking place against a background of rising unemployment in European economies deep in the throes of recession. Seeking respite from their troubles, steel industry representatives have been pressing the European Commission to come up with a rescue plan similar to that administered in the 1980s. In a climate of intensifying international trade conflict, particularly with the US, the Commission faces the delicate problem of meeting the needs of its domestic industry without provoking retaliation from abroad.

The Economics of Steel Making

In the last several decades, the steel industry has split into three distinct sub-industries, each with its own production process, cost structure, and product range. The three are the integrated mill, the mini-mill, and the specialty mill.

Integrated Mills

An integrated steel mill performs all the steps in the process of making steel shapes from iron ore. This process begins with mining the ore. The mined ore is then refined

This case was written by Pamela Denby, Research Associate, under the supervision of
H. Landis Gabel, Professor at INSEAD, and Olivier Cadot, Assistant Professor at INSEAD.
It is intended to be used as a basis for class discussion rather than to illustrate either effective
or ineffective handling of an administrative situation.

to increase the iron content and to remove impurities. A second basic ingredient is coal which is charred in the absence of oxygen to make coke. These two raw materials and a third, limestone, are then fed into a blast furnace which reduces the iron ore into pig iron. The pig iron is transferred to another furnace to be refined into molten steel, primarily by reducing the carbon content. Today, this process usually takes place in a basic oxygen furnace. There are, however, some of the older, less efficient and more polluting open hearth furnaces still being used for this process.

The molten steel is moulded either through ingot-making or continuous casting. In the ingot method, the molten steel is poured into a ladle which fills moulds for casting ingots of about 60 tonnes. Once cast, the ingots are taken from their moulds and re-heated to an even temperature throughout before going through a breakdown mill that shapes them into intermediate forms: slabs, billets, and blooms. Each of these intermediate forms then goes through a series of mills before reaching some final shape. Many of the steps in the ingot making process can be circumvented by continuous casting, where the intermediate forms are made directly, cutting costs by about 30 percent.[1] Producers have increasingly adopted continuous casting since its introduction in 1963, see Exhibit 7.1.

Steel-making in an integrated facility as described above involves a significant capital investment, estimated to be between $960 and $1,500 per metric tonne of annual capacity.[2] With such high capital costs, integrated steel making must be performed on a large scale to be economic. In the post-war years, the minimum efficient scale for an integrated plant has grown significantly with the development of new, productivity-enhancing technologies such as the basic oxygen furnace (first used in 1952) and continuous casting. The minimum efficient scale for a new, 'greenfield' plant using the latest technologies is estimated to be between 5.4–6.4 million metric tonnes of annual production.[3]

Exhibit 7.1 *Continuous casting usage as a percentage of crude steel produced*

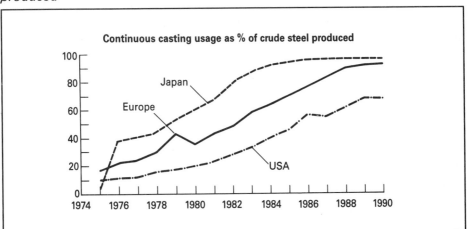

Mini-mills

A mini-mill effectively bypasses the first few steps of an integrated facility by using steel scrap as its primary raw material. Because the quality of the steel they can produce is limited by impurities often found in scrap, most mini-mills at present specialize in a limited range of lower-grade products. With technological advances, however, mini-mills have been progressing into the higher value added range of standard steel products and should continue to do so.

Mini-mills benefit from significantly lower capital costs, estimated to be between 16–21 percent of those for an integrated mill.[4] Lower fixed costs mean that mini-mills can operate economically on a smaller scale than integrated mills, usually between 300,000 and 1.2 million tonnes per year.

By cutting costs in a number of ways, mini-mills are able to compete on price. Mini-mills' energy costs are one-third those of integrated mills because they bypass the energy-intensive blast furnaces.[5] By not using the polluting blast furnace, mini-mills can enjoy lower pollution control costs. Because they are smaller in scale, mini-mills can be located in relatively 'thin' regional markets, which helps save transportation costs. In the US, high per unit labour costs are reduced through use of non-union labour and by tying pay to productivity. In addition, by using exclusively continuous casting and other modern techniques, mini-mills can produce a tonne of steel in two or three man hours compared to an average of six in integrated mills. Such savings mean that mini-mills can produce steel products for 17–23 percent less than integrated producers.[6]

The combination of lower start-up and other costs has fed mini-mill growth in recent years. Furthermore, because of mini-mills' lower fixed costs and their dependence on steel scrap, they are better able to weather an economic downturn when the cost of scrap drops. Nevertheless, there is a limit to how much of the steel market mini-mills can take, since their product range is limited[7] and their proliferation will push up the historically low price for steel scrap.[8]

Although some integrated producers also operate electric arc furnaces, the graph in Exhibit 7.2 gives a good indication of recent growth in mini-mills, the primary users of electric arc furnaces.

Speciality Steel Mills

Similar to a mini-mill, the speciality steel mill is relatively small and primarily scrap-based. It benefits from the same cost savings as a mini-mill, but specializes in making custom, high-quality steel to meet a particular customer's specifications. Producing only a small percentage of world steel output, speciality steel mills account for relatively more profits. Competitive advantage is maintained through product differentiation, quality control, and meeting specific users' requirements. Product innovation and technology also play an important role.

One technology that may be increasingly adopted in the future by both

Exhibit 7.2 *Electric arc furnace usage as a percentage of total production*

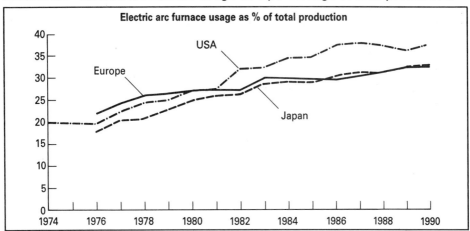

mini- and speciality steel mills is direct reduction, as indicated in Exhibit 7.3 summarizing the steel making for all types of producers. Direct reduction would reduce electric furnace users' dependence on scrap but would be on a much smaller scale than the integrated mill's blast furnace. As mini-mills grow in production capacity, expand product range, and adopt direct iron making, the distinction between them, integrated producers, and speciality steel makers will diminish, see Exhibit 7.3.

Exhibit 7.3

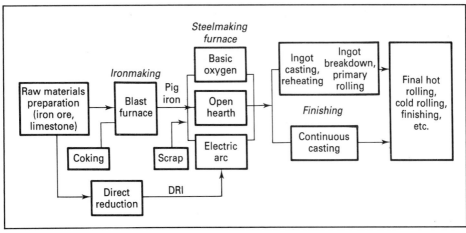

Industrial Policy Responses to the Oil Shocks of the 1970s

Before 1974, steel was considered a steady growth industry as demand consistently outpaced GNP growth.[9] In the wake of the first oil shock in 1973, however, the world economy experienced a severe contraction. Steel consumption as a percentage of industrial production declined as users in industrialized countries substituted alternative materials (in the transport sector, for example, where lighter weight alternatives meant better fuel economy) and reduced quantity through use of higher quality steels, see Exhibit 7.4.

For traditional producers in industrialized countries such as the US, Japan, and the EC, steel became a declining industry beset with structural problems, excess capacity being paramount. The adjustment process in each took on different forms.

European Community

The European Community steel industry is subject to the Treaty of Paris (1951), which founded the European Coal and Steel Community (ECSC), rather than the Treaty of Rome (1958), which established the European Economic Community (EEC). Since 1967, the ECSC and EEC have been united in the European Communities (EC) whose Commission administers the separate treaty provisions and acts as the 'High Authority' of the ECSC.[10] The Treaty of Paris invests the High Authority with supranational powers of intervention in the steel industry not provided to the Commission in the Treaty of Rome.

There are significant differences between the Treaty of Rome and the Treaty of Paris. Both explicitly forbid state aids, especially those that distort competition. While both provide for specific exemptions, however, the Treaty of Paris has significantly more (see Exhibit 7.5). For example, the High Authority can provide

Exhibit 7.4

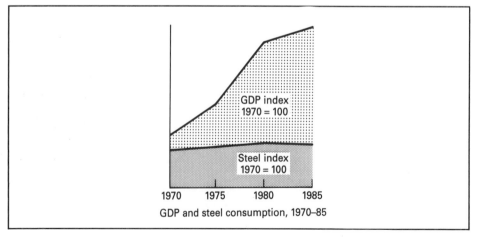

GDP and steel consumption, 1970–85

Exhibit 7.5 *Legal restrictions on state aids*

Treaty of Rome

ARTICLE 92

1. Save as otherwise provided in this Treaty, any aid granted by a Member State or through State resources in any form whatsoever which distorts or threatens to distort competition by favouring certain undertakings or the production of certain goods shall, in so far as it affects trade between Member States, be incompatible with the common market.

3. The following may be considered to be compatible with the common market:

(a) aid to promote the economic development of areas where the standard of living is abnormally low or where there is serious underemployment;

(b) aid to promote the execution of an important project of common European interest or to remedy a serious disturbance in the economy of a Member State;

(c) aid to facilitate the development of certain economic activities or of certain economic areas, where such aid does not adversely affect trading conditions to an extent contrary to the common interest . . .

(d) such other categories of aid as may be specified by decision of the Council . . .

Treaty of Paris

ARTICLE 4

The following are recognized as incompatible with the common market for coal and steel and shall accordingly be abolished and prohibited within the Community, as provided in this Treaty: . . .

(c) subsidies or aids granted by States . . . in any form whatsoever.

Treaty of Paris: Selected Exemptions

ARTICLE 56

1. If the introduction . . . of new technical processes or equipment should lead to an exceptionally large reduction in labour requirements in the coal or steel industry, making it particularly difficult in one or more areas to re-employ redundant workers, the High Authority: . . .

(b) may facilitate . . . the financing of such programmes as it may approve for the creation of new and economically sound activities capable of reabsorbing the redundant workers into productive employment;

(c) shall provide non-repayable aid towards:
   – the payment of tideover allowances to workers;
   – the payment of resettlement allowances to workers;
   – the financing of vocational retraining for workers having to change their employment.

Exhibit 7.5 *continued*

---

2. If fundamental changes, not directly connected with the establishment of the common market, in market conditions for the coal or the steel industry should compel some undertakings permanently to discontinue, curtail or change their activities, the High Authority, on application by the Governments concerned:

(a) may facilitate, in the manner laid down in Article 54, either in the industries within its jurisdiction or, with the assent of the council, in any other industry, the financing of such programmes as it may approve for the creation of new and economically sound activities or for the conversion of existing undertakings capable of reabsorbing the redundant workers into productive employment;

(b) may provide non-repayable aid towards:
 – the payment of tideover allowances to workers;
 – the payment of allowances to undertakings to enable them to continue paying such of their workers as may have to be temporarily laid off as a result of the undertakings' change of activity;
 – the payment of resettlement allowances to workers;
 – the financing of vocational retraining for workers having to change their employment.

The High Authority shall make the provision of non-repayable aid conditional upon payment by the State concerned of a special contribution of not less than the amount of that aid, unless an exception is authorized by the Council, acting on two-thirds' majority.

---

aid for modernization and conversion of plant and for retraining redundant workers. The High Authority has the authority to raise funds on the international markets for such investments as are allowed by the Treaty.

As far as its powers to restrict illegal state aids, the High Authority must be notified of any planned investment in the steel industry. It is at this point that the High Authority determines whether the investment involves subsidies. The High Authority has no power to stop such investments, however, except by requiring that they are paid for from the company's own resources.

In the event of a decline in demand precipitating a 'manifest crisis' in the industry, the High Authority's powers are enhanced (see Exhibit 7.6). The High Authority is then vested with power to control the market by setting minimum prices and production quotas with the threat of fines to violators.[11] In addition, quantitative import restrictions can be set against imports that 'cause or threaten to cause serious injury to production' within the ECSC. Before resorting to crisis measures, however, the Commission is instructed to use 'indirect means of action', such as 'cooperation with government to regularize or influence general consumption' and 'intervention in regard to prices'. With a declaration of a manifest crisis, the Commission is in effect empowered to direct the EC steel market as a cartel – precisely what the ECSC was formed to abolish (see Exhibit 7.7). Beyond a decline in demand, however, the characteristics of a manifest crisis are not defined.

Policy Response
The Treaty of Paris was signed in a climate of ever-increasing steel demand. Indeed,

Exhibit 7.6 *Crisis cartel provisions in the Treaty of Paris*

ARTICLE 57
In the sphere of production, the High Authority shall give preference to the indirect means of action at its disposal.

ARTICLE 58
1. In the event of a decline in demand, if the High authority considers that the Community is confronted with a period of manifest crisis and that the means provided for in Article 57 are not sufficient to deal with this, it shall, after consulting with the Consultative Committee and with the assent of the Council, establish a system of production quotas, accompanied to the necessary extent by the measures provided for in Article 74.

2. The High Authority shall, on the basis of studies made jointly with the undertakings and associations of undertakings, determine the quotas on an equitable basis. It may in particular regulate the level of activity of undertakings by appropriate levies on tonnages exceeding a reference level set by a general decision.

The funds thus obtained shall be used to support undertakings whose rate of production has fallen below that envisaged, in order in particular to maintain employment in these undertakings as far as possible.

ARTICLE 61
On the basis of studies made jointly with undertakings and associations of undertakings . . . and after consulting with the Consultative Committee and the Council as to the advisability of so doing and the price level to be so determined, the High Authority may, for one or more of the products within its jurisdiction: . . .

(b) fix minimum prices within the common market, if it finds that a manifest crisis exists or is imminent.

Antidumping

ARTICLE 74
In the cases set out below, the High Authority is empowered to take any measure which is in accordance with this Treaty:

(1) if it is found that countries not members of the Community or undertakings situated in such countries are engaging in dumping or other practices condemned by the Havana Charter;

(2) if a difference between quotations by undertakings outside and by undertakings within the jurisdiction of the Community is due solely to the fact that those of the former are based on conditions of competition contrary to this Treaty;

(3) if one of the products referred to in Article 81 (coal and steel) of this Treaty is imported into the territory of one or more Member States in relatively increased quantities and under such conditions that these imports cause or threaten to cause serious injury to production within the common market of like or directly competing products.

However, recommendations for the introduction of quantitative restrictions under subparagraph 2 may be made only with the assent of the Council, and under subparagraph 3 only under the conditions laid down in Article 58.

Exhibit 7.7 *Legal restrictions on cartels*

Treaty of Rome	**Treaty of Paris**
ARTICLE 85	ARTICLE 65 (EXTRACT)

Treaty of Rome

ARTICLE 85

1. The following shall be prohibited as incompatible with the common market: all agreements between undertakings, decisions by associations of undertakings and concerted practices which may affect trade between Member States and which have as their object or effect the prevention, restriction or distortion of competition within the common market, and in particular those which:

(a) directly or indirectly fix purchase or selling prices or other trading conditions;

(b) limit or control production, markets, technical development, or investment;

(c) share markets or sources of supply;

(d) apply dissimilar conditions to equivalent transactions with other trading parties, thereby placing them at a competitive disadvantage;

(e) make the conclusion of contracts subject to acceptance by the other parties of supplementary obligations which, by their nature or according to commercial usage, have no connection with the subject of such contracts.

2. Any agreements or decision prohibited pursuant to this Article shall be automatically void.

3. The provisions of paragraph 1 may, however, be declared inapplicable in the case of:

● any agreement or category of agreements between undertakings;

● any decision or category of decisions by associations of undertakings;

Treaty of Paris

ARTICLE 65 (EXTRACT)

1. All agreements between undertakings, decisions by associations of undertaking and concerted practices tending directly or indirectly to prevent, restrict or distort normal competition within the common market shall be prohibited, and in particular those tending:

(a) to fix or determine prices;

(b) to restrict or control production, technical development or investment;

(c) to share markets, products, customers or sources of supply.

2. However, the High Authority shall authorize specialization agreements or joint buying or joint selling agreements in respect of particular products, if it finds that:

(a) such specialization or such joint buying or selling will make for a substantial improvement in the production or distribution of those products;

(b) the agreement in question is essential in order to achieve these results and is not more restrictive than is necessary for that purpose; and

Exhibit 7.7 *continued*

> • any concerted practice or category of concerted practices; which contributes to improving the production or distribution of goods or to promoting technical or economic progress, while allowing consumers a fair share of the resulting benefit, and which does not:
>
> (a) impose on the undertakings concerned restrictions which are not indispensable to the attainment of these objectives;
>
> (b) afford such undertakings the possibility of eliminating competition in respect of a substantial part of the products in question.
>
> (c) the agreement is not liable to give the undertakings concerned the power to determine the prices, or to control or restrict the production or marketing, of a substantial part of the products in question within the common market, or to shield them against effective competition from other undertakings within the common market.
>
> 5. On any undertaking which has entered into an agreement which is . . . prohibited by paragraph 1 of this Article, the High Authority may impose fines or periodic penalty payments.

throughout the 1960s, ECSC producers could not add capacity fast enough. However, after the boom year of 1974, when steel producers worldwide enjoyed the highest demand ever and were operating at full capacity, demand fell precipitously. Because of the five-year time lag between investment decisions and completion of projects, however, capacity continued to be added throughout the 1970s. The resultant structural crisis presented the first occasion to interpret the full extent of treaty provisions.

The Davignon Plan   By 1975, European producers were calling for an officially declared manifest crisis and thus the formation of a crisis cartel under the provisions of Article 58 of the Treaty of Paris. In December 1976, the Commission concurred and established a producers' cartel called Eurofer. The Commission and Eurofer jointly agreed to voluntary production quotas in January 1977. In May 1977, 'guidance' prices on most products, and mandatory minimum prices on some, were in force under the first 'Davignon Plan'.

To maintain price discipline, it was necessary to protect the EC market from cheap imports. Between 1974 and 1977, import penetration into the EC had increased from 6 percent to more than 11 percent. Therefore, voluntary restraint agreements (VRAs) limiting volumes based on 'traditional' patterns of trade were negotiated with most of the primary exporters to the ECSC, starting with Japan in 1976 and including Hungary, Poland, and Czechoslovakia by 1978. Exporting nations were compelled to enter into VRAs under threat of antidumping proceedings. These VRAs were renegotiated annually. Other nations that did not enter into VRAs were subject to a 'basic price' system, similar to a trigger price mechanism (discussed later). If imports entered the ECSC below a predetermined 'competitive' price, they would trigger an expedited antidumping investigation.

OECD members were highly concerned about capacity increases in lesser developed countries hampering their efforts to coordinate supply and demand. In an attempt at multilateral coordination to address the problem of world over-capacity, the EC initiated the formation of a Steel Committee at the OECD in 1977.

In the wake of the second oil shock in 1979, US producers filed the first of a series of antidumping lawsuits against EC producers. Faced with a decline in demand coupled with closure of the US market, the first Davignon Plan fell apart as prices collapsed due to competitive price cutting. In October 1980, the Commission formulated the second Davignon Plan entailing a combination of mandatory and voluntary production quotas, minimum prices, and guidance prices for certain steel products.

These market controls were coupled with attempts to reduce the level of state subsidies. From the formation of the ECSC up to 1974, in the period of increasing demand and rapid expansion, the prohibition on state aids had not been strictly enforced and the Commission's authority to do so had been progressively diminished. The Commission therefore attempted to clarify its policy prohibiting state subsidies through a series of Aids Codes. After an ineffective first attempt in 1980, the Commission promulgated a Second Aids Code in the middle of 1981 forbidding aid for continuing operations after 1984 (later extended through 1985) and for investment after 1985. Any operations or investment subsidies thereafter would have to be part of a 'systematic restructuring programme' of capacity reductions, modernization, and financial restructuring.[12] In June 1983, the Commission laid down the specific goal of reducing ECSC capacity by at least 26.7 million metric tonnes.[13] Permission to provide subsidies for research, environmental protection, plant closures, and regional development remained.

Despite these seemingly strict prohibitions on state aids, European steel makers received an estimated $36 billion in subsidies between 1980 and 1985. Nearly two-thirds of this was 'aid for continued operation' rather than for worker retraining or investment in modernization, as provided for in the treaty.[14] The costs of worker retraining and early retirement programmes, largely borne by public funds, are not included in the $36 billion figure. The magnitude of state aids to the steel sector became so great under the Davignon Plan as to be characterized as a 'subsidy steeplechase' among member states[15] (see Exhibit 7.8).

There was a consensus, however, that the solution to the problem was reduced capacity, though no member state wanted to bear that burden. State aids were used in an attempt to counter the effects of Commission policy and shift the burden of adjustment onto another member state. The Commission repeatedly threatened to terminate quota protection if producers did not come up with a viable restructuring scheme. While mandatory minimum prices were eliminated in 1986, however, production quotas were renewed until July 1988. Besides, use of manifest crisis market controls was no longer possible in 1988 since demand had picked up that year, and the conditions for application of Article 58 were no longer present.

Exhibit 7.8

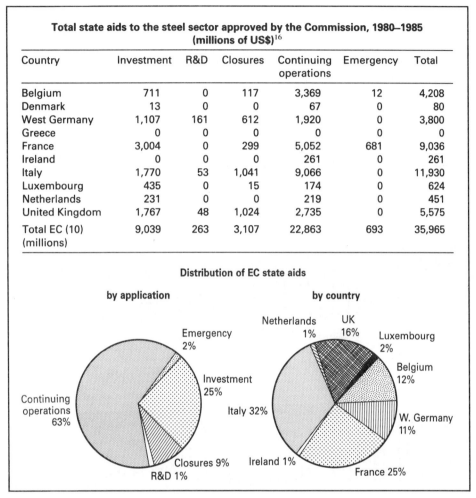

Total state aids to the steel sector approved by the Commission, 1980–1985 (millions of US$)[16]

Country	Investment	R&D	Closures	Continuing operations	Emergency	Total
Belgium	711	0	117	3,369	12	4,208
Denmark	13	0	0	67	0	80
West Germany	1,107	161	612	1,920	0	3,800
Greece	0	0	0	0	0	0
France	3,004	0	299	5,052	681	9,036
Ireland	0	0	0	261	0	261
Italy	1,770	53	1,041	9,066	0	11,930
Luxembourg	435	0	15	174	0	624
Netherlands	231	0	0	219	0	451
United Kingdom	1,767	48	1,024	2,735	0	5,575
Total EC (10) (millions)	9,039	263	3,107	22,863	693	35,965

Distribution of EC state aids

by application

by country

Emergency 2%

Investment 25%

Continuing operations 63%

Italy 32%

Closures 9%

R&D 1%

Netherlands 1%

UK 16%

Luxembourg 2%

Belgium 12%

W. Germany 11%

Ireland 1%

France 25%

Effects

Between 1978 and 1989, net capacity in the nine EC countries initially covered by the Davignon Plan was reduced by 40 million metric tonnes, or by 20 percent. Employment was reduced by 443,500 jobs, or 44 percent. The addition of Greece to the EC in 1981 and Portugal in 1986 did not significantly affect over-capacity. Spain's accession in 1986, however, added another 22 million metric tonnes of capacity, 2.5 million of which were eliminated by 1989 (see Exhibits 7.10 and 7.11). With such capacity reductions and massive modernization efforts (see Exhibit 7.9) effectuated by the time demand picked up in 1987, European steel producers were well placed for a return to profitability, and the Davignon Plan was declared a success.[17]

Exhibit 7.9   *Adoption of production methods as a percentage of total production and percentage reductions in employment from 1974 level*

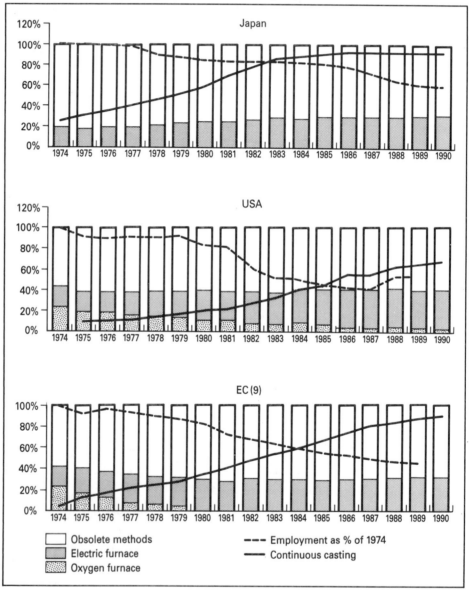

USA

The average integrated steel mill in the US has an annual production capacity of less than 3 million tonnes, and no greenfield integrated plants have been built since the

Exhibit 7.10 *Production and capacity trends in the EC: 1974–1990*[18]

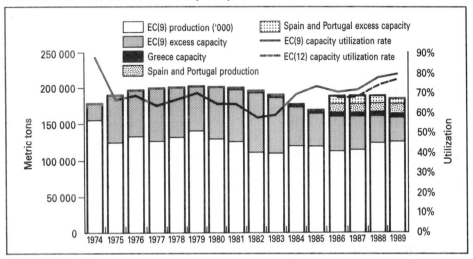

Exhibit 7.11 *Percentage capacity reduced by each member state (as a percentage of 1980 total capacity and as a percentage of total capacity reduced 1980–1990)*

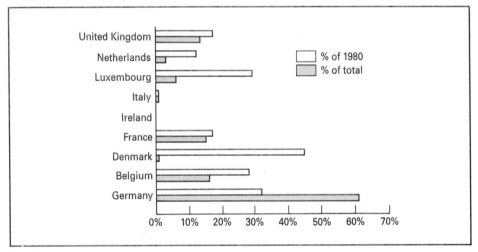

1950s. The combination of the recession of 1958 followed by a six-month strike in 1959 marked a turning point in the US steel industry. Foreign producers, whose more modern technologies were just coming on stream at that time, were able to penetrate the US domestic market, and the US has been a net importer of steel ever since. The US steel industry responded to the crisis of the 1970s with increasingly vociferous cries for protection from allegedly unfair imports.

Policy Response

In an effort to curb trade disruption and the diplomatic repercussions from antidumping and countervailing duty proceedings, various administrations negotiated other means to offer the US industry protection.

Trigger Price Mechanism By the end of 1977, American steel firms had filed over 20 petitions under the provisions of the Antidumping Act of 1921 as amended by the Trade Act of 1974, claiming injury as a result of alleged European and Japanese dumping on the American market.

Steel imports into the US from the EC and Japan had been subject to voluntary restraint agreements since 1968. After the VRAs expired in 1975, however, imports steadily gained market share to reach nearly 20 percent of domestic consumption. In the amended Act, dumping was defined as selling at less than fair value: either below domestic market prices in the country of origin or below the cost of production plus an allowance for reasonable profit (8 percent) and general expenses (10 percent). The cost of production criterion was to be used if the US price was lower than the cost of production 'over an extended period of time and in substantial quantities'. Under US law, if the government finds dumping has occurred and has caused 'material injury' to the US industry, the prescribed remedy is the imposition of antidumping duties.

The Carter administration, concerned about the inflationary impact of import duties and their political repercussions on the Tokyo Round of multilateral trade negotiations, convened a task force to formulate alternate protection measures that would persuade US industry to withdraw its petitions. The resultant Solomon Report recommended a system of trigger prices. Imports sold at less than a calculated trigger price would set off an immediate, fast-track antidumping investigation, without the need for the domestic industry to file petition.

The trigger prices were calculated based on the costs of the most efficient producers in the world, the Japanese. Production costs were based on an 80 percent capacity utilization rate, the historic average. To this was added the cost of transport to the US.

In addition to the trigger price mechanism, the US industry was offered loan guarantees and relaxation of some of the environmental regulations imposed by the 1977 Clean Air Act. Furthermore, the Treasury Department promised to consider speeding up the capital equipment depreciation schedule for tax purposes.

The industry accepted the Carter administration's offer and withdrew its petitions. The trigger price mechanism functioned from 1978–79 until it grew increasingly difficult to administer because of exchange rate movements and growing pressure by US industry to raise the trigger price. Unsatisfied with the level of protection provided by the arrangement, the largest US integrated producers filed antidumping petitions against seven European producers in March 1980, and the administration immediately withdrew the trigger price policy. It was reintroduced later in the year with a 12 percent increase in prices and it ran until January 1982 by which time a total of 96 antidumping and countervailing duty petitions had been filed by the US steel industry against EC producers.[19]

Voluntary Restraint Agreements In response to the mass of petitions filed, US government and EC Commission representatives entered into negotiations in an attempt to avert a full-blown trade crisis. If agreement could be reached, the antidumping and countervailing duty investigations would be suspended.[20] The negotiations resulted in a collection of VRAs effective November 1, 1982, which would limit EC exports of certain steel products to a set percentage of US consumption. The expressed goal of the VRAs was '. . . to give time to permit restructuring and therefore to create a period of trade stability.'[21] There was, however, no government assistance in, policy for, nor participation in such restructuring.

After more than 300 petitions were filed in 1984 against countries not covered by the EC–US Steel Arrangement, a more comprehensive set of VRAs was negotiated, and the EC's were extended. In September 1984, President Reagan announced the conclusion of a series of agreements to restrict imports into the US to 18.5 percent (later expanded to 20.5 percent) of the market. The VRAs were valid until September 30, 1989, at which time they were renegotiated until March 31, 1992, in fulfillment of an election-year pledge made by George Bush in 1988. At the time, however, Bush noted that they would not be renewed after 1992 and that the only 'permanent solution to the domestic steel industry's problems' lay in negotiating an end to foreign subsidies.[22]

Effects
Between 1978 and 1989, net capacity in the US steel industry was reduced by 37 million metric tonnes (26 percent) through market forces (see Exhibit 7.12).

Exhibit 7.12 *Production and capacity trends in the USA: 1974–1990*[25]

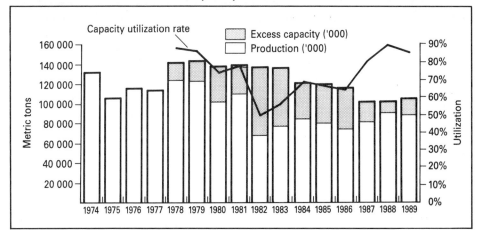

Employment was reduced by 249,600 jobs (53 percent). The capacity reduction was exclusively of integrated mills. Mini-mills actually expanded, raising their market share to 22 percent by 1988. This was a four-fold increase in market share in ten years.[23] Increased competition from domestic mini-mills prompted US integrated producers to modernize and to retreat into the higher value-added, flat-rolled products that account for 50 percent of US consumption. In a break from the traditional domain of mini-mills in the lower end of the product line, however, the leading US mini-mill, Nucor, adopted the latest technology for making flat-rolled sheet in the mid-1980s.[24] In 1992, US mini-mills had a 21 percent market share as compared to 17 percent for imports.

Rest of the World

Japan
Built almost entirely during the post-war period, the Japanese steel industry has an average plant capacity of 6.7 million metric tonnes per year.[26] Through use of the latest production methods, continual improvement as a result of a high level of investment, and optimal sitings at deep-water ports, Japanese producers are the most efficient in the world.

Japan exports roughly 40 percent of its steel. Although Japanese steel has been subject to voluntary export restraints to its main markets since the 1976 VRA with the EC, its high efficiency allows it to maintain profitability even at 70 percent capacity utilization. Reduction of the export market for steel has been counteracted somewhat by exporting steel technology to the newly industrialized countries (NICs) in the form of turn-key plants.

Non-market Economies
The non-market economies of Eastern Europe and the USSR have traditionally been massive producers of steel. For example, Czechoslovakia was perhaps the highest per capita producer of steel in the world with over 15 million metric tonnes of annual production in a country of roughly 15 million people.[27] Most of the steel produced in these countries, however, has gone to serve intra-Comecon trade. Such steel producers use antiquated, inefficient techniques and have an output per worker 40–50 percent that of Western countries.[28] In 1988, for example, open hearth furnaces accounted for nearly 50 percent of steel produced. Use of continuous casting accounted for only 23 percent of production in Czechoslovakia and 28 percent in Poland.[29]

Newly Industrialized Countries
Many of the petrodollars from the first oil shock were recycled as loans to lesser developed countries like Taiwan, China, South Korea, Brazil and Mexico and used to construct steel mills. These NICs enjoyed the advantages of modern technology and optimal plant siting near ocean transport, reducing transport costs for both

purchase of raw materials and sale of finished product. Low labour costs, low cost indigenous raw material sources, and lax environmental regulations gave a competitive advantage to these countries.

While demand for steel has been declining in the industrialized world, it has been increasing in the NICs (see Exhibit 7.13). Economic growth tends to be steel-intensive in the early stages of development which emphasize heavy industry and infrastructure. NICs have increasingly met this demand themselves rather than by importing from traditional steel producers in the industrialized countries. Demand is nevertheless still small compared to production capacity. With insufficient domestic demand, there is an incentive to export in order to benefit from economies of scale and to earn foreign exchange to repay the loans from abroad.

Debate

With the recession hitting the US in 1991 and spreading to Europe in 1992, the steel industry faced another significant decline in demand. In this context, several events have conspired with powerful trends in the industry to put EC steel producers again in a state of crisis.

The Fall of the Iron Curtain

Association Agreements Signed
The first order of the day after the victory of the Democratic Forum in the April 1990 Hungarian elections was to declare a priority to joining the European Community. This sentiment was echoed by the other emerging democracies in

Exhibit 7.13 *World crude steel production has shifted to NICs*

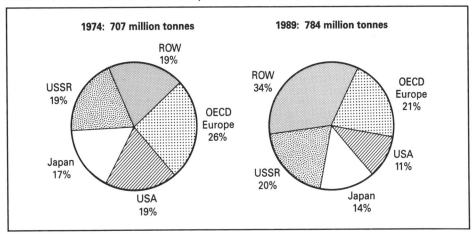

Eastern Europe as traditional markets with the former Soviet bloc countries collapsed.[30] The President of the European Commission, Jaques Delors, responded favorably in June 1990, declaring that 'We can do no more but to help them help themselves'.[31] By the end of the year, the EC Commission had begun negotiations with Hungary, Czechoslovakia, and Poland over the terms of association agreements to open EC markets to those countries' exports.

In their final declaration after the July 1991 London summit, the Group of Seven industrialized nations also agreed to 'undertake to improve further [Central and East European countries'] access to our markets and for their products and services, including in areas such as steel, textiles, and agricultural produce.'[32] The European countries, through the European Bank for Reconstruction and Development, were given the task of administering the Western nations' aid programmes to the emerging democracies.

After eight months of negotiations over the association agreements, however, the French blocked agreement in September 1991 by refusing to allow free trade in agricultural products. It was a surprise move since Germany had made significant concessions on steel and Portugal on textiles. Exasperated by the French move, the Dutch Foreign Minister said, 'This is a disgrace. There seems to be a small faction here that is living on another planet.'[33] The earlier compromises rapidly broke down, and steel and textiles won a 'safe-guard' clause that allowed the EC Commission to impose quota restrictions if imports of those products surged. The association agreements were signed with the safe-guard clause in place and went into effect in January 1992.

The Paradoxes of Help
Four months later, in April 1992, Eurofer filed a complaint with the European Commission charging that Czechoslovakian steel exports to EC countries had increased by 126 percent and threatened to 'destroy' the EC steel industry.[34] EC steel producers charged that Eastern European exports, which accounted for less than 5 percent of EC consumption, were undercutting EC prices by 20–25 percent and thereby contributing to an overall 40 percent drop in steel prices in 1992. In August, the Commission responded to Eurofer's complaint by putting a temporary quota of 20 percent per annum on the growth of Czech steel exports to the EC. In December, EC member states informally agreed to continue the quota in 1993 at the same level.

The EC Commission was caught in a dilemma – coordinating Western aid to Eastern Europe on the one hand, and limiting trade on the other. 'For 40 years, we heard that the free movement of trade is a basic value of the democratic society,' said the Foreign Minister of the newly independent Czech Republic, 'but we are finding trade blocked by quotas and tariffs, especially in Western Europe.'[35] In January 1993, the EC Commission proposed increasing the quotas 35 percent above what was sold in 1991. Some member states, however, were opposed and wanted to stick to the 20 percent level. 'You cannot sacrifice a job in Lorraine to protect one in Bohemia,' said the French Minister of Industry.[36] 'Once the market improves, we'd be happy to remove the quotas on Eastern imports,' conceded an official at the German Steel Federation.[37]

Transatlantic Trade War: Expiry of VRAs – and US Protectionism Renewed

As the VRAs limiting EC exports to the US were set to expire on March 31, 1992, negotiators at the GATT talks (aimed at reaching the long-sought-after Multilateral Steel Accord) had reached an impasse. The Multilateral Steel Accord was intended to replace the VRAs and reduce the massive distortions in the international steel trade resulting from national subsidy and tariff policies. The US wanted the steel accord to compel all signatories to eliminate steel tariffs, subsidies, and other unfair trading practices within 10 years. Japan, on the other hand, led major steel exporters in demanding that the US soften its antidumping and countervailing duty laws in exchange. Several NICs, for their part, wanted exemptions from the proposed rules. The negotiations broke down and the VRAs were not renewed.

By June, the 'Big Six' integrated producers in the US had submitted 84 petitions alleging unfair trade by 21 countries, including 12 producers in 6 EC countries. In November, the US Commerce Department issued a preliminary finding that steel from 12 countries had received unfair subsidies, and countervailing duties were imposed. In January 1993, the Commerce Department announced a preliminary finding of steel dumping by 19 countries, including the 12 EC producers. The findings required the immediate posting of bond to cover antidumping duties ranging as high as 110 percent and affecting 2 million metric tonnes of EC steel imports into the US. Although the bond would be returned if the final determination was negative, it effectively curtailed affected imports.

The EC argued that the dumping duties were unwarranted since they covered a period when EC producers were subject to the VRA quotas, which the EC said were fully respected. Furthermore, the EC argued that US integrated producers were actually being injured by their own domestic mini-mills. The Commerce Department is scheduled to make its final determinations by mid-June 1993.

EC Steel in Crisis

In November 1992, the EC Commission came to the help of its steel industry. It announced $1.1 billion in possible funding to help ease the cost of restructuring,[38] and it named Ferdinand Braun as its 'steel envoy' to survey the industry and identify where capacity cuts could be made.

As the resultant Braun Report was reaching completion, European steel producers began lobbying the Commission to again declare a manifest crisis. In January 1993, after reporting 'catastrophic' losses, the German steel maker Thyssen Stahl called for the formation of a 'crisis cartel' under the provisions of Article 58 stating that 'the situation now is worse than it was even during the 1970s and 1980s.'[39] A delegate from the French steel federation summed up the industry's sentiment: 'We can't export to the US anymore; the European Community lets our market be invaded by Eastern Europe; prices are so low that they're no longer profitable . . . It's a very critical situation.'[40]

The Braun Report detailed possible capacity cuts throughout the EC industry totalling about 30 million metric tonnes, and envisaged the loss of 50,000 jobs over three years. The total cost of restructuring was estimated to be $7.1 billion. The EC Commission met with industry representatives in February to discuss the report. The Commission declined to allocate capacity reductions and stated that it would only provide funding if the industry itself came up with a definite capacity reduction programme by September 30, 1993, to be carried out by the end of 1994. The Commission would provide $290 million to match member states' funds for worker retraining.

The proposed job reductions set off labour protests in Germany. The head of the largest union repeated the call for a crisis cartel, stating 'The restructuring in Europe cannot be left just to a dubious corporate cartel. The government have put market-economy ideology above the concerns of people . . . It's time for politics to come to its senses and to introduce a social turnaround.'[41]

With the EC Commission once again charged with pulling the steel industry out of a crisis, several questions are raised.

- Would another crisis cartel along the lines of the Davignon Plan of the '70s and '80s serve to rescue the EC steel industry from its doldrums?

- On the contrary, have the 'solutions' of the '70s and '80s caused the crisis of the '90s?

- Would a Multilateral Steel Agreement better serve the needs of the European industry?

- What other instruments might the European Commission have at its disposal?

Notes

1. *The Competitive Status of the US Steel Industry: A Study of the Influences of Technology in Determining International Industrial Competitive Advantage* (Washington, DC: National Academy Press, 1985): pp. 156–57.
2. Estimates are in 1978 dollars by the US government's Office of Technology Assessment. Quoted in Jack Robert Miller, 'Steel Minimills', *Scientific American*, Vol. 250, No. 5 (May 1984): p. 29.
3. Robert W. Crandall, *The US Steel Industry in Recurrent Crisis* (Washington, DC: Brookings, 1981): p. 11.
4. Estimates are in 1978 dollars by the US government's Office of Technology Assessment. Quoted in Jack Robert Miller, 'Steel Minimills', *Scientific American*, Vol. 250, No. 5 (May 1984): p. 29.

5. Jack Robert Miller, 'Steel Minimills', *Scientific American*, Vol. 250, No. 5 (May 1984): p. 33.
6. 'Ideas from Indiana recast face of steel', *Financial Times* (London: 28 July 1992): p. 10.
7. One observer has estimated that mini-mills will peak with 34 per cent of the US market share some time around 1995. Jack Robert Miller, 'Steel Minimills', *Scientific American*, Vol. 250, No. 5 (May 1984): p. 35.
8. The low price of scrap relative to pig iron in the 1980s (35 percent of the cost of pig iron in the early 1980s as compared to 70 percent in the 1950s) accounts for almost one-third of the cost advantage of mini-mills versus integrated mills. Martin T. Katzman, 'From horse carts to minimills', *The Public Interest*, No. 392 (summer 1988): p. 129.
9. Sources: World GDP data are from *United Nations National Accounts Statistics* (New York: UN, 1990); world crude steel production data from *United Nations Statistical Yearbook*, 37th issue (New York: UN, 1992).
10. . . . together with the European Atomic Energy Community (Euratom).
11. Through Articles 61 and 58. See Exhibit 7.6 for full text of relevant articles.
12. *Bulletin EC*, No. 6(1981), pp. 18–19.
13. *Bulletin EC*, No. 6(1983), point 1.1.1 to 1.1.12 and 2.1.66.
14. Report from the Commission to the Council on Application of the Rules on Aids to the Steel Industry, COM(86) 235 final, August 6, 1986. In Thomas R. Howell, *et al.* *Steel and the State* (Boulder, CO: Westview Press Inc., 1988): p. 69.
15. Thomas R. Howell, *et al.* *Steel and the State* (Boulder, CO: Westview Press Inc., 1988): p. 64.
16. Source: *Report from the Commission to the Council on the Application of the Rules on Aids to the Steel Industry*, 1984–1985. EC Commission. COM(86) 235 final, 6 August 1986. ECU's converted to US$ using average rate for 1980–1985.
17. 'From Smokestack to Cutting Edge', *The Economist* (London: 10 March 1990): pp. 79–80.
18. Greece joined the EC in 1981; Spain and Portugal, in 1986. All data are gathered from relevant annual issues of *The Iron and Steel Industry* (Paris: OECD).
19. US countervailing duty law under the Tariff Act of 1940 had been substantially amended by the Trade Agreements Act of 1979. Under US countervailing duty law, the Commerce Department must first find that a foreign producer has benefitted from subsidies towards manufacture, production, or export of a certain product. If the International Trade Commission separately finds that such subsidies threatened to or did cause material injury to the US industry, or materially retarded the establishment of the US industry, then the prescribed remedy is a countervailing duty, in addition to any other duties, equal to the amount of the net subsidy.
20. US law allows the suspension of antidumping and countervailing duty investigations if a settlement is reached whereby the foreign government or producer agrees to terminate exports, discontinue or offset any subsidies, or to remove the 'injurious effect' of subsidized exports. Such agreements are conditioned on being able to be effectively monitored and on being in the public interest. Such agreements must be reached before the Department of Commerce's final determination – in this case, on August 24, 1982.
21. As quoted in Frank Benyon and Jacques Bourgeois, 'The European Community – United States Steel Arrangement', *Common Market Law Review*, Vol. 21 (The Hague: 1984), p. 351.
22. 'How George Bush may Recast Quotas on Steel Imports', *Business Week* (20 March 1989): p. 44.

23.   'US Minimills Launch a Full-Scale Attack', *Business Week* (13 June 1988): p. 54.
24.   'Ideas from Indiana recast face of steel', *Financial Times* (London: 28 July 1992): p. 10.
25.   Comparable capacity figures for 1974–1977 are not available. For the years 1978–1989, the sum of production and excess capacity equals total capacity. All data are from relevant annual issues of *The Iron and Steel Industry* (Paris: OECD).
26.   The Iron and Steel Industry (Paris: OECD), p. 13.
27.   '"Velvet Revolution" Opens Door for Steel Investment', *American Metal Market* (7 December 1990): p. 4.
28.   Ibid.
29.   'Steel Production Practices Vary in East Europe', *American Metal Market* (10 September 1990): p. 4.
30.   Vaclav Havel, 'The Paradoxes of Help', *New York Times* (14 July 1991): §4, p. 19.
31.   From a speech given in Brussels, June 8, 1990, 'L'Europe à la croisée des chemins: la CE dans un environment politique et économique en plein changement'.
32.   'Summit in London; Excerpts from Group of Seven's Declaration', *New York Times* (18 July 1991): §A, p. 12.
33.   'French Sink East Europe Trade Deal', *New York Times* (7 September 1991): p. 35.
34.   'Germany gets OK for Curb: Commission Clears way to Break Czech Steel Exports', *American Metal Market* (20 August 1992): p. 4.
35.   'Pillar of European Unity, Steel, Now Divides East and West', *International Herald Tribune* (28 January 1993): pp. 1–2.
36.   'EC Will Tax Steel From East as Part Of a Crisis Plan', *International Herald Tribune* (26 February 1993).
37.   'Steelmakers in Eastern Europe Court New Prospects, to the Dismay of West', *Wall Street Journal* (23 June 1992): §A, p. 16.
38.   'European Steel: Hot Blast', *The Economist* (London: 21 November 1992): p. 91.
39.   'Thyssen Calls for Steel Cartel', *International Herald Tribune* (20 January 1993).
40.   Yves-Thibault de Silguy, delegate general of the French steel federation, quoted in 'Steelmakers in Eastern Europe Court New Prospects, to the Dismay of West', *Wall Street Journal* (23 June 1992): §A, p. 16.
41.   'German Union Urges EC aid for Steelmakers', *Wall Street Journal* (17 February 1993).

CASE 8

Television Without Frontiers (A)

Jonathan Story

On October 23, 1989, the US House of Representatives voted unanimously (342 to 0) to denounce a European Community Directive on broadcasting, 'Television Without Frontiers', which stated that the majority of television programming broadcast in EC countries should come from within the community. Congress believed that such a quota was in violation of the General Agreement on Tariffs and Trade (GATT), and that the EC was infringing the right of the US film and television industry to market its goods in the European Community.

The general rancor in the US was understandable, given that the EC directive threatened to curtail US broadcasting industry exports, one of the few American sectors that enjoyed a large trade surplus ($2.5 billion annually), and to close the door on the ever growing European market, which was expected to buy $1.47 billion worth of American programs in 1989.[1]

The Television Without Frontiers Directive

The European Commission first began to study the regulation of trans-European broadcasts in 1974. This was the year during which the Court of the European Community, in the Saatchi case, decided that broadcasting was a service, and as such should fall under Article 59 of the Treaty of Rome, which stated that services should circulate freely within the Community.

The Commission's main goal was to allow for programs developed within the member states to be received and transmitted without restriction, by cable, satellite or hertzian signal, in other countries of the Community.

In 1984, the Commission ordered a study of the European broadcasting industry, 'The Green Paper on the Establishment of the Common Market for

This case was written by Kathy Burton, Research Assistant, under the supervision of Jonathan Story, Professor at INSEAD. It is intended to be used as a basis for class discussion rather than to illustrate either effective or ineffective handling of an administrative situation.
Copyright © 1992 INSEAD Fontainebleau, France.
Financial support from Sandeep Sander, Director, Sander & Co. A/s, Denmark, and Jan O. Froeshaug, Ceo Egmont, Denmark, is gratefully acknowledged.

Broadcasting, Especially by Satellite and Cable'. The Green Paper presented the main arguments for developing cross-border broadcasts, and discussed barriers to meeting this goal. A directive on broadcasting was necessary, the paper argued, because television would be an important tool in the integration of Europe and the opening of a single market in 1993. The Commission also recognized the economic importance of the European broadcasting industry, and thus saw a need to support and protect both the manufacturing of European broadcasting equipment and the production of European programming. The latter was of particular concern, given the large number of American television programs on European airwaves.

The Green Paper outlined measures that would need to be settled before border-free broadcasting could became a reality, including the regulation of the content and number of minutes of advertising, the need to protect children and adolescents from violent and pornographic programming, and an agreement on laws concerning the rights of authors and the right of reply (the right of an individual to respond to any facts broadcast about him or her).

The desire to establish trans-European broadcasting had been established with the Green Paper, but the realization of this goal was neither certain nor evident. Apart from differences in regulations, philosophies about states' role in broadcasting varied wildly within the community. Britain and Luxembourg, for example, had had private television channels since the 1950s, while Spain still had only government-run stations. Denmark allowed only 105 minutes of advertising a week, while Italy allowed 7,189 minutes. Legislation concerning author's rights and the right to reply also differed from country to country (see Exhibits 8.1 and 8.12 (pp. 109–13), National Broadcasting Legislation, c.1983).

The Commission proposed setting down minimum requirements according to the basic broadcasting rules of the member states. Individual countries were then free to write stricter laws that would apply only to broadcasters operating from that country.

But the issues surrounding free broadcasting throughout Europe were far thornier than just the question of regulating advertising or protecting author rights. The production and broadcasting of television programs, after all, is not only a business but also an integral part of a country's culture. The Commission, therefore, saw a need to restrict access by outsiders – specifically producers from the United States – to European airwaves as a means of protecting the member states' culture. As Jacques Delors, then the newly appointed president of the EC, said in a speech in 1989 to the Assises de l'Audiovisuel:

> Culture is not merchandise. We cannot treat culture in the same way we treat refrigerators or automobiles. Laissez-faire and a market economy aren't enough in this case . . . Don't we have the right to exist? Don't we have the right to perpetuate our traditions, our patrimony, our language? How can a country of, say, 10 million inhabitants stand against the universality offered by satellites and maintain its language, which is a vehicle of its culture as well as its culture?

The final directive, 'on the coordination of certain provisions laid down by law, regulation or administrative action in member states concerning the pursuit of

Exhibit 8.1   *National broadcasting legislation as of 1983*

Country	Organization	Programs	Advertising
West Germany	9 Länder services 2 federal stations ZDF + Lower Saxony's commercial network	Fed–Land regulation Promote political values	Carry advertising, but controls
Belgium	RTBF, BRT, BRF Public corporations Political appointments	Government and community regulation. Must promote cultural/ crit. values. Impartiality.	Forbidden
Denmark	Denmark's Radio Radio council (listeners' views)	Radio council scrutiny Freedom of speech, + information	Forbidden
France	July 1982 law on audiovisual TDF at national level – Radio France; TF1; Antenne 2; FR3 do programs – SF production INCA responsible for commercial code. State is sole shareholder. Also local/reg. companies + Radio Fr. Internationale Law ends monopoly	Ensure public interest (arts) Haute Autorité issues licences – 9 members appointed by president – To represent pluralism	Regulation by the MA + Régie Française de Publicité
Greece	ERT, ERT 2 State is sole shareholder	Impartiality, democratic, cultural	Advertising
Eire	RTE Broadcasting authority PTT	Irish unity, cultural Democratic values Arouse interest in UC	Advertising
Italy	April 1975 – Private licensing RAI – 99.5 percent IRI owned 350 private TV stations Board of Directors elected by IRI + Parliament's supervisory committee	Respect pluralism Parliamentary committee monitors	Advertising
Luxembourg	GTL at Radio-Télé-Lux (RTL) – a joint stock company	Government supervision	Advertising
Netherlands	Minister for Cultural Affairs grants broadcasting time NOS is the broadcasting foundation.	Openness, diversity, cooperation Program committees of NOS commissioner monitors	Advertising

Exhibit 8.1 *continued*

Country	Organization	Programs	Advertising
UK	BBC – Board approved by privy council IBA – 15 independent TV companies: IBA approved by HS TV-AM Channel 4 Home Secretary supervises BBC has 54 advisory committees	Wide variety; quality; impartiality; public taste	BBC: no advertising

Source: European Commission

television broadcasting activities', better known as 'Television Without Frontiers', was signed in October of 1989 and addresses in large part the issues outlined in the Green Paper. The directive states that advertising cannot exceed more than 20 percent of any half-hour segment, and cannot comprise more than 15 percent of a programming day. Advertisements for alcohol are restricted, and those for tobacco and pharmaceutical products banned altogether, as are advertisements found offensive to religious or political beliefs or those that encourage discrimination on grounds of race, sex or nationality. The directive also states that children's programs must not contain pornography or excessive violence.

The protection of European programming is addressed in Article 4 of the directive (see Exhibit 8.2):

> Member states must ensure, where practical and by appropriate means, that broadcasters reserve for European works, within the meaning of Article 6, a majority proportion of their transmission time, excluding the time appointed to news, sports events, games, advertising and teletext services.

As of 1991, the guidelines would apply to prime time – 6 pm to 11 pm daily – as well as non-prime viewing hours.

European works, as outlined in Article 6 of the directive, are defined as any works originating from the member states of the community, from East Germany, or from European countries that signed the Council of Europe's European Convention on Transfrontier Television (which stipulates the same guidelines as the directive in terms of quotas, advertising, etc.). Co-productions with non-EC production companies are allowed, but the broadcast works must be made, supervised and majority-financed by one or more producers within the EC or from countries that signed and ratified the Council of Europe convention (see Article 6 of the directive in Exhibit 8.2).

EC countries were given three years to attain a majority of European broadcast works in their broadcasts, but the directive demands that broadcasters not let their

Exhibit 8.2

CHAPTER II

General provisions

Article 2

1. Each Member State shall ensure that all television broadcasts transmitted

– by broadcasters under its jurisdiction, or
– by broadcasters who, while not being under the jurisdiction of any Member State, make use of a frequency or a satellite capacity granted by, or a satellite up-link situated in, that Member State,

comply with the law applicable to broadcasts intended for the public in that Member State.

2. Member States shall ensure freedom of reception and shall not restrict retransmission on their territory of television broadcasts from other Member States for reasons which fall within the fields coordinated by this Directive. Member States may provisionally suspend retransmissions of television broadcasts if the following conditions are fulfilled:

(a) a television broadcast coming from another Member State manifestly, seriously and gravely infringes Article 22;

(b) during the previous 12 months, the broadcaster has infringed the same provision on at least two prior occasions;

(c) the Member State concerned has notified the broadcaster and the Commission in writing of the alleged infringements and of its intention to restrict retransmission should any such infringement occur again;

(d) consultations with the transmitting State and the Commission have not produced an amicable settlement within 15 days of the notification provided for in point (c), and the alleged infringement persists.

The Commission shall ensure that the suspension is compatible with Community law. It may ask the Member State concerned to put an end to a suspension which is contrary to Community law, as a matter of urgency. This provision is without prejudice to the application of any procedure, remedy or saction to the infringements in question in the Member State which has jurisdiction over the broadcaster concerned.

3. This Directive shall not apply to broadcasts intended exclusively for reception in States other than Member States, and which are not received directly or indirectly in one or more Member States.

Article 3

1. Member States shall remain free to require television broadcasters under their jurisdiction to lay down more detailed or stricter rules in the areas covered by this Directive.

2. Member States shall, by appropriate means, ensure, within the framework of their legislation, that television broadcasters under their jurisdiction comply with the provisions of this Directive.

CHAPTER III

Promotion of distribution and production of television programmes

Article 4

1. Member States shall ensure where practicable and by appropriate means, that broadcasters reserve for European works, within the meaning of Article 6, a majority proportion of their transmission time, excluding the time appointed to news, sports events, games, advertising and teletext services. This proportion, having regard to the broadcaster's informational, educational, cultural and entertainment responsibilities to its viewing public, should be achieved progressively, on the basis of suitable criteria.

2. Where the proportion laid down in paragraph 1 cannot be attained, it must not be lower than the average for 1988 in the Member State concerned.

Exhibit 8.2 *continued*

However, in respect of the Hellenic Republic and the Portuguese Republic, the year 1988 shall be replaced by the year 1990.

3. From 3 October 1991, the Member States shall provide the Commission every two years with a report on the application of this Article and Article 5.

That report shall in particular include a statistical statement on the achievement of the proportion referred to in this Article and Article 5 for each of the television programmes falling within the jurisdiction of the Member State concerned, the reasons, in each case, for the failure to attain that proportion and the measures adopted or envisaged in order to achieve it.

The Commission shall inform the other Member States and the European Parliament of the reports, which shall be accompanied, where appropriate, by an opinion. The Commission shall ensure the application of this Article and Article 5 in accordance with the provisions of the Treaty. The Commission may take account in its opinion, in particular, of progress achieved in relation to previous years, the share of first broadcast works in the programming, the particular circumstances of new television broadcasters and the specific situation of countries with a low audiovisual production capacity or restricted language area.

4. The Council shall review the implementation of this Article on the basis of a report from the Commission accompanied by any proposals for revision that it may deem appropriate no later than the end of the fifth year from the adoption of the Directive.

To that end, the Commission report shall, on the basis of the information provided by Member States under paragraph 3, take account in particular of developments in the Community market and of the international context.

Article 5

Member States shall ensure, where practicable

and by appropriate means, that broadcasters reserve at least 10% of their transmission time, excluding the time appointed to news, sports events, games, advertising and teletext services, or alternately, at the discretion of the Member State, at least 10% of their programming budget, for European works created by producers who are independent of broadcasters. This proportion, having regard to broadcasters' informational, educational, cultural and entertainment responsibilities to its viewing public, should be achieved progressively, on the basis of suitable criteria; it must be achieved by earmarking an adequate proportion for recent works, that is to say works transmitted within five years of their production.

Article 6

1. Within the meaning of this chapter, 'European works' means the following:

(a) works originating from Member States of the Community and, as regards television broadcasters falling within the jurisdiction of the Federal Republic of Germany, works from German territories where the Basic Law does not apply and fulfilling the conditions of paragraph 2;

(b) works originating from European third States party to the European Convention on Transfrontier Television of the Council of Europe and fulfilling the conditions of paragraph 2;

(c) works originating from other European third countries and fulfilling the conditions of paragraph 3.

2. The works referred to in paragraph 1 (a) and (b) are works mainly made with authors and workers residing in one or more States referred to in paragraph 1 (a) and (b) provided that they comply with one of the following three conditions:

(a) they are made by one or more producers established in one or more of those States; or

Exhibit 8.2 *continued*

(b) production of the works is supervised and actually controlled by one or more producers established in one or more of those States; or

(c) the contribution of co-producers of those States to the total co-production costs is preponderant and the co-production is not controlled by one or more producers established outside those States.

3. The works referred to in paragraph 1 (c) are works made exclusively or in co-production with producers established in one or more Member State by producers established in one or more European third countries with which the Community will conclude agreements in accordance with the procedures of the Treaty, if those works are mainly made with authors and workers residing in one or more European States.

4. Works which are not European works within the meaning of paragraph 1, but made mainly with authors and workers residing in one or more Member States, shall be considered to be European works to an extent corresponding to the proportion of the contribution of Community co-producers to the total production costs.

Article 7

Member States shall ensure that the television broadcasters under their jurisdiction do not broadcast any cinematographic work, unless otherwise agreed between its rights holders and the broadcaster, until two years have elapsed since the work was first shown in cinemas in one of the Member States of the Community; in the case of cinematographic works co-produced by the broadcaster, this period shall be one year.

Source: European Commission Directive 3/10/89: On the co-ordination of certain provisions laid down by law, regulation for administrative action in Member States concerning the pursuits of television broadcasting activities (89/552/EEC)

proportion of European works fall below their 1988 level (1990 for Greece and Portugal). Member states are also required to report to the Commission every two years, starting in October 3, 1991, on the application of Article 4. If a country fails to achieve a majority proportion of European works, explanations must be provided, but the directive indicates that the Commission will not rule with an iron fist. 'The Commission may take account in its opinion, in particular, of progress achieved in relation to previous years, the share of first broadcast works in the programming, the particular circumstances of new television broadcasters and the specific situation of countries with a low audiovisual production capacity or restricted language area' (Article 4.4).

The directive states that as long as a broadcaster complies with the rules of its own country, and with EC regulations, it can send its signal anywhere within the EC. This ensures that the stricter laws established by some countries will only apply to broadcasters operating from that country, and not a foreign broadcaster sending its signals to that country.

The European Broadcasting Industry

The 1980s brought great change to the European broadcasting industry, both because the television market, once controlled by state monopolies (with the exception of Luxembourg and the UK, which had private stations since the 1950s), was opened to privately-owned stations, and because of the explosive growth in cable and satellite broadcasting.

The Increase in Broadcasting Hours

These changes meant an enormous increase in broadcasting hours. US Market research firm Frost & Sullivan, in its annual study 'The US & International Programming Production Market for TV and New Video Technologies', estimated that European programming hours would increase from 250,000 in 1987 to 440,000 in 1992, and the number of terrestrial stations would increase from 61 to 86. The European Community Commission predicted that by 1993, there would be 200 European television channels, including satellite and cable, each broadcasting anywhere from 10 to 24 hours per day.

To fill the increasing number of broadcast hours, EC member countries bought more and more of their programming from outside the European Community. Eighty percent of all European programs never left their country of origin, and American producers and distributors were the main providers of programming, supplying roughly 45 percent of all European television programs (series, movies, documentaries, etc.) and 60 percent of all the films imported by European television stations.[2]

The balance of television programs came from the UK (15 percent), West Germany (7 percent), France (5 percent), other European countries (8 percent), Eastern European countries (3 percent), exchanges via Eurovision – an exchange program set up by the European Broadcasting Union – (7 percent), international joint productions (4 percent) and from the rest of the world (6 percent).[3]

Cost was the reason for the large influx of American programs. In France, for example, the cost of producing a one-hour original show averaged 400,000 ECUs, while the cost of buying one episode of Dallas was 30,000 ECUs.[4] And production costs were rising as television viewers, accustomed to seeing high-quality productions in their home on video cassettes, demanded high-quality production values from television shows. In 1984 it cost 700,000 ECUs to make a feature film in the EC. In 1986, that figure had jumped to 1 billion ECUs.

The trend toward outside purchasing as against internal production seemed destined to continue because broadcasters' expenditures on programs were expected to grow at a much slower rate than the total number of broadcast hours. In addition, the majority of new commercial stations did not have big inhouse production budgets, nor – since they were new – did they have a stock of old programs and films they could rebroadcast. Thus, they were forced to buy rather that produce. One strategy, used extensively by Italian and French private channels when they first started operating, was to buy huge stocks of mostly American film and series – some of them 20 or 30 years old. This practice delighted US broadcasters with large film libraries. 'As Europe expands, there is an enormous demand for a product that is both audience-attractive and economical. Americans have that product ready on the shelf,' said Don Wear, senior vice-president, CBS Broadcast International.[5]

Just as European broadcasters were forced to buy cheaper American products, Americans were compelled to sell more programs in Europe to recoup their own higher production costs. In 1990, European markets were expected to contribute 70 percent of US producers' profits and European TV program imports from the US were expected to reach $1.47 billion. This was up from $675 million in 1987 and $212 million in 1983 according to Frost & Sullivan[6] (see Exhibits 8.3 and 8.4 for further information).

European spending on programs produced by European broadcasters was expected to grow by 8 percent between 1989 and 1995, from $7.51 billion to $8.125 billion, after which it would remain relatively stable, at least over the next several years. Spending on co-productions over the same period was forecast to rise 69 percent, from $1.82 billion to $3.075 billion, and purchases from independent European producers were projected to climb 66 percent, from $1.325 billion to $2.199 billion.[7] Imports from outside Europe, especially from Latin America, Canada and Australia were also expected to grow.

The television programs in highest demand by audiences were works of fiction, namely series, soap operas, and feature length films. These programs drew the most viewers, and made up almost 40 percent of all programs broadcast in Europe.[8] They were also the most costly for broadcasters to produce. Matteo Maggiore, author of a European Community Commission document on audiovisual production in the single market, estimated that by the mid-1990s, 500,000 hours of works of fiction might be broadcast every year in Western Europe. Even if half of those hours represented rebroadcasts, Maggiore reckoned that the EC would need to produce 125,000 hours of fiction to meet the demand and stay within EC directive regulations. A relatively tall order, considering that in 1987, only around 57,000 hours of fiction were broadcast in the EC countries, and each country, on average, filled only 23 percent of its needs from within its own borders. The US, the largest exporter of television programs and films, supplied roughly 35 percent of fictional works in Europe. Germany and the UK were the only two countries that produced more programs than they bought (see Exhibit 8.5 for further information).

Technological Advances

(a) Satellites Television programs broadcast via satellite, a practice which began roughly 30 years ago, were first transmitted with telecommunications satellites, which emitted very weak signals that were then picked up by a large dish and distributed to viewers via cable or ground transmitters. Most satellite transmission was used for sending video signals of news events around the globe.

But as early as the 1970s, the potential for television viewers to receive programs directly in their homes with their own satellite dishes became apparent. With direct broadcasting by satellite in mind, the World Administrative Radio Conference (WARC) met in Geneva in 1977 to set broadcast 'footprints' for Europe, Asia and Africa.[9] 'Footprints' are the zones in which a satellite, on the basis of the power and strength of its beam, can send signals which can be clearly received by a 90 cm (35 inch) satellite dish (the norm for home use). The Conference,

Exhibit 8.3 *Studio revenues derived from exports*

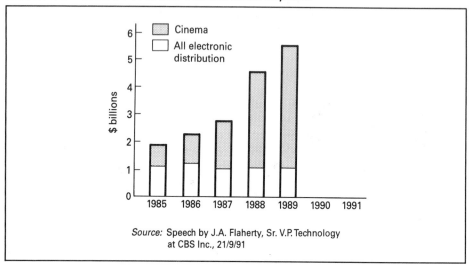

Source: Speech by J.A. Flaherty, Sr. V.P. Technology
at CBS Inc., 21/9/91

Exhibit 8.4 *Studio revenues from program distribution – 1989*

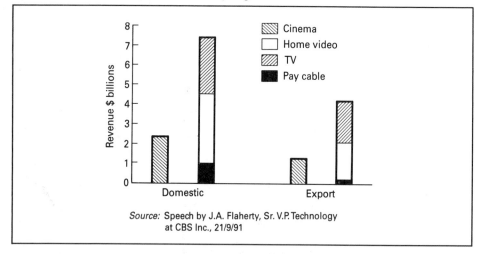

Source: Speech by J.A. Flaherty, Sr. V.P. Technology
at CBS Inc., 21/9/91

concentrating on national, rather than transnational, broadcasting service awarded each country five channels, regardless of country size or population. The footprints and regulations established at the conference were due to expire in 1994.

The strength of satellite beams – even the relatively weak beams of telecommunications satellites – were such that the satellite's footprint often extended over several nations. However, the footprints defined by the conference

Exhibit 8.5 *Importation of works of fiction by country/channel (1987)*

Country/Channel	1987 Imports from		1985 Imports from	
	EC (%)	USA (%)	EC (%)	USA (%)
West Germany				
ARD (films only)	14.3	37.1		
ZDF	33.2	36.1*	33	36
SAT1 (films only)	31.5	48.1		
Belgium				
RTBF	51.3	48.7	51	49
Denmark				
DR	35.5	58.6	43	46
Spain				
RTVE	27.2	48.0	30**	35**
TV 3 Catalan	11.7	20.1		
France				
TF1	1.7	44.1*	34	37
A2	4.0	29.3*	26	35
FR3	6.8	30.9*		
Italy				
RAI	27.6	57.4	28	57
Luxembourg				
RTL-TV1 (includes Bel. & Lux. production)	45.0	55.0		
RTL Plus (films only)	86.0	9.3		
Netherlands				
NOS	30.0	56.0	30	56
United Kingdom				
BBC1 (films/series only)	4.0	24.0		
BBC2 (films/series only)	5.0	9.0		
ITV	5.8	13.8	5***	38***
Channel 4	5.0	12.0		
Sky Channel	5.8	35.6		

*   1988 figures
**   feature films only
*** 1982 figures
Source: International Institute of Communications 'Stories Come First' and *The Political Economy of Communications*, edited by Kenneth Dyson and Peter Humphreys, Routledge, 1990

were set along country borders. The part of the footprint which lay beyond the target area was referred to as overspill. Overspill was inevitable, especially over smaller European countries, and it was destined to become even greater as the technology for receiving satellite transmissions improved.

As early as 1983, the European Commission was considering the effects of overspill. In a report dated May 1983, it stated 'In theory, a government could prohibit its citizens from watching foreign transmissions, although this would be unthinkable in Western democracies. Indeed the European Convention on Human Rights, ratified by all the member states of the Community (signed in 1950), guarantees every person the freedom to receive and impart information and ideas without interference by public authority and regardless of frontiers.'[10] Thus, the advances in satellite broadcasting technology forced the European Community to tackle the regulations of trans-European broadcasting (see Exhibits 8.6 to 8.9 for footprint maps).

The first broadcaster to latch on to the idea of pan-European broadcasting via satellite was Rupert Murdoch. In 1981 he created Satellite Television plc in London to broadcast programs across Europe with low-powered satellites. At first the channel broadcast for two hours a day, beaming programs in English to cable networks in Norway, Finland, Malta and Switzerland. This experiment in multi-country transmission was renamed Sky Channel in 1984, and the number of broadcast hours were increased. By January 1988, more than 11 million homes in 19 countries received the channel.[11]

Exhibit 8.6 *Area covered by the Luxembourg satellite beam*

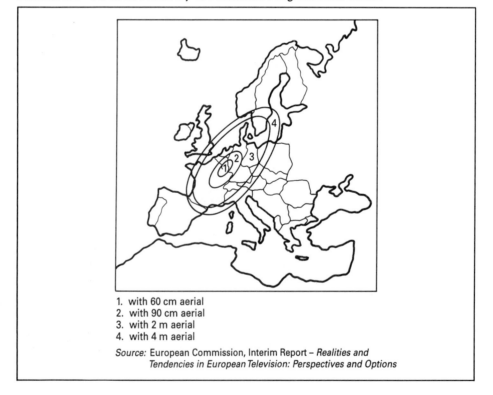

1. with 60 cm aerial
2. with 90 cm aerial
3. with 2 m aerial
4. with 4 m aerial

Source: European Commission, Interim Report – *Realities and Tendencies in European Television: Perspectives and Options*

Exhibit 8.7   *Reception areas for the French satellite beam*

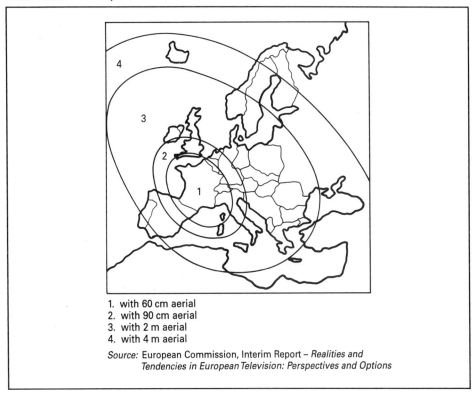

1. with 60 cm aerial
2. with 90 cm aerial
3. with 2 m aerial
4. with 4 m aerial

Source: European Commission, Interim Report – *Realities and Tendencies in European Television: Perspectives and Options*

Toward the end of the 1980s, telecommunications satellites – capable of sending stronger signals and therefore of being received over a greater area – were launched, but television programming was still distributed via cable or ground networks and mostly (but not entirely) stayed within the borders of its country of origin. British companies still dominated satellite broadcasting with Sky Channel, Super Channel and MTV Europe, although broadcasters in France (M6 and La Cinq) and Germany (RLT Plus), among others, also transmitted programs via satellite.

The first operational direct broadcasting satellite, ASTRA, was launched in December 1988 by the European Satellite Society, a private company based in Luxembourg. By 1989, five other direct broadcast by satellite services existed: TV-SAT in Germany; TDF in France; TELE-X in Scandinavia; OLYMPUS for the European Space Agency; and BSB in the United Kingdom. Together, these were broadcasting 39 channels directly by satellite. Many channels were still only received in their country of origin, although ASTRA's footprint covered 77 percent of Western Europe and provided access to 99 percent of all French, German and

Exhibit 8.8   *Reception areas for the United Kingdom satellite beam*

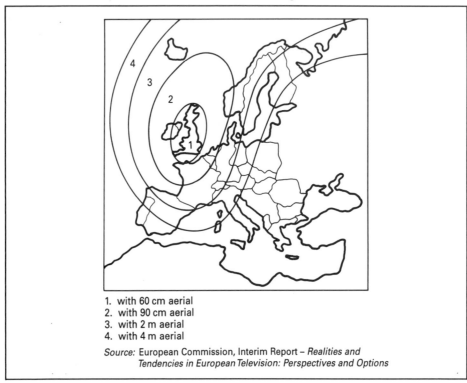

1. with 60 cm aerial
2. with 90 cm aerial
3. with 2 m aerial
4. with 4 m aerial

Source: European Commission, Interim Report – *Realities and
Tendencies in European Television: Perspectives and Options*

English-speaking homes. Rupert Murdoch (who moved his channels from a telecommunications satellite to ASTRA) was ASTRA's most important client, with Sky Channel, Eurosport, Sky Movies, Sky News and the Disney Channel (joint venture with Walt Disney Studios). Because of the large number of English programs on ASTRA, Murdoch concentrated most of his marketing efforts on the United Kingdom. By 1990, he projected that his channels would be seen in 1.5 to 2.5 million homes UK homes. After three months of broadcasting (April 1989), 81,000 homes in the UK had reception equipment, but a survey conducted by an English marketing group found that 80 percent of British people had no intention of buying special individual satellite equipment, despite the fact that a complete satellite reception kit was being sold for only £199.[12]

The regulation of satellite transmission is covered in Article 2 of the 1989 directive and states that any EC broadcaster transmitting programs via satellite, must respect laws laid down in the state where it has its operational headquarters. If US or other non-EC broadcasters, for example, use the frequency or satellite capacity granted by an EC-member country, or use a satellite link-up situated in an EC country, they must follow the broadcasting laws of that country (see Article 2 of the directive in Exhibit 8.2).[13]

Exhibit 8.9 *Reception areas for the German satellite beam*

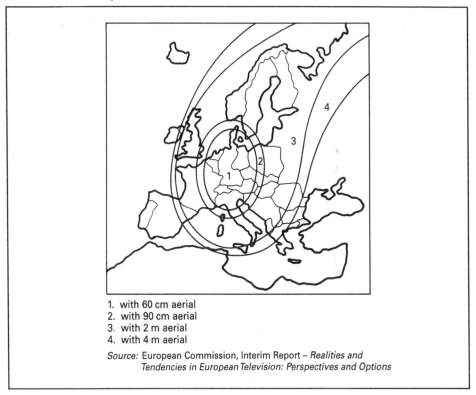

1. with 60 cm aerial
2. with 90 cm aerial
3. with 2 m aerial
4. with 4 m aerial

Source: European Commission, Interim Report – *Realities and Tendencies in European Television: Perspectives and Options*

(b) Cable   At the end of 1988, about 16 million European homes were wired for cable television, or roughly 18 percent of the 130.1 million homes with televisions in Europe. Cable TV, however, was not equally popular in all European countries. Cable television was developed for rural areas, where the geography of an area made reception of standard television signals difficult. Countries where several languages are spoken (like Switzerland) saw an early development of broadcasting via cable. But cable was also the ground network for much satellite transmission, so expansion in non-direct satellite broadcasting depended in large part on cable penetration (see Exhibit 8.10).

(c) High-definition Television (HDTV)   In 1985, the Japanese announced to the International Radio Consultative Committee (CCIR) – the body responsible for setting the standards for broadcasting – that it wanted to propose a world standard for high-definition television (HDTV). Japan's model was incompatible with existing technology, meaning that both broadcasters and consumers would have to invest in new cameras and television sets. Sparked by this announcement, the Europeans

Exhibit 8.10 *Homes with cable television and satellite in the EC*

Country	Homes with TV	% of homes with cable TV*				Percentage with satellite dish*	
	1987 in thousands	1987	1988	1990	1995	1990	1995
W. Germany	23,510	13.6	19.6	27.6	56.1	0.2	4.7
Benelux	3,354	12.6	15.2	18.0	22.5	0.1	0.1
Denmark	2,200	27.3	29.5	38.6	54.5	2.7	11.4
Spain	10,693	NA	2.7	5.6	14.0	0.2	0.5
France	20,000	0.5	0.7	1.8	9.5	1.5	9.4
Greece	2,900	NA	0.4	NA	NA	0.3	0.7
Ireland	942	31.8	34.0	42.5	55.2	1.2	14.9
Italy	19,667	0.0	0.0	NA	NA	0.0	0.1
Holland	5,547	60.4	69.4	73.9	82.9	1.8	4.5
Portugal	3,090	NA	1.7	NA	NA	0.3	0.7
UK	20,886	0.2	0.3	2.5	7.1	7.2	33.5

* Based on percentage of homes with TV, 1987 figures
Source: Audiovisual Production in the Single Market, by Matteo Maggiore, European Community Commission, 1991

moved to create a standard of their own, and thus began the HDTV battle. In 1986, European companies presented their own plans to the CCIR, which was scheduled to select the world production standard for HDTV in the Spring of 1990. The European group was composed of four European manufacturers: Philips (Netherlands), Thomson (France), Thorn-EMI (UK) and Bosch (Germany). Its standard, unlike the Japanese version, would be evolutionary, meaning it would allow for HDTV programs to be received on existing European television sets (but not on US sets, which operated under a different broadcasting standard).

Throughout the mid-1980s, the US had still not entered the HDTV contest, but in 1988, the US made two important announcements. The first, in February 1988, was that it would begin research on its own HDTV standard. The second, in September 1988, was that the Federal Communications Commission (FCC) had ruled that any HDTV system used in the US must be compatible with existing television equipment. In essence, the FCC's decision meant a rejection of both the Japanese and the European standard under development.

In May 1989, the Americans requested that the CCIR postpone its decision from 1990 to 1994. This delay gave both the Japanese and the Europeans time to perfect their own systems, but also provided the Americans with four more years in which to develop their own HDTV model.

In the US, seven different groups of researchers were working on HDTV development, two of which had European connections: the North American Philips System (with Dutch consumer electronics company Philips) and the Sarnoff Research Center ACTV System (with Thomson and RCA, its US affiliate). Other signs of a US/European cooperation were evident. Robert Mosbacher, the secretary of state for trade, met with an EC commissioner in May 1989 to discuss the need to develop a standard acceptable to both the EC and the US. The result of that meeting was a planned symposium later the same year that would include European and American broadcasters, industrialists and government authorities discussing ways to cooperate on HDTV development.

Internationalization of the Television Industry

New technology and the deregulation of television throughout Europe encouraged the globalization of European media companies. Not only did the largest European media firms buy into private channels throughout Europe, but many also expanded their activities, producing programs for television as well as feature-length films to be distributed in theaters and on video as well as to be broadcast on television.

The biggest European media companies developed US-style programming houses, which integrated the production, financing and distribution of programs. Berlusconi's three networks in Italy, for example, were supplied programs by another Berlusconi subsidiary, Reteitalia, which also created products for cinema distribution and foreign markets. France-based Hachette, and Leo Kirch in Germany also had similar subsidiaries.

Alliances between media moguls were formed at all levels. Broadcasters like Rupert Murdoch joined forces with SES, a Luxembourg satellite company. Broadcasters also purchased shares in each other's companies, such as the Italian firm Fininvest (majority owned by media mogul Silvio Berlusconi) purchasing shares in French (La Cinq and Canal Plus) and German (Tele 5) channels.

The EC Commission tended to back such partnerships, as proven by its lenient merger regulations. EC officials can veto a merger equaling more than 5 billion ECUs, but that represents a level higher than any possible coupling of European media firms. 'Europe is used to having cartels and they have never been illegal in the way they are in the United States,' said Neal Weinstock, author of the Frost & Sullivan report on television.[14]

By 1989, there were at least four main alliances involving European media giants:

1. News International (Murdoch, UK)–Walt Disney (US).

2. Havas (France)–CLT (Luxembourg) – Canal Plus (France)– TVS (UK).

3. Fininvest (Italy)–Bouygues (France)–Kirch (German)–Pathé (France)–Maxwell (UK)

4. WH Smith (UK)–Compagnie Générale des Eaux (France).[15]

(See Exhibit 8.11 for company profiles.)

But while these large mergers were taking place, most production houses, apart from those owned directly by broadcasters, remained small. In the UK, for instance, there were 31 production houses in 1988. In Germany there were 44, France 70, and Spain, 32. Even the largest producers, like France's Hamster

Exhibit 8.11 *Companies*

Bertelsmann

This group, which began as a publisher of hymnals, was, until the Time-Warner merger, the largest communications group in the world. In 1987, its sales were 5.243 billion ECUs, 50 percent of which came from books, 40 percent from newspapers and magazines, and 10 percent from audiovisual and other media. In the audiovisual domain, Bertelsmann holds 38.5 percent of the German channel RTL Plus. With the cooperation of Canal Plus (French pay television channel), they planned the launch of Canal Plus Deutschland. In addition, Bertelsmann, in 1988, won the five year rights to broadcast the German championship soccer matches (until then run only on German state-owned television) and Wimbledon.

Other electronic media investments in Germany include: UFA Film, Universum Film, Stern TV, GEO films, Gruner & Jahr Film, and 33 percent of KMG, a company specializing in television (hertzian and cable).

Fifty-eight percent of Bertelsmann's sales came from outside of Germany in 1987, and 29 percent came from sales in the US and Canada.

News Corporation Worldwide (Rupert Murdoch)

Murdoch controls two-thirds of the Australian press and is number four in the US television market through his establishment, in 1986, of Fox Television (former Metromedia television). His US acquisitions also included 20th Century Fox, the movie studio. His 1987 sales were 3.956 billion ECUs, made of the following activities: daily newspapers, 38 percent; cinema, 26 percent; television, 13 percent; magazines, 11 percent; publishing, 3 percent; other sectors, 9 percent.

Murdoch launched four direct broadcasting by satellite channels in 1989 – Sky Channel, Eurosport, Sky Movies and Sky News – and established a joint venture with Disney to launch Disney Channel. Initially his Sky Channel had been targeted throughout Europe, but subsequently Murdoch changed his focus to the UK and Ireland. Only Eurosport is seen across Europe.

Compagnie Luxembourgeoise de Télédiffusion (CLT)

CLT, which had sales of 299 million ECUs in 1987, is the oldest commercial television company in Europe.

CLT's RTL channel is broadcast throughout Luxembourg, in 73 percent of Belgian households and in eastern regions of France. It also broadcasts German language programs via RTL Plus in Germany. In addition, CLT has interests in the following companies:

> M6 (France), 25 percent; RTL Plus (Germany), 46.1 percent; Compagnia di Distribuzione Cinematografica Italiana (Italy), 80 percent; Stand'Art Production (France), 100 percent; three television production groups: Cristal, DIC, World Entertainment Group Luxembourg

CLT also has plans to create channels in Spain and Holland and has obtained a concession for Channel 3 in the UK (1992).

In 1987, CLT's president said, 'We don't ask for any subsidy, we only ask that we be not held back by different rules in each country.'[1]

1. *Le Figaro*, November 19, 1987, 'Pour une télévision sans frontière'

Exhibit 8.11 *continued*

Fininvest

Fininvest is 51 percent owned by media magnate Silvio Berlusconi.

In 1987, it was the fourteenth largest communications group in the world, with 2.917 billion ECUs in revenues.

Fininvest dominates Italian television, owning three of the five national television chains: Canale 5, Italia 1 and Rete 4 (50 percent owned with Mondadori), which bring in $1 billion a year in advertising revenues. Other audiovisual investments include 25 percent of La Cinq (French television stations), a 45 percent stake in the West German company Kabel Media which owns Tele-5. Berlusconi is also a minority shareholder of Music Box in West Germany.

Walt Disney Studios

In 1989, revenues for the theme park and entertainment group Walt Disney were $4.6 billion dollars. Operating profit for Walt Disney Studios, the division that included the Disney Channel, syndicated television, video sales and motion pictures topped $256 million (including video sales), about 20 percent of net operating income for the entire Disney Group. Its pay television channel, The Disney Channel had captured nearly five million subscribers and box office revenues for Disney films approached $5 billion, of which $445 million came from overseas theaters.

Gulf & Western

Gulf & Western, an American entertainment, publishing and consumer/commercial finance concern reported net revenues for 1988 of $5.1 billion. Its entertainment division produced, financed and distributed motion pictures, television programming and videos internationally, and operated theaters and sports and entertainment facilities, made up $1.9 billion or 37 percent of revenues, as well as 37 percent of the company's operating income.

Its production and distribution arm for television programming and motion pictures was Paramount Pictures Corp., which produced 20.5 hours of television programming weekly in 1988/1989.

Time Warner

Time Warner, the product of the merger between Time Inc. and Warner Communications, is the largest communications company in the world, with revenues of $7.642 billion in 1989.

Operating income of $1.4 billion broke down as follows:

magazines, 23 percent; filmed entertainment, 12 percent; recorded music and music publishing, 17 percent; cable television, 38 percent; programming – HBO, 12 percent; books, 2 percent.

Warner Brothers Television licensed over 13,000 hours of programming to over 100 countries in a dozen languages, and was the world's largest distributor of television programming. In 1989, Time Warner cable company had 6.14 million subscribers in the US, 12 percent of the 49.4 million homes cabled in the US.

productions or Germany's TV-69, only boasted a 1988 turnover of 135 million French francs and 15 to 20 million DM respectively.

Nationalized and Pan-European Television

Despite the growth in private multimedia companies, state-run channels continued to exist in every country, although many were experiencing financial problems, caused both by a loss of advertising dollars to commercial stations, and to the higher costs of buying or making television programs. The *raison d'être* of these nationalized channels was to defend, if not strengthen, the cultural identity of a nation. In order to compete with commercial channels, they began forming alliances. The first was the European Co-production Association, established in 1985. Seven national channels – Channel 4 (UK), ORF (Austria), RAI (Italy), SRG/SSR (Switzerland), ZDF (Germany), RTVE (Spain) and Antenne 2 (France) – created an organization to produce fictional programs for television jointly. By 1989, the group had produced 42 hours of programming, with an investment approaching 270 million French francs.

One of the problems of such joint ventures was language. Most broadcasts that were transmitted to several countries simultaneously were usually dubbed or subtitled depending on the preferences of viewers in each country. People in France, Germany and the UK, for example, preferred dubbing, while people in smaller countries, or where cable penetration was great, were used to subtitles.

The nationalized channels biggest experiment with pan-European television, and its most blatant failure, came with Europa TV, created in 1985. Started by five countries – Germany (ARD), Ireland (RTE), Italy (RAI), Netherlands (NOS) and Portugal (RTP) – the channel's goal was to be the first multilingual, pan-European station, broadcasting simultaneously (by dubbing the programs into the five different languages) via a communications satellite.

Europa TV tried to reflect 'European' culture. It devoted 15 percent of air time to news or information programs, viewed from a European rather than nationalistic perspective. The rest of its six hour per day schedule included entertainment, cultural, sports, music and religious programs. Europa TV was financed through advertising, contributions from member countries, a subsidy from the Government of the Netherlands (where it was headquartered), and aid from the European Commission. The channel's break-even point was 6 million viewers, but its audience reached, at most, only 1.8 million out of a possible 3.5 million viewers connected to cable in the five countries. Advertisers soon fled because of the lack of audience, and the channel folded after only one year of operation. Reasons for the failure were not only to an insufficient number of cable viewers, but the overriding national interests of viewers and the inadequacy of certain programs.

The EC took the initiative in organizing several programs in the late 80s to support a European Audio-Visual 'Space'. The largest was MEDIA, first established in April 1986. The MEDIA plan consisted of several projects co-financed by the European community and aimed at defending and promoting the European film and television industry. The first projects were launched in 1988 with a budget of

5.5 million ECUs. The projects included: financial support for the distribution of low-budget films to cinemas, funds to dub or subtitle television programs and education services to teach independent film-makers about the business/financing side of the industry. The results of MEDIA, as of the end of 1988 were: 75 launchings of 20 films in 13 countries, 20 films or TV series dubbed or subtitled, the promotion of 1,000 independent production companies in seven international markets and 2 million ECU spent to develop 100 scripts.

The Intra-EC Battle

Many issues were disputed in the six years of debates that led to the final directive, such as whether to allow alcohol advertising, how sponsored programs should be identified to viewers, whether news programs and political information programs could be sponsored and how to protect the rights of authors in programs retransmitted by cable. But by far the biggest point of contention between EC countries was over quotas for EC programming. The initial text for the directive, proposed by the European Commission in Brussels in 1986, had called for a quota stipulating that 30 percent – rising to 60 percent after several years – of all programs broadcast must come from EC countries. This quota was the darling of the French delegation and was generally supported by the Italians, but lacked the backing of the majority of other countries. Greece and Portugal opposed the quotas as too stringent (because their industries were not big enough to support such a high ratio of expensive European television). Denmark, Germany and the UK also opposed the quotas, the first two for internal political reasons, and the latter because the government was generally anti-protectionist.

By November 1988, the European Commission was feeling pressure to complete its negotiations on the broadcasting directive. The main impetus came from the Council of Europe, an organization comprising 22 European nations (including the 12 members of the EC), which was negotiating a parallel agreement that would regulate the transmission of television programs between its member countries. The European Commission was fearful that differences in the way the two organizations viewed pan-European broadcasting would find the 12 EC members faced with signing two very dissimilar documents. The EC met with heads of states of the European Council in Rhodes in December 1988 to demand that the Community Directive and the European Council texts be convergent.

However, the European Commission was not simply worried about a consensus. In fact, it wanted its directive to be the model for the European Council's text. The Commission was fearful that the European Council had a much less protectionist view of television broadcasting, and would not allow programming quotas unless the European Commission signed a directive first and thus forced its hand. But the Council of Europe beat the European Commission to the punch. It pushed through its version of a television directive on March 17, 1989. The biggest blow to the European Commission was that the Council's regulation concerning

European works had been watered down from a 60 percent quota to 'a majority portion of a broadcaster's transmission, whenever possible'.[16] The Commission was thus obliged to adopt the same text for the EC directive.

To make matters worse, the European Commission continued to be deadlocked in its negotiations over the directive, due to Belgian, German and Danish disagreement over the text. Belgium rejected the directive because it desired the inclusion of a payment scheme whereby private channels would contribute money to a state fund to promote independent productions, until a Community-wide fund could be created. All the other EC countries disagreed, fearing such aid would violate EC laws against the state-funding of an industry. In prior months, the Belgian delegation had opposed the directive because they wanted to be allowed to impose a tax on foreign television broadcasters.

Germany rejected the directive because it wanted no quotas. Firstly, broadcasting in Germany was not controlled by the central government, but by the Länder, and the central government did not want to interfere in their domain. Further, the German delegation did not believe the Commission should have a say in the content of programming. Finally the delegation rejected the definition of 'European works', because it did not include programs produced in East Germany.

Denmark opposed the directive because it believed that the Commission should not have a say in cultural issues. The Dutch were also afraid that with the adaptation of the directive, its highly complex broadcasting system, which to date included no purely commercial broadcasters, would be destroyed. The Dutch feared that commercial stations would flood the market, taking advertising away from the country's quasi-nationalized channels.

On April 13, 1989, the directive text was approved by the EC's Council of European Ministers by a vote of nine to three, with Denmark, Belgium and Germany voting against the directive (although Germany had received the concession that East German works would be considered European).

Although the ministers had agreed to send the text to Parliament for ratification, there were still rumblings over certain issues, especially quotas. A member of the Portuguese delegation, for example, said 'For us, whether we buy French or American programs, we are submitting to colonization by a foreigner. On the other hand, series from North or South America, or Japan cost us much less.'[17] And France still wanted stricter quotas. 'This is without a doubt an over-timid compromise that we have adapted,' said Edith Cresson, Minister of European Affairs for France, 'but it constitutes a dynamic start in helping us save our culture and our productions.'

European producers, directors and actors, however, were furious. They wanted quotas to combat American and Japanese domination. They lobbied the European Parliament in Strasbourg to reintroduce a 50 percent minimum for European production. Parliament refused, knowing there was no chance that the Council of Ministers would accept it.

On June 15, 1989, on the eve of the final ratification of the directive – which had been approved by the European parliament a month earlier – France, Holland

and Greece backed out. France because Mme Cresson had been pressured by Jack Lang, the French Cultural Minister, to insist on concrete quotas. The Dutch had been subjected to heavy pressure from the Americans, who saw the directive as 'protectionist'. The Americans had threatened to tie the directive to their support of the European standard for high-definition television (HDTV). The Dutch and the Germans, both heavily involved in HDTV research, knew that if the Americans jumped to Japanese technology or created an HDTV of their own without the Europeans, that European HDTV would never get off the ground. The spokesperson for the German delegations said, 'On this issue, we would prefer to have the USA on our side.'[18]

European film makers and directors had been clamoring for quotas, but they were far from happy with the failed vote. The ministers, by law, had only a limited time to ratify the directive. If this one failed, a new text would take two or more years to write. Without any sort of regulation, the industry feared that the laws of the jungle would reign, and that European television would soon become extinct. But negotiations dragged on. During the final vote in October 1989, England and Germany fought to remove all reference to a majority proportion of European works, but finally a compromise was reached, and the directive was passed on October 3, 1989. Germany however, insisted that the Commission furnish a written declaration stating that the quotas were only 'politically binding', rather than legally binding – a request the Commission honored.

Reaction by the Industry

The European broadcasting industry gave a mixed reaction to the quotas. The general director of Gamma-Television, a French company, blamed the industry itself for not being international enough in its programming. The Americans, he reckoned, were not at fault: 'We have to think internationally before we think French, and that's true for the subject, for the style, for the rhythm, and also for the language.' He even proposed that Gamma produce programs directly in English, creating, in essence, its own series in the American image.[19]

In June of 1989, five of the biggest broadcasters in Europe – French TF1, Luxembourg's CLT, Italian Fininvest, British ITV, and German SAT 1 – formed ACT (Association for Commercial Television) to lobby for their cause before the Commission in Brussels. Their main concerns were to attain the most lenient terms for advertising (the most advertising time and the fewest restraints on issues like bartering, sponsorship, etc.) and the lowest possible quotas.

However, a number of trade groups pushed for quotas: the European Federation of Audiovisual Professionals (producers and directors) lobbied to have quotas established when it looked like the directive would not specify limits. German producers meeting with their counterparts in Paris in April, 1989 also asked for quotas, as did Spanish producers.

The US Reaction

US producers and distributors were fearful of broadcasting quotas because the deregulation and privatization of European television had expanded the European market enormously, and they did not want to lose access to this gold-mine. 'The European marketplace is bigger now, driving up prices and increasing demand for programming', said Regina Dantas, senior vice-president for international sales for Qintex Entertainment, a television production and right-distributing company.[20]

For these reasons the Americans, both producers and government officials, campaigned against European quotas of any kind, calling them protectionist. Nor did they buy the cultural argument. 'We do not understand why the Spanish culture is more protected by a film produced in Germany by "Europeans" than by a Spanish film of Mexican origin, or why the English culture is promoted more by a film produced in France by "Europeans", than by a film of New Zealand origin', said Carla Hills, the US Trade Representative, adding that 'the definition of European works is economic, not cultural.'[21]

The United States took the argument before the ruling council of GATT, contending that Article 4 of the EC directive violated the agreement. Firstly, GATT states 'any advantage, favor, privilege or immunity granted by any contracting party to any product originating in or destined for any other country shall be accorded immediately and unconditionally to the like product originating in or destined for the territories of all other contracting parties.'[22] GATT also states that 'the products of the territory of any contracting party imported into the territory of any other contracting party shall be accorded treatment no less favorable than that accorded to like products of national origin in respect of all laws, regulations and requirements affecting their internal sale, offering for sale, purchase, transportation, distribution or use'[23] (although GATT does not specifically cover television programming, it does allow for screen quotas for works of national origin).

The European Commission countered with the following arguments:

1.   The US excludes cultural products in its free-exchange agreement with Canada, and agrees to very strict quotas from Canada.
2.   The Organization for Economic Cooperation and Development (OECD) has a code on the Liberalization of Invisible Operations that allows screen quotas and production subsidies for audiovisuals works, a code the US supports.
3.   Television programming is a service and not a product, and thus does not fall under the GATT rules.
4.   The quotas are not legally binding, and therefore not in violation of GATT.

In addition to these formal protests, US broadcasters and producers had begun cooperating with their European counterparts to establish commercial ties before 1993. US broadcaster ABC, for example, acquired a minority stake in Tele-Munchen KG, a German production and distribution company in 1989. It also has

Exhibit 8.12 *Countries*

France

Television Market

In France, revenues from television reached $3.8 billion in 1989 and 20 million households, or 96 percent of all households, had at least one television.

Number of Channels

Six terrestrial channels (one of which is subscription) and one satellite channel.

History

In 1986, the French government restructured the television industry, selling TF1, a state-owned channel to private investors; awarding franchises to two other commercial stations (M6 and La Cinq), awarding a franchise to Canal Plus (subscription TV), allowing advertising on public channels and increasing advertising time from 5 percent to 10 percent of broadcast hours, and introduced French program quotas. The state kept Antenne 2 and FR3 as state-owned channels.

Regulations

The French boast the most stringent regulations in Europe: 50 percent of television programs must be French, that is made in France, in French and using French resources (lowered to 40 percent in 1991), 60 percent must be EC made (70 percent for TF1 feature films). From October 1991, this applied to prime time as well. In addition, France implemented $10,000 fines for every hour of programming that violated the quota.

Productions

Private channels can produce only 33 percent of their dramas and series in house (although FR3 can produce 70 percent and M6 100 percent).

They can produce only 50 percent of their other programs (FR3 can produce 75 percent).

Investment

Private channels must invest minimum required levels in French feature films, documentaries and cartoons; TF1, La Cinq and M6 must spend at least 15 percent of revenues on original French language production.

Scheduling

Films cannot be shown on Wednesday, Friday evening or Saturday before 8.30 pm. A minimum of three years must elapse between theatrical release and broadcasting release (two years if the channel was involved in co-production and one year for Canal Plus).

Channels must meet these minimum hours for documentaries: 300 hrs/year for A2, La Cinq, and M6; 250 hrs/year for TF1 and 120 hrs/year for FR3.

Exhibit 8.12   *continued*

Germany (West)

The TV Market

West Germany had $3.5 billion television revenues in 1989, and has a household penetration of 24.4 million, or 97 percent.

History

Deregulation in German television began in 1984 with the introduction of two private networks, SAT-1 and RTL-Plus, to compete with the two public networks ARD and ZDF. Later, Tele-5 and Pro 7 networks were also added. Germany has a rapidly expanding cable system, and it is estimated that in 1989, 28 percent of the households were cabled, much higher than France (1.2 percent) or the UK.

Regulation

Regulation is under the authority of the Länder, which has been very protective of its rights and fought hard to keep the federal government out of broadcasting issues and which long opposed private television. The Länder impose no EC or German quotas on either their public or private networks, and no quotas for commissioning programs from independent producers.

Great Britain

Commercial television has existed in Great Britain since 1954. The British Broadcasting Corporation (BBC) is the public service station, created by a Royal Charter in 1926, comprised of two television channels (BBC 1 and BBC 2). The BBC is administered by a board of twelve governors, named by the Queen, who hold office for five years.

The Independent Broadcasting Authority (IBA), a para-public authority, controls the private sector, comprised of two channels, ITV (Independent Television) and Channel Four, both of which are financed by advertisements. ITV awards concessions to roughly fifteen companies who broadcast regionally. Channel Four, a completely private channel, has operated since 1983.

Private companies ITV and Channel 4 export to Denmark, the US and New Zealand, as does the BBC. In addition, British companies are known for their involvement in all domains of television and film. For example, Granada has its hands in distribution and leasing of satellite equipment; the sale and co-production of programs; the production of feature-length films; and the participation in new public channels in France, Spain and Portugal, and new satellite channels (Super Channel, and BSB-direct satellite).

Both cable and satellite television are very strong in the UK, with major satellite stations run by Rupert Murdoch (Sky Channel and Disney Channel) and Robert Maxwell (MTV Europe, Super Channel).

Regulations

The United Kingdom has no legal quotas, but BBC and ITV voluntarily limit programming coming from outside the EC to 14 percent of all prime-time shows and 25 percent of shows

Exhibit 8.12   *continued*

at night. In 1993, 65 percent of all shows, excluding news, sports and game shows, must come from the EC and 35 percent can come from the rest of the world.

Italy

Italy had $4.2 billion in television revenues in 1989, and a household penetration equal to that of France in terms of gross numbers (20 million) although higher in terms of penetration (99.2 percent of all households). In 1989, satellite and video were non-existent.

Italy boasts three public channels, RAI I, RAI II, and RAI III, five commercial national networks, and 1,100 local channels. However, three commercial networks, all owned by Berlusconi (Canale 5, Italia 1 and Rete 4), and all founded in 1984, dominate the sector.

Regulations

Italy has the least stringent broadcasting restrictions of any EC country. It has no quota for EC or Italian programs, and no quotas for supporting independent products. There are no guidelines regulating relations between broadcasters, distributors and producers.

In 1990, a new law did set down some barriers, but still less than in many European countries.

Cross-media holdings are now limited to: three television networks, or two channels and newspapers selling less than 8 percent of the total, one channel plus newspapers selling less than 16 percent of the total market, no channels and newspapers selling over 16 percent of the total market. No group is allowed to hold more than 20 percent of the total media, a level extended to 25 percent if the media provides more than two-thirds of a companies income. Advertising time was also limited and theatrical releases cannot be broadcast for two years, unless the broadcaster is a co-producer (one year).

Spain

Spain has television penetration of 98 percent or 10.7 million households in 1989. Cable penetration was 9.3 percent of all households in 1989 and satellite penetration was 0.3 percent of households.

History

Television was a state monopoly under Franco, and commercial television was relatively late coming to Spain. Regional stations began springing up in the 1980s, and large networks, Tele 5, Antene 3 and Canal Plus (pay TV) were introduced only in 1990. Apart from these three commercial channels, Spain has two national public channels, TV1 and TV2 (TVE) and seven regional channels run by local governments.

Regulations

The commercial stations are required to buy 40 percent of their programming in Spain and 50 percent of their television films in the EC. The quotas do not apply to the regional stations or the two public channels. In addition, the commercial channels must produce 10 percent of their own programming, although the specifics about what constitutes an inhouse

Exhibit 8.12   *continued*

production are fairly vague, so that many stations make minimum investments in inexpensive programming produced by outside companies to satisfy this quota.

Ownership of any channel by any one group, national or foreign, is limited to 25 percent.

On TVE, advertising is limited to 10 percent of total broadcast hours per day (its broadcast day is 19 hours per day for each station), 8 minutes in any one hour, with breaks no less than 26 minutes apart. Commercial stations are limited to 10 percent of total hours (12 hours for Telecinco, 18 hours for Antenna 3) and no more than 10 minutes in any one hour.

Belgium

Belgian television was reformed in the 1970s, when the control of radio and television were taken out of the hands of the state, and although still public, were given over to the French, Flemish and German communities within Belgium. The French have two channels, RTBF and Tele 2, as do the Flemish, BRT 1 and TV2; and the Germans have a radio station and also produce several television programs. A 1987 law allowed the creation of private channels, and RTL-TV1, a French-language station began broadcasting in September 1987.

Belgium has the highest penetration of cabled households in the world. By 1989, 90 percent of households with televisions had cable. Viewers in Belgium, depending on the region in which they live, can see Dutch, German, French and British television.

Quotas

As of 1987, 20 percent of BRT's programming had to be Flemish productions. By 1992/93 that level was to rise to 50 percent. RTL-TV1 was obliged by law to produce 20 percent of what it broadcast.

Denmark

Television and radio broadcasting until the 1980s was dominated by national public television, local stations and mini-cable networks. Danmarks Radio, which controlled radio and television broadcasts of public service programs, had a monopoly until the 1970s, after which the government encouraged private citizens to organize small local companies with collective antennas and local area cable networks. Sixty percent of the Danes relied on these mini-networks in the 1980s to get programs from neighboring countries like Norway, Sweden and Germany, as well as to receive local programs. In 1983, Kanal 2, the first pay television channel, was introduced, and in 1986, a second public channel TV2, supported by advertising, was launched. The government recently decided to construct a national network of fiber optics to join the mini-networks.

Greece

Since 1987, the three Greek channels ET1, 2, and 3 have been under the control of ERT, a company 100 percent owned by the state.

Exhibit 8.12 *continued*

Ireland

RTE is the public service television channel, owned by the state, alongside two national channels. Because of the limited choice in viewing, 60 percent of the population has cable, which allows them to receive the four British channels, and the Ulster channel (UTV).

Quota

RTE voluntarily produces or commissions a minimum of 30 percent of its yearly output.

Luxembourg

In 1954, the government granted a monopoly television concession to Compagnie Luxembourgeoise de Télédiffusion (CLT), which benefits from no public funding and depends on advertising for its revenue. CLT broadcasts under the name RTL (Radio Télé Luxembourg), and sends signals into Belgium (RTL-TV1). It also owns part of the French channel M6, has a German-language channel (RTL Plus), and is associated with Rupert Murdoch in the United Kingdom.

Netherlands

Under the broadcasting law of 1988, the three national public channels (Nederland 1,2 and 3) are non-profit operations. Air time is given to religious organizations, political parties and educational organizations. The NOS, the foundation for radio and television broadcasts, organizes the programming provided by these organizations, and ensures the availability of general interest programs like news and children's shows. Only the Foundation for advertising by radio and television (STER) can run advertising spots. The Netherlands has large cable penetration.

Quota

A minimum of 50 percent of new programs broadcast each year over national public channels must be inhouse productions or new commissions; however, programs can be commissioned from foreign producers.

Portugal

Television is constitutionally a monopoly of the state. RTP (Radiotelevisao Portuguesa) is a government-owned company with four channels: RTP 1, RTP 2, RTP-Madeira and RTP-Acores. Portugal already has 2,000 parabolic antennas, and one-tenth of the population receive broadcasts via satellite.

---

a minority stake in Tesauro, Spain's largest supplier of television programs, and Hamster, a French independent TV producer. Through its stake in Tele-Munchen, ABC also has interest in Tele-5, a private German satellite channel. Co-productions between American broadcasters like Harmony God, Fox Broadcasting and Tribune Broadcasting and European broadcasters or producers like Leo Kirch and Silvio Berlusconi had also been launched.

Questions

1. What's at stake in the TV film market?
2. What should European producers do?
3. What should the EC do?
4. What should the US do?

Notes

1. Frost & Sullivan, a market research film, in their report: 'The US and International Programming Production for TV and New Video Technologies', 1991.
2. Amm Eckstein, *Europe and the Future of Television*, Club de Bruxelles, 1989.
3. Ibid.
4. Action program for the European audio-visual media products industry, Communication by the Commission to the Council, Commission of the European Communities (COM (86) 255 final, May 12, 1986).
5. 'Europe is Klondike for TV Gold Rush', *Variety*, January 20, 1988.
6. As quoted in *World Screen News*.
7. Ibid.
8. The International Institute of Communications, as quoted in *Audiovisual Production in the Single Market*, by Matteo Maggiore, Office of Official Publications of the European Community, Luxembourg, 1991.
9. North and South America opted to wait until the next regional conference in 1983.
10. Interim Report, Realities and tendencies in European Television: perspectives and Options Commission of the European Communities COM(83) 229 Final, Brussels, May 25, 1983.
11. Europe and the Future of Television, Club de Bruxelles report.
12. *Europe and the Future of Television*, Club de Bruxelles.
13. The International Telecommunications Union (a specialized agency of the United Nations) grants frequency and orbital position for satellites. Since the ITU grants the air space over Europe to European countries, US or foreign broadcasters would be forced to use European satellites if it wanted to broadcast directly by satellite to Europe.
14. 'Unveiling the New Europe', *World Screen News*.
15. Matteo Maggiore, *Audiovisual Production in the Single Market*, Commission of the European Communities, 1990.
16. The Council of Europe convention was signed by Austria, Spain, Liechtenstein, Luxembourg, Norway, Holland, San Marino, Sweden, Switzerland and the UK on May 5, 1989. It would not take effect until it had been ratified by the parliaments of all seven states.
17. *Libération*, April 14, 1989, 'La CEE donne son feu vert à la télé sans frontières ni quotas', page 14.
18. *Libération*, June 16, 1989, 'La télévision sans frontières tombe en panne', page 2.
19. *Le Monde*, July 8, 1988.
20. *International Herald Tribune*, March 18–19, 1989 'Television: transformation begins in Europe', page 18.
21. Associated Press, 'US Complains About European Limits on Imported TV Programs', October 11, 1989.
22. GATT, Article 1, section 1.
23. GATT, Article 3.

Television Without Frontiers (B)

Aftermath

Jonathan Story

The Television without Frontiers directive failed to be a complete success. Due to the many compromises made to ratify the directive, the regulations outlined in the document are fairly minimal. And so much power was left in the hands of the states that an EC-wide television regulation still barely exists; broadcasters in member states continue to be bound more by regulations made by the government in the countries where they have their operational headquarters, than by transnational law.

This situation raises some sticky legal questions. Say a satellite service sets up shop in Luxembourg, known for its very lax copyright laws. According to Luxembourg law, this service could legally broadcast imported movies across Europe even if other European broadcasters had paid for exclusive rights to the movie. A new EC law proposed in July 1991 would rectify this situation by demanding a common level of copyright protection for works broadcast throughout Europe, but the law, even if adopted, will not become effective until January 1995, and not until 1998 for services already in operation.

'You still have to deal with rules in every single country,' said Lee Steiner, a senior partner and entertainment lawyer at Loeb & Loeb, a US law firm. 'Each country is trying to protect its own special interests, and as a result, at the start of 1993, there will be very few common rules' (quoted in 'Unveiling the New Europe', *World Screen News*).

According to the EC commission, most countries, as of March 1992, had adopted legislation stipulating that broadcasters broadcast a 'majority share' of EC programs when possible, the same wording found in the directive (only Spain, Greece and the Flemish sector of Belgium still had not passed any such legislation). Other countries, like France and Britain, had written laws including specific quotas, but France's were by far the strictest in the community: demanding that 60 percent

This case was written by Kathy Burton, Research Assistant, under the supervision of Jonathan Story, Professor at INSEAD. It is intended to be used as a basis for class discussion rather than to illustrate either effective or ineffective handling of an administrative situation.
Copyright © 1992 INSEAD Fontainebleau, France.
Financial support from Sandeep Sander, Director, Sander & Co. A/s, Denmark, and Jan O. Froeshaug, Ceo Egmont, Denmark, is gratefully acknowledged.

of television programs be of European origin and 50 percent of French origin, which in essence limited non-French European works to 10 percent. So tough were the quotas that the French legislation had come under attack not only from French broadcasters and producers, but also from the EC Court. Under pressure from the EC, France reduced the French works quota to 40 percent in July 1991, but in exchange, the EC allowed it to apply a more stringent definition of French works (principally shot in the French language and 25 percent financed and produced in France).

French broadcasters were against quotas because their production budgets had swelled at a time of increased competition over advertising (which in France is limited to one break per hour of drama, much more stringent than the 20 percent per hour allowed under the EC directive). Many analysts believed that the quotas helped to push French station La Cinq to the brink of bankruptcy.

Producers, who a few years before had vehemently defended quotas, now feared that their ability to co-produce, which had become the most popular way to finance the making of television and films, would be greatly curtailed by the new definition of a French work. Producers were thus obliged to spend more money on productions so they would be considered French. French producer Jacques Dercourt, for example, shot some episodes of a co-produced program, 'Love at First Sight', in both French and English in order to qualify the production as French. 'We ended up with two negatives,' said Dercourt. 'For a budget per episode of 4 million French francs, we incurred an overcost of 1.1 million French francs per episode, including post-production' (quoted in 'French without Frontiers', *Broadcast*, October 10, 1991). And French producers do not buy the government's argument that the extra 10 percent of programming time now allotted to European works will help boost their co-production.

Broadcasters and producers are now hoping that the French parliament will modify the broadcasting legislation. 'The future of French production is inextricably linked to European production,' said Jacques Dercourt. 'We cannot succeed on our own' (quoted in 'Law of Change', *Moving Pictures International*, October 3, 1991).

PART 2

Trade, Industrial Policy and Technological Change

Case: The US Machine Tool Industry

The US Machine Tool Industry case raises the claim that the Japanese government 'targeted' the industry, and thus has threatened the survival of US producers. The case concludes with a question faced by the American president: What should he do?

Case analysis invariably turns on answers to several questions. Is the charge of targeting valid on the basis of the evidence, or are there other more plausible explanations for the plight of the US industry? What precisely does the term 'targeting' mean? If the Japanese are in fact targeting the machine tool industry, what would their objectives be? In what ways, if any, would they harm American interests? In answering this last question, the reader must decide what is of greatest American national interest: local manufacturing, local research, local ownership and control, or simply access to competitively priced equipment irrespective of where work is performed? Finally, if acceptable answers to all these questions suggest that some valid US is threatened, what policy response from President Reagan is most appropriate?

This case complements several others in this volume. One is the Boeing *vs.* Airbus case where targeting is again claimed but by the Americans against the Europeans and in an industry with very different economic structures. The case complements the Television without Frontiers case because both present situations in which it is difficult to sort out plausible justifications for trade intervention from pure industry protectionist self-interest. And it complements the Ford and local content regulations case where import protection may have some unintended consequences.

117

Cases: Fair trade in commercial aircraft: the case of Boeing *vs* Airbus Industrie; Boeing's case against Airbus; In defence of Airbus Industrie

The three Airbus cases, designed for role-playing, consider the trade dispute brought up by Boeing against the Airbus consortium for unfair State aids. The cases are set at a time when Airbus Industrie, after a slow start with the A-300, is finally getting commercial success with its new A-320. As a result, it is becoming a real threat for Boeing, which then decides to lobby the United States government to initiate a trade dispute at the GATT. Is this a case of unfair subsidies? The reader must sort out complex arguments centring around economies of scale, conflicting views about cost and sales projections, and the opaque legal structure of the Airbus consortium.

As in the machine tool case where Japanese industrial targeting was the focus, the reader must form a judgment about what European governments are trying to achieve with Airbus. Are they trying to make money selling airplanes, or maximizing spillovers from technology development, or simply breaking a US monopoly over a profitable sector? Are the above objectives in conflict with each other? Clinton advisor Laura Tyson recently argued that Airbus is a replicable model of successful industrial policy. Is it? And is it legitimate? Finally, how do results so far measure up to the objectives?

Cases: High definition television in Europe, Philips, Thompson, BSkyB

This four-case set, designed for role playing, centres on Europe's attempt to develop its own system of high-definition television. Technical issues are daunting, and the reader must first struggle with them before attempting to form an opinion on the corporate strategy and industrial-policy issues. What is the nature of the high-definition television market? Does it have special characteristics that make strategic interaction among players particularly important? What are the key players and constituencies? What are their agendas?

While 'High-definition television in Europe' may be viewed as another case of European targeting of a strategic industry, the challenge here is to understand the complex tangle of corporate and government strategies. For Philips and Thomson, the difficulty is to devise a strategy that is viable technically and credible commercially while appealing to other key actors. Critical to success or failure is the ability to build a consensus around a 'European strategy'. Did they succeed? How does their approach compare to that of Japanese manufacturers? The reader must also identify the interests of broadcasters, represented here by BSkyB. Do these interests conflict with those of manufacturers, and why? Do broadcasters have an alternative strategy to offer? Is this strategy appealing to European governments?

Case: Alcatel

The main theme of the case, *Alcatel, France Télécom and the French Government*, is the relationship between the state and the economy. In most modern democratic states, the role of the state in the economy became more and more important after the First, and especially after the Second, World War. Whether as an owner of enterprises (and therefore supplier of goods and services), as a regulator, as a client, or as a redistributor of resources through taxation and government spending, the state became a central actor in economic affairs. However, the degree of state intervention in the economy displayed significant variations, both across countries and across economic sectors. Among the Western industrial democracies France, thanks to a massive extension of the public sector after the Second World War and the launching of numerous initiatives to develop 'national champion' firms in a range of industrial sectors, displayed the highest level of state intervention. Among economic sectors, telecommunications equipment was one of those in which the state's role was most prominent. In all the West European countries, the supply of telecommuniations services was a state monopoly. The PTTs (Postal, Telephone and Telegraph administrations) or other state agencies – abroad as well as on the domestic market – were the equipment manufacturers' sole important clients. There was hardly any other country in the West and, in France, hardly any other sector, in which the conditions were so favourable for the state to influence the behaviour of private enterprise.

The US Machine Tool Industry

H. Landis Gabel and Damien Neven

The Price of National Security

In late April 1986 President Reagan sat in the Oval Office browsing through a file prepared by his Chief of Staff titled, 'US Machine Tool Industry and the National Defense'. Every now and then he looked up at the photo of the F-18 fighter on his desk, and reflected on the importance of this industry not only to national defence, but also to economic growth and productivity.

The file contained newspaper cuttings and a summary of various studies undertaken on the industry. It was to help the President decide upon what action to invoke arising from a petition that had been filed in March 1983 by the National Machine Tool Builders Association (NMTBA – the major trade association of US machine tool manufacturers). The Association had petitioned the US Commerce Secretary, Malcolm Baldridge, to restrict imports of machine tools for the following five years under the National Security Clause, Section 232 of the Trade Expansion Act of 1962 (19 USC Section 1862). The Act allows for protection from imports whenever it is found that 'an article is being imported into the United States in such quantities or under such circumstances as to threaten to impair the national security'. The purpose of the petition was a last ditch attempt by the Association to stop the flood of machine tool imports which had gone from 16.8 percent of consumption in 1977 to 26.4 percent in 1982, and had since risen even further. At the same time, US production of machine tools had fallen from $5.1 billion in 1981 to $3.8 billion in 1982. The quotas proposed by the Association in its petition would limit US machine tool imports to 17.5 percent of the total value of domestic consumption of machine tools.

The main question facing the President were: did the US need a viable machine tool industry in order to maintain national security? If it did, were the proposed quotas the best means by which to halt its decline? The President was sensitive to the ramifications import quotas might have on major trading partners. Rather than

This case was prepared by John F. Thomas, Research Associate, under the supervision of H. Landis Gabel, Associate Professor, and Damien Neven, Assistant Professor at INSEAD. It is intended to be used as a basis for class discussion rather than to illustrate either effective or ineffective handling of an administrative situation.

imposing quotas, could he persuade the major machine tool exporting countries to voluntarily restrict their imports to the US?

Background to Requests for Government Assistance

The first major public exposure to the plight of the domestic machine tool industry came back in 1977. Houdaille Industries, a domestic machine tool builder, through its Los Angeles based Burgmaster division, had filed a lawsuit against a Japanese machine tool builder, Yamazaki Machinery Works Ltd, for alleged violation of a licensing agreement, patent infringement, use of trade secrets, and improper use of its promotional and advertising material, when the latter began exporting its V-15 vertical machining centres to the US. Houdaille had always complained that the 1970 licensing agreement with Yamazaki was the only means by which it could get its machine tools into the Japanese market. They alleged that Yamazaki redesigned Houdaille's machine tools and then exported them to the US market, using Houdaille's trade marks. Houdaille's action had sparked an investigation by the US International Trade Commission into Yamazaki's alleged unfair import competition. The matter was finally settled out of court, as neither attorneys for Houdaille nor the International Trade Commission were permitted visas to enter Japan to obtain further evidence of the alleged practices. The out of court settlement was for less than $1million and ended the 1970 agreement in which Burgmaster licensed its automatic tool changer to Yamazaki.

Then in May 1982, Houdaille filed a petition requesting that President Reagan remove the investment tax credit of 10 percent on machine tools imported to the US from Japan. The President's power in this matter rested with an obscure and never-before-used provision in the Revenue Act of 1971. To invoke the Act, it had to be proved that products had been sold in the US through the efforts of an illegal cartel. Houdaille in its petition had alleged that the Japanese Ministry of International Trade and Industry (MITI) had targeted the machine tool industry as a growth industry and as such the Japanese government had provided the industry with unfair tax breaks, lending concessions, assistance in shaping production strategies, protection from imports while the industry prepared to launch an export drive, and in 1980 had diverted $100 million from bicycle-betting proceeds to subsidise industry R&D – practices Houdaille claimed had helped Japanese exporters of machine tools price 25–30 percent below their US competitors and which constituted a Japanese machine tool cartel. Mr Philip O'Reilly, Houdaille's CEO did not believe that the petition was protectionist or anti-trade, but claimed that it would restore the free trade that he thought the Japanese had tried to take away. In its review of Houdaille's evidence, the US government agreed that the Japanese action did constitute unfair trade practices and deplored their effect on the US machine tool industry. However, the Administration was split over how to deal with the issue – those supporting Houdaille's petition were the US Trade Representative's Office, the National Security Council, Department of Defense, and Malcolm Baldridge, the Secretary of Commerce. Those against the petition included the Treasury, the State Department, and the US Office of Management and Budget.

In April 1983, after much debate in the Administration over the petition in particular and industrial targeting issues in general, and after personal approaches from the Japanese Prime Minister, the President rejected the plea for relief. Soon after, Houdaille approached MITI for help in finding a Japanese partner. MITI bureaucrats tried not to gloat, but Houdaille's request for advice must have been sweet vindication. MITI had been outraged by Houdaille's arguments that the Japanese machine tool industry had been unfairly subsidised and that a MITI-directed cartel had led the Japanese industry's export drive. MITI played the role of intermediary in talks lasting nine months which ended in an agreement between Houdaille and Japan's Okuma Machinery Works Ltd on joint US production. MITI cited the agreement as a case of Japanese cooperation on transfer of technology to the US. However, when the agreement fell apart in early 1985, Houdaille decided to sell all its machine tool operations to a management group, and to concentrate its manufacturing efforts on engineered sealing, industrial pumps, and engineered industrial products.

Meanwhile a decision on the Association's March 1983 petition had languished awaiting a number of independent studies on the plight of the US industry – the National Research Council had commissioned two studies (one of which was under a contract with the US Department of Army), along with reviews by Department of Commerce, National Security Council, US Trade Representative's Office and US International Trade Commission. Now in April 1986, after three years, during which the machine tool industry had invested $800,000 in a lobbying effort led by Nancy Reynolds (a close friend of the President and Mrs Reagan) it was time for the President finally to resolve the matter.

Current State of the Domestic Industry

The executive summary of the 'US Machine Tool Industry and the National Defense' file stressed from the outset the severe state of the industry. Since 1982, 25 percent of the US companies that made machine tools had folded, a result of declining orders, excess capacity, foreign competition and shrinking profits. Many other tool making operations had been consolidated: a third of the industry's jobs had vanished. Against this was the continued relative strength of the Japanese industry which boosted its exports to the US from $683.3 million in 1984 to $854 million in 1985 – an increase of 25 percent.

The US industry was on its knees. Total US industry output in value of shipments had fallen to $2.7 billion in 1985, down from $4.8 billion in 1980. From 1980 to 1985, the US share of the world market had fallen from 20 to 12 percent. Meanwhile, imports' share of the US market had increased from 23 percent in 1980 to 40.9 percent in 1985. For its entire history up until 1978, the industry had a positive balance of trade. By 1985, it produced a negative balance of trade of more than $1.2 billion.

Identification of the Industry

At the outset, the various studies on the industry had recognized that it was undergoing fundamental restructuring. A structurally more complex and techno-logically dynamic industry was replacing a mature, less complex one. Traditionally, the NMTBA had described a machine tool as 'a powered device, not hand-held, which cuts, forms, or shapes metal'. Such machines are highly diverse in nature – ranging from boring, grinding, and threading implements to pressing, bending, and die-casting devices. Essentially every major manufactured product was produced on machine tools or on machines built by machine tools.

Although basic metal-cutting and metal-forming machines are still a critical element in the manufacturing process, the machine tool industry is becoming part of a new, automated manufacturing industry that is producing new types of products, such as computer-driven, integrated production systems, that did not exist 15 years ago. In describing these changes, one of the recent studies[1] had noted that 'advances in microelectronics, robotics, systems engineering, computer science, and substitute materials have altered the character of manufacturing and changed the nature of the machine tool industry, making machine tool construction one of the world's high tech industries'. The study identified new strategic groups which have emerged in the industry. According to the study, the effect of these new groupings was that 'traditional machine tool firms produce in an environment in which their products are more like commodities than products of greater technological sophistication. In this traditional market sector, which is now actually part of a larger machine tool market, this strategic group will have to adjust its capabilities to meet intensified competition on the basis of price, delivery time, and reliability: factors where such US firms have shown comparative weakness in recent years. Because this is one group where Japanese manufacturers have tended to compete heavily, competitive conditions will probably require US firms in this group to become competitive worldwide like the Japanese and to develop economies of scale in production'.

The number of potential US manufacturers thins out quickly once one leaves the lower left corner of the strategic map. Relatively few conventional machine tool companies have the range of necessary skills to compete successfully in the middle group, which currently comprises primarily the large machine tool manufacturers who account for a sizeable portion of US machine tool production capacity. It may well be that this group is, as a practical matter, open only to larger firms that have the resources to offer more comprehensive after-sales service and to gain better access to capital markets.

The rapid industry changes were confirmed by Mr James A. D. Geier, the chairman of Cincinnati Milacron Inc., the nation's largest machine tool manufac-turer: 'Fifty percent of the products we sold last year did not even exist five years ago. We've gone from being an industry with very little change in products to one with a revolutionary change in products. I'm not so sure that all the companies are capable of making the necessary changes.' Geier added: 'The traditional machine tool industry that has been the cornerstone of Milacron is as dead as a doornail.

Milacron's prospects are now pegged to the company's transition from producing the traditional lathes, boring mills and broaching machines to turning out robots, laser equipment, plastic-processing machines and computer-controlled machines that produce aircraft parts.'

These industry changes had attracted large, US-based, multinational firms to the industry such as Westinghouse and Rockwell International (both of whom entered the industry through joint ventures with Japanese machine tool builders). Whilst these companies have not entered the business of manufacturing machine tools themselves, they do supply Flexible manufacturing Systems (FMS) and automated factory customers with machine tools which they purchase from machine tool builders. As the markets for FMS and other factory automation systems develop, these new entrants will be formidable competitors with machine tool builders for the ancillary products needed in factory automation (e.g. computer software), which in many systems will be of greater value than the machine tools themselves. Indeed, some of the new entrants have gained experience in automating their own facilities, and are well placed to compete successfully in the new technology of factory automation. A few of them alone, have greater financial resources than the entire traditional US machine tool industry. They also have had extensive experience in international trade, including international joint ventures. Moreover, by their machine tool purchasing decisions, these companies determine whether a substantial portion of the machine tools consumed in the US are produced locally or overseas. Examples include Westinghouse – Mitsutoki, Rockwell International – Ikegai Iron Works, Bendix – Murata, and the joint venture between General Motors and the Japanese FMS manufacturer, Fanuc (which, according to Merrill Lynch, is one of the most profitable Japanese companies with an operating profit margin in 1985 of about 35 percent).[2] Fanuc also has a joint venture with Siemens, the West German electrical giant, called General Numeric Corp.

These industry changes have also been accompanied by changes in the ownership of machine tool manufacturing capacity within the industry. As one of the studies had noted:[3]

> Sound business decision making today may dictate that a corporation shift its machine tool production to a foreign venture partner, seek foreign machinery to complement its own peripheral devices such as controllers, or relocate its own manufacturing facilities overseas. The danger exists that as business comes closer to realizing true economies of production on a worldwide scale, the US could lose some productive capacity which is valuable to the national security.

Among competitive moves, several US machine tool makers have established operations in Japan, e.g. when Bendix (then a subsidiary of Allied Corp.) acquired Warner & Swasey, one of its first actions was to transfer nearly all of its machine tool production to the Murata joint venture in Japan (Allied Corp. finally sold their ailing Bendix Automation Group to Cross & Trecker in 1984). Richard T. Lindgren, chief executive of Cross & Trecker Corp., believes: 'there probably isn't any way a North American producer is going to be able to compete with the Japanese on the basis of price.'[4] Cross & Trecker's solution was to introduce a machining centre made by a Japanese producer (50 percent owned by Cross & Trecker) but fitted with Cross & Trecker controls. At the same time, European and Japanese toolmakers, in order to consolidate their market position, are building both manufacturing and assembly plants in the US. Since the mid-1970s, at least 15 foreign companies have gone this route. At the same time, foreign companies are buying up US toolmakers. In 1979, Oerlikon-Buhrle Holding, a Swiss producer, bought Motch & Merryweather Machinery Co., a manufacturer and the largest US distributor of machine tools. In 1981 the Japanese firm Makino Milling Machine Ltd bought a 51 percent stake in the US machine tool builder, LeBlond Inc. (now called LeBlond Makino). They, like the general trend in the industry, buy, sell, and share technology with scant regard to national boundaries. They assemble machining centres in the US that have half US and half Japanese parts and labour.

Industry Structure

As part of this changing face of the industry, there is a growing dichotomy between the few large firms and the large number of small firms in the industry. The industry has traditionally consisted of many small businesses (fewer than 20 employees) given that in the past many young and talented entrepreneurs with new ideas could start small machine tool businesses with relatively small amounts of capital in the hope of cashing in on once healthy market opportunities. In 1982, 67 percent of all machine tool businesses fell into this category yet they only employed 7 percent of the industry's workforce. However, for at least the past six years, the 15 largest companies in the industry have produced approximately 75 percent of the industry's output and employ approximately 18 percent of the industry's workforce. This compares to Japan where the industry is dominated by large companies and captive shops (i.e. which produce exclusively for one major customer, e.g. the Japan Machine Tool Builders Association includes the following members: Citizen Watch Co. Ltd, Brother Industries Ltd, Hitachi Seiko Ltd, Komatsu Ltd, Mazda Motor Corp., Mitsubishi Heavy Industries Ltd, NEC Corp., Sanyo Machine Works Ltd). However, experiences in both Japan and Germany suggest that technologically innovative, small firms can compete quite effectively with larger firms. The main problem they face however is access to sufficient levels of R&D funding and credit. These firms therefore are usually dedicated to relatively narrow product lines in which they have been able to build reputations for quality in software, customer support, customer training, and applications engineering.

   As one of the industry studies noted,[5] among the small firms, the industry is still extremely fragmented with minimal concentration having occurred through mergers and acquisitions. The study listed a number of factors which account for this structure, e.g. frequently the financial skills and strategies predominant in an acquiring conglomerate do not substitute for the technical and engineering acumen necessary for successful management of a machine tool company; machine tools are highly specialized items sold to equally specialized markets therefore limiting the advantage of offering a broad line of machine tools, and hence denying merging companies economies of scale in either marketing or manufacture. The study even admitted that often the best produced, specialized high technology machine tools come from small, independent companies.

Main Industry Customers

The main purchasers of machine tools are: US Department of Defense approximately 3.5 to 4 percent of domestic orders in 1978;[6] automotive industry 28 to 30 percent; and the civilian aerospace industry's 10 to 12 percent. An analysis conducted by Data Resources, Inc. for the NMTBA however indicates that defence related purchases account for closer to 20 percent of all machine tool purchases in the US when indirect and induced capital purchases are taken into account.

Industry–Military Relationship

The industry's close association with the military has been both beneficial and at times disastrous to the continued well-being of the industry. During wartimes, the industry benefitted from massive increases in demand, an example being during the Second World War when some 800,000 machine tools were produced. However, at the end of the war, approximately 300,000 US government-acquired machine tools were dumped on the domestic market. This had a severe dampening effect upon the vitality of the industry, and it had not yet recovered when the Korean War once again heightened demand for machine tools. Additionally, these wartime experiences with government management and allocation procedures left a legacy of suspicion among machine tool builders that still persists.

One major benefit to the industry has been the development and diffusion of state of the art technology, carried on outside the industry mostly as a result of Department of Defense initiatives. Perhaps the most important was the technological shift to numeric control (NC), for which the US Air Force funded research and, following the early 1950s, helped to diffuse throughout the industry by means of a 'big buy' strategy, i.e. the placing of orders by the Department of Defense for large numbers of NC machines with a number of major machine tool companies to ensure that the new technology diffused throughout the industry. The Manufacturing Technologies Program of the Department of Defense (ManTech), dating from the early 1950s, played an instrumental role in the development and diffusion of this new technology, and now spends an average of $225 million annually on R&D on manufacturing technology including computer aided design and manufacturing systems, robotics and flexible manufacturing systems. This compares with $15 million spent by the Japanese government in 1982 on research and development on flexible manufacturing technologies.[7]

In addition, under the Defense Industrial Reserve Act (Public Law 93-155), the government is authorized to procure and manage a stockpile of weapons parts and also of manufacturing equipment such as machine tools. The Department of Defense's stockpiled machine tools consist of two categories: the General Reserve, which is centrally managed by the Defense Logistics Agency; and various idle packages for mobilization, which are managed by each of the three services. As of July 1983, the General Reserve had an inventory of 12,286 machine tools, which were valued at $334 million. However, the average age of these tools was 29 years, with less than 2 percent less than 10 years old. Longstanding Department of Defense policy has aimed at replacing 5 percent of this inventory each year, but because of lack of funds, this goal has not been met. As of July 1983, the Idle Packages for Mobilization numbered 13,489 machine tools, with an inventory value of $382 million. They had a similar average age to those in the General Reserve. This total Department of Defense-owned stockpile of 25,775 machine tools is down from an estimated 32,000 tools in 1981 – again due to a lack of funds. One of the industry studies[8] asserted that thus far, the stockpile concept had tended to discourage technological advances while running up substantial carrying costs for the government. They cited an 1982 Army report which asserted that use of the stockpile to provide machine tools for M1/M60 tank production would 'cost a great deal of money [in machine tool rehabilitation] and would not improve manufacturing methods above those used for the last 50 years'.[9]

The role played by defence contractors must also be taken into account in addressing the issue of national security. As one industry study noted:[10]

> It is misleading to assume that machine tool capability relevant to the Department of Defense rests entirely with the conventional machine tool industry. In point of fact, many defense contractors are highly capable of developing their own sophisticated tools. Although individual contractors have often developed sophisticated machines inhouse, it has usually been machine tool companies that have built such machines, transforming prototypes into heavy-duty equipment suitable for high-volume production and making more standard models available for purchase. It is this role of technology transfer among defense contractors that may be the most important contribution of the domestic machine tool industry, and the one that would be most sorely missed if the domestic industry were to deteriorate further. It would be undesirable, too, to pass on this role to foreign suppliers, however competitive they might be.

Cyclical Nature of the Industry

The nature of the products of the industry results in a higher than average cyclicality in demand. The main reason for this cyclicality is what may be called an accelerator effect regarding purchases of major capital equipment. Relatively small changes in the demand for commercial products induce great changes in the demand for capital equipment. For example, a company uses lathes for the manufacture of its products.

Assume that its manufacturing base consists of ten such lathes and that, because of wear, one replacement lathe is purchased each year. If the company's response to a change in demand is to increase output, it may find that a relatively small production increase, say 10 percent, may require the purchase of an additional lathe beyond the yearly replacement unit. Here a modest increase in production can lead to a 100 percent increase in the company's lathe demand. This can, and of course does, work in the opposite direction when the company's demand falls. These fluctuations destabilize the machine tool market when they occur on an economywide scale. Whilst in reality individual companies can adopt strategies of production (overtime and backlogs) that might act to buffer this accelerator effect, its impact can never be fully suppressed.

A major source of cyclicality has traditionally been the very durability of machine tools themselves. As long lived products, replacement orders have not generally been a strong foundation of industry sales. Instead it has been only major business growth or product changes that has spurred large orders of new machine tools. The numerous studies of the industry[11] regard the US industry as poorly suited to the cyclical market. The relatively high skill requirements, long production lead times and high work-in-process inventories that characterize the local industry pose great problems when confronted with oscillations in demand.

US machine tool builders in the past have relied primarily on backlogs to suppress the effects of the cyclicality of demand. This has resulted in major backlogs in the delivery of orders during peak periods. In 1979, orders for the industry reached $5.5 billion with a backlog of more than $2.2 billion or about 16 months at prevailing shipment rates. Severe backlogs during periods of intense demand put great pressure on the industry to satisfy its large domestic customers, particularly US car makers. For these customers, delivery date can be a more important purchasing variable than price. This lack of sufficient domestic capacity at peak times was a major factor in the increased capture by imports of the domestic machine tool market, as well as the loss of US industry sales abroad. A survey of machine tool customers undertaken as part of one of the industry studies,[12] revealed that US machine tool users were able to obtain delivery of Japanese machines within 1 or 2 months during the late 1970s, when some domestic builders were requiring an 18 to 24 month wait. For many of those customers, lead time was the prime factor in the decision to purchase a Japanese machine.

Importance of the Industry for Economic Prosperity

Whilst the industry is not important in terms of output, producing less than 0.6 percent of US Gross National Product in 1985, or numbers of people employed, much of the domestic economy's ability to grow is closely related to the availability of machine tools for the manufacture of new products. This technology is both process and product related. In relation to manufacturing technology, the use of machine tools with computer numeric control has allowed major increases in the automation of assembly line processes. Many major US industries, such as the automobile industry, are closely dependent upon machine tools for the maintenance of their competitiveness in domestic and world markets, e.g. a new swivelling cutter head that sculpts dies from computer aided designs has reduced by two thirds the time it takes General Motors to make dies. Until this innovation came along, diemaking technology hadn't changed much in 50 years. In addition, advances in machine tool technology has facilitated new products in electronics, optics and aerospace (e.g. the increasing use of graphite epoxy, a material lighter than aluminium and stronger than steel, in aircraft, is as a result of the development of graphite tape laying machines that eliminate expensive manual labour and can build wing parts five times faster than workers doing the job by hand).

The NMTBA has always argued that machine tools are crucial elements in heightening national defence and industrial productivity and as a result, if the US machine tool industry is unable to take the lead in the development of the newest innovations, the prospects exist that important advances in manufacturing technology for many industries might be significantly delayed, or escape development at all, in the US relative to overseas competitors. As put by Mr James A. Gray, President of the NMTBA:

> If the Japanese get control of the machines that go into state-of-the-art manufacturing for such things as cars and trucks, then they'll sell us yesterday's technology while keeping today's for themselves. They will be better able to compete in those industries, which won't bode well for American industry.

Additionally the NMTBA claims that a great deal of engineering and manufacturing knowhow would be lost if the domestic industry disappeared. Mr Harley Shaiken, a research fellow at the Massachusetts Institute of Technology, who helped prepare one of the industry studies, claims that:

> The machine tool industry is the core industry in any advanced manufacturing economy. If you have an industry that is as pivotal as machine tools, and if something goes wrong there, if innovation is slower there, that can directly affect all other industries.

Causes of the Demise of the US Machine Tool Industry

There has been much public debate over the plight of the industry during the past three years with both critics and supporters of the industry voicing their opinions.

National Machine Tool Builders' Association's Case

The NMTBA had argued that the cause of the industry's demise had, by and large, been exogenous factors outside the control of the industry, e.g. the cyclicality of domestic demand, a stronger Japanese industry which was due to the differences between US and Japanese government approaches to industrial policy, the Japanese economy being stronger than the US economy, and US government policy which acted as a disincentive to exporting. Insofar as the Japanese government's industrial policy key areas included:

- The close industry–government cooperation in planning industrial development in Japan. MITI, with an annual industrial investment fund of over $2 billion (1980), exerts strong influence over many sectors of the Japanese economy in line with national goals and its own economic forecasts. MITI's influence has been likened to American basketball – the league officials establish regulations about size of team, recruitment and rules of play that result in relatively equally matched teams of great competitive abilities. They do not interfere in internal team activity or tell a coach how to run his team, although they do try to provide information that should enable the coach to improve. Many decisions made by MITI might more properly be viewed as MITI enunciation of a consensus among the most significant actors. But when a new foreign technology is available for purchase, MITI officials try to see that it is bought at the lowest possible price by the Japanese company that can best use it without overwhelming its competitors. MITI will decide 'it's Mitsubishi's turn for this one, the rest of you don't bid against it'.[13] MITI's subsidies are not overt, but everybody knows which firm in the top league of each industry will be in line for the next favours when they request licences, permissions to break particular environmental restrictions, etc. In 1968 the Japanese were signing international conventions about throwing their market open to foreign competition, and not meaning much of what they wrote. When a journalist from *The Economist* asked a MITI planner which industry he would really like to liberalize for foreigners, the journalist was told 'probably wooden clogs'.[14] The machine tool industry was one in which MITI had encouraged heavy investment and which benefited, from among other things, government-encouraged financial support – either in the form of direct low-interest loans, or loans in a rationed capital market in which interest rates were well below market-clearing level – an important, if hard-to-measure, subsidy.

- *Special depreciation allowances:* as the boss of one US automated assembly line says: 'at present this equipment is very expensive, technological progress is rapid, there is danger our competitors will have even better equipment before this is depreciated'.[15] MITI knows this and hence the Japanese government introduced special depreciation allowances to ensure customers could update at the same pace as technological change.

- The less restrictive application of antitrust laws in Japan, with the effect of allowing vertical integration of larger companies, and horizontal coordination among actual and potential competitors for R&D, and product specialization. This encouraged extensive collaboration on joint projects, associations formed between companies to work jointly on government-sponsored projects, promoted research on novel machining systems, or the submission of joint bids on large domestic or overseas commercial orders. In the US, however, the antitrust laws stifled such cooperation. An example of this was when the Justice Department's Antitrust Division filed a suit in 1979 against the proposed merger of two machine tool companies, Cross Co. and Kearney & Trecker Corp., which were not direct competitors in any product line; however, the antitrusters argued that 'potential competition' between them would be eliminated.[16] After the courts finally rejected the charge, the two companies merged.

- MITI has offered strong support to the machine tool industry, particularly in the area of government sponsored R&D. One major cooperative project was the Flexible Manufacturing System Complex (FMC), a seven year undertaking to establish a manufacturing system for the rapid commercial production of machine components in small batches. The project was pursued by three government research institutes and 20 companies with a total budget estimated to be approximately $65 million.

- The Japanese domestic machine tool industry had been protected by import duties on foreign-made machine tools which were not abolished until April 1983, i.e. by which time the Japanese industry had become a major world participant.

In addition the NMTBA argued that specific US government policies had been detrimental to the industry. These included:

- *US trade restrictions:* one factor accounting for the decline in the machine tool balance of trade had been US government initiated trade restrictions on the export of strategic and high-technology items to the Soviet Union and Eastern European nations along with trade embargoes and sanctions following the Soviet's invasion of Afghanistan.

- *US government export policy:* the lead story in *Business Week*, July 21, 1980 sums up the feelings of many on the general state of US export policy: 'The new export policy works like the old – badly'. This article, as do many of the studies on the industry, claims the US Department of Commerce has discouraged and confused the industry because of inconsistency in its export licensing regulations, internal jurisdictional fragmentation, and its inconclusive trade policy interactions with other executive agencies. Some comments made in the *Business Week* article include one by Warren E. Kraemer, McDonnell Douglas Corp.'s corporate vice-president for Europe:

  > Before we can pay an expense of an agent, which may be a taxicab ride, he
  > has to have his expense account validated by an American consular authority.
  > If you are required to spend weeks in clearing approvals for any given
  > situation, as opposed to your competitor's ability to make instant decisions,
  > you obviously suffer.

This administrative nightmare was a result of the Foreign Corrupt Practices Act, a law aimed at curbing bribery by US companies. Adds Kraemer:

> Any person who has any association with us must certify practically every time he answers the phone, that what he is doing is not immoral, illegal, or an attempt to influence or bribe someone with whom he is in contact.

Yet another by Reginald H. Jones, the then chairman of General Electric Co.:

> To provide an American employee in Saudi Arabia with $40,000 worth of salary, GE must pay him roughly $140,000.

And one from Senator William V. Roth Jr. (R-Del) on US foreign policy objectives:

> When we want to give the appearance of doing something, the first thing we always do is cut off trade.

- *Product Liability and Occupational Safety and Health Administration (OSHA) regulations:* as pointed out in one industry study,[17] these regulations, which are not duplicated in other nations, raise the production and overhead costs of US builders relative to international competitors. Whilst OSHA type regulations will most likely eventually be adopted by other nations, hence diminishing the impact on US exports, the threat of product liability legal action remains a burden to the industry. The uncertainty concerning the potential hazards of new technologies and product designs acts to dampen the adoption of innovations within the machine tool industry and among its customers.

- *Investment tax credit policy:* as one study on the industry pointed out, fluctuations in the US government's investment tax credit policy has done much to amplify the cyclical market fluctuations that have plagued the industry. Furthermore, the NMTBA claimed that economic management also had an effect on the state of the domestic industry. This claim was supported by one of the studies[18] which noted:

> The slow growth of the American economy in the 1970s expressed itself in a sluggish demand for machine tools – as for capital goods generally. This weak demand for machine tools has been a significant factor in the slow productivity growth in the machine tool industry itself. Conversely, in Japan, rapid growth in aggregate output has been accompanied by higher rates of investment and more rapid productivity growth in machine tool production. Thus, to some extent, the performance of each country's machine tool sector has been consistent with the differential growth rates of each economy.

Critics of the Industry

The industry certainly had its share of critics. Mr Shaiken of MIT claims:

> Domestic machine tool makers keep saying they're an innocent victim of a Japanese onslaught. But they have much to do with bringing about their own problems.

And Margaret B. W. Graham, a professor of management at Boston University and vice chairman of one of the committees that studied the industry, comments:

> By and large, the companies involved in these protectionist arguments are spending too much of their energy trying to get protection and far too little trying to become competitive.

This criticism has been backed up by numerous examples of major mismanagement on the part of machine tool builders that have failed, and at the same time, examples of machine tool builders who are succeeding in these 'difficult times'. There was the example of the once mighty Mesta Machine Co. whose success and decline, as the *Wall Street Journal* claimed in their January 3, 1984 edition, in many ways symbolized the story of Smokestack America. Started in 1897, Mesta's major output during its heyday of the 1940s and '50s was the machinery that made the US an industrial powerhouse – machines that even today can be found in factories around the world. Recalled Mitchell Bowers, engineering chief of the Alcoa forging press:

> If you had the nerve to ask them to do something, they could find some way to do it.

Mesta was a company where the employment policy was based on human relations and whose workers rejected union representation until 1967. But in the early '60s, the company failed to see the new wave of technology that was upon the steel industry – continuous casting. Mesta lost the engineering edge that had distinguished it from other machinery builders. In the end Mesta was caught selling something that nobody wanted to buy – rolling mills. And along with other US machinery makers, it did not have the expertise to design and sell its own casters. By the end of the '70s, when Mesta could ill afford featherbedding, the company was stuck with union work rules that institutionalized excess employment levels, once used to boost output in times of high demand. A new breed of aloof top management and increasingly distrustful rank and file workers proved disastrous for Mesta in the '70s. This differed greatly from the old employment policy, which was more akin to present day Japanese cooperative labour – management relations, which cover such things as lifelong employment, extensive dissemination of information regarding company problems and performance to workers at the lowest level, and peer group reinforcement of productivity and quality control. After $60 million worth of losses over the preceeding four years, Mesta filed for Chaper 11 in 1983.

Against the example of Mesta, is the story of Ingersoll Milling Machine Co., whose CEO, Edson Ingersoll Gaylord, complains:

> It makes me mad to see that association (NMTBA) as a lobby for government favours. Protection will take the heat off an industry that needs reform.

Ingersoll competes like the fittest, but not on all fronts. Only a small part of the company's production consists of standard machine tools designed for all-purpose industrial use. The company gets most of its revenues (which totalled about $200 million in 1984) from large-scale custom-made machines or machining systems for special applications. Ingersoll's success stems in part from the fact that they stay at the forefront of technology, e.g. since the early 1970s Ingersoll has spent more than $100 million to build and equip new shops and offices in the US and Germany, where the company has three machine tool subsidiaries. Ingersoll, a family-owned company, prides itself on investing in the latest technology – 80 of Ingersolls's 100 metalworking machines are less than five years old, and almost all the rest are less than ten years old. Ingersoll started using computers in design and production well ahead of most machine tool builders, and the company is now thoroughly computerized. Designers draw blueprints on computer screens, programmers write machining instructions to accompany a design, and the company's central computer generates tape containing these instructions, which in turn controls the machinery that shapes the metal. And while his machine-tool-building colleagues huddle in Washington with their petition, Gaylord has met the foreigners head on, beating formidable opponents like Mitsubishi Heavy Industries and Toshiba in competition for big orders from General Motors, General Electric, and Boeing.

Both critics of the industry and in fact some of the studies on the industry have pointed to some major self-induced reasons for the demise of the industry. These included:

- *Export markets:* although each country's machine tool market is highly cyclical, worldwide oscillations are not as severe. The export market therefore represents an important means by which all countries can buffer the cyclical nature of domestic demand, by offsetting sales to a world market in which aggregate demand is relatively stable. It is this potential stabilizing opportunity that is lost to the US industry with the decline in its share of world machine tool exports. US machine tool builders have traditionally not had a strong export orientation as a large domestic market had removed much of the incentive of the industry to look overseas. The inability of the industry to gear up and maintain a workforce and production capacity suited to periods of peak demand, results in backlogs that, as mentioned above, seriously jeopardize world competitiveness. In addition, critics of the industry claim there has been a general failure of the industry to take advantage of existing US government export assistance, e.g. the Export Administration Act of 1979 reduced the application process time for export licences and significantly simplified the paperwork associated with a new 'Qualified General' export licence. A similar indifference greeted the Federal Trade Adjustment Assistance Program, under which Trade Adjustment Assistance centres were established to offer financial and technical aid to small manufacturing firms that had been hurt in competition with foreign imports.

- *Service and maintenance levels:* as part of one of the industry studies,[19] a survey was carried out of machine tool users. Respondents to the survey 'stressed the superior reliability of Japanese machine tools over the

American counterparts, and the meticulous attention to after-sales service'. The study noted that: 'in particular, the Japanese attention to quality is substantially at odds with the pressures on American business to maximize production, sometimes at the expense of quality'. What one Committee member described as a 'get-it-out-the-factory-door, we'll-fix-it-in-the-field' attitude. Product reliability had become one of the major selling points of Japanese machine tool products, according to prime defence contractor respondents to the same survey, who had bought Japanese tools in the late 1970s and early 1980s. It is not only the Japanese who have competed against US producers on the basis of quality. Although West German producers are not at the forefront of technical progress in machining centres, computer numeric controls, industrial robots and flexible manufacturing systems, they produce quality goods which sell well. In fact, the West German industry is the second largest machine tool producing nation after Japan. In 1985 it accounted for 17 percent of world production and 21 percent of world exports of machine tools. For many years it has been the largest machine tool exporting nation. The industry provides a positive balance of payments, exporting $1,970 million worth of production, and importing only $636 million (35 percent of domestic machine tool consumption) in 1985.

- *Capital investment:* US machine tool industry outlays for capital spending have generally lagged behind those of other US industries. This confirms the assertion that local machine tool builders have tended to rely on stretched out order backlog management, rather than increased capacity to accommodation cyclical changes in demand. Faced with shortages of skilled labour, the industry has been pushed in the direction of more automated production technologies but not, claims one of the industry studies,[20] to the degree of some of their overseas competitors. US machine tool builders in general, still have relatively labour intensive operations. This is at a time when US machine tool industry productivity has actually declined and direct wage compensation among US machine tool workers is still the highest among major machine tool producing nations. The industry argues that it has been undercapitalized for the expansion of its production, the modernization of its equipment, and the research and development necessary to remain competitive in both product and process technology due to traditionally low profit margins in the industry and, of course, the cyclical market variations that make the industry in general a relatively high credit risk. These arguments are validated in part by Exhibit 10.1 which shows the volatility in earnings of the industry compared to all US manufacturing industries for the period 1967 to 1985, and also the industry's lower average returns (5.5 percent *vs* 7.3 percent net income before tax to sales, and 8.0 percent *vs* 9.8 percent net income before tax to assets). However, the US machine tool industry's returns compare more than favourably to Japanese machine tool builders who survive on a low

Exhibit 10.1 *Average net income of all manufacturing corporations and machine tool companies surveyed, 1967 to date (US)*

	Net income before taxes			
	As percentage of sales		As percentage of assets	
Year	All manufacturers	Machine tool manufacturers (a)	All manufacturers	Machine tool manufacturers
1967	8.3%	12.1%	10.9%	16.6%
1968	8.8	11.6	11.7	15.1
1969	8.4	8.9	10.7	10.6
1970	6.8	3.8	8.3	4.8
1971	7.0	(2.7)	8.7	(2.7)
1972	7.4	(1.3)	9.5	(1.4)
1973	8.0	4.3	11.0	4.8
1974	7.7	5.6	10.7	7.2
1975	6.7	8.9	8.8	12.7
1976	7.8	9.3	10.6	12.3
1977	7.8	7.6	13.5	12.5
1978	7.8	7.4	10.7	11.5
1979	7.5	12.0	11.1	16.9
1980	6.7	12.9	9.5	19.4
1981	7.4	12.2	10.5	18.0
1982	5.3	5.0	6.7	6.1
1983	6.3	(9.6)	7.9	8.7
1984	7.1	(3.2)	8.9	(3.4)
1985	5.9	(0.6)	7.1	(0.7)

(a) Data based on the machine tool activities of 111 companies and divisions.
Note: Figures in parentheses represent negative figures.
Sources: National Machine Tool Builder's Association. US Department of Commerce, Bureau of Census. 'Quarterly Financial Report on Manufacturing Corporations' (Quarterly).

return on sales, ranging from 1 to 3 percent. In addition, compared with durable goods manufacturers, the industry has done reasonably well. Whilst the industry has traditionally spent only 1.6 percent of sales on R&D (rising to 3.7 percent in 1979), the US electronic component industry spends approximately 5 percent of sales on R&D.

- *Manpower shortages:* the cyclicality of the domestic market, and the inability of the domestic machine tool builders to use the export market to smooth out demand fluctuations, has created serious manpower planning problems. If employment must be cut significantly, some segment of the highly skilled labour force is irretrievably lost; then when orders rise again, there is a serious shortage of skilled workers. This was clearly the case during the surge of activity in the industry in 1980. Declared Mr W. Paul Cooper, president of Acme-Cleveland Corp.:

> The main problem in getting output up rapidly is manpower. Today we have
> the plant and equipment to produce considerably more than we are producing.
> The limiting factor is engineers and skilled workers.

This uncertainty in employment prospects makes recruitment and training
of new workers difficult. The training of a skilled toolmaker may take four
to five years, a period that could easily extend beyond the life of the
demand cycle. Future prospects for skilled machinists appear gloomy given
that in 1983, the estimated average age of machinists in the US was 58. In
addition there is a new requirement for skilled manpower in engineering
and product design as customers increasingly demand total manufacturing
systems. Due to its inability to stabilize employment levels, the industry
has a bad employment record and thus finds it difficult to attract and hold
both skilled labour and management.

● *Production processes:* critics of the US industry point to the different
  production philosophy of the Japanese firms to their US counterparts – a
  commitment to small-lot production, very carefully scheduled, with very
  low work-in-process inventories. US firms, by contrast, have much less
  control over inventories in the production process. This results from
  having little control over critical production timings and schedules (e.g.
  supplier deliveries). These production process deficiencies result in lower
  output at higher cost.

● *Lack of industry cooperation:* it is claimed that many machine tool builders
  are not aware of, and do not exploit fully, their legal possibilities for
  cooperation in pursuit of increased sales abroad (e.g. the Webb-Pomerene
  Act, for instance, specifically permits joint sales abroad). Yet, says George
  P. Sutton of Lawrence Livermore Laboratories, who headed a two year
  study of the machine tool industry:

> Cooperative research could also be beneficial in an industry of small units,
> although this too, runs into antitrust problems. There is a lot of general
> technology they would like to get together on if they were not so worried about
> the Justice Department.

It is claimed by industry studies that machine tool builders of other nations
have used joint export trading companies successfully to boost export
sales, whereas those cooperative ventures undertaken in the US have not
been encouraging. One such effort, described in a study on the industry,[21]
was the formation of the International Technical Assistance Corporation
(ITAC) by 12 members of the National Tooling and Machining
Association, a US trade association that represents primarily tool and die
companies. Quotes the study:

> ITAC was designed to act as an export management company for trade with
> Eastern Bloc and Latin American nations. Set up in 1973 as a public
> corporation with over-the-counter stock, ITAC was from the outset cash-poor

relative to its large start up costs. The consultants it hired to aid in export negotiations either were preoccupied with the needs of much larger clients or did not have sufficient technical and trade representation in the target nations. ITAC was also victimized by what some observers termed questionable legal advice and ceased independent existence in 1975.

- Domestic market acceptance of innovations: machine tool builders have been slow to bring new innovations into the domestic market. For example, despite its widely accepted importance for manufacturing, numerical control has diffused slowly among machine tool customers partly as a result of machine tool builders being slow to introduce this technology into their own production processes. The trade journal, *American Machinist*, concluded in 1977 that: 'NC has so far fallen well short of its potential impact in enhancing the nation's productivity'. The early development of NC machine tools gave the US industry a considerable jump on foreign competitors in international markets, but in recent years this advantage has eroded considerably. As the numerical control case illustrated (i.e. the development of new technology by the US Air Force), many technological innovations in US machine tools come from outside the US industry, diffuse slowly due to industry and user resistance, and are subject to quick capture by competing industries abroad.

Conclusion

As he finished browsing through the 'US Machine Tool Industry and the National Defense' file, the President looked up at the photo of the F-18 fighter. Now he had to decide.

- Was it necessary for national security to have locally based machine tool manufacturers?
- Would these manufacturers, if protected, be able to 'deliver the goods' in time of mobilization?
- Would US economic growth benefit more from ready access to overseas machine tool technology?
- Was the world market for machine tools sufficiently competitive to ensure that US users could be assured of the best machine tools at the lowest price?
- How freely did machine tool and associated technology cross national boundaries?
- What would be the backlash from companies such as Boeing, General Motors, Ford and General Electric, if they no longer had ready access to overseas machine tools?

- Should protection be against locally based, foreign firms?
- Should imports from overseas based, locally owned firms be exempted from any protection?
- What was the most efficient structure for the local industry?
- Would the industry stagnate if protected?

Notes

1. 'The US Machine Tool Industry and the Defense Industrial Base'. Committee on the Machine Tool Industry Manufacturing Studies Board, Commission on Engineering and Technical Systems National Research Council. Published by National Academy Press, Washington DC, 1983.
2. *Financial Times*, Monday, February 3, 1986.
3. See footnote 1.
4. *The Wall Street Journal*, Tuesday, September 4, 1984.
5. 'The Competitive Status of the Us Machine Tool Industry: A Study of the Influences of Technology in Determining International Industrial Competitive Advantage' prepared by the Machine Tool Panel, Committee on Technology and International Economic and Trade Issues, Office of the Foreign Secretary, National Academy of Engineering, and Commission on Engineering and Technical Systems, National Research Council. Published by National Academy Press, Washington DC, 1983.
6. US Department of Commerce.
7. 'What is all this about "Industrial Targeting" in Japan'. By Gary R. Saxonhouse, *The World Economy*, Vol. 6, No. 3, September 1983. Trade Policy Research Centre, London. Mobilization Study, Final Report by General Dynamics, Land Systems Division, June 1982. Vol.1, page 4.
8. See footnote 1.
9. 'M1/M60 Tank Systems Industrialization Preparedness Mobilization Study, Final Report' by General Dynamics, Land Systems Division, June 1982. Vol.1, page 4.
10. 'The US Machine Tool Industry and Defense Readiness: An Agenda for Research'. Report of the Committee on the Machine Tool Industry, Manufacturing Studies Board Assembly of Engineering National Research Council. *National Academy Press*, Washington DC, 1982, *The Economist*, February 23, 1980, page 28.
11. See footnote 4.
12. See footnote 4.
13. *The Economist*, February 23, 1980, pages 27–28.
14. *The Economist*, February 23, 1980, pages 27–29.
15. *The Economist*, February 23, 1980, page 28.
16. 'Getting machine tools humming once more' by Lewis Beman and Steven E. Prokesch, *Business Week*, September 1, 1980.
17. See footnote 4.
18. See footnote 1.
19. See footnote 1.
20. See footnote 4.
21. See footnote 4.

Fair Trade in Commercial Aircraft

Boeing *vs* Airbus

H. Landis Gabel and Damien Neven

Since March 1986, the General Agreement on Tariffs and Trade (GATT) Committee on Trade in Civil Aircraft has been examining an American complaint against Airbus Industrie. The Americans have accused Airbus and the governments behind it – France, West Germany, Britain, and Spain – of contravening two articles of the GATT agreement on trade in civil aircraft. These articles, numbers 4 and 6 (shown in Exhibit 11.1), are intended to ensure that international trade in commercial aircraft is not distorted by political pressures on customers or by uneconomic pricing.

Specifically, Boeing and McDonnell Douglas allege that since Airbus Industrie's inception in 1969, it has received or been promised government loans and assistance worth between $12 and $15 billion – support, they claim, that was not made on commercial terms. Thus, Airbus has been able to price unfairly in competition with them. 'They are pricing 15 percent below the MD-11 for a comparable aircraft,' complained John McDonnell, President of McDonnell Douglas.[1] Examples of instances in which Boeing believes that political influence was improperly used to sell Airbus aircraft are noted in Exhibit 11.2.

The complaint was prompted by the growing success of Airbus' sales which has forced the Americans to take its competitive threat seriously. (Exhibit 11.3 shows shows aircraft deliveries.) This threat was reinforced by Airbus Industrie's announcement at the 1987 Paris Air Show that it would proceed with its A330 and A340 aircraft projects. Airbus' member governments had agreed to provide development loans for these airplanes despite the high probability – in Boeing's opinion – that earlier loans to Airbus would never be repaid.

In March 1987, representatives from the US Department of Commerce and Airbus Industrie's member governments met at GATT's headquarters in Geneva to try to resolve the conflict short of a trade war that would be costly to both sides. In

---

This case was prepared by John F. Thomas, Research Associate, under the supervision of H. Landis Gabel, Associate Professor, and Damien Neven, Assistant Professor at INSEAD. It is intended to be used as a basis for class discussion rather than to illustrate either effective or ineffective handling of an administrative situation.
Copyright © 1987 INSEAD-CEDEP, Fontainebleau, France.

Exhibit 11.1

Article 4, Government-directed procurement, mandatory sub-contracts and inducements

4.1 Purchasers of civil aircraft should be free to select suppliers on the basis of commercial and technical factors.

4.2 Signatories shall not require airlines, aircraft manufacturers, or other entities engaged in the purchase of civil aircraft, nor exert unreasonable pressure on them, to procure civil aircraft from any particular source, which would create discrimination against suppliers from any Signatory.

4.3 Signatories agree that the purchase of products covered by this Agreement should be made only on a competitive price, quality and delivery basis. In conjunction with the approval or awarding of procurement contracts for products covered by this Agreement a Signatory may, however, require that its qualified firms be provided with access to business opportunities on a competitive basis and on terms no less favorable than those available to the qualified firms or other categories.[1]

4.4 Signatories agree to avoid attaching inducements of any kind to the sale or purchase of civil aircraft from any particular source which would create discrimination against suppliers from any Signatory.

Article 6, Government support, export credits and aircraft marketing

6.1 Signatories note that the provisions of the Agreement on Interpretation and Application of Articles VI, XVI and XXIII of the General Agreement on Tariffs and Trade (Agreement on Subsidies and Countervailing Measures) apply to trade in civil aircraft. They affirm that in their participation in, or support of, civil aircraft programmes they shall seek to avoid adverse effects on trade in civil aircraft in the sense of Articles 8.3 and 8.4 of the Agreement on Subsidies and countervailing Measures. They shall also take into account the special factors which apply in the aircraft sector, in particular the widespread governmental support in this area, their international economic interests, and the desire of producers of all Signatories to participate in the expansion of the world civil aircraft market.

6.2 Signatories agree that pricing of civil aircraft should be based on a reasonable expectation of recoupment of all costs, including non-recurring programme costs, identifiable and pro-rated costs of military research and development on aircraft, components, and systems that are subsequently applied to the production of such civil aircraft, average production costs, and financial costs.

---

[1] Use the phrase 'access to business opportunities . . . on terms no less favourable . . .' does not mean that the amount of contracts awarded to the qualified firms of one Signatory entitles the qualified firms of other Signatories to contracts of a similar amount.
Source: General Agreement on Tariffs and Trade Agreement on Trade in Civil Aircraft, Geneva 1985.

Exhibit 11.2   *Quotes – political leverage/linkage*

Korea

'It was Charley (Charley Cho, President of Korean Air) who negotiated with the French for entry into Paris in exchange for the purchase of Airbus aircraft,' says a South Korean banker. (*Business Week*, December 9, 1985)

India

'The list, recently presented to the French Government by US officials, includes: promises of French technical assistance in cleaning up the Ganges River; French support in the World Bank for securing soft loans for India; French support in the United Nations for India's claim of establishing a nuclear-free zone for the Indian Ocean; and acceleration of delivery schedules of French mirages jets to India.' (*International Herald Tribune*, October 31, 1985)

Canada

'What the French were insisting on is that we commit Air Canada (to the purchase of A320s). That's just not a policy that's followed in Canada.' (Quote attributed to an unidentified federal official.) (*Financial Post*, March 10, 1984)

Turkey

'Turkey's purchase of the Airbus will undoubtedly enhance the emergence of new possibilities for traffic and technical development in Turkey.' (EEC Representative for Turkey, J. Morgan.) (*Hurriyet*, February 16, 1984)

'Once it became clear that both Airbus and Boeing were offering almost exactly equivalent financing terms – attention switched to political implications of the deal. The Airbus and proposals of Kraftwerk Union to build Turkey's first nuclear plant figured in talks between Mr Ozal and his West German hosts.' (*Financial Times*, October 24, 1984)

Portugal

'Portuguese Prime Minister Mario Soares told his French counterpart – during a recent visit – that TAP–Air Portugal will not sign a contract for four Airbus A310s unless the nation succeeds in its seven year bid to join the EEC.' (*Flight International*, February 18, 1984)

Source: Boeing Company

Exhibit 11.3 *Commercial jet transport aircraft deliveries*

	'65	'66	'67	'68	'69	'70	'71	'72	'73	'74	'75	'76	'77	'78	'79	'80	'81	'82	'83	'84	'85	'86	Total
US manufacturers																							
707	61	83	118	111	59	19	10	4	11	21	7	9	8	13	6	3	2	8	8	8	3	4	576
727	111	135	155	160	115	54	33	41	92	91	91	61	67	118	136	131	94	26	11	8			1,730
737			4	105	114	37	29	22	23	55	51	41	25	40	77	92	108	95	82	67	115	141	1,323
747					4	92	69	30	30	22	21	27	20	32	67	73	53	25	23	16	24	35	663
757																		2	25	18	36	35	116
767																		20	55	29	25	27	156
DC-8	31	32	41	102	85	33	13	4															341
DC-9/MD-80	5	69	152	203	121	53	45	32	29	48	42	50	22	22	39	23	78	43	51	44	71	85	1,327
DC-10							13	52	57	47	43	19	14	18	36	40	25	11	12	10	11	17	425
L-1011								17	39	41	25	16	11	8	14	24	28	14	6	4	2		249
Subtotal	210	319	470	681	498	288	212	202	281	325	280	223	167	251	375	386	388	244	273	204	287	344	6,906
European manufacturers																							
Comet	1		1																				2
Caravelle	18	18	20	15	11	9	4	5	3														103
Trident	10	11	1	11	9	2	13	11	7	4	6	9	7	4									105
VC-10	12	7	10	9	2	1																	41
BAC-111	34	46	20	26	40	22	12	7	2	4	2	6	6	3	3	3							236
F-28					10	11	10	13	19	9	22	10	13	11	10	13	14	12	17	19	13	13	239
Mercure										6	4	1											11
A300										4	9	13	16	15	24	39	38	46	19	19	16	10	268
A310																			17	29	26	18	90
BAe 146																			10	10	18	23	61
Concorde											1	6	2			5							14
Subtotal	75	82	52	61	72	45	39	36	31	27	44	45	44	33	37	60	52	58	63	77	73	64	1,170

Source: Boeing Company

1986, the EEC imported American civil aircraft valued at just over $3 billion while the EEC's aircraft exports to the US totaled just over $1 billion.

The Characteristics of the Industry

The boundary of the aircraft industry encompasses manufacturers of military and commercial aircraft, their engines, and accessories. The broader aerospace industry includes the aircraft industry and also missiles and space. In the US, the total aerospace industry sales in 1985 were $96.5 billion, of which 55 percent was to the US Department of Defense, 7 percent to NASA, and the remaining 38 percent to commercial customers. In Europe, sales in 1985 totaled $30 billion of which 75 percent was to the military and other government buyers and the remaining 25 percent to commercial clients (see Exhibit 11.4).

The US aircraft industry consists of 15,000 companies which employ more than 1.3 million people. By contrast, the European industry's workforce in 1979 was about 420,000 people. The US industry has run a trade surplus of $10 to $13 billion annually for the first half of this decade (see Exhibit 11.5) and $17 billion in 1987. The industry as a whole is the largest single US exporter, accounting for 9 percent of total US exports in 1985. Of all US manufacturers, Boeing is the largest single exporter.

The aerospace industry market in the free world between 1987 and the end of the century is forecast to be about $1,400 billion. Military procurement should constitute about $800 billion ($500 billion for military aircraft and $300 billion for guided missiles). Of the remaining $600, close to $300 billion is forecast for purchases of approximately 5,400 commercial aircraft of all kinds.

The prevalence of advanced technologies both in design and in manufacture (e.g. electronics, metallurgy, and composite materials), the relationship between civilian and military work, and the value of international trade in aircraft has made the industry immensely important to governments of the developed countries. To quote Jean Pierson, the President and Chief Executive of Airbus Industrie, 'Why is the American government supporting and subsidizing the US aircraft industry through defense contracts? Simply because the future of the US, and of Europe in our case, is not in perfume or popcorn. The future is in electronics, computers, aircraft, missiles, and space.'[2]

Pierson's allusion to US military support for commercial aircraft is both an acknowledgment that all major producers of commercial aircraft do related work for the military and a rebuttal of the American claim that government support for Airbus is unfair. But it is difficult to quantify the advantages that accrue to either US manufacturers or to their European counterparts from military procurement. In 1981, the Aerospace Industries Association of America complained that a decrease in military spending was a problem for the industry. 'The modest defense procurement and R&D increases of the late 1970s have taken their toll as military technology had long been a significant ingredient (now decreasing in importance) in the formula for US superiority in the commercial transport business.'[3]

Other studies of the industry echo the same theme. 'During the postwar period the commercial aircraft industry has benefitted from substantial direct (NASA and its predecessor NACA) and indirect (military research and independent R&D reimbursement allowed as part of the overhead costs of military contracts) federal

Exhibit 11.4 *US aerospace industry sales by product group, calendar years 1971–1985 (millions of dollars)*

Year	Total sales	Aircraft			Missiles	Space	Related products and services
		Total	Civil	Military			
Current Dollars							
1971	22,775	12,213	3,764	8,449	3,678	4,361	2,523
1972	23,610	12,516	4,181	8,335	4,285	4,163	2,646
1973	25,837	14,144	5,742	8,402	4,224	4,126	3,343
1974	27,454	14,867	6,320	8,547	4,108	4,412	4,067
1975	29,686	16,433	6,463	9,970	3,775	4,686	4,792
1976	29,825	16,056	6,007	10,049	3,671	4,787	5,311
1977	32,199	16,988	6,183	10,805	4,106	5,001	6,104
1978	37,702	21,974	8,222	12,852	4,098	5,717	6,813
1979	45,420	26,382	13,227	13,155	4,778	6,545	7,715
1980	54,697	31,646	16,285	15,179	6,469	7,945	8,819
1981	63,974	36,062	16,427	19,635	7,640	9,388	10,884
1982	67,576	35,484	10,982	24,502	10,368	10,514	11,390
1983	79,975	42,431	12,373	30,058	10,269	13,946	13,329
1984	83,486	41,905	10,690	31,215	11,335	16,332	13,914
1985	96,571	50,482	13,730	36,752	11,438	18,556	16,095
Constant Dollars (Aerospace composite price deflator, 1982 = 100)							
1971	59,934	32,139	9,905	22,234	9,679	11,476	6,639
1972	61,484	32,594	10,888	21,706	11,159	10,841	6,891
1973	60,226	32,970	13,385	19,585	9,846	9,618	7,792
1974	58,165	31,498	13,390	18,108	8,703	9,347	8,617
1975	56,011	31,005	12,194	18,811	7,123	8,842	9,041
1976	51,422	27,683	10,357	17,326	6,329	8,253	9,157
1977	51,850	27,356	9,957	17,399	6,612	8,053	9,829
1978	57,648	32,223	12,572	19,651	6,266	8,742	10,417
1979	62,822	36,490	18,295	18,195	6,609	9,052	10,671
1980	68,116	39,183	20,280	18,903	8,056	9,894	10,983
1981	70,768	39,891	18,171	21,720	8,451	10,385	12,040
1982	67,756	35,484	10,982	24,502	10,368	10,514	11,390
1983	76,239	40,449	11,795	28,654	9,789	13,295	12,706
1984	76,733	38,516	9,825	28,691	10,418	15,011	12,788
1985	87,872	45,934	12,493	33,441	10,408	16,885	14,645

Source: Aerospace Industries Association

Exhibit 11.4 *continued*

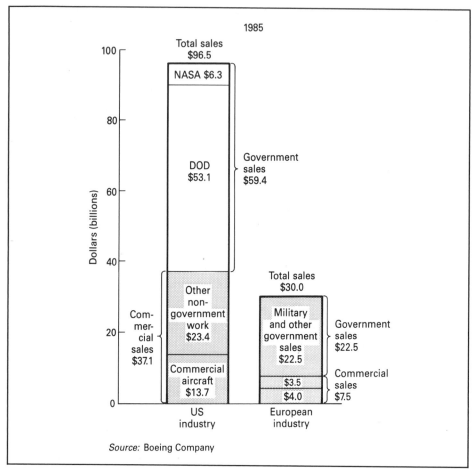

Source: Boeing Company

financial support for research. The size of the federal R&D investment within this
industry, as well as the existence of a dedicated civilian technology development
program, render the aircraft industry unique among US manufacturing industries.
NACA and NASA played an important role as centers for generic research, and
they reduced total industry R&D costs through operation and construction of costly
testing and research installations. Moreover, both the civilian and military research
programs encourage the wide diffusion within the aircraft industry of technological
knowledge, supporting the development of a readily accessible industry knowledge
base.'[4]

But the results of NASA-funded aeronautical research are unclassified and
widely disseminated. NASA holds the patents on discoveries it funded even if the
work was done by a private company. For example, McDonnell Douglas worked

Exhibit 11.5 *US total and aerospace foreign trade[a] calendar years 1981–1985 (millions of dollars)*

Year	Total US merchandise trade			Aerospace		
	Trade balance	Exports	Imports	Trade balance	Exports	Imports
1981	(30,051)	228,961	259,012	13,134	17,634	4,500
1982	(35,182)	207,158	242,340	11,035	15,603	4,568
1983	(60,710)	195,969	256,679	12,619	16,065	3,446
1984	(110,932)	212,057	322,989	10,082[r]	15,008	4,926[r]
1985	(136,627)	206,925	343,552	12,592	18,724	6,132

Source: Bureau of the Census, 'Highlights of US Export and Import Trade', report FT990 (Monthly); 'US Exports, Schedule B, Commodity by Country', Report FT446 (Annually); 'US Imports for Consumption and General Imports, TSUA Commodity and Country of Origin', Report FT246 (Annually).

[a] Total US and aerospace foreign trade are reported as (1) exports of domestic merchandise, including Department of Defense Shipments, f.a.s. (= free alongside ship) basis, not seasonally adjusted, (2) imports for consumption, customs value basis, not seasonally adjusted, and (3) the difference (surplus or deficit) between exports and imports.
[r] Revised.

with NASA on a program to develop 'winglet' attachments to reduce the draft created at aircraft wing tips. For each DC-10 and MD-11 that McDonnell Douglas equips with these winglets, the company pays NASA. Airbus' A300 was the first commercial airplane to make use of NASA research in supercritical airfoils.

The extraordinarily high research and development costs, the economies of scale, scope, and experience, and the level of commercial risk undertaken with each new airplane have led to a progressive reduction in the number of manufacturers. In 1960 there were 17 manufacturers of commercial transport aircraft in the Western world. Today there are only three builders of large airframes – Airbus Industrie, Boeing, and McDonnell Douglas. Few firms can assume the burden of a $3 billion initial cash outflow that a major new aircraft program entails, and consortia are becoming progressively more common in the industry. (The same is true with the engines.)

Despite the trend to fewer and fewer producers, the industry is intensely competitive. The intensity of competition is a consequence of forces that ensure that more than one manufacturer's airplane is launched into each market segment and that the subsequent competition within each segment is fierce.

The cost structure of large civilian aircraft suggests that each market segment (customarily defined by range and capacity) should be occupied by only one aircraft model. Nevertheless, there have usually been multiple models in direct competition. Examples include the DC-8, 707 and Conair 880; and DC-10 and L-1011; the DC-9 and 737; and large numbers of intermediate and stretched models.

Several factors contribute to the surprising frequency of this direct competition.

First, on the introduction of a new technology (e.g. jet engines or wide fuselages), all the major airlines are anxious to launch new models quickly, and their first orders are usually large. Producers, however, have a strong motive to limit their rates of production. This is because if a fixed number of units are to be produced over the lifetime of an aircraft model, it is generally cheaper to spread that production out over time than to build them all in a hurry. Thus, different prospective producers can compete with each other in terms of delivery dates.

Related to this, a producer can 'tailor' its design to the specifications of the airline that agrees to be a launch customer. For example, Boeing's 707 fuselage design was widened at the request of American Airlines which proposed to buy 30 aircraft. This again may provide all that is necessary to entice a number of firms into production, each promised large first orders by specific airlines, and each hopeful of follow-on orders.

In addition to the pull of the airlines, there can be a push from the engine manufacturers. As an illustration, after the Lockheed L-1011 took an early lead in orders over the DC-10, General Electric, the prospective engine maker for the DC-10, offered United Airlines financial aid to purchase DC-10s. United's DC-10 order was sufficient to push McDonnell Douglas into production.

Another factor that contributes to direct model competition is the procurement strategy of the airlines. It is conceivable that all the airlines could make a common decision on a single airplane model for each market niche – thus affording the producers significant cost savings – and then exploit their market power to push purchase prices down. In fact, United Airlines once tried to do just this by forming a buyers' cartel to make a common industry choice between the DC-8 and the 707. But the cartel was sabotaged by Pan Am which placed orders for both models. Presumably, Pan Am reasoned that it would be impossible for the many airlines to retain their bargaining power in follow-up orders.

A final factor is the advantage all producers see in having a basic model in each major market segment from which derivatives can be developed for subsegments or newly identified major segments. Although the basic models are occasionally unique, with little shared design or production, often even they have some commonality. The derivatives invariably share designs, production facilities, and purchased components, which make them relatively inexpensive to develop and manufacture. They can expand a model's market, extend its lifetime, and lead to economies of scale and experience. (See Exhibit 11.6 for an estimate of the economies of experience.) For example, it is estimated that the incremental development cost of stretching an aircraft design rarely exceeds 25 percent of the original development cost.

Boeing has been exceptionally able to exploit these economies. Its 'basic' 707, 727, 737 and 757 models have similar fuselage shapes which has reduced design costs and allowed them all to be built with common production facilities. The 727-100 was stretched to the 727-200. The 737-100 was stretched to the -200 and -300 (and a -400 is planned) as well as shrunk to the -500.

In summary, although there are clear economies to a single airplane model for

Exhibit 11.6 *The learning effect*

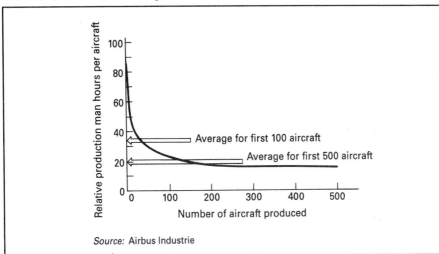

Source: Airbus Industrie

each market niche, these economies have historically proven insufficient to guarantee that result. Quite commonly, two or more models are introduced. And once introduced, models' development costs are sunk and their designs are frozen. The early rush for a place in the order queue is past. In this situation, it has proven impossible for the firms to mitigate price competition.

There are a number of reasons why price competition is intense after the aircraft are on the market. One is that cost is highly dependent on total lifetime sales. This means that there is very strong competition for market share, especially early in an airplane's life. This competition is exacerbated by the large and infrequent orders that characterize the industry and by the secrecy surrounding sales negotiations. Furthermore, aircraft cost characteristics imply that it is virtually impossible to define in any meaningful way the 'cost' of a specific airplane. Thus, there is no reliable benchmark on which to base industry pricing. Finally, even if there were, the fact that most purchase contracts also include financing and after-sales support means that it is difficult to compare prices even after the fact.

Another reason for intense price competition is that there is little product differentiation that might otherwise divert competition from pricing. Two different manufacturers' aircraft, if of the same technological vintage and in the same market segment, are very nearly homogenous. This is because many of the critical systems are made by outside contractors and thus are available to both manufacturers. The cost of developing these systems and the safety and financial risks inherent in radical technological change ensure that the systems are all reasonably conservative and standardized. Aircraft engines are the most obvious example, but communication and navagation electronics, air conditioning, de-icing systems, etc., are others.

Finally, although an airline – especially a small one – may experience some efficiency in flying a single manufacturer's family of aircraft, this efficiency is rarely sufficient to ensure customer loyalty.

Originally, this efficiency derived indirectly via engine standardization. For example, Boeing aircraft traditionally used similar versions of Pratt and Whitney engines. This afforded the airlines substantial economies in spare parts inventory since engine parts constitute the most costly inventory component. Maintenance was also much more efficient when all the engines were of similar design. But this source of benefit has disappeared now that virtually all airplanes are offered with a choice of engines. (For example, a 747 can be purchased with Pratt and Whitney, General Electric, or Rolls Royce engines.) That is, it is possible now for an airline to mix manufacturers' airframes yet retain engine standardization. This has reduced the airlines' cost of switching suppliers and has increased their ability to pit one aircraft maker against another.

There can still be some efficiencies in crew training and aircraft service, however, when operating only one maker's aircraft. For example, the A300 and A310 have crew cross-qualification. And it is less expensive for an airline to upgrade with a stretched version of its existing fleet than to choose another manufacturer's airplane. Many spare parts are interchangeable between derivatives, and the same ground equipment can be used. Economies of this sort, although not as significant as the economies of engine standardization, can save airlines money. Boeing estimates that if an airline buys an airplane of a new type, the retraining and new equipment needed will make it 10–20 percent more expensive than a similar airplane of a familiar type. This saving may, however, come at the expense of the improved technology that a wholly new model might incorporate.

The result of the frequent and intense competition between different producers' models in a single market segment is sometimes a clear winner and a clear loser (as in the case of the 707 and the DC-8) and sometimes only losers (as in the case of the DC-10 and L-1011). And ever since the beginning of the jet age, only a couple of Boeing models have ever made a profit.

The Post-war Background of the US Aircraft Industry

From the end of the war to the mid 1970s, three US firms – Douglas (which became McDonnell Douglas), Lockheed, and Boeing – virtually controlled the free world's commercial aircraft market. The origin of this dominance was an agreement within the Western Alliance during the war whereby European aviation production capacity was to be concentrated on fighter aircraft while all transport aircraft were to be produced by US manufacturers. Furthermore the biggest bomber contracts, which required the construction of facilities for and afforded experience in building very large aircraft, were American.

Immediately after the war, the majority of commercial aircraft were derivatives of the US military aircraft. In Boeing's case, the B-29 bomber and the C-27 military transport became the Boeing 377 'Stratocruiser', Boeing's entry into post-war air transport competition. (Ironically, although the 377 was a commercial failure, it was later adapted for use by Airbus to carry large airplane sections to Toulouse for assembly.) For Douglas, an Air Force contract in the 1930s to develop a super bomber, the XB-15, resulted in the C-54 military transport which developed into the DC-4.

McDonnell Douglas and Lockheed

Douglas was the leading commercial aircraft producer from the time of its DC-3 before the war to the DC-7 in the 1950s. All of its models but the DC-7 made money. But Douglas miscalculated on the prospects for jet aircraft and lost its leadership of the industry forever. The company was persuaded by its two best customers – American and United – that the market was not yet ready for jet airplanes and that Douglas should not worry about Boeing's competition since no one would ever buy commercial aircraft from Boeing.

Although Douglas was still able to produce a successful jet aircraft (the DC-9), by January 1967 the company was on the verge of bankruptcy and had to merge with the McDonnell Corporation – a military aircraft manufacturer without commercial airplane experience.

Shortly after the merger, the newly formed McDonnell Douglas found itself living a nightmare. Both it and Lockheed were competing in a market niche that was too small to support them both. Their airplanes, the DC-10 and the L-1011, were virtually identical in length, width, wing span, capacity, range, speed, eingine thrust, and seat-mile costs. As late as 1968, after three US airlines' orders launched the L-1011, McDonnell Douglas seriously considered cancelling the DC-10 launch. 'There was no chance both aircraft could succeed, because their prices were going to be ratcheted down by the airlines. Remember, these were $2 billion programs,' said Jackson McGowan, then head of McDonnell Douglas' commercial aircraft division.[5] But McGowan's forecast was ignored.

The competition between the DC-10 and the L-1011 drove Lockheed from the commercial aircraft business and nearly into bankruptcy. McDonnell Douglas survived. It eventually sold 381 DC-10s and 60 of its military version, but analysts believe that it lost a substantial amount of money on the program. Between 1980 and 1983, it lost $315 million in the commercial aircraft business. But like Lockheed, McDonnell Douglas is primarily a defense contractor.

The bitterness of the international trade dispute between the Americans and the Europeans now is in good part due to the memory of the DC-10 and L-1011 disaster. McDonnell Douglas is poised to repeat its earlier nightmare. Its proposed MD-11 (a derivative of the DC-10) is targeted at the same market niche as is the proposed Airbus A340. The niche has been estimated to be worth only about 1,200 units which is not big enough to support both contenders profitably. The MD-11 program was started in 1986, and just one year later the Europeans announced their A330/A340 program.

McDonnell Douglas and the other American critics of Airbus reason that Airbus's folly will have a clearly predictable result. Airbus, with its government-guaranteed loans, will 'dump' aircraft on the market at a loss, it will fail to pay its loans, the European tax payer will absorb the financial loss, and McDonnell Douglas will be driven from the market like Lockheed before it. Airbus's strategy, according to an insider, is 'to go for the kill . . . The A340 won't be a commercially successful aircraft, but it can really hurt McDonnell.'[6] Early indications based on estimates of purchase contracts bear out the fear. The MD-11 has a price of about $100 million while the A340, a more costly airplane to produce since it is entirely new, is being priced at about $80 million.

Boeing

In the fall of 1950, William Allen, President of Boeing, took his first flight in a jet – one of Boeing's B-47s. The experience convinced him that the commercial airlines could be made customers for a passenger jet. A week later when he was in England for the Farnborough Air Show, he saw another reason why Boeing should develop a commercial jet airplane – the new DeHavilland Comet jetliner.

Because of pressure to complete the B-52 project, it was not until 1952 that Boeing started work on a dual purpose jet tanker and transport prototype. There was no Air Force contract for the tanker – the $15 million prototype was financed entirely by Boeing. The plane was given a dual designation to match its dual role – the 367-80 ('Dash Eighty') and the 707. In May 1954 the Dash Eighty made its debut, and in September of that same year the Air Force placed an initial order for 29.

Those 29 were so successful with the Air Force that it followed up with orders for a total of 732 more with delivery taken between 1956 and 1965. With cash flow ensured by the military contracts, Boeing modified its early 707 design to improve its passenger comfort and its economics. Initial orders for the 707 were booked in 1955, and with that successful airplane, Boeing took the lead in the industry that it has yet to relinquish.

The next major Boeing model was the 727. With it, Boeing demonstrated the strategy of developing a family of aircraft that would sustain its leadership.

In 1964, the Pentagon approached Boeing, Douglas, and Lockheed with the idea of an aircraft more than twice the size of any other – a true 'jumbo jet'. Boeing and Lockheed were each awarded a $6 million Air Force contract for design studies for the airplane which was designated the C-5A. Although Boeing assigned 500 engineers to the job and was judged to have the better design, its bid was too high, and the contract for the airplane went to Lockheed.

Boeing, aware early in the competition that its bid would probably be too high, began to look for some application of the technology it just developed. It approached Pan Am which agreed in 1966 to be the launch customer for a new and extraordinarily large commercial aircraft – the 747. TWA, which had tried unsuccessfully to persuade Boeing to build a smaller aircraft, was another launch customer, albeit a relatively reluctant one. Other US airlines found themselves in the same position – not enthusiastic about the 747's huge size but afraid of losing a competitive position to rival carriers.

It was clear from the start that if the 747 program were unsuccessful, it would bankrupt both Boeing and Pan Am. Boeing committed $750 million – virtually its entire net worth – to the project. It originally offered General Electric the engines, but GE did not want to develop a commercial version of its contract-winning C-5A engine design until the military had largely absorbed the cost of the prototypes. Boeing then offered the contract to Pratt and Whitney which, like Boeing, was looking for a use for its losing C-5A design.

The 747 program was troubled from the beginning by the aircraft's excessive weight (allegedly the result of rushing the design). If the engine were not altered, the 747's range, altitude, climb rate, and runway length requirement would all suffer. By the summer of 1967, the 747 program's troubles had become serious. Pratt and Whitney and Pan Am wanted to delay the program for six to nine months while the engine was modified to create greater power. Boeing, which eventually prevailed, wanted to hold to schedule and squeeze more thrust from the existing engines. Boeing destroyed 60 of its 87 engines in tests of the 747, and it nearly destroyed itself as well. At one time it had four airplanes to test and only enough working engines to get one off the ground at a time. Each new test required transferring the engines between airframes. Despite its decision to try to keep to its production plan, Boeing inevitably found that engine problems caused deliveries to fall behind schedule. This meant that Boeing was slow to receive the large final purchase installments – money needed to finance the rising inventory of partly built aircraft.

With the recession of 1969 came cancellation of orders and options, and over the next three years Boeing did not receive a single order for a 747 from a domestic US airline. The company began to sink beneath the burden of too many people, too many unfinished 747s, and too much inventory. Boeing was kept alive by the immensely popular 727, the Minuteman missile program, and its own draconian cost reductions. The company cut employment at all levels of the company from 101,000 in 1968 to 37,000 three years later. A sign on a major highway from Seattle, Boeing's home town, read, 'Will the last person leaving Seattle please turn out the lights.'

The story of its years of crisis and survival has become a Boeing legend, and the episode did indeed profoundly affect the company. Boeing emerged a much more efficient aircraft producer. The changes in production methods necessitated by fewer people increased the actual time that an employee spent working productively by 170 percent. That improvement and the workforce reduction resulted in Boeing being able to produce a 747 in 1978 with only a quarter of the man-hours that were required five years earlier.

The 747 trauma led to an important change in aviation industry practice as well. Previously, airplanes had been designed for a single engine type. Because of the disputes between Boeing and Pratt and Whitney, Boeing decided that it wanted an alternative engine for the 747. Boeing was able to persuade the formerly reluctant GE to modify its C-5A engine for use with the 747. Today, all major manufacturers offer a choice of two or even three different engines. As was explained above, the result was to lessen substantially the loyalty of an airline to any single airplane producer.

The Post-war Background of the European Aircraft Industry

Great Britain, a world leader in the aircraft industry before the war, was unable to re-establish its position subsequently. Economies of scale in production were increasing, yet Britain's naturally small domestic market was divided among several companies. Neither corporate nor government policy in the aviation industry dealt effectively with the problem. According to a private research report on the industry in 1965, 'Many of Britain's aircraft fiascos could be blamed on the indecisions and confusions of governments, and the disorganization of an industry with too many companies. . . . The sheer wastefulness of the British resources was extravagant.'[7]

It is significant that the report did not mention poor technology. In fact, Britain commercialized the world's first passenger jet, the Comet 1, and had a chance to capture a major share of the world market from Douglas or Boeing. But the airplane suffered from metal fatigue which caused two crashes, and the entire program was grounded from 1954 to 1957. In 1957, when the Comet IV was launched, the Americans had leap-frogged the Comet's technology.

The British were also the first to offer a medium range commercial jet, the Hawker Siddeley Trident. Although a potential competitor of the later Boeing 727, the Trident was designed specifically for the British market and did not suit US airlines. Britain's sole commercial success, which came in the decade of the 1950s, was the Vickers Viscount. It was the only British aircraft able to repay its government development loans.

In the years just after the Second World War, the French government pursued a consistent policy of protecting and rebuilding its aircraft industry. But the French, like the British, faced the disadvantage of a small home market. Also like the British, French technological successes like the Caravelle, the first short-range commercial jet aircraft, were unsuited to the US market. (It accommodated too few passengers.)

In 1970, sales by the European firms were only $3.8 billion. Sales by the three US commercial aircraft makers exceeded $25 billion. That year, 90 percent of the free world's commercial aircraft were of American manufacture.

The Emergence of Airbus Industrie

The year that Boeing and Pan Am agreed to the 747 launch, 1966, was also the year that Frank Kolk, the CEO of American Airlines, presented plans to the industry for a very different airplane. Specifically, he wanted a much smaller and more efficient aircraft designed to suit the Civil Aeronautics Board (CAB) regulation of the US airline industry. The CAB's rules prohibited price competition among existing carriers, they prohibited the entry of new carriers, but they did not constrain the number of flights the existing carriers could schedule. The result was rapid growth in the number of flights between popular city pairs. To fly these efficiently would require, in Kolk's view, a wide-body, twin-aisle, twin-engine aircraft that could carry 250 passengers 2,100 miles. If its design were executed properly, the airplane should be able to offer seat-mile costs as much as 30 percent lower than Boeing's 727-200. Kolk called his concept the 'Jumbo Twin' and sent its specifications to Boeing, Douglas, and Lockheed.

Although Boeing was uninterested, both Lockheed and Douglas developed wide-body planes – the L-1011 and the DC-10 respectively. But both turned out to be larger than Kolk wanted. They had three engines instead of two, and although their capacity was 250 persons, they each had a range of 3,500 miles. So the US manufacturers left an important market niche unfilled (see Exhibit 11.7).

Kolk's plans were also of interest to a group of European companies that were beginning talks about forming a consortium to produce large commercial aircraft. The consortium, born at a meeting of government and industry officials in London in 1966, was to consist of three companies – one from Britain, one from France, and one from West Germany. France would have the lead role in work on the airframe (through Sud Aviation) with Britain (through Rolls-Royce) taking the lead role with the engine. By April 1967, the companies had received government funds and were starting to cooperate seriously. On July 20, Roger Beteille, formerly Chief Engineer at Sud Aviation, was appointed Director of Europe's new Airbus Industrie.

Two critical issues had to be faced in 1968. One was the size of the first Airbus and the other was the choice of an engine. At one point, each of the European airlines wanted an airplane of a different size. France and Britain were at the two extremes. Compromise was reached on a 250 seat, wide-body airplane. Ironically, although the compromise was on the size that Frank Kolk had specified, it did not represent convergence of opinion on the ideal airplane. Rather, it was due to problems with Rolls-Royce.

Rolls-Royce had found itself forced to choose between developing the Airbus engine or starting a new engine for the Lockheed L-1011. The company did not have the ability to execute both programs simultaneously. It chose to drop Airbus and to joint the Lockheed program.

Rolls-Royce then tried to interest the Europeans in a more powerful version of the L-1011 engine, designated the RB211. But once out of the Airbus consortium, Rolls-Royce found political obstacles to its readmission. It had a reputation as being less 'European' than other British aerospace firms and had poor relations with France's engine supplier, the government-owned SNECMA. In addition, the UK partner in the Concorde program, British Aircraft Corporation, angered the French by advocating a strictly British Airbus. Finally, the French preferred an American engine because they felt that it would improve Airbus' sales to US airlines.

The clear French preference for an American engine was not shared by the Germans, however. Although they acknowledged the importance of penetrating the US market, the Germans were worred that the choice of a US engine would force

Exhibit 11.7   *The A300 opportunity – size/range*

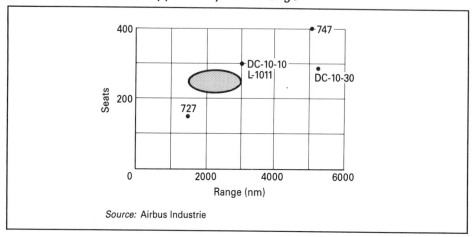

Source: Airbus Industrie

Britain to withdraw from the Airbus program entirely. Britain's exit from the Airbus program could have two very unattractive consequences. First, Germany, with a small aerospace industry and only a 20 percent share of the program, would risk being overwhelmed by the French unless it increased that share – a prospect it did not like. Second, there could be a serious problem with Airbus's wing. The wing was to be built by the British firm, Hawker Siddeley. But without government funds, Hawker Siddeley might be unable to develop the wing, and neither the French nor the Germans had an equivalent level of expertise.

Nonetheless, the Germans finally voted with the French in favor of a US engine. And it was this choice of an American engine that decided the size of the first Airbus. The three American engine programs that were then underway (for the 747, DC-10, and L-1011), if mated to a twin-engine airframe, set the capacity at 250.

The American winner of the engine competition was General Electric, largely because of its willingness to give SNECMA a sizeable share of the work. (Approximately 25 percent of all work on GE's big engines is now done by SNECMA.)

The postscript to the engine story was that Britain withdrew from the Airbus program which was restarted in May 1969 with France and Germany as equal partners. The Germans agreed to finance Hawker Siddeley's continuing participation in the wing production at a cost of $70 million. As was recounted above, the Lockheed program proved a disaster and contributed to Rolls-Royce's bankruptcy in 1971. It was then nationalized by the British government.

The Airbus made its first test flight in October 1972 and its commercial debut with Air France on May 24, 1974. Because the total development costs of the A300 had exceeded the initial target by less than 5 percent, the program was expected to turn profitable after the sale of 360 units.

The launch order for the A300 came from Air France. (As one Air France official put it, 'It would have to fly backwards for us not to buy it.'[8]) This was followed by orders from Lufthansa and a few non-European carriers. But sales in the first few years were alarmingly low. During an 18-month period from early 1976 to late 1977, not a single order was received. The sales problem was exacerbated by a cost problem. European employment policy made the partners unwilling (or unable) to stop production and lay off workers. They continued to build aircraft which were parked on the tarmac at Toulouse. At one point, there were 16 unsold A300s waiting for buyers. Despite a recovery later, sales of the A300 have not fulfilled expectations and from 1974 through 1986 totaled only 268 airplanes.

In May 1978, Airbus launched a $1 billion development program for a derivative of the A300 – the A310. The aircraft would be smaller (218 passengers *vs* 250 for the A300), but it would have 50 percent commonality with the A300, including a common final assembly line. The goal was to introduce the A310 at a price 15 percent below that of the A300. (Airbus's accounting methods allocated to the A310 only the development costs specific to it. All the development costs of the parent A300 were still borne by that model.)

The A310 was the first of the necessary extensions to Airbus's product line, extensions that would reduce average production costs and expand market share. But whereas the A300 had a market niche to itself (the wide-body, short-to-medium haul market that Kolk had defined), the A310 would enter service in direct competition with Boeing's proposed 216 seat 767.

The latest addition to the Airbus family, the 150-passenger A320, will first be delivered in 1988. Airbus says its break-even point is 600 aircraft. It may achieve that goal even before the airplane's first commercial flight. It has more than 440 orders and options in hand, and the A320 is the fastest selling airplane in aviation history.

In 1987 Airbus was selling three models – the A300, A310, and A320. It had delivered more than 375 airplanes to 61 airlines around the world for an estimated $40 billion. Its backlog consisted of more than 730 firm orders. But despite these seemingly impressive figures, Airbus was still experiencing a large negative cash flow.

Airbus has now started work on the A330 and A340. The sponsoring governments have promised $3.5 billion of the $4 billion that the projects will need. (This sum is included in the estimated $12 to $15 billion worth of government support mentioned above.) The money from the governments will be in the form of development loans. The one-half billion dollars not covered by the government sponsors is privately funded.

Airbus Industrie's A330 and A340 models will fill Airbus's product line at the larger and longer range end of the market, and they will complete airbus's family of aircraft. The A330 is a 310-seat medium to long range aircraft while the A340 is a 260-seat very long range aircraft. Each employs the existing A300/A310 fuselage cross section and tail fin as well as an advanced version of the A320 cockpit and control systems. The development of the A330 and A340 models is actually one program since 85 percent of the two airframes is common. The principal difference is that the A330 has two engines while the A340 has four.

The Present Structure of Airbus Industrie

Airbus Industrie is a partnership comprising four European aerospace manufacturers – Aerospatiale, Deutsche Airbus, British Aerospace (BAe), and Constructions Aeronauticas SA (CASA).

Aerospatiale

Aerospatiale was founded in 1970 through the rationalization of state-owned Nord Aviation and Sud Aviation. Aerospatiale is 97 percent owned by the French government and is the largest aerospace company in France. Its sales in 1986 exceed $4.4 billion,[9] and its employment exceeded 38,000. Commercial and military aircraft constitute 34.4 percent of sales, helicopters 24.2 percent (of which 59 percent is military and 41 percent is commercial), missiles 21.6 percent, and strategic systems and satellites (e.g. the Ariane program) 19.8 percent. Currently, the company's commercial aircraft activities include Aerospatiale's involvement in Airbus and a joint venture with Aeritalia to produce the ATR 42/72 commuter aircraft. Aerospatiale has a 37.9 percent equity share of the Airbus program and is responsible for the development and production of nose sections, wing roots, and engine pylons, and for final assembly of the aircraft. By 1983, the French government had advanced Aerospatiale $786 million for the development of components for Airbus aircraft. The French government also provided general capital and credit guarantees to Aerospatiale to help defray production costs. The French government covered all of Aerospatiale's commitment to the A300, but this dropped to 75 percent for the A310. For the A320, the French government provided 85 percent of Aerospatiale's requirement of $928 million, and for the A330/A340 program the French government has pledged $855 million in loans to assist Aerospatiale's development costs. (This was only 60 percent of the amount Aerospatiale requested.)

The French 'Sixth Plan' of 1970 changed the means by which government support was provided to the industry. Direct contracting was replaced by 'reimbursable advances', a method of repayable aid to cover non-recurring costs similar to the British system of launch aid.

Deutsche Airbus

Deutsche Airbus is a wholly-owned subsidiary of Messerschmitt-Boelkow-Blohm (MBB), West Germany's largest aerospace group. MBB's equity is widely held by private interests, although the company is heavily dependent on Federal and Länder governments for risk capital and for financial guarantees.

Extensive domestic rationalization has resulted in the West German airframe industry being centered around MBB. MBB is involved in a wide range of aerospace programs including military fighter aircraft (e.g. the Tornado, built in partnership with BAe and Aeritalia); trainers and transports; missiles; commercial and military helicopters; and space equipment (e.g. the Ariane program). In 1985, MBB earned a profit of $65 million on sales of $3.6 billion. In 1986, MBB suffered a loss of $62 million on reduced sales of $3.3 billion.

MBB's major commercial aircraft activity is its 37.9 percent equity involvement in the Airbus program (via Deutsche Airbus) in which it is responsible for the development and production of most of the fuselage sections, the fin sections, and the flaps. The German government has provided Deutsche Airbus with $1.4 billion in long term government loans (with interest payments deferred until 1994) and has guaranteed an equivalent amount of commercial bank loans to help cover production costs. In the early 1980s, the government allowed Deutsche Airbus to suspend the loan repayments which were based on a share of the proceeds of Airbus aircraft sales. (A combined total of $3 million for each A300 and A310 is earmarked by Deutsche Airbus and Aerospatiale as repayment of initial loans to their respective governments.)

Deutsche Airbus has only provided about 15 percent of its share of Airbus development costs. The balance has come from the West German government. For the A320, the West German government advanced Deutsche Airbus $740 million in aid and credits. For the A330/A340 program, the West German government is providing $1.8 billion – 90 percent of Deutsche Airbus's development costs – in the form of repayable grants. It also agreed to provide a further $1.1 billion in repayable funding to offset accumulated loans and guarantees previously granted to Deutsche Airbus for the A300 and A310. As part of the agreement, however, MBB itself is committed to invest $179 million in Deutsche Airbus.

British Aerospace

British Aerospace is the largest aerospace company in the UK. It was formed in 1977 by the amalgamation and then nationalization of Hawker Siddeley Aviation, British Aircraft Corporation, and Scottish Aviation. The company was then privatized between 1980 and 1985. In 1986, its sales were $5.9 billion (of which exports accounted for more than 66 percent) and pre-tax profits were $341 million.

BAe produces a wide range of aerospace products including military fighter aircraft, refueling aircraft, airborne early warning systems, missiles, commercial aircraft (e.g. a range of feederliner and commuter aircraft consisting of the four-engined BAe-146, twin-turboprop Jetstream 31, ATP, and the BAe-748), business jets, and space equipment (e.g. Ariane).

BAe's commercial aircraft business also includes a 20 percent equity share of the Airbus program in which it is responsible for the development and production of the wings. The British government claims that it has not directly financed either the A300 or the A310. However, when a nationalized company, BAe received money voted under various Acts of Parliament to fund its share of the A310, as well as a non-recurring payment of $47 million towards its Airbus-related work in progress. When privatized, these assets and financial obligations were absorbed into BAe's accounts. In 1983, BAe wrote off $188 million from its commercial research and development account, much of which was attributable to its work on the Airbus program. BAe received $469 million in launch aid towards its estimated requirement of $820 million for development work on the A320. The terms of the A320 launch aid made it clear that BAe will have to meet stringent repayment schedules. In particular, 50 percent of the launch aid takes the form of a fixed obligation and will have to be repaid by BAe over three years starting in 1990 with the balance repayable from the sales of individual aircraft, irrespective of how many are sold. For the A330/A340 program, the British government pledged $844 million in loans to BAe – far short of the $1.4 billion originally requested.

Construction Aeronauticas SA (CASA)

CASA is Spain's only aircraft manufacturer. It is 72 percent state-owned via the public-sector holding company, INI, and minority shares are held by Northrop Corporation of the US and MBB of West Germany. In 1986, its sales were $418 million with losses of $77 million. In 1985, it had made a profit of $14 million. Of all Airbus partners, CASA relies the least on home-govenment purchases which account for only 20 percent of its sales. The company has designed and produced three aircraft – a high-wing 25-passenger turboprop, an updated, bigger and longer range version of that plane (which is produced in a joint venture with Nurtanio of Indonesia), and a basic military jet trainer. Together, they make up less than 50 percent of its total sales.

CASA's commercial activities also include a 4.2 percent equity share of the Airbus program in which it is responsible for developing and producing the carbon fiber stabilizers (horizontal tailplanes). This business accounts for about 25 percent of CASA's total sales. The carbon fiber technology has become a company speciality, and it is a subcontractor for similar parts to McDonnell Douglas. Other sub-contracting work comes from Boeing, Dassault, Canadair, and from the Ariane program.

The Spanish government provided all the funds required by CASA for its A320 development activities (CASA was not part of the A300) and has pledged $160 million for CASA's involvement in the A330/A340 program. In addition there are two associate members of Airbus Industrie:

● Fokker, a private Dutch company.
● Belairbus, a group of Belgian aviation and industrial interests formed in 1979 to coordinate that country's participation in the Airbus program.

Bringing the Partners Together

The objective of Airbus Industrie's organizational structure was to strike a balance between the benefits of collaboration and the independent interests of the four partners. The solution was an organization unique to French law – a 'Groupement d'Interet Economique' (GIE) which translates as a 'Grouping of Mutual Economic Interest'. This structure for Airbus Industrie allows the four partner companies to develop and manufacture aircraft sub-assemblies which are then assembled by one of the partners (Aerospatiale). The four partners act as subcontractors to Airbus Industrie. Airbus Industrie, in turn, is responsible for coordinating the design, development, financing, and production activities of the partners, for contracting with some outside suppliers (e.g. the engine manufacturers), and for sales and product support of the aircraft. It has a workforce of about 1,100. Airbus Industrie does not maintain any autonomous design or production facilities – these functions remain in the hands of the partners.

Decision-making Process

The ultimate decision-making body for Airbus Industrie is its General Assembly of Members which ratifies major decisions such as whether to start a new program. In practice, however, the functions of the General Assembly are assumed by the Supervisory Board. This Board is composed of 17 representatives from the four partner companies (six each from Aerospatiale and Deutsche Airbus, four from British Aerospace, and one from CASA). One representative acts as Chairman (currently this is Franz-Josef Strauss). Much of the detailed day-to-day supervision is delegated to an Executive Committee.

The Role of the Governments

Government involvement in Airbus Industrie is at the level of the partners. The partners deal with their respective governments on issues like launch aid for new aircraft programs. In addition, Airbus Industrie's programs are guaranteed against default by inter-government agreements signed at the start of each program. Finally, numerous government committees exist to monitor the overall commercial status of the programs, to negotiate intergovernmental agreements like the levies on the sale of aircraft that repay development loans, and to settle work sharing arrangements between the partner companies.

Implications of the Structure

One of the major advantages of the Airbus Industrie structure is that it allows the group to exploit the specific technical strengths of each of its partners (for example, BAe's expertise in wing design and construction and CASA's expertise in carbon fiber technology).

At the same time, however, a disadvantage of the structure is that there is a potential conflict of interest between a member's role as a partner and as a subcontractor. As a partner, it is in the interest of each firm to ensure that Airbus fulfill the terms of the original 1969 Franco-German Memorandum of Understanding that specified that Airbus Industrie had to build aircraft according to strict commercial criteria. That is, it had to choose components and equipment from the best source irrespective of nationality. But as a subcontractor, each firm has a motive to increase its share of the work even if it is not the most efficient producer. And Airbus Industrie can exert little power over the partners. They are not analogous to subsidiaries or divisions of an integrated company on whom the results of a 'make or buy' decision can be forced.

To cite an example of the political pressure for work allocation, when the A320 program was started, the British and German partners complained that the French share of the equipment subcontracting work was too great. Although the French reduced their share, the American share (which went as high as 40 percent of A300/A310 aircraft) was reduced as well to make room for expanded work for the British and Germans. (This is one of the sore points with the Americans.)

Another conflict arises from a different source. The partners collectively determine the cost of each element of the airplane. This determination is based on detailed studies of development and production processes, the complexity of the work, its commonality with earlier programs, man-hour and material requirements, etc. But if one of the subcontracting partners beats a cost estimate, it has no incentive to reveal that fact to the others since it could result in a reduced price. This is an inevitable consequence of consortium development and a major difference between Airbus and Boeing. Nevertheless, over the last decade, the companies have improved their efficiency considerably and have repeatedly renegotiated internal pricing.

Financial Reporting

Because Airbus Industrie is a 'GIE', with the majority of its costs incurred by the partners, it faces no legal requirement to publish annual financial statements. Legally it is simply a sales and administration organization for the combined products of the partners. This lack of financial reporting has provoked the Americans who want to know the overall revenues and costs of the different Airbus programs to prove their charge that Airbus violates GATT agreements. The US delegation to the current round of GATT discussions has asked that the whole system of financial reporting be altered to provide this information routinely.

Collaboration and Competition in the Last Decade

In the 1970s, world aircraft markets began to shift from the US to other countries.

Between 1971 and 1976, the five major US airlines, which accounted for 30 percent of the world's passenger traffic, placed only 4 percent of the world's orders for new aircraft. Roughly 70 percent of Boeing's orders were coming from foreign airlines. Anxious to draw more sales from Europe, Boeing began to explore with the French the possibility of a European joint venture. But Boeing was prepared to proceed only if the French could enlist British and German involvement. All parties to the discussions were undoubtedly aware that international cooperation on this scale would probably kill Airbus.

The major obstacle to the Europeans, however, was Boeing's concept of how the work was to be shared. Boeing insisted on overall control with the Europeans acting simply as risk-sharing subcontractors. 'We've got the smarts, they've got the money,' explained a Boeing executive.[10] The Airbus partners eventually dropped negotiations, but Boeing did strike an agreement with the Italians to develop a new aircraft. The project was later abandoned by Boeing with the Italians 'compensated' by a contract to make the trailing edge of the wing and some tail sections for the 767 (about 10 percent of the work on the 767).

Boeing's other foray into trans-Atlantic cooperation came at the end of the 1970s. In 1978, when Airbus launched the A310 program, Britain was not a member of the consortium. This afforded Boeing the opportunity to draw the British into its programs and to sabotage Airbus. Boeing wanted three big nationalized British companies tied to trans-Atlantic rather than Continental collaboration. The three were British Airways, Rolls-Royce, and BAe. With British Airways involvement, Boeing could preempt a major customer, and with BAe involvement, Boeing might be able to deny Airbus's access to crucial wing technology. Without BAe providing the wing, the French would have to develop it – a change that would set the A310 program back a year.

Boeing's strategy was related to its planned 757 model. This twin-engine, narrow-body aircraft was to be based on a stretched 727 fuselage, a newly designed wing, and new high bypass engines. Boeing offered BAe the wings and Rolls-Royce the engines.

But Boeing faced many problems with its scheme. First, the 757 was conceived as a 155-seater which would replace airlines' aging fleets of 727s. This market would eventually become huge, but Boeing wanted to forestall its development as long as possible to avoid cannibalizing the 727 which was still selling over 100 units yearly. Unfortunately, the British wanted a credible commitment from Boeing to proceed with the 757. Second, the financial burden of the 767 and 757 programs running simultaneously was daunting to Boeing. Third, British Airways wanted a larger airplane, one to carry 185 passengers. The only other carrier to express any interest in this was Eastern. Fourth, BAe, which was profitably making wings for the Airbus, preferred full membership in Airbus Industrie to Boeing's offer of a subcontractor's role in the 757. Fifth, costs in Britain were above those at Boeing so that any work done in the UK would raise the 757's price. And finally, Prime Minister Callaghan wanted Britain in the Airbus partnership. (Callaghan actually wanted either Boeing or McDonnell Douglas in it as well.) The

French and the Germans wanted Britain in Airbus, too, but the French set a price on its re-entry. They insisted that re-entry be conditional on British Airway's purchase of A310s rather than 757s.

All of these complex problems were eventually resolved although generally not in Boeing's favor. In order to minimize the impact of the 757 on the 727's sales, and under pressure from British Airways, Boeing finalized the design of the 757 as a 185-seat aircraft. Rolls-Royce produced one of two engine types Boeing offered with the 757, and British Airways put the 757 into service in 1982.

The French relented on their demand that British Airways buy A310s when Laker Airways unexpectedly bought 10 A300s. (It was rumored that Laker did so under duress. It was petitioning the EEC for rights to Continental routes which both the French and British governments were in a position to thwart. Laker Airways later went bankrupt.) With that problem solved, British Aerospace joined Airbus Industrie in early 1979.

Unfortunately for Boeing, the nascent market demand for a 150-seat airplane was left unsatisfied.

The other major Boeing program of the 1970s was the 767. It was an entirely new aircraft positioned to fill the gap between the 727 and the A300 – the same target that Airbus had for its proposed A310. The 767 incorporated a wide-body, twin-aisle fuselage, a new wing, a new tailplane, and the use of high bypass engines. For the 767 program, Boeing sought Japanese rather than European collaboration. In 1976, a study instigated by MITI had suggested that the best means by which the Japanese could enter the aviation industry was to start as a minor member of a consortium of manufacturers and then expand the share of work within it. There were three major prospective Japanese participants – Mitsubishi, Fuji, and Kawasaki Heavy Industries.

Following the study, Japan began extensive negotiations with Boeing concerning participation in the 767 program. The result was a risk-sharing subcontractor relationship in which Japan would manufacture a major portion of the fuselage (about 15 percent of the total value of the aircraft). Boeing succeeded in getting access to the Japanese government's industry subsidies and to Japan's manufacturing expertise without compromising its control over research and development, product design, marketing, or service.

The Boeing 767 entered service in 1982, one year ahead of the Airbus A310. The two airplanes are very similar and are competing in a market segment that is not large enough for both. The competition is so fierce that in order to finalize an early order from TWA, Boeing agreed to pay a penalty if the 767 did not match the fuel efficiency of the A310. In the later trade dispute between the companies, Airbus cited this as a hidden discount to TWA since both Boeing and TWA knew the A310 to be the more fuel efficient of the two aircraft.

Airbus now holds 65 percent of the twin-aisle twin-engine aircraft market with 457 A300s and A310s sold. Boeing's sales of 247 of its 767 constitute the other 35 percent.

The Battle to Fill the 'Hole in the Sky'

Since the early 1980s, the world's airlines have been asking the manufacturers for an airplane to fill such an obvious gap in the market that it has become known as 'the hole in the sky'. The hole is the 150-seat, medium range market segment. It has been created by the obsolescence (and the objectionable noise level) of the DC-9, Trident, and 727. Nearly 1,500 aircraft (out of a total of 6,000 commercial jet airliners in service) are due to be replaced within the next ten years.

As has been explained, Boeing originally intended the 757 for this market niche but decided instead to increase the airplane's size to 185 seats. The combined financial burden of that airplane and the 767 has kept Boeing from restarting a new 150-seater program. Furthermore, Boeing has said (and clearly hopes) that the US airlines are not financially prepared to reequip themselves with new 150-seaters. Boeing's strategy to serve 'the hole in the sky' is to develop inexpensive derivatives of the 737 as temporary palliatives until it can commence a wholly new program. By that time, improvements in engine technology will allow it to eclipse the A320. The new program has an official Boeing designation – the 7J7, but it is little more than a promise to the airlines at present.

Boeing has stretched its 737-200 into the new 737-300 which entered commercial service in 1984. It can carry 128 passengers. And there are plans for a further stretch into the 737-400 to carry 145–155. The 737-400 should enter service in March 1989. In addition to stretching the airplane, Boeing incorporated changes to the original 737 wing, new cockpit avionics, engine mountings, and landing gear. Most importantly from a competitive viewpoint, Boeing adopted the new GE/SNECMA CFM56-3 engine (which is similar to the A-320's engine).

Boeing's efficiency in producing the 737 (which is surpassing the 727 as the most successful airliner ever produced) and the natural economies of a derivative airplane means that it can price the 737-300 relative to a development cost of $300–$400 million compared to the $1.7 billion development cost of the A320. It is Boeing's hope that the resulting price differential will offset the undisputed technological superiority of the A320, and that the airlines will postpone their demand for entirely new technology until the 7J7 is completed.

One factor in Boeing's favor is the changing cost structure of the airlines in the last few years. In the early 1980s, fuel constituted 40 percent of an aircraft's operating costs. That has falled to only 16 percent. Financing now constitutes more than half of an airplane's lifetime cost.

McDonnell Douglas, having lost $275 million in the commercial aircraft business over the past three years, is even less able than is Boeing to start a new project (although it has a 'paper' 150-seater). Like Boeing, its marketing strategy is to sell a derivative. This is a stretched DC-9 that can accommodate 142 passengers and is designated the MD-80. Although its technology is outdated compared to the A320, the MD-80 was available in 1983 and has a much lower capital cost.

Airbus's 150-seat A320 is, of course, positioned exactly in the hole. The A320 was launched in 1984 for entry into service in 1988. Its sales prior to delivery have exceeded those of any aircraft ever produced. A320 customers include major American airlines like Pan Am and Northwest. The sale of the A320s to US airlines is a reminder of Airbus Industrie's taunt that its 'captive' home market is not its sole success. In fact, fewer than one quarter of its A300/A310 sales are to home customers. This compares to 68 percent for Boeing's 767.

The Current Situation

Between 1985 and 1986, Boeing's market share dropped from 58 to 46 percent, McDonnell Douglas's rose slightly from 19 to 20 percent, and Airbus's jumped from 11 to 25 percent. And Airbus is still not selling a full family of models. With the existing A300 and A310, the imminent introduction of the A320, and the planned A330/A340, Airbus could anticipate achieving its goal of a 30 percent share of the free world market by the mid-1990s.

To Boeing and McDonnell Douglas, the competition is not fair. As a Boeing executive said in 1987, 'Behind the Airbus facade are Europe's leading defense contractors, supported by government investments, orders, loans, guarantees, facilities, tax advantages, research funding, and political ties. The Airbus governments claim to their taxpayers that civil transport is, or could be, commercially viable. After 17 years of supporting Airbus, the European taxpayer is entitled to ask: Where is the bottom line for Airbus?'[11]

Notes

1. *Business Week,* July 6, 1987.
2. *Time,* August 3, 1987.
3. Aerospace Research Center, 'The Challenge of Foreign Competition to the US Jet Transport Manufacturing Industry', Aerospace Industries Association of America, Inc., 1981, p. 10.
4. Mowery, D., 'Federal Funding of R&D in Transportation: The Case of Aviation', Carnegie Mellon University, 1985, p. 21.
5. Newhouse, J., *The Sporty Game,* New York, 1982, p. 155.
6. *Business Week,* July 6, 1987.
7. Sampson, A., *The Arms Bazaar,* Coronet Books, 1978, p. 105.
8. Newhouse, *op. cit.,* p. 217.
9. Currency translation here and elsewhere in the case is made at 1988 exchange rates.
10. Ibid., p. 197.
11. Ibid.

Boeing's Case Against Airbus

H. Landis Gabel and Damien Neven

The Boeing Company, with $16 billion in annual sales, dominates the non-communist civilian aircraft industry. It is the largest commercial aircraft manufacturer in the Western world and has produced 5,061 of the 9,201 commercial jet aircraft delivered between 1952 and 1986. Boeing is the only profitable commercial jet aircraft producer, and over the last five years it has averaged a 12 percent return of shareholders' equity. (For a five year summary of Boeing's financial performance, see Exhibit 12.1.) Even more significantly, it is the only producer ever to launch a profitable commercial jet. By most estimates, its 707, 727, 737, and 747 either were or will be profitable. According to a *Fortune* magazine survey, Boeing is America's third most respected corporation.

Boeing's commercial success is in sharp contrast to the succession of failures that has characterized European commercial aircraft in the post-war period – the Mercure, Comet, VC-10, Concorde, Trident, BAC-111, and VFW-614. Between 1945 and 1974, successive British governments spent $2.8 billion (at 1974 prices)[1] on civil aircraft projects, yet they have received less than $281 million in repayments. French public sector spending averaged more than $375 million annually from 1962 to 1977 compared to repayments of about $11 million per year.

This legacy of failure has not driven European firms from the industry, however, nor has it deterred European governments from supporting those firms with taxpayer's money. Airbus Industrie, Europe's latest commercial aircraft venture, has received about $10 billion in public sector support over the seventeen years of its existence, and despite little reason – in Boeing's view – to believe that financial success can be achieved, the member governments have just agreed to commit $3.5 billion more to the launch of two new aircraft – the A330 and A340.

Boeing's pessimistic view of Airbus Industrie's future is based on Boeing's market forecasts and estimates of the price/cost relationships of Airbus's programs. These data suggest that there is no prospect that the government loans that have been made to Airbus will ever be repaid. These loans therefore contravene

---

This case was prepared by John F. Thomas, Research Associate, under the supervision of H. Landis Gabel, Associate Professor, and Damien Neven, Assistant Professor at INSEAD. It is intended to be used as a basis for class discussion rather than to illustrate either effective or ineffective handling of an administrative situation.

Exhibit 12.1   *The Boeing Company, five year summary,*
$ million (except per share data)

	1986	1985	1984	1983	1982
Operations					
Sales:					
Commercial	10,957	8,893	6,026	7,618	5,829
US Government	5,384	4,743	4,328	3,511	3,206
Total	16,341	13,636	10,354	11,129	9,035
Operating profit					
Commercial Aircraft Division	411	376	17	na	na
Military Aircraft Division	367	317	346	na	na
Missiles and Space	55	68	131	na	na
Other industries	(9)	3	15	na	na
Total operating profit	824	764	509	na	na
Corporate income	304	184	153	na	na
Corporate expense	(100)	(85)	(93)	na	na
Earnings before tax	1,028	863	569	na	na
Federal taxes on income before					
DISC adjustment	363	297	179	na	na
Net earnings	665	556	390	355	292
Per primary share	4.28	3.75	2.67	2.44	2.02
% of sales	4.1	4.2	3.8	3.2	3.2
Cash dividends paid	186	157	136	136	135
Per share	1.20	1.04	0.93	0.93	0.93
Other income					
(principally interest)	407	293	241	179	171
R&D expenses	757	409	506	429	691
General and admin. expenses	606	477	420	374	348
Add. to plant and equipment	795	551	337	223	331
Deprec. of plant and equipment	433	356	337	337	324
Salaries and wages	4,374	3,442	3,011	2,825	2,983
Average employment	118,500	98,700	86,600	84,600	94,700
Financial position at Dec 31					
Identifiable net assets					
– Commercial Aircraft Division	3,691	3,689	4,831	na	na
– Military Aircraft Division	2,285	1,673	1,420	na	na
– Missiles and Space	434	235	210	na	na
– Other industries	364	314	328	na	na
– Corporate	4,294	3,335	1,696	na	na
Total net assets	11,068	9,246	8,485	7,471	7,593
Working capital	2,819	2,349	2,130	1,957	1,800
L/T customer financing	195	514	541	539	339
Cash and S/T investments	4,172	3,209	1,595	1,095	294
Total borrowings	277	34	299	383	473

Exhibit 12.1   *continued*

	1986	1985	1984	1983	1982
Long term debt	263	16	284	301	315
Long term deferred taxes	219	326	322	743	666
Stockholders' equity	4,826	4,364	3,695	3,038	2,813
Per share	31.12	28.12	25.34	20.89	19.42
Common shares outstanding (000s)	155,095	155,189	145,837	145,442	144,884
Firm backlog					
Commercial	20,084	18,637	15,949	12,845	14,913
US Government	6,304	6,087	5,562	5,198	4,112
Total	26,388	24,724	21,511	18,043	19,025

Article 6 of the GATT Agreement on Trade in Civil Aircraft which requires that there be a reasonable expectation that such loans be repaid. This article is intended to ensure that public sector financial support of a country's commercial aircraft industry does not distort international trade.

Boeing also believes that the European governments have violated Article 4 of the GATT Agreement which is intended to ensure that aircraft sales are made on a purely commercial basis and not as a result of political influence. As an indication of the political nature of Airbus's market, Boeing notes that from 1978 to 1985, 65 percent of Airbus's sales of wide-body, twin-engine aircraft (213 A300s and A310s) went to government-owned airlines. This compares to only 20 percent of Boeing's sales (67 757s and 767s).

European Government Assistance to Airbus

The direct and indirect subsidies provided by European governments to Airbus have taken a variety of forms which, due to Airbus's lack of financial disclosure, cannot easily be quantified. They include research and development funding, development grants, program launch funding, special production loans (with conditional repayment and low interest rates), and equity infusions. The 'Report to the President of France on the Activities, Management and Financial Results of State-Owned Companies, 1982' candidly referred to 'serious unknowns' in Airbus's financing and to the unreliability of the apparent loss reported by Aerospatiale in its Airbus accounts. So far the European governments have received only about $1.1 billion in loan repayments ($3 million for each A300 and A310 sold).

Boeing's belief that Airbus will be an inevitable commercial failure is based on estimates of cumulative Airbus cash flows. In estimating these cash flows, Boeing used published Airbus data on launch costs, US industry data on recurring production costs, and Airbus's published actual deliveries and estimated future deliveries by model.

The A300/A310 Program

The typical cash flow for a successful US aircraft program of comparable size to the A300/A310 is shown in Exhibit 12.2a. Assumptions include a four year development period, 700 aircraft delivered during the 10 years following development, typical production costs, and a total of about 950 aircraft delivered over a 25 year program lifetime. (This represents market penetration similar to that achieved by the McDonnell Douglas DC-9 and the Boeing 727 and 737.)

In contrast to this stereotype, the A300 program only delivered 223 airplanes over its first 10 years, its development period was five years, and under optimistic assumptions it is likely to sell only 424 airplanes in total.

The poor cash flow that results is further aggravated by allegedly high European production costs. These high costs allegedly arise first from inflexible employment policies that compel Airbus to produce for inventory when sales drop and secondly from an inefficient international allocation of work. This allocation is inefficient both in terms of transport costs (for example, empty Airbuses are flown from France to Germany for their interiors, then returned to France for more detailed work and delivery to customers) and in terms of the productive efficiency of the different partners.

The complexity inherent in any multinational decision making organization is also costly. For example, a 1981 study of the US Air Force's F-16 fighter aircraft program reported that co-production between the US and European nations

Exhibit 12.2a *Cumulative cash flow, medium-size aircraft*

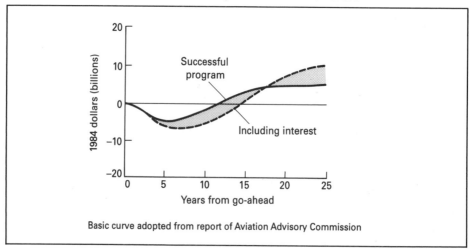

Basic curve adopted from report of Aviation Advisory Commission

increased costs by about 5 percent.[2] Finally, Airbus models incorporate relatively costly new technologies – technologies that Boeing believes are not cost-effective and whose costs are not recovered in the aircraft's prices.

Boeing believes that the net impact of these factors is to raise Airbus's airframe costs (i.e. excluding engines and avionic equipment) 20 percent above those of comparable US aircraft.

Exhibit 12.2b shows the result of Boeing's cash flow projections for the A300 with and without its A310 derivative. Although the A310 is assumed to increase the number of aircraft deliveries in the combined program by about 420 units, its launch costs and high recurring costs result in an even worse cash flow than the A300 experiences alone.

Boeing validates this cash flow projection by comparing the A300/A310 program with the commercially ill-fated Lockheed L-1011. During the first ten years of the two programs, total deliveries were almost identical – 223 L-1011s and 240 A300/A310s. (The A300/A310 actually had a slower delivery schedule than the L-1011 over the first three years.) When the L-1011 program was finally cancelled in 1981, Lockheed announced losses of $2.6 billion for the program. Because the L-1011 and A300/A310 are similar in size and design and were developed at the same time with similar technologies, it is reasonable to assume that the A300/A310's cash flow must suffer similarly.

The A320 Program

Despite the favorable publicity that the A320 has received, Boeing believes that it too will be a commercial failure. McDonnell Douglas, which had lengthy discussions

Exhibit 12.2b *Cumulative cash flow, medium-size aircraft*

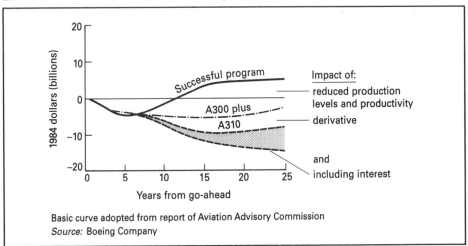

with Airbus about sharing production of the A320, estimated that if the A320 were priced at $31.9 million (in 1984 dollars), it would break even at 600 aircraft – a figure commonly quoted in the press. However, in order to compete with the purchase prices of US derivative models like Boeing's 737-300 and -400 and McDonnell Douglas' MD-80, instances exist where Airbus has been known to have discounted the price of the A320 to $25 million. (Exhibit 12.3 shows the effect of such a reduction in price on the cash flow for the A320 program.) At this lower price, the A320 does not break even before 1000 aircraft are sold, and when interest is taken into account, the program never breaks even.

The A330/A340 Program

Finally, Boeing believes that the proposed A330/A340 program is doomed to the same pattern of losses. Boeing's estimate of the program's financial viability is based on a comparison with the McDonnell Douglas MD-11, its closest competitor. The terms of the comparison are as follows.

- The launch cost of the A300/A340 is $4 billion compared to $700 millon for the MD-11 – a differential of $3.3 billion.

- The A340 has four engines to the MD-11's three, implying $3 million higher costs for each aircraft.

- Based on 1986/1987 exchange rates, production of the A330/A340 will incur a 10 percent labor cost disadvantage.

Assuming sales of 400 of each model, the A340 will therefore suffer a total unit

Exhibit 12.3   *A320 program cash – McDonnell Douglas study (constant 1984 dollars)*

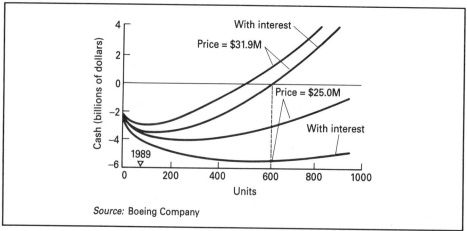

Source: Boeing Company

production cost penalty of over $11 million compared to the MD-11. Boeing acknowledges that the A340 will offer customers substantial operating cost savings compared to the MD-11. These savings have a capitalized value of $9 million. So to be comparably priced, the A340 should command a $9 million price premium in the market. Yet McDonnell Douglas's market information indicates that the A340 will be priced about 25 percent below the MD-11. Estimates for the A300/310 and the A320 programs show a negative cash flow of $10 to $12 billion (in 1984 dollars). The launch of the A330/A340 increases that to a $15 to $22 billion negative cash flow by 1994, 25 years from start of the first Airbus program (see Exhibit 12.4).

Boeing's Response to Airbus's Unfair Competition

Boeing claims that for each $50 million in sales lost by US aircraft manufacturers to Airbus, the nation incurs a $30 million trade loss, a $90 million total negative economic impact, and a loss of 3,500 jobs. But more seriously, the US loses by degrees its world leadership in one of the highest technology industries in the economy.

The company stresses that unlike Airbus, it does not want government financial support. Rather, it wants the US government to pressure the Europeans to end their support of Airbus and thus ensure that the international trade competition to which Boeing is subject is fair. Boeing has actively supported the

Exhibit 12.4 *Cumulative cash flow, current and planned airbus programs*

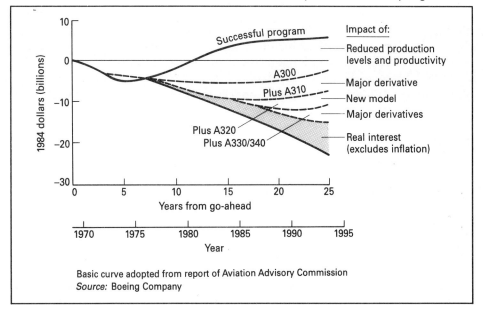

position of the US Trade Representative in the GATT and has urged that the US government threaten trade sanctions against the Europeans unless they comply with GATT rules.

To rebut a counterargument that sales to the US Department of Defense subsidize Boeing's commercial aircraft business, Boeing notes that its last major military aircraft program was the B-52. Between 1952 and 1962, the company built 744 of the bombers. But today it has no major military aircraft programs, and almost 70 percent of its sales are of commercial aircraft. NASA contracts and the Department of Defense have accounted for about 4 percent and 3 percent respectively of Boeing's commercial research and development in the last 10 years. McDonnell Douglas and Lockheed rather than Boeing have been the major beneficiaries of military aircraft programs, and ironically each has suffered massive losses in its commercial aircraft division.

If military business can be imagined to support commercial aircraft, then the Europeans should be the greatest beneficiaries. From 1980 to 1985, the Airbus partners recorded $39.8 billion in military sales compared to Boeing's $19.5 billion (see Exhibit 12.5). And beyond military business, the European firms benefit from government sponsored research as does Boeing. For example, the German government funds research into composite materials, and BAe has worked closely with the government-owned Royal Aircraft Establishment (whose low-speed wind tunnel is among the most modern in the world) on wing aerodynamics and the design of high lift systems. A final misleading claim by the Europeans is that Boeing is the giant against which they must compete. In actual fact, the manpower and assets of the Airbus partners exceed those of either Boeing or McDonnell Douglas (see Exhibit 12.6).

In addition to its political initiative, Boeing has embarked on major internal efforts to ensure the continuation of what it believes to be its superiority over its rivals. It has invested over $2.2 billion in the last five years in plant and equipment in order to increase its already impressive level of manufacturing efficiency. The company's stated goal is to cut 25 percent off its cost structure by 1990. Part of that effort entails a production reorganization patterned on that of the Japanese.

Boeing has also become more aggressive in the marketplace. It won part of a 40-aircraft order from American Airlines (Boeing sold the airline 15 767s to Airbus's 25 A300s) by agreeing to leasing terms so liberal that American Airlines could, if it chose, cancel the deal on just one month's notice. And in another startling departure from its past marketing practices, Boeing agreed to take $700 million in convertible Allegis Corporation notes in payment for 747s sold to Allegis's subsidiary, United Airlines.

Notes

1. Currency translation here and elsewhere in the case is made at 1988 exchange rates.
2. Rich, M., *et al.*, 'Multinational Coproduction of Military Aerospace Systems', Rand, 1981, p. 122.

Exhibit 12.5 *Sales of commercial aircraft vs. government sales, 1980–1985*

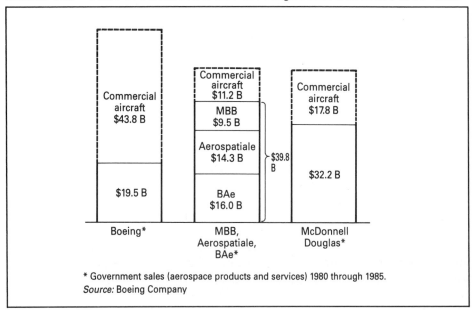

Boeing*

Commercial aircraft $43.8 B

$19.5 B

MBB, Aerospatiale, BAe*

Commercial aircraft $11.2 B

MBB $9.5 B

Aerospatiale $14.3 B

BAe $16.0 B

$39.8 B

McDonnell Douglas*

Commercial aircraft $17.8 B

$32.2 B

* Government sales (aerospace products and services) 1980 through 1985.
Source: Boeing Company

Exhibit 12.6

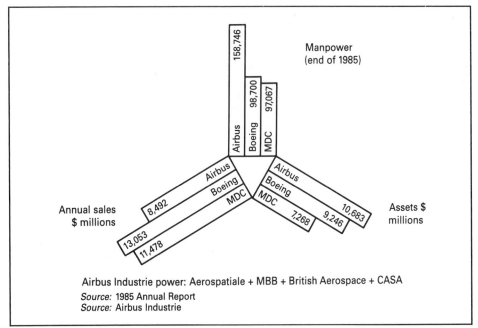

Manpower (end of 1985)

Airbus 158,746
Boeing 98,700
MDC 97,067

Annual sales $ millions

Airbus
Boeing
MDC
8,492
13,053
11,478

Assets $ millions

Airbus
Boeing
MDC
10,683
9,246
7,268

Airbus Industrie power: Aerospatiale + MBB + British Aerospace + CASA
Source: 1985 Annual Report
Source: Airbus Industrie

CASE 13

In Defense of Airbus Industrie

H. Landis Gabel and Damien Neven

Although attacked by the US Trade Representative in the GATT, Airbus Industrie has yet to issue any general defense of its existence, structure, or method of financing. Nevertheless, the elements of that defense, should it ever be made, can be pieced together from interviews with Airbus personnel and from public statements made by Airbus supporters.

The case for Airbus Industrie can be summarized as follows. The dominance of the civilian aircraft industry by the United States is the direct consequence of a variety of government policies undertaken during the Second World War and subsequently. This dominance and the way it is maintained distorts international trade and justifies both in economic and political terms the entry of additional competitors into the marketplace. European firms were leaders in the industry prior to the Second World War and have every reason to believe that they possess the resources necessary to restore their former position. Airbus – the organization to do so – is a commercial enterprise, competing on a purely commercial basis with larger American firms in a market that is large enough to sustain three major competitors.

If Airbus is successful, as it anticipates, not only will Europe profit in terms of technological advancement, an improved trade balance, and job creation, but the customers of the aircraft manufacturers will profit by having more choices between better products at lower prices than prevailed before the US monopoly was broken. That European governments have made loans to Airbus does not change the essence of the case. It only illustrates the obvious fact that the industry never was nor ever will be independent of government interest and involvement. Indeed, the US industry has received much larger sums for a longer time than has the European industry.

This case was prepared by John F. Thomas, Research Associate, under the supervision of H. Landis Gabel, Associate Professor, and Damien Neven, Assistant Professor at INSEAD. It is intended to be used as a basis for class discussion rather than to illustrate either effective or ineffective handling of an administrative situation.

The Specifics of Airbus's Defense

Industry Size Differential

As Exhibit 13.1 shows, the US industry is many times the size of the European industry. Because the aircraft/aerospace industry is one in which there are large economies of scale, scope, and experience, this size differential creates a significant competitive advantage for the Americans.

American manufacturers have also benefitted from a home market that has accounted for over half of the world's traffic and hence commercial aircraft sales (see Exhibit 13.2). The huge and integrated domestic market has provided the US manufacturers with virtual assurance of large initial orders from their domestic customers. Orders from just two of the larger US airlines could easily finance the launch of a new aircraft. For example, the launch orders from Eastern Airlines and United Airlines for a total of 80 Boeing 727s in 1960 were worth $420 million. If a US firm could win 25 percent of its home market, a project could be launched with confidence in the production efficiences that would translate into commercial success. But for a European manufacturer, even 100 percent of its home market would leave a cost disadvantage relative to the US manufacturer. Whereas the possibility of exports to the US were in no sense blocked, political obstacles and natural 'buy American' sentiments all conspire to obstruct the European sales in North America.

Exhibit 13.1 *Comparative size of aircraft/aerospace industries, based on 1981 sales*

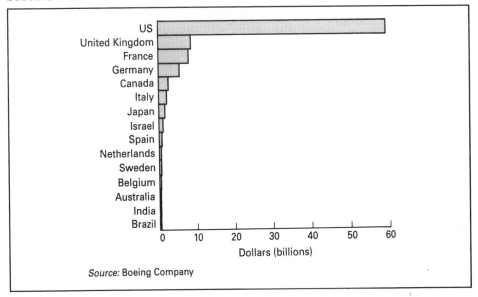

Source: Boeing Company

Exhibit 13.2 *Historical domination of the US market*

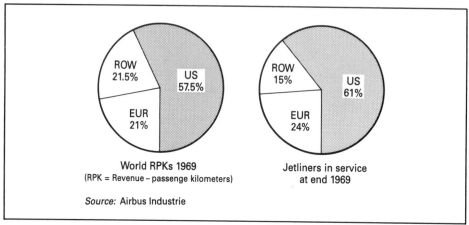

World RPKs 1969
(RPK = Revenue – passenge kilometers)

Jetliners in service
at end 1969

Source: Airbus Industrie

The Benefits of US Government Support

Since the beginning of the Second World War, the US commercial aircraft industry
has received substantial benefits from the US government – especially from the
Department of Defense.

One major source of benefit has been government-funded research and
development for military aircraft which spills into commercial aircraft. A recent
study of federal research and development funding noted that total US investment
in aircraft from all sources between 1945 and 1982 amounted to $103 billion (in 1972
dollars). Of this total, $77 billion (75 percent) was provided by the military, $17
billion (16 percent) was financed by industry, and the remaining $9 billion (9 percent)
was government non-military funding. According to the study, 'US government
policy in the aircraft industry not only supported pre-commercial research in civilian
and military aircraft technologies, but also played a major role in supporting the
diffusion of the results of this research'[1] (see Exhibit 13.3).

Research work carried out by NASA has enabled the US industry to stay at
the forefront of aeronautical technology. In the past five years, NASA has spent
$1.5 billion to support basic aeronautical research and development. Much of the
development and flight testing of the new generation of ultra-high bypass engines is
being carried out on NASA-supplied aircraft. In addition, NASA maintains its own
test facilities, saving the commercial industry the cost of duplicating research
programs. This saving has been to be worth nearly $1 billion (in 1972 dollars) from
1982 to 1991.

US military contracts let on a cost-plus basis have allowed the aircraft
manufacturers to earn high rates of return on military programs and thus to initiate
commercial aircraft programs whose risk-adjusted prospective rates of return are
below what would ordinarily be required.

Exhibit 13.3 *US annual R&D investment, 1945–1982 (1972 dollars)*

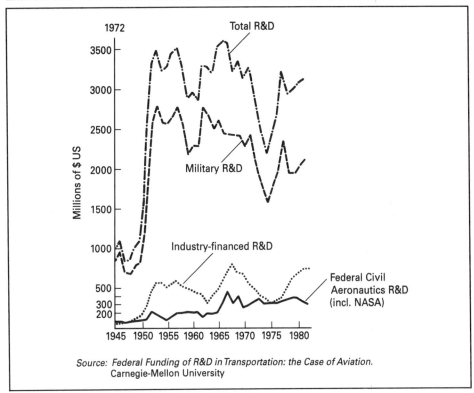

Source: *Federal Funding of R&D in Transportation: the Case of Aviation.*
Carnegie-Mellon University

In addition, the contract price of military aircraft programs generally includes funding for manufacturing facilities. For example, Boeing's Renton plant, which was built on government funds to produce military aircraft during the Second World War, was subsequently used to produce the 707, 727, 737, and 757 models. And Boeing's Military Airplane Company in Wichita produces fuselage panels for the 737 and 757 aircraft.

Not only have military contracts built production facilities for commercial airplanes, but military aircraft programs have also helped defray the initial design costs of commercial aircraft. For example, the design team for the 747 was originally funded by the US Department of Defense's 'Heavy Lift' program that resulted in the Lockheed C-5A transport.

Finally, high volume military work can increase a contractor's purchasing power in the markets for the materials, components, and capital equipment common to both military and commercial aircraft.

The history of the Lockheed L-1011 provides an unusually clear example of the link between US commercial and military businesses. Ernest Fitzgerald, a Pentagon official assigned to investigate mismanagement by defense contractors, published a detailed and candid account of the L-1011/C-5A relationship. He showed how Lockheed, with the connivance of the US Air Force, was able to transfer money authorized for the C-5A to aid the ailing L-1011. As Fitzgerald wryly observed, 'With Lockheed's commercial ventures underwritten by the taxpayer and its military programs safely tucked back into the Pentagon's cost-plus womb and hooked up to the Treasury's umbilical cord, the "Great Plane robbery" was an accomplished fact'.[2]

Another example is offered by the McDonnell Douglas DC-10. In November 1983, with the imminent closure of the DC-10 production line, McDonnell Douglas was on the verge of abandoning large commercial aircraft production. However, the US Air Force then ordered a tanker/transport version, the KC-10, and McDonnell Douglas was able to keep its DC-10 production line open. The 44 tankers ordered by the Air Force did not make money for McDonnell Douglas, but they did sustain the company until, in May 1984, Federal Express ordered 6 DC-10s, and McDonnell Douglas was able to restart commercial production. Moreover, the combination of the KC-10 and the Federal Express order carried McDonnell Douglas to the MD-11, the derivative of the DC-10 now being developed for the commercial market.

In contrast with the American firms, Airbus has never derived an airplane from a military model, nor is Airbus supported by sales of any military derivatives.

The Importance of Competition in the Industry

A recurring argument of the Europeans is that Boeing has a monopoly in the commercial aircraft market. Although McDonnell Douglas is ostensibly a competitor, it has such a narrow range of models (only the MD-80 and the DC-10/MD-11 series) that it does not constitute competition sufficient to diminish Boeing's market power. Furthermore, the barriers to enter the industry are so high that potential competition does not constitute a restraint on Boeing either.

As evidence to support its argument, Airbus cites the example of the Boeing 747, the sole aircraft model in the long range, high capacity market segment. Airlines complain that the standard 747-200's price of between $100 and $120 million (compared to a 1966 launch price of less than $50 million in inflation adjusted terms) represents an exploitation of monopoly power.

Effective competition would not only reduce prices, but it would also increase the rate of technological improvement in the industry. For example, the US manufacturers were reluctant to introduce commercial jet aircraft because, as the established market leaders, they had little to gain by embarking upon a new and high-cost technology before its advantages had been proven. So it was the British who took the lead with the Comet, the world's first commercial jet. Only an order from Pan Am for British Comet 3s in 1952 spurred the US industry into action. Boeing launched its 707 and Douglas quickly followed with the DC-8. These two long haul jet aircraft triggered the rapid conversion of world's airlines fleets to jets. A more recent example that Airbus often cites is its introduction of all-electronic flight controls – what it calls 'fly-by-wire' technology. This innovation allows, among other benefits, the reduction of the flight crew from three to two. Boeing is now introducing similar electronics into its new 747-400.

Implicit US Government Protection of Boeing

Boeing contends that Airbus represents unfair competition because its viability is guaranteed by its member governments. It cannot go bankrupt. Yet the counterargument is that Boeing, too, has a government guarantee against insolvency, albeit a less explicit one. Every government, including that of the United States, is understandably concerned about its major defense and high technology businesses, and there is every reason to expect – and evidence to support the expectation – that the US government would prevent Boeing's bankruptcy.

The Nixon Administration provided a federal loan guarantee of $250 million to prevent Lockheed's bankruptcy from the L-1011 crisis in 1971. (The legislation passed the Senate by one vote.) Lockheed and its supporters had argued that the commercial L-1011 and the military C-5A were interdependent and that the firm's collapse would have serious implications for the entire US aerospace industry.

Lockheed's plea for government assistance was aided by the precedent set in the mid-1960s when the government rescued Douglas. The company faced a financial crisis caused by the high cost of producing both the DC-8 and DC-9, and it made a successful application for an emergency loan under the 1950 Defense Production Act.

Both the Lockheed and Douglas cases were clearly unusual, and each had significant military implications. Furthermore, in both cases, the loans were ultimately repaid with interest. But this is a retrospective view. The US government acted to prevent the bankruptcy of two commercial aircraft manufacturers with military contracts, it had no guarantee that its support would be repaid. Boeing surely knows that it, too, could make the same case for help were it necessary.

Benefits Derived by Boeing from Other Governments

Boeing even benefits from the support of other governments. Japan's Ministry of International Trade and Industry (MITI) launched three of its industrial giants in to the commercial airframe business just a few years ago. Mitsubishi, Kawasaki, and Fuji Heavy Industry collectively formed the Civil Transport Development Corporation (CTDC) of Japan. The high start-up costs and risks were mitigated when MITI arranged financing on easy terms and relieved the companies of many other burdens. From 1978 to 1982, MITI provided $61 million in loans to CTDC to assist it to become a subcontractor to the Boeing 767 program. The loans are similar to those provided to the Airbus partners by their respective governments because they are to be repaid from proceeds of the sale of CTDC subassemblies to Boeing. Yet Boeing has not complained of these loans.

Recently, Boeing's commuter aircraft subsidiary, de Havilland of Canada, began discussions with Shorts of Northern Ireland about the possibility of jointly developing and producing a new generation of commuter aircraft. At the time the press reported that Shorts would be requesting assistance from the UK government for launch aid if the joint program were to proceed.

Notes

1.   Mowery, D., 'Federal Funding of R&D in Transportation: the Case of Aviation', Carnegie-Mellon University, 1985, p. 13.
2.   Hayward, K., *International Collaboration in Civil Aerospace*, St Martin's Press, 1986, p. 158.

CASE 14

High-definition Television in Europe

H. Landis Gabel and **Olivier Cadot**

Decision Point

It is May 14, 1991 – less than three weeks before the European Commission (EC) will propose a new directive on satellite broadcasting policy to replace the current one that expires at the end of the year. At stake is whether the EC will require use of the D2-MAC transitional standard for high-definition television for all satellite broadcasts. The stakes are particularly high for three companies: Thomson Consumer Electronics of France, Philips NV of the Netherlands, and British Sky Broadcasting.

Technical Considerations

How your TV Works

Television receivers produce an image by firing electrons across a cathode ray tube to light up the phosphorous coating on the screen in a distinct pattern of dots. The electrons sweep across the screen in horizontal lines, from left to right, drawing every other line from top to bottom, first the even, then the odd. This interlaced scanning structure (notated 2:1) means it takes two complete sweeps to draw all the lines and produce a complete image, or frame. The process is repeated either twenty-five or thirty times per second (25 Hz or 30 Hz) at a frequency called frames per second. The number of sweeps made per second is called the field frequency and, with an interlaced scanning structure, it is necessarily twice the number of frames per second (50 Hz or 60 Hz). The eye's tendency to retain images fills in the missing information between frames.

This case was written by Pamela Denby, Research Associate, under the supervision of H. Landis Gabel, Professor at INSEAD, and Olivier Cadot, Assistant Professor at INSEAD. It is intended to be used as a basis for class discussion rather than to illustrate either effective or ineffective handling of an administrative situation.

The quality of the image's reception depends on the integrity of the broadcast signal between the television transmitter and your receiver. Today's analog signals are subject to numerous common forms of interference. For example, a building along the transmission path can deflect part of the signal and cause it to arrive late at your TV, producing duplicate images, or 'ghosts', on your screen. Other notorious culprits are household appliances like vacuum cleaners, blenders, and hair dryers that run at a set frequency and can cause 'snow' to appear in the image.

The quality of the image's display on your TV screen depends on the combination of spatial and temporal parameters that are set in the TV's technical standard. The image is broken into horizontal lines, each of which is divided into picture elements (pixels). Image resolution improves with an increase in frames per second, lines per frame, or pixels per line. Each pixel receives three types of information: two on its colour (chrominance) and one on its brightness (luminance). If provided simultaneously in a composite signal, the chrominance and luminance information can interfere and produce poor colours or banding. In some standards, the chrominance/luminance information is separated by either time phase or sequence in order to prevent such distortions. At the time of the change from black-and-white to colour television broadcasts, composite signal technology, called frequency division multiplex, was chosen so that owners of black-and-white televisions could continue to receive broadcasts, and transmissions could be sent within the existing channel allocations. Advances in filters, hue control, and screen technologies since then have helped to ameliorate some of the composite signal's inherent problems.

Today's Regional TV Standards: NTSC, SECAM, and PAL

NTSC has been the television transmission standard in the US since 1941 when it was selected by the National Television System Committee for black-and-white television. It has 525 scanning lines drawn in an interlaced scanning structure at a field frequency of 59.94 Hz (notated 525/59.94/2:1). It has been the basis of the US colour transmission standard since 1953. Chrominance/luminance information is provided simultaneously. Japan, Canada, Mexico, and parts of Latin America also use this standard.

SECAM (Séquentiel Couleur à Mémoire) was developed between 1958 and 1960 for colour television in France and is also used in francophone Africa, Eastern Europe (including East Germany), and the countries of the former Soviet Union. It has 625 scanning lines and a 50Hz field frequency in an interlaced scanning structure (625/50/2:1). SECAM uses a composite signal, but the chrominance/luminance signals are separated by sequence. The receiver has a memory so that it can reconstitute the information and display it simultaneously on your screen.

PAL (Phased Alternation by Line) was developed in Germany in 1962 and became the standard in all of Western Europe except France. Like SECAM, it has 625 scanning lines interlaced at a 50 Hz field frequency (625/50/2:1) in a composite signal. Unlike SECAM, however, the chrominance/luminance information is separated by phase. PAL is also used in Brazil and Australia.

Exhibit 14.1 summarizes the technical differences and relative advantages of each standard.

How HDTV Works

High-definition television (HDTV) improves image resolution primarily by increasing the number of lines on the screen. It also can make improvements by increasing pixels per line, by sending colour and luminance information as separate components, and by scanning the image, one line after another so one sweep makes one frame (1:1) and the eye has to fill in less information. An increase in field frequency can help to decrease flicker and to improve screen brightness but it is not considered practical because the eye cannot perceive improvements above 80 Hz and because it is convenient to tie it to the frequency of the alternating current power source. With higher resolution, HDTV avoids image degradation on large screens of cinematic, wide-screen proportions in a 16:9 aspect ratio rather than today's 4:3.

Exhibit 14.1   *Current colour television standards*

	NTSC	PAL	SECAM
Full name	National Television Systems Committee	Phased Alternation by Line	Séquentiel Couleur à Mémoire
Date	1953	1962	1958–1960
Principal countries of use	USA Japan Canada	Western Europe except France Brazil	France former Soviet bloc countries francophone Africa
Market share (see end note 1)	40%	39%	21%
Scanning structure	525/59.94/2:1	625/50/2:1	625/50/2:1
Pixels/line	530	720	720
Colour signals	Sent together	Sent separated by phase	Sent separated by sequence
Channel bandwidth	6 MHz	7–8 MHz	8 MHz
Advantages	Brighter screen, less flicker, stereo sound possible	Better colour and resolution, stereo sound possible	Better colour and resolution
Disadvantages	Colour distorts easily	Dim screen, more flicker	Dim screen, more flicker, no stereo sound

Reception can be improved by digital transmission of either the sound signal, the image signal, or both. All of these improvements require the transmission of significantly more information, pushing the limits of channel capacity (measured in terms of megahertz (MHz) of bandwidth).

Technical Factors and their Impact

Analog or Digital Format

In an analog format, a signal is sent as a wave that is modulated, for example, by frequency (FM) or amplitude (AM), to convey information. The analog wave varies constantly with the source. A digital signal is made by sampling an analog signal at regular intervals and assigning each sample a numeric value. Regardless of what it conveys, any digital signal is sent in the binary code of computers, which is made up exclusively of 0s and 1s.

Digital format for HDTV means that a programme is much easier both to manipulate, for example for editing and special effects, and to duplicate. For transmission, the digital format facilitates error checking because the degradation of a 1 signal, for example, would have to be greater than 50 percent before it could be misconstrued as a 0. Uncompressed, a digital transmission takes up much more bandwidth than an analog transmission of the same signal. On the other hand, the binary encoding also provides a much greater capacity for signal compression by using a mathematical formula to summarize the information it carries. For multimedia applications, a digital format implies that all data sources – compact disc, television, radio, telephone, and computer – can be designed to be compatible.

Bandwidth Constraints

Television signals can be transmitted terrestrially, over cable, by satellite, or by a combination thereof, such as satellite transmission for onward distribution by cable (see Exhibit 14.2). Each of these transmission media has progressively more bandwidth capacity.

The electromagnetic spectrum is a limited resource, and only a certain segment is suitable for terrestrial, over-the-air transmission of signals. Much of this segment is already taken up by existing services, such as broadcast television, radio, portable and cellular telephony, military communications, police, taxi, shipping and trucking fleets, etc. New products that are best suited to terrestrial, over-the-air transmission, such as cellular phones, compete for space in the already crowded spectrum. Government regulation determines how this resource is allocated.

The physical limitations and government regulation of the electromagnetic spectrum together affect the development of transmission methods for high-definition television. For example, television broadcasters in the US are allotted 6 MHz of bandwidth per channel, and each channel is separated by another 6 MHz in the VHF (very high frequency) range of the spectrum to minimize interference.[2] Any increase in bandwidth given to television broadcasters by regulators means

Exhibit 14.2 *Television transmission media*

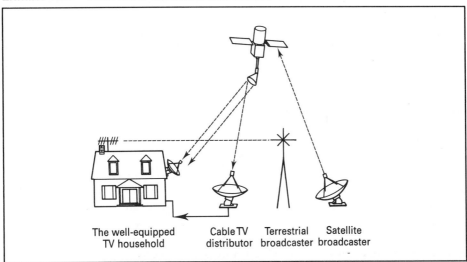

| The well-equipped TV household | Cable TV distributor | Terrestrial broadcaster | Satellite broadcaster |

there is less available to other services. For HDTV to be transmitted over the terrestrial airwaves without reallocating channels, the signal must be compressed to fit into a system originally designed for traditional television. In the US, this means fitting the HDTV signal into the 6 MHz band between existing channels and designing the transmission standard in such a way as to avoid interference. In Europe, TV channels have 7–8 MHz of bandwidth. Because of the way channels have been assigned to existing national services in Europe, however, accommodation of a trans-European HDTV signal may only be possible through a reallocation of channels.

Cable transmission is not limited by the constraints on over-the-air, terrestrial transmissions – only by the type of cable used. The coaxial cables most common today are divided into channels of between 7–8 MHz. Since cable companies decide the allocation of their systems' capacity, one could conceivably merge two 8 MHz channels into a single 16 MHz HDTV channel. Hyperband cable systems, which have channels of about 12 MHz, are currently proposed for Germany, France and the Netherlands, and the European Commission is expected to recommend them for all future cable systems. The fibre optic cables of the future will have almost limitless capacity for broadband HDTV transmissions over integrated services digital networks (ISDN).[3]

Satellites have the capacity to handle broadband transmissions since the higher frequency segment of the electromagnetic spectrum suitable for satellite transmission of signals is currently uncrowded. Because satellite transmissions cross national boundaries, the allocation of satellite channels is handled by international agreement. Segments of the spectrum have already been set aside for HDTV transmission by satellite.

The advantage of sending an HDTV signal by cable or satellite is that it does not crowd out other uses of the terrestrial spectrum, and it need not be as compressed, thereby obviating possible compromises in quality due to the shorthand of compression. The disadvantage is that the network of viewers connected to cable or to satellite receivers is currently small.

HDTV Standards in Contention: HiVision, MAC Packet, and Digital

HiVision
HiVision, the first HDTV standard to be commercialized, is already running in Japan. It is an analog system of 1,125 scanning lines interlaced at 60 Hz (1125/60/2:1) in a 16:9 aspect ratio. Programmes produced in HiVision are transmitted by satellite in a 8.1MHz bandwidth using the MUSE compression method, a technique based on devoting relatively more bandwidth to stationary objects and cutting out seemingly redundant motion information. MUSE broadcasts cannot be received on existing NTSC television sets without a converter.[4]

MAC Packet
'MAC Packet' refers to the evolutionary family of inter-compatible standards, from D2-MAC to HD-MAC, that was designed to enable a two-step approach to the introduction of HDTV in Europe. The first step entails distributing enough D2-MAC transmissions and compatible equipment to establish the momentum needed to drive the second step, the introduction of HD-MAC.

D2-MAC was designed for satellite transmissions with the potential for onward distribution by cable. Although D2-MAC could be transmitted terrestrially, there are no immediate plans to do so. Europeans can receive D2-MAC broadcasts on their existing PAL/SECAM sets at the same resolution as existing transmissions, provided they have either a cable hook-up or a satellite dish, a D2-MAC decoder, and a television receiver that has a socket able to accept the decoder.[5]

To be able to appreciate the improvements to be found in the D2-MAC signal, consumers must purchase, in addition to the D2-MAC decoder and satellite dish, an improved definition television receiver (IDTV).[6] The D2-MAC signal improves upon existing PAL and SECAM transmissions three ways: better colour, wider picture, and compact disc quality sound. It does this by separating the chrominance and luminance information by time multiplex into a component signal, by using a 16:9 aspect ratio, and by sending the sound signal in digital, two-channel stereo.[7] At 625 scanning lines interlaced at 50 Hz, the D2-MAC signal does not necessarily provide higher horizontal resolution, but it can do so with some receivers. For example, some IDTV models use line doubling to increase horizontal resolution,[8] while others double the field frequency to 100 Hz to reduce flicker.[9] All IDTVs continue to receive PAL and SECAM broadcasts in their 4:3 aspect ratio unless fitted with a blow-up feature that stretches the format to fill the screen at the loss of some resolution.

Once HDTV sets become available (the second step) IDTV owners will be able to purchase a second, HD-MAC decoder to allow HDTV viewing on their IDTV receiver. Even with the HD-MAC decoder, however, IDTV models that double frequency rather than lines will display HD-MAC programmes at distinctly lower resolution than an HDTV set. To appreciate fully the qualitative differences, viewers would have to purchase an HDTV set.

HDTV sets in the MAC standard will display 1,250 scanning lines interlaced at 50 Hz – twice as many lines as D2-MAC. The HD-MAC production standard is intended to evolve eventually into a progressive scanning structure (1250/50/1:1). An HD-MAC programme is produced entirely in digital; then the image is converted into an analog signal for transmission. A section of the bandwidth is reserved for digital transmission of a DATV (digitally assisted television) signal that is sent together with the analog signal (up to four different language tracks in stereo or eight in mono plus encryption/decryption codes for pay-TV distribution). The DATV signal is the key to the evolutionary characteristic of the MAC packet of standards, for it also includes instructions to the decoder on how to reconstitute the signal. A D2-MAC decoder will receive instructions on how to process the signal into a 625-line display. The HD-MAC decoder, on the other hand, will have additional capability to interpret data provided by the DATV signal on how to reconstitute the compressed, 625-line D2-MAC transmission into the 1,250 lines of the original HD-MAC production. Once the HD-MAC information is included in the DATV signal, the total transmission bandwidth required will expand from 8.5 MHz to 12 MHz.

US Digital

The Federal Communications Commission (FCC) is currently conducting tests on five different rival systems in order to select the US standard for terrestrial, over-the-air broadcasts by June 1993. Because of the FCC requirement that current NTSC receivers not be stranded, whichever HDTV standard is selected will be simulcast together with the NTSC signal in no more than 6 MHz of additional bandwidth. Such narrow constraints spurred the development of digital systems and digital compression techniques by four of the five contenders. The FCC is not involved in determining standards for cable and satellite transmissions, but the related industries are nevertheless awaiting the decision on terrestrial broadcasting before commercializing a standard for their own use. Although proposed standards vary in number of lines, depending on the scanning structure, the primary difference will be found in the compression technique. Exhibit 14.3 delineates the technical characteristics of the latest proposals for the US standard with the European and Japanese standards for comparison.

Competitive Differences in HDTV Systems

Time until Available on the Market

A whole range of products based on the Japanese HiVision/Muse standard is already

Exhibit 14.3 *High definition television standards*

Country	Proponent	Companies	Standard	Scanning structure	Pixels	Signal type	Signal bandwidth
Europe	Eureka 95	Thomson Philips Nokia Bosch	HD-MAC	1250/50/2-1:1		mixed	12 MHz
Japan	NHK	NHK Sony	HiVision	1125/60/2:1		analog	8.1 MHz
USA	American Consortium	Zenith AT&T	Digital Spectrum Compatible HDTV	787.5/59.94/1:1	square	digital	6 MHz
	American TV Alliance	General Instrument MIT	ATVA Progressive System	787.5/59.94/1:1	square	digital	6 MHz
			DigiCipher	1050/59.94/2:1		digital	6 MHz
	Advanced TV Research Consortium	Philips Thomson NBC Sarnoff Research	Advanced Digital TV	1050/59.94/2:1		digital	6 MHz
	NHK	NHK	MUSE 6	1125/59.94/2:1		analog	6 MHz

on the market, including lightweight HDTV cameras and other studio equipment considered essential to the production of programmes. The Japanese state-owned public broadcasting network, NHK, began offering one hour per day of HDTV demonstration broadcasts beginning in August 1990. In November 1990, Sony introduced a 90cm, 16:9 MUSE receiver. In November 1991, NHK expanded the broadcasts to eight hours daily. The Japanese also have products available for non-broadcast HDTV applications, such as large, high resolution displays for computer aided design on an HDTV interface.[10]

Prototypes of a complete HDTV line on the European standard were first demonstrated at the International Broadcasting Convention in September 1988, but there have been delays in making available studio equipment that is sufficiently portable and low-priced to encourage production of programmes. D2-MAC receivers have been available on the European market since February 1991, but there is a dearth of D2-MAC programmes being broadcast. Nevertheless, the EC has set a target date of 1997 for the introduction of HD-MAC broadcasts.

In the US, because the FCC has not yet selected a broadcast standard, equipment engineered on the proposed digital standards is at the prototype stage. The introduction of HDTV broadcasts could be expected to follow the policy-directed time line for terrestrial broadcasting, putting it between 1996 and 1999. The competitive forces of pay-per-view, home video, subscription cable services, and satellite distribution, however, could spur earlier introduction.[11] Consumer equipment for non-broadcast programming could be introduced by late 1994.[12]

Cost

The initial price of any HDTV will be high but can be expected to fall significantly as companies compete to reduce component costs. The most expensive components of an HDTV are the screen and the integrated circuits (ICs). Traditional screens based on cathode ray tubes (CRTs) have size limitations. As CRTs are made larger, they become too heavy and too large for household use. For these reasons, several companies have embarked on ambitious R&D programmes in advanced screen technologies with the ultimate goal of developing a large, flat screen that could be hung on a wall.[13]

Once standards are set, the development of application-specific integrated circuits (ASICs) will help to reduce the IC component cost. Japanese companies have already established a number of joint ventures with American chip makers in the expectation of reducing the number of ICs required for MUSE by about 85 percent through the development of ASICs.

Quality

Comparisons of display quality are difficult to make since no production standard is being transmitted in its full high definition. With current transmissions, one can only compare the results of compression techniques. HD-MAC is considered superior to MUSE, since it better depicts motion. For example, MUSE is reported to have difficulty following a soccer player through a quick play sequence involving movement and stops: while the player moves, the abundance of data needed for the motion causes the playing field in the background to appear blurred. When he stops, the grass suddenly springs back into focus.[14] Furthermore, the HiVision production standard is interlaced, while the European standard, although interlaced now, will evolve into progressive scanning. Indeed, the Secretary General of the Japanese government-affiliated HiVision Promotion Center has said, 'Actually, I have to admit there's not really that much difference in picture quality between present broadcasts and MUSE.'[15]

Under studio conditions, in a side-by-side comparison conducted in Moscow, on the other hand, the Japanese standard was considered superior to HD-MAC 'in virtually every subjective test conducted.'[16] The Europeans disputed the test results since testing was conducted on a Japanese monitor that did not have the capability to compensate for the slower European 50 Hz field frequency by doubling the frame rate. In sum, since quality comparisons are difficult to make at the present time, more telling comparisons must be made based on other criteria.

Compatibility Considerations

Whenever the transition to a new technology is made, the question arises whether the new will be compatible with the old. This issue of retrocompatibility becomes pertinent in the case of a product involving hardware and software components (TVs and programmes, for example) and crucial when the product is part of a network of users. In the case of television, the issue last arose in the transition from black-and-white to colour. It is raised again with the transition to HDTV. Exhibit 14.4 outlines the compatibility choices made by the different standards.

As important as retrocompatibility is forward compatibility. A standard that is not potentially forward compatible may be very good at bringing HDTV to market quickly, yet it could stifle the development of still more advanced technologies. For example, the futuristic concept of an open architecture receiver envisions a bare-bones HDTV receiver into which separate modules could be added, permitting use also as a videophone, a personal computer, or a link to on-line services – depending upon which applications the consumer wanted to use. Such a receiver could render moot any debate over the number of scanning lines and field frequency because the receiver would be intelligent enough to adjust these parameters according to the input and the application.[17] For this concept to be realized, the basic HDTV standard must be compatible with computers and with future plans for telephone networks. This would require, at the very least, that the HDTV standard be fully digital. The production and manufacturing opportunities provided by such a device would be much greater than simply renewing the base of television receivers. It would, of course, require a delay in the introduction of high-definition television for this concept to be realized.

Exhibit 14.4

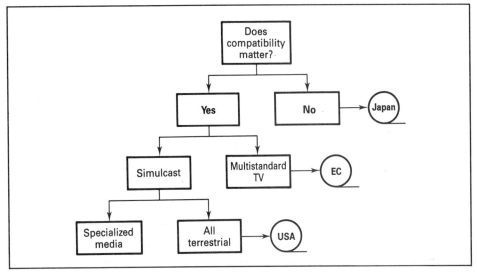

Along with the consideration of retro and forward compatibility is the issue of compatibility between national or regional markets. As the market size of a standard increases, so does the market size for the whole range of hardware and software products and the ease with which those markets can be entered by producers. Experts have argued that the European TV industry was protected to some extent from imports from Japan in the era of colour TV because its standards – PAL and SECAM – had much smaller markets than did NTSC, the standard in both Japan and the US. Thus it was not coincidental that the Japanese manufacturers came to dominate the US market but not the European. Whether an incompatible HDTV standard would protect the European industry in the 1990s was yet to be seen.

Industrial Policy and the Development of HDTC Standards

NHK and the Development and Promotion of HiVision

HDTV was developed in Japan through a joint effort of government and industry that included broadcasters, manufacturers, and providers of programmes. Japanese researchers began work on high definition systems in the late 1960s. NHK embarked upon the development of high-definition television by contributing 15 percent of the $500 million total that, in 1970, launched a joint R&D effort with manufacturers such as Sony, Toshiba, and NEC.[18] For NHK, HDTV was a way both to justify higher viewers' fees to the Japanese Diet and to compete against emerging private stations. Television manufacturers were interested because they saw an opportunity to renew the saturated market for television receivers. In all, manufacturers added at least $670 million of their own funds to the government's $400 million to support HDTV research and development.[19] As the result of their efforts, Sony, Matsushita, Hitachi, and NHK were able to demonstrate a working HiVision system in 1981. By 1984, they had reached agreement on the MUSE transmission standard.

The Japanese have a liberal patent policy for their HiVision production standard with no discrimination among countries. There are no royalties for patents related to the production standard or to conversion between HiVision and existing systems. This strategy was intended to gain *de facto* acceptance of the system standard with royalties reaped later from the MUSE transmission system.[20]

To secure adoption of their production standard, the Japanese promoted it in the United States, where they lobbied for support from the relevant US standards-making bodies, and from CBS with whom Sony had existing commercial relationships.[21] CBS in turn lobbied the State Department, which represents the US at the CCIR.

The Japanese also attempted to gain support for their standard by supplying equipment to important users. For example, equipment was loaned on a trial basis starting in 1982 to Hollywood directors such as Francis Ford Coppola.[22] Through the CBS technical centre in Rome, Sony obtained the support of the Italian state broadcasting network RAI, which was lent HiVision production equipment. Another production system was sold to Captain Video, the Paris advertising production house.[23]

By the time of the May 1986 plenary session of the CCIR in Dubrovnik, the Japanese had garnered enough support to propose that HiVision be adopted as the worldwide production standard. The Japanese proposal was supported by the US, Canada, Brazil, and Chile. However, the Europeans, together with a number of African countries, the USSR, Brunei, and Iran, successfully blocked the effort. A decision on a standard was postponed at least until the May 1990 plenary session.

Despite the setback in Dubrovnik, the Japanese continued their effort to establish HiVision as the *de facto* production standard and to gain support for adoption of the MUSE transmission standard as well. The HiVision Promotion Council, comprised of the Ministry of Posts and Telecommunications, broadcasters, and manufacturers, organized a project to record the 1988 Summer Olympics from Seoul in HiVision and to distribute the production via satellite to public viewing locations in Japan. In conjunction with this event, NHK negotiated an agreement with the South Korean government to license HiVision technology to four South Korean manufacturers, including Samsung.[24] NHK also lobbied the Chinese and Soviet governments to consider adopting the Japanese HDTV standard.

The Japanese used substantial public funds to support HDTV on other fronts as well. Manufacturing interests joined forces with the Ministry of International Trade and Industry (MITI) to target $400 million between 1988 and 1992 for the re-tooling of manufacturing plants to build cathode ray tubes in the 16:9 aspect ratio. MITI also funded 70 percent of an $80 million effort to develop large, flat screen technology for HDTV by 1995.[25]

Meanwhile, Sony and Matsushita set their sights on Hollywood studios and their libraries of films. Sony purchased Columbia with its 2,700-film library for $3.2 billion in 1989. Matsushita followed suit with the 1990 purchase of MCA for $6.13 billion.[26] The objective was to integrate quickly into software by transfering films to HiVision for either broadcast or high-definition videodisc viewing.[27] And to promote its production equipment, Sony encouraged Columbia to shoot productions in HDTV. This demonstrated the advantages of HDTV in post-production editing and special effects even though the productions would then have to be converted to 35 mm film for distribution.

For all of its efforts, however, NHK was not able to forge a united Japanese front. Perhaps as the result of NHK's overwhelming influence in the Japanese HDTV development process, private Japanese broadcasters countered in August 1989 by offering ClearVision broadcasts – a lower cost NTSC-compatible IDTV standard – and manufacturers followed suit with compatible equipment. Then, in August 1990, Japan Victor Company (JVC) joined the ranks of those displaying D2-MAC prototype receivers at the Internationale Funkausstellung in Berlin, Europe's biggest consumer electronics show.[28]

The FCC Policy Process

The US had a late start in HDTV research and development as a result of having less public support for industrial R&D, stricter antitrust regulations, and only one US-owned television manufacturer (Zenith).[29] It was only when it became clear that HDTV was being developed for satellite and, perhaps, cable transmission only that the US terrestrial broadcasters' interests catalyzed an American HDTV effort characterized as a government-directed patent race.

After a powerful lobbying effort and a petition to the FCC in February 1987, terrestrial broadcasters convinced the FCC to become actively involved in HDTV. The FCC's first step was to freeze both the allocation of new TV channels and the proposed reallocation of UHF channels to cellular telephony. In January 1988, the FCC established an Advisory Committee on Advanced Television Service, and in September 1988, the FCC announced that HDTV broadcasts would have to fit into the existing spectrum allocations of 6MHz. The FCC then announced in March 1990 that the HDTV signal would have to be simulcast in the 6MHz band between existing channels together with the NTSC signal.

The FCC said it would begin testing systems that fit these specifications in April 1991. The tests would be carried out by the independent but industry-funded Advanced Television Systems Committee (ATSC). Entrants would be required to pay a $1.4 million testing fee and to submit a proposal by June 1990. As long as entrants made the deadline and could develop a prototype in time to keep the testing schedule, any modifications to the original proposal could be made. Thus, when General Instrument filed an all-digital proposal two days before the FCC deadline, three of the other contenders were able to change to digital systems as well. The

FCC planned to render its decision in June 1993 based on the recommendations of the ATSC.

Since the licensing of proprietary technology is one of the requirements in the FCC standards approval process,[30] the goal for contenders in the US competition is to secure the most patents to be used in the eventual standard. Even though the patents would have to be licensed, the patent-holders would earn royalties whenever another manufacturer made a product based on its patent. At least one proponent suggested merging the best components of each proposal into an FCC system standard.[31]

Once the standard is selected, the FCC will offer each existing terrestrial broadcaster the option of an extra 6 MHz of spectrum space, which it must take up within three years. After that, the broadcaster has three years in which to begin simulcast HDTV/NTSC broadcasts, putting the market introduction for broadcast programmes no later than 1999. The FCC will require a phase-out of NTSC broadcasts over 15 years in order to reclaim the original 6MHz of the terrestrial broadcast spectrum and make it available for other uses in 2008.

Although the FCC became actively involved in HDTV in 1988, industry groups wanted a more comprehensive US industrial policy to catch up with the Japanese. In late 1988, they were feverishly lobbying the Commerce Department and Congress to release funds for HDTV research, to relax antitrust laws to allow research and production consortia, to decrease capital gains taxes, and to legislate a permanent R&D tax credit. By early 1990, a total of seven HDTV-related bills had been introduced in Congress and ten committees had held HDTV hearings.[32] Proposals included mandated use of US semiconductor chips and exclusive licensing rights to US companies. Arguments were cast in apocalyptic terms, with HDTV cited as the last make-or-break chance for the US electronics industry.[33] Proponents had the government's ear until the American Electronics Association put a $1.35 billion price tag on government support and got Commerce Secretary Mosbacher's ire in return for asking 'Uncle Sugar' for handouts.[34] In the end, they were unable to make their case. The only immediate funding came in the form of $30 million between 1989 and 1992 through the Defense Advanced Research Project Agency (DARPA) for research on display technologies suited for defense applications. In 1991, Congress extended funding to include $74.5 million through DARPA for more general research on 'high-definition systems'. Terrestrial broadcasters would have to foot the estimated $10–12 million per station conversion bill themselves.[35]

Given its progress on a separate transmission standard, the US changed its official position at the CCIR and withdrew its support for the Japanese standard at the CCIR Extraordinary Meeting of May 1989. With the adoption of several regional transmission standards thus appearing more and more likely, the US's move shifted debate within the CCIR from whether to adopt the Japanese or the European production standard to whether to establish a 'common image format' or 'common data rate' to facilitate the international exchange of programmes. A common image format would set virtually all the video parameters except for field frequency, the single irreconcilable parameter between 50 Hz and 60 Hz countries.

The fact that the US transmission standard was to be decided based on the terrestrial broadcasters' needs infuriated the computer industry and led to a second debate over the standard. Besides digital format, computer compatibility would be facilitated by a progressive scanning structure with square pixels and resolution defined in terms of lines per inch rather than lines per frame – the parameters used in computer graphics. The standard could increase its lifetime if it included the flexibility to adjust definition according the needs of the application in order to be compatible with new applications as they emerged.[36] This debate blocked any decision at the March 1990 Atlanta interim working party of the CCIR.[37]

At the 1994 CCIR plenary session, the issue of an international production standard will be taken up again. The US is expected to propose adoption of a common image format with progressive scanning and square pixels in the 16:9 aspect ratio.

Eureka and the EC-led Development of the MAC Packet

Just six months before the May 1986 plenary session of the CCIR in Dubrovnik, the Europeans began organizing their defence against the Japanese standard. Alerted by the state-run broadcaster TDF, the French Ministry of Industry took up the case just in time for the French government to let their opposition be known at the CCIR's preliminary meeting in Geneva. By the time of the Dubrovnik meeting, the European Community had formulated a common position against the Japanese proposal. The ostensible reason for the opposition was that the Japanese standard was not compatible with existing systems. Adoption of the Japanese production standard would render obsolete the existing base of TV sets and create a replacement market for an exclusively Japanese technology, possibly shutting out European television manufacturers. In addition, the field frequency would have to be converted from 60 Hz to 50 Hz to be compatible with European power sources which the Europeans claimed was an unfair burden. The Europeans succeeded in postponing any decision by the CCIR until the next plenary session, in 1990, by which time they hoped to offer a counter-proposal.

By mid-1986, the Europeans had started work on their own HDTV system. The research programme, led by the European TV makers Philips, Thomson, and Bosch, got 30 to 50 percent of its funding from the EC through the European Research Coordinating Agency (Eureka).[38] The goal of the HDTV programme, called Eureka 95, was to develop a European system that would allow the introduction of HDTV in an evolutionary way without stranding owners of PAL and SECAM receivers. It became apparent that the two-step approach would be the only way to sell enough receivers to assure broadcasters and programme producers the minimum audience needed to justify an investment in infrastructure conversion.[39]

With a budget of $450 million in public funds during the first four years, Phase 1 of Eureka 95 aimed to work out a European HDTV based on the MAC standard, and to produce prototypes in time for the May 1990 plenary session of the CCIR.

MAC was an all-European standard for direct broadcasting by satellite developed by the British Independent Broadcasting Authority from earlier German research. As early as 1982, the European Broadcasting Union had proposed that MAC be adopted as the standard for direct broadcasting by satellite in an attempt to bridge the PAL/SECAM divide in Europe.

Phase 2 of Eureka 95, with a budget of $150 million between July 1990 and December 1992, aimed to complete the development of the chain of hardware from production to reception in time to produce and distribute coverage of the 1992 Winter Olympic games from Albertville, France.

Like the Japanese, the Europeans have devoted significant public funds to their HDTV development programme. Eureka was not the only channel of funding. The EC invested $4.65 billion in eight years in Siemens, Thomson, and Philips through the JESSI[40] project to develop semiconductors, including ones specifically designed for HDTV. Through the RACE (Research on Advanced Communications for Europe) project, the EC pumped $690 million over eight years into research on broadband ISDN, which eventually will include fibre optic delivery of digital high-definition television.

Besides funding for R&D, the companies participating in the Eureka 95 project will have free access to patents developed as a part of the collaborative project. Third parties, such as Japanese manufacturers, must negotiate a licensing fee to produce equipment on the MAC standards. One proposal has been put forth for a licensing fee of $6 per decoder manufactured in Europe, $9.50 per unit manufactured outside the EC, and something in between if partly manufactured in the EC.[41]

While the Eureka consortium was working out the details of the MAC standards, the European Commission promulgated directives intended to support its adoption in Europe. To this end, in November 1986, the EC Commission put forth a directive requiring all high-powered broadcast satellites to use the MAC standard for television transmissions.

The Debate

EC member states had to agree to a new directive before the existing one expired on December 31, 1991. The deadline for drafting a proposed directive was June 3, 1991. The new directive had to satisfy the various industrial interest groups if a European standard was to be successfully set. The 1986 directive had two faults. First, it did not apply to low-powered telecommunications satellites, which have subsequently become able to transmit TV signals. Second, it had no provision to ensure that manufacturers would produce the equipment needed by broadcasters to comply with the directive. Events stemming from these faults set satellite broadcasters and manufacturers in conflict.

In June of 1988, when Rupert Murdoch announced that his Sky channel network would begin PAL broadcasts off the Société Européennes des Satellites'

(SES) Astra satellite, the seam that the original directive had tried to sew between manufacturers and broadcasters was ripped apart. SES had tried to purchase MAC equipment from Philips but was told none was available.[42] Since Sky could not broadcast in MAC as scheduled, it slipped right through the loophole in the 1986 directive by broadcasting off Astra, a low-powered telecommunications satellite not covered by the directive.

The license of Sky's competitor British Satellite Broadcasting (BSB), however, mandated that it use MAC. With the loss of Sky, MAC proponents thus pinned their hopes on the success of BSB. 'We knock on wood every morning, praying that BSB will be successful. If they go down, the MAC standard will go down,' said a senior vice-president at Thomson Consumer Electronics.[43] Due in part to delays in the availability of MAC equipment, however, BSB did not get on the air until March 1990. By the time Murdoch's Sky channel had signed up one million subscribers, BSB floundered with just 180,000.[44] In November 1990, BSB announced a merger with Sky. Murdoch stated that the new company, British Sky Broadcasting (BSkyB), would transmit exclusively in PAL off the Astra satellite when the mandatory simulcasting period imposed by British regulators ended on December 31, 1992. When BSB's orders for MAC decoders were cancelled, Philips laid off 250 employees at its Le Mans plant in France[45] and filed an $87 million lawsuit against BSB for its losses.[46] Thomson wrote off $38 million in unsellable D2-MAC dishes.[47]

Satellite broadcasters like Sky have built up an audience of 2.6 million households receiving broadcasts over 61 channels in PAL,[48] with 26 million more receiving their broadcasts via cable.[49] In contrast, only 170,000 households receive satellite broadcasts over the 13 D2-MAC channels.[50] A switch to MAC would not only compel PAL satellite broadcasters to incur substantial costs in converting transmission equipment, but it might also cause them to lose audience share since subscribers would have to change their reception equipment. Furthermore, broadcasters are wary of investing in MAC conversion now since another switch to digital may be required some years hence. It is for these reasons that BSkyB and other satellite broadcasters operating in PAL or SECAM oppose legislation forcing them to use D2-MAC.

Meanwhile, Philips and Thomson continued their efforts to promote adoption of the HD-MAC standard. In May 1990, the two companies announced an accord to pool $3.45 billion into a joint HDTV research and development programme. Thomson, with French government help, would contribute $1.55 billion while Philips would contribute $1.9 billion. The announcement was timed strategically, just one week before the May 1990 CCIR plenary session where a world production standard for HDTV, an issue that had been forestalled in 1986, was due to be reconsidered.

The CCIR plenary session in Dusseldorf resulted in agreement on most parameters of production and programme interchange. A decision on the two parameters most linked to transmission standards, the number of scanning lines and field frequency, was put off with a call for further study. Neither the HiVision nor the HD-MAC standard was endorsed, and consideration of digital HDTV was deferred.

Satisfied that it had blocked the Japanese in the CCIR, the European Commission went about promoting its own standard by making production equipment available. It established a European Economic Interest Group (EEIG), a separate legal entity in EC law allowing both public and private companies to form consortia to pool part of their economic resources while maintaining economic and legal independence. The Vision 1250 EEIG was launched in July 1990 with a $48 million annual budget funded one-third by the EC, one-third by national governments, and one-third by manufacturers and broadcasters. Comprised of fourteen electronics manufacturers, broadcasters, and programme producers, Vision 1250 set as its first goal the production and distribution of HD-MAC coverage of the 1992 Olympic Games and the Seville '92 World Expo.

To settle an earlier controversy over which standard would be used on the TVSAT-2 satellite over Germany, the French and German governments signed a memorandum of understanding in support of D2-MAC in August 1990. Only a month later, in complete disregard of that memorandum, German terrestrial broadcasters announced their intention to develop PAL Plus, an enhanced version of PAL.

While the European consensus supporting the D2-MAC transitional standard was unravelling, recent events in the US called into question the wisdom of the final stage high-definition standard, HD-MAC. In June 1990, General Instrument stunned industry observers by submitting to the FCC an all-digital proposal for the US transmission standard. The logic of the European two-step approach was to block the Japanese standard by forcing D2-MAC receivers into the marketplace quickly and thereby reserve the future for HD-MAC sometime between 1995 and 1997. But the logic assumed that all-digital HDTV was a distant dream. As digital HDTV became more of a reality, the argument for MAC began to crumble on its foundations.

In November 1990, while continuing to promote their part-analog standard in Europe, Philips and Thomson, together with their American partners in the Advanced Television Research Consortium, changed their US proposal to all-digital. All the other contenders for the US transmission standard except for the Japanese eventually either switched to digital or dropped out of the race.

The first European wide-aspect television receiver was made available on February 12, 1991, after Thomson introduced its Space System TV at a glittery Paris reception in La Défense the night before. In his remarks to the 4,000 invited guests, France's Minister of Industry Roger Fauroux proclaimed, 'we are meeting the Japanese challenge [and] stepping ahead.'[51] At $6,000, the 93 cm screen IDTV increased resolution by doubling the number of lines in the input signal to 1,250. While it could receive PAL and SECAM broadcasts and display them in wide-aspect format (by cutting off the top and bottom of the picture) it contained no advanced TV decoders and thus was not linked to any specific standard for HDTV. The separate D2-MAC decoder and satellite dish were priced at $900. Thomson geared up to make 1,000 sets per month at its Villingen plant in Germany, with tubes being sourced from its Anagni Videocolor plant in Italy. The ICs would be sourced from its Thomson-SGS subsidiary in Grenoble, France. About the same time, press reports speculated that negotiations were taking place between Eureka 95 members and Sony over licensing fees for the MAC patents. Other Japanese manufacturers adopted a wait-and-see attitude.[52]

Just a few hours before Thomson introduced its Space System TV, a skillfully leaked internal report of the French Ministry of Foreign Affairs made its way into that day's newspaper coverage. The report questioned the need for a D2-MAC transitional standard in the light of digital development in the US. 'Born at the beginning of the 1980s, the analog MAC family was introduced much too late as a transmission standard . . . The hour of truth for . . . D2-MAC is thus very near. Europe . . . must prepare itself from this moment on to envisage the eventual end of D2-MAC . . .'[53] The head of Thomson Consumer Electronics retorted, 'I didn't know that there were any competent electronic engineers at the Ministry of Foreign Affairs.'[54] In later newspaper editions, a government spokesperson claimed, 'That study does not reflect the policy of the Ministry of Foreign Affairs and does not at all correspond to the position of France.'[55]

By this stage, various interest groups had coalesced in the debate over the new EC Directive. Philips lobbied the European Commission to establish a much stricter directive and publically accused SES of sabotaging the European HDTV effort. On February 22, 1991, SES director general Pierre Meyrat responded at a press conference in Brussels by stating that both industry and consumers should be allowed to choose their own path to an HDTV standard and that D2-MAC was an unnecessary step along the way. Meyrat accused Philips of trying to mislead the Commission: 'There are 130 million homes with PAL TV sets,' he said, 'and no HDTV system is compatible with any of them.'[56] 'Millions of TV screens throughout Europe will go blank.'[57]

The EC Commissioner for research and technology, Filipo Maria Pandolfi, began an arduous task to find common ground between the various industry groups. On February 28, 1991 representatives of the consumer electronics industry, broadcasters, and governments began meetings in Brussels with Pandolfi to discuss strategy, burden sharing, and the implications of digital HDTV in the US. Pandolfi's goal was to reach a consensus in time to present a draft directive for the EC telecommunications ministers to consider at their meeting on June 3.

On April 9, the EC Commission launched an enquiry to determine the legality of French state aid for Thomson after France's Minister of Industry announced a plan to pump $345 million in cash into Thomson and to give it a $103.4 million research grant for HDTV. Thomson's ability to fulfill the financial obligation of its joint research project with Philips was thus called into question.

Pandolfi's attempts to forge consensus in the industry working group have reached an apparent impasse. Nevertheless, EC telecommunications ministers are scheduled to meet on June 3 to consider Pandolfi's draft of the proposed directive. In the interim, companies such as BSkyB, Philips, and Thomson have much to consider.

- What is at stake for each of the players?
- What arguments can each put forth to convince the EC to take its interests into account?
- Keeping in mind its policy goals, what options does the EC have?
- How can each of the players best position itself to emerge in good shape regardless of which scenario ensues?
- Depending on what happens, how should each of the players respond?

Glossary

analog	An analog signal carries data in the form of a wave that varies constantly with its source.
aspect ratio	The ratio of width to height of a television screen. Today's television screens have an aspect ratio of 4:3 – the same as movies at the time that standard was selected. A 16:9 ratio would better accommodate the proportions of most movies today.
bandwidth	The measure of the amount of electromagnetic spectrum needed to transmit a signal in terms of megahertz. The more information being transmitted through a channel, *ceteris paribus*, the higher capacity bandwidth required.
broadband ISDN	Broadband Integrated Services Digital Network. A fibre optic network for transmission of wide bandwidth voice and data communications.
CCIR	Comité Consultatif International de Radio-Diffusion/International Radio Consultative Committee. The voluntary standard-setting committee of the International Telecommunications Union, part of the United Nations.
chrominance	The part of the video signal indicating saturation and hue of colour.
component signal	A signal in which the two chrominance signals and the luminance signal are sent separately.
composite signal	A signal in which the chrominance parts of the television signal are sent together with the luminance signal, as in existing television standards.
D-MAC	The transitional standard adopted in Britain for transmission by satellite. Because it has twice as many digital audio channels as D2-MAC, it has a wider bandwidth and can only be used for satellite transmissions.
D2-MAC	The European transitional transmission standard to HDTV, officially adopted by France and Germany. The D refers to the duo-binary nature (-1, 0, 1) of the DATV and digital

audio portions of the signal. The 2 refers to the fact that these portions of the signal are halved to fit better into the bandwidth restraints of cable. This division means that D2-MAC has eight-channel sound, rather than the sixteen-channel sound of D-MAC. D2-MAC is nevertheless still too wide to be transmitted over a single terrestrial broadcast channel.

digital
A digital signal is made by sampling an analog signal at regular intervals and assigning each sample a numeric value. Regardless of what it conveys, any digital signal is sent in the binary code of computers, which is made up exclusively of 0s and 1s.

EEIG
European Economic Interest Group. A separate legal entity formed by a consortium of companies that allows companies, both public and private, to pool part of their economic resources while maintaining their economic and legal independence. Vision 1250 is one example.

Eureka
European Research Coordinating Agency.

FCC
Federal Communications Commission. The regulatory body of the US with jurisdiction over the airwaves.

fibre optic
Transmission of a signal using pulses of light conducted over an extremely thin, flexible thread of glass that has signal frequency capacity in the order of 1 billion MHz.

field frequency
The number of sweeps per second made by the electron beam. In an interlaced scanning structure, it is the frequency at which one-half of the scanning lines are drawn per second, because it takes two interlaced sweeps to make a complete picture, or frame. In a progressive scanning structure, one sweep equals one frame, and so the field frequency equals the frame rate. Up to about 80 MHz, a higher field frequency improves perceived resolution by reducing flicker.

forward compatibility
A characteristic of a standard that allows enough flexibility for it to evolve with new applications as they are developed. Also called extensibility.

frames per second
The number of complete pictures per second. With an interlaced scanning structure, it is necessarily one-half of the field frequency in PAL/SECAM (25 frames per second) and NTSC (30 frames per second) systems. 35 mm film runs at 24 frames per second.

HD-MAC
The European HDTV production standard.

Hertz
The measure of frequency per second, abbreviated Hz; e.g. a 60-hertz phenomenon is something occurring 60 times each second.

HiVision
The Japanese HDTV production standard.

hyperband cable	Cable delivery systems of wider channel bandwidth capacity (12 MHz) than standard cable systems (7–8 MHz).
interlaced scanning structure	In scanning an image that is broken up into horizontal lines, every other line is scanned in two sweeps. Assuming the same field frequency, this method results in more flicker but requires less bandwidth than a progressive scanning structure (see below).
JESSI	Joint European Submicron Silicon Programme.
luminance	The part of the TV signal indicating intensity of light.
MAC Packet	Multiplexage Analogique en Composante/Multiplexed Analog Components. The European hierarchical family of compatible standards for HDTV, from the intermediary D2-MAC standard to the high-definition, HD-MAC standard.
multimedia	A general term, used in this context to describe a computer that can process video, audio, and text data from various sources.
MUSE	Multiple Sub-Nyquist Encoding. The Japanese HDTV transmission standard.
NHK	Nippon Hoso Kyokai. The state broadcasting company of Japan.
NTSC	National Television Standards Committee; used to mean the US television standard.
PAL	Phased Alternation by Line. The television standard developed by AEG Telefunken in 1962.
pictures per second	See frames per second.
pixel	Picture element.
progressive scanning structure	In scanning an image that is broken up into horizontal lines, every line is scanned sequentially, one after the other, such that one sweep of the image includes all the lines. This method results in higher resolution by reducing flicker but requires more bandwidth.
RACE	Research and development in Advanced Communications technologies in Europe.
Retrocompatibility	A characteristic of a standard that allows it to be compatible with the previous vintage of product.
SECAM	Séquentiel à Mémoire. The television standard developed by the French between 1958–60.

Notes

1. Market share is based on UNESCO estimates of number of viewers in each standard in 1988. Of the estimated 280 million NTSC viewers, 195 million are in the US, 14 million in Canada, and 71 million in Japan – of the estimated 150 million SECAM viewers, 22 million in France, 107 million in the former USSR, and 22 million in Eastern

Europe. Thirty million of the estimated 270 million PAL viewers are found in the UK, 23 million in Western Germany, 22 million in Italy, and 13 million in Spain.

2. Each channel in the UHF (ultra high frequency) part of the radio spectrum is divided by five channels because of the increased tendency for interference in that range. These extra channels are commonly referred to as taboo channels.

3. Broadband is a general term used to describe advanced applications that require enormous bandwidth. In this context, we will use it to connote uncompressed HDTV transmissions. Regarding ISDN, we are referring to broadband ISDN (B-ISDN) over optical fibres, since it does not seem likely that today's ISDN standard would be able to support full-motion video in a multimedia context over standard, twisted-pair wires.

4. Mitsubishi has a HiVision to NTSC downconverter on the market for $148, and other companies are working on developing downconverters as well. 'A Broadcasting Delay', *Electronics* (October 1990): p. 52.

5. In Europe, the average cable penetration rate is 16 percent, while only 3 percent of European television households have satellite receivers. The rate varies widely between European countries, from near full penetration in the Netherlands and Western Germany to virtually no cable in Italy, Spain, Greece, and Portugal. A full 80 percent of European television households receive signals exclusively by over-the-air broadcast. Source: *The Impact on Consumers of the Proposed Council Directive on the Adoption of Standards for Satellite Broadcasting of Television Signals*, Coopers & Lybrand, 1991.

6. IDTVs are also sometimes called Intermediate Digital TVs, because they use digital processing to translate an image into higher definition. If improvements are also made at the broadcasting end, they are often called EDTVs (for extended or enhanced definition television, although sometimes a distinction is made by reserving extended definition TVs for those in 16:9 aspect ratio). The source of the confusion is that official classifications vary depending on whether they are those of the EC, the CCIR, the Japanese Telecommunications Technology Council, or the FCC (which simply calls everything advanced television). Thus, while the terms are and often can be used interchangeably, we will use solely IDTV for the purposes of this case.

7. The sound signal also could be sent in four-channel monophonic sound, or eight-channel low quality sound. This has important applications in Europe, since different language tracks could be sent simultaneously in each channel, and the viewer could select which language desired at the flip of a switch.

8. The Thomson Space System IDTV interpolates extra lines between existing ones using a technique called line shuffling. Although this results in the same number of lines as HD-MAC, it does not result in the same quality of resolution.

9. Philips EDTV 100 Hz.

10. Ford UK, for example, purchased $10 million of Sony HDTV equipment in order to use HDTV CAD to cut down the design cycle of a new car from 64 to 48 months. Referred to in 'Japan's HDTV: What's wrong with this Picture?' *Business Week* (April 1, 1991): p. 52.

11. Cablevision Systems planned to test HDTV delivery by cable in selected test markets starting September 1991. See 'HDTV on cable in September', *Television Digest* (March 18, 1991): p. 8.

12. For example, Zenith has stated that if its standard is selected, it could have HDTV sets on the market by 1994. Comments of Jerry Pearlman, chairman and president of Zenith, quoted in 'Zenith goes digital for HDTV', *Appliance Manufacturer* (March 1991): p. 65.

13.   Although liquid crystal display (LCD) technology is under the most research at present, it is very difficult to manufacture in large sizes since a single defect would black out an entire pixel. Thus, there are also several other technologies being explored at the moment. Japanese manufacturers predicted that the market for advanced screen technologies would be $8 billion by 1995. Such display systems have wide-ranging applications besides HDTV; most importantly, in portable computers, but also in air traffic control and defence, to name just two examples. 'High Definition Look at the Future', *Electronic News* (December 3, 1990): p. 4.

14.   'La Haute Définition: Évolution ou Révolution?' *Science et Technologie* (April 1990).

15.   Hiroshi Akiyama quoted in 'Japan HDTV: Static Before the Start', *International Herald Tribune* (October 9, 1991).

16.   '1,250/60 Standard Wins', *Television Digest* (July 30, 1990): p. 6.

17.   For a summary of the open architecture receiver concept, see Richard Jay Solomon, 'On the Threshold of a Dream', *Byte* (June 1990).

18.   'TV's High-Stakes, High-Tech Battle', *Fortune* (October 24, 1988): p. 116.

19.   Estimate of Japanese companies' financial contributions to HDTV R&D vary widely, with some as high as $1.3 billion. Heather Hazard, HBS study, p. 13.

20.   Jacques Pelkmans and Rita Beuter, 'Standardization and Competitiveness: Private and Public Strategies in the EC Color TV Industry', ed. H. Landis Gabel, *Product Standardization and Competitive Strategy* (Amsterdam: North Holland, 1987): p. 202; Adam Watson Brown, 'The Campaign for High Definition Television: A Case Study in Triad Power', *Euro–Asia Business Review* (April 1987): p. 6.

21.   The relevant standards-making bodies that initially supported NHK were the Society of Motion Picture and Television Engineers (SMPTE), which represents the production industry, and the Advanced Television Systems Committee (ATSC), which represents both manufacturers and broadcasters. A joint venture between CBS and Sony to distribute records in Japan is attributed as the basis for their cooperation in HDTV, along with CBS's ownership of patents for tape-to-film transfer. See A. W. Brown, p. 7.

22.   Coppola's latest film, *Bram Stoker's Dracula*, uses HDTV production techniques for some of its special effects.

23.   Adam Watson Brown, p. 8.

24.   'NHK: A Tale of Dreams', *Tokyo Business Today* (November 1988): p. 47.

25.   'High-definition Television is Rallying a Digital Revolution', *Business Week* (January 30, 1989): p. 47.

26.   'Big Mat goes to Hollywood', *Business* (UK: December 1990): p. 87.

27.   See, for example, 'Why Sony is Plugging into Columbia', *Business Week International* (October 16, 1989): pp. 23–24.

28.   Hervé Marchal, p. 82.

29.   The importance of ownership is, however, debatable. Zenith, though US-owned, manufactures its TVs in Mexico, while most television manufacturing done in the US if by foreign-owned companies.

30.   Heather A. Hazard & Herman P. Daems, 'Technical Standards and Competitive Advantage in World Trade: The Case of Television' (undated): p. 54.

31.   Jae Lim, head of MITI's Advanced TV Project, suggested that the proponents form a National Television Alliance in *Television Digest* (April 22, 1991): p. 4.

32.   Cynthia A. Beltz, 'How to Lose the Race: Industrial Policy and the Lessons of HDTV', *The American Enterprise* (May/June 1991): p. 23.

33.   Referred to in 'Political Lightning Rod', *Electronics* (October 1990): p. 57. Indeed, the

US government's Office of Technology Assessment forecast the entire HDTV market, including chips, transmission systems, and receivers, to be worth $12 billion by the year 2003.

34. *Wall Street Journal* (June 6, 1990): p. 1. Quoted in Hazard, HBS study, p. 10. By September 1990, the AEA had performed a climb-down and learned not to include specific funding levels in its recommendations.

35. Or, stations could spend an estimated $1.5–2 million to be able to pass through a network feed. Results of the PBS and CBS studies are discussed in 'HDTV Cost Estimate Cut', *Television Digest* (October 8, 1990): p. 6. Although widely quoted, these estimates could be lowered, since the lower power of digital transmission would mean fewer stations needed new towers. Furthermore, all estimates are initial prices and do not take into account potential cost reduction in volume production.

36. In short, an open architecture that is scaleable and extensible.

37. Richard Jay Solomon, 'HDTV: Digital Technology's Moving Target', *Intermedia* (March–May, 1990).

38. E. Cohen, p. 319.

39. 'L'Aventure de la Télévision Haute Définition', *Télécoms Magazine*, No. 34 (May 1990).

40. Joint European Submicron Silicon program.

41. 'Favorable EC Ruling over Standard Expected', *Electronic World News* (February 18, 1991): p. 3.

42. The delay in MAC equipment may be attributable in part to the fact that Britain had split off from continental Europe with its D-MAC variant.

43. Comments of Ronald Blunden in 'Power game with too much to lose', *Financial Times* (London: July 17, 1990): p. 12.

44. Source: Continental Research. Quoted in Karel Cool and Ingemar Dierickx, 'British Sky Broadcasting (BSkyB)' (Fontainebleau, France: INSEAD-CEDEP, 1992).

45. 'Philips: En Panne Pour le DMAC', *Electronique-Actualités* (November 16, 1990): p. 2.

46. 'Philips in £50 million claim against Sky and BSB', *The Daily Telegraph* (London: November 29, 1990): p. 27.

47. 'MAC attack', *The Economist* (March 16, 1991): p. 71.

48. 'This Satellite Company Runs Rings Around Rivals', *Business Week* (February 11, 1991): p. 52.

49. 'Broadcasters Clash over Satellite Rules', *New Scientist* (March 9, 1991): p. 14.

50. Data from CIT Research (London) quoted in 'MAC attack', *The Economist* (March 16, 1991): p. 71.

51. 'Widescreen HDTV set – Europe now, US in 1992?' *Television Digest* (February 18, 1991): p. 12.

52. 'Favorable EC ruling Over Standard Expected: Backers of D2-MAC May Get a Lift', *Electronic World News* (February 18, 1991): p. 3.

53. 'Selon un rapport du ministère des affaires étrangères: La stratégie européenne pour la télévision haute définition devrait être réorientée', *Le Monde* (February 12, 1991): p. 19.

54. Bernard Isautier in 'Le D 2 Mac et le "poil à gratter"', *Le Figaro* (February 13, 1991).

55. 'Le gouvernement minimise le rapport mettant en cause la norme D2 Mac', *Le Monde* (February 14, 1991).

56. 'Broadcasters Clash over Satellite Rules', *New Scientist* (March 9, 1991): p. 14.

57. 'EC Fine-tunes HDTV Standard', *Marketing* (June 6, 1991): p. 4.

High-definition Television in Europe

Philips Consumer Products

H. Landis Gabel and **Olivier Cadot**

Philips Consumer Products is a division of the Philips Group, Philips NV, a publically traded, $28 billion multinational enterprise headquartered in the Netherlands. Founded over 100 years ago, Philips has traditionally had a reputation for strength and stability. In recent years, however, it has been on shaky ground. Since 1987, the company has been undergoing a massive restructuring, the full benefits of which have yet to be realized.

When Cornelius Van der Klugt took over as Chairman in 1986, Philips made everything from toothbrushes to defence electronics. Through a management shake-up, sell-offs, 24,000 lay-offs, and extensive streamlining of product lines, Van der Klugt focused Philips on four core businesses: consumer electronics, lighting, computers, and chips. This restructuring, however, was not sufficient to forestall the effects of recession. During Van der Klugt's tenure, net margins failed to exceed 2 percent and, indeed, hit a ten-year low of 0.9 percent in 1989. In May 1990, Philips stock dropped 11 percent in one day upon the announcement that first quarter profits had plummeted to $3.25 million from $121 million the year before. In a move intended to placate investors, the board of directors forced Van der Klugt to retire one year ahead of schedule and speedily replaced him with his hand-picked successor, Jan Timmer.

Upon taking charge on July 1, 1990 Timmer announced 'We are going to change the way we work',[1] and initiated Operation Centurion, a bold attempt to transform Philips' feudal corporate culture into that of a dynamic international competitor. 'We must learn the real value of money,'[2] Timmer lectured managers in an effort to get them to cut costs and focus on profits. Further rationalizations would be tied to performance so that Philips will concentrate only on what it does best. As one managing director explained, the new 'approach is to fight on what

This case was written by Pamela Denby, Research Associate, under the supervision of H. Landis Gabel, Professor at INSEAD, and Olivier Cadot, Assistant Professor at INSEAD. This is a satellite case to accompany 'High-Definition Television in Europe'.
Copyright © 1993 INSEAD, Fontainebleau, France.

we're good at. Not on what other people are good at.'[3] Recently, Timmer promised to resign if the company did not turn around soon.

Timmer had earned a reputation as a turnaround specialist during his 39-year career at Philips, particularly after his last assignment before becoming chairman: revitalizing the group's largest division, consumer electronics, which accounts for 40 percent of group sales. Through a massive restructuring, including 7,000 job cuts, Timmer increased profitability dramatically and brought the consumer electronics division to number two status in the world (behind Matsushita), second in the US, and first in Europe.

The success of the consumer electronics division, however, has been encumbered by lacklustre performance in the group's other divisions. Margins have been shaved in the traditionally profitable lighting division by a price war with Siemens and General Electric. In addition, the recession in the US combined with exchange rate movements during 1990 hit the lighting division particularly hard. Most significant, however, are the huge losses in the computer and semiconductor divisions, which together made up 45 percent of the group's sales. Prospects for 1991 are uncertain due to the Gulf War, but first quarter profits of $68 million were higher than expected and the stock has rebounded somewhat.

Philips has systematically sold off non-performers since the start of Operation Centurion. 'We must stop labelling something "strategic" as a cover-up for mal-performance,' says Timmer.[4] Although number one in the European semiconductor market with the prospect of sourcing its own chips for HDTV, the substantial losses in semiconductors prompted Philips to call a retreat from that sector. Philips laid off 4,000 workers from the chip division in 1989 after its world market share slipped from 3.4 percent in 1988 to 3 percent in 1989. Many of the current restructuring's job reductions of between 45,000 and 55,000 by the end of 1991 will come from the computer and semiconductor divisions. In September 1990, Timmer announced that Philips would withdraw from the memory-chip programme of the JESSI Mega-Project and would halt its own SRAM production. Furthermore, Philips sold off much of its defence manufacturing business to Thomson and has been looking for a buyer for its ailing computer division.

From now on, Philips will look for joint ventures to source key components it cannot make profitably, such as semiconductors. One starting point might be the 35 percent stake in the components subsidiary of Matsushita that Philips has held since 1952. Another may be through its collaborative R&D effort with Thomson. 'For 95 years, we did everything on our own,' explained senior vice-president for video products Peter Groenenboom. 'Now the technology jumps are too big and risky.'[5]

After the video cassette recorder (VCR) debacle, Philips earned a reputation for inventing new technologies only to have other companies reap the profits. The company took a similar beating with audio cassettes and CDs. Known within the company as the 'Gerard and Anton syndrome', the gulf between research and profitable commercialization reportedly dates back to Anton Philips, who founded the company, and his brother, Gerard, who was in charge of research. Through

Operation Centurion, Timmer has tried to ameliorate this problem through forming 'concern' product committees.

Philips is counting on several new products in the pipeline to pull it out of its doldrums, including HDTV. In the spring of 1992, Philips is planning to introduce the digital compact cassette, which it co-developed with Matsushita and for which it has already lined up several software deals. As with CDs, Philips probably stands to earn the most profits from software, through the deals and from its 80 percent-owned Polygram records division. In addition, after eight years and perhaps $500 million of R&D, Philip's much-vaunted Interactive Compact Disc is scheduled for an autumn 1992 European market introduction.

Philips plans to introduce its wide-screen MAC receiver in the summer of 1991 and an HD-MAC version in 1995. The large-screen segment of the television receiver market has seen a growth in demand in recent years. Of the 20 million colour TV sets sold annually in Europe, however, only 1 percent are in a comparable size category to Philips' wide-screen MAC receiver. Although demand is small now, the promise of HDTV is so far-reaching that it could revive the floundering European consumer electronics industry, including Philips. 'That is why the Japanese have targeted HDTV as a key strategic technology. They wish to dominate tomorrow's economic world,' according to Peter Groenenboom.[6]

Philips has invested a significant amount of capital in the European HDTV standard, perhaps $250 million so far. About one-third of Philips HDTV R&D has been funded by the EC. In its joint HDTV R&D effort with Thomson, Philips has promised to invest $1.9 billion more. The funds that Thomson expects from the French government to cover its part, however, may be limited by what the EC Commission's Competition Directorate determines as legitimate behaviour for government shareholders.

Concurrent with its R&D in the European HDTV standard, Philips has been involved in other activities that are not necessarily linked. The 100 Hz field frequency of its MAC receiver, for example, improves the quality of any picture, including PAL and SECAM, and has already been introduced as a feature in Philips' 'flicker-free' line. Much of its HDTV R&D activity has been in studio production equipment, advanced flat panel displays, integrated circuits, and wide-screen CRTs. Philips is working together with Thomson on liquid crystal display (LCD) screen technology in an effort to catch up with the Japanese. Philips has also put R&D in both Pal Plus in Europe and digital TV through its US proposal.

Notes

1.   *Business Week* (November 12, 1990).
2.   'Philips' Big Gamble', *Business Week* (August 5, 1991): p. 17.
3.   Barrie Mead quoted in *Marketing* (April 11, 1991).
4.   'Philips' Big Gamble', *Business Week* (August 5, 1991): p. 17.
5.   Ibid., p. 18.
6.   'Satellite groups' merger clouds HDTV picture', *Financial Times* (December 3, 1990).

High-definition Television in Europe

Thomson Consumer Electronics

H. Landis Gabel and **Olivier Cadot**

> Free-trade doctrine . . . rested on the notion that competitive advantages were
> given out fairly by God – Portugal made wine, England cloth, and so forth –
> for the benefit of the whole world market. But when you get to high tech,
> anyone with the necessary will and means can grab the advantage. Once they
> have it, they can keep it.
>
> So let's forget about Adam Smith and David Ricardo. Comparative
> advantage is not an excuse sent by God for being subdued. It's something to
> be conquered or, in our case, recovered. And for that you need money and
> time, which equals protection.
>
> *Alain Gomez, Chairman of Thomson[1]*

Thomson Consumer Electronics is part of Thomson SA, a multinational enterprise
nationalized by the French government in 1981. When President Mitterrand
appointed Alain Gomez as Chairman and CEO in 1982, Thomson was a sprawling
industrial conglomerate on the verge of bankruptcy.[2] Gomez has since transformed
it dramatically by selling off 20 product areas, trimming costs, and cutting jobs,
mostly in Europe. 'I did not have to shake them out of the trees,' Gomez said about
the lost employees. 'Most of them were already senile and fell out on their own.'[3]
Today, Thomson's activities are focussed on two core businesses: Thomson
Consumer Electronics and Thomson-CSF (defence electronics), which account for
44 percent and 49 percent of the group's activities, respectively.[4] Both are what
Gomez considers strategic industries. 'You can always buy more from other
companies if you can develop and produce yourself what they might be selling,'
according to Gomez. However, 'if you are out of the game, they will blackmail you'.[5]

Thomson Consumer Electronics (TCE) became a world competitor in

---

*This case was written by Pamela Denby, Research Associate, under the supervision of
H. Landis Gabel, Professor at INSEAD, and Olivier Cadot, Assistant Professor at INSEAD.
This is a satellite case to accompany 'High-definition Television in Europe'.
Copyright© 1993 INSEAD, Fontainebleau, France.*

211

television manufacturing under Gomez's tenure primarily through acquisition of market share. TCE is now first in the US market for television receivers, second in Europe (behind Philips) and third in the world (behind Matsushita and Philips). Television manufacturing accounts for over one-half of TCE's activities. Half of TCE's revenues come from the US.

Gomez was rumored to be negotiating to sell TCE to either Daewoo or Toshiba back in 1987, when the opportunity to buy RCA and Ferguson presented itself. In late 1987, Gomez swapped $800 million in cash and Thomson's medical electronics group for General Electric's RCA television division. In his address via satellite to the 17,000 newly acquired employees, Gomez foretold of huge profits with HDTV on the horizon. 'This is our opportunity,' he proclaimed. 'We cannot miss it.'[6] As a result of the RCA acquisition, TCE gained a 22 percent market share and number one status in the American market. At the time, this made TCE number two in the world, behind Philips. Some industry analysts, however, scoffed at Thomson's move as a Pyrrhic victory. Before the deal, GE had spun off the prestigious David Sarnoff Research Center. Furthermore, Thomson had to postpone majority acquisition of RCA Licensing, which manages the patents of Thomson and RCA, until 1999. In exchange, GE is to post a $208 million payment to Thomson in 1991. Some analysts felt that Thomson got the raw end of the deal by getting stuck in an unprofitable market while GE was just shearing off dead weight.

In the European market, TCE has systematically bought out competitors, starting with the acquisition of AEG Telefunken in 1983 and followed by the purchase of Ferguson from Thorn-EMI in 1987. Such growth has not been without cost. Thomson carries a significant debt burden, estimated to be in the order of $2.13 billion. Meanwhile, it is investing about $30 million per year in HDTV research in the US in addition to its HDTV R&D activities in Europe. Thomson funds about one-half of its overall research budget; the rest is financed by the government.

In addition to televisions, Thomson has aggressively entered the semiconductor market, starting with the purchase of Mostek from United Technologies in 1985. In 1987, Thomson-CSF's semiconductor unit formed a 50:50 joint venture with Italy's state-owned IRI to form SGS-Thomson Microelectronics. The following year, SGS-Thomson acquired Thorn-EMI's undercapitalized semiconductor business, INMOS, in an asset swap. SGS-Thomson competes head-on with the Japanese in every segment of the chip business and has about 3 percent of the world market, ranking thirteenth in the world and second in Europe after Philips. Five percent is generally considered the critical market share needed to survive in the semiconductor industry, and thus Thomson has looked for further growth in this division. TCE has planned to source its HDTV chips from SGS-Thomson.

With prices of televisions falling faster than those of components, television manufacturers have been cutting costs and focussing on higher-end, more value added models. Even though the market for television receivers is generally considered saturated, the large-screen segment has been growing. In this market environment, Japanese manufacturers have initiated rounds of competitive price cuts in a fight for market share. Thomson's attempts to raise prices by 3 percent have thus met little success. TCE's 2.2 percent operating margin is much lower than Sony's 7 percent.

The recession in the US combined with 15 percent drop in the dollar in 1990 have hit TCE hard, with TV unit sales dropping between 4–5 percent. TCE is expected to post a $549 million loss in 1990, after writing off $365 million in restructuring costs. 1989 losses were $36 million. The defence division, on the other hand, is expected to post a $430 million profit in 1990, down from $526 million in 1989. With defence orders down due to the Gulf War, not to mention the long-term effects of the end of the Cold War, prospects for 1991 do not look good.

In sum, TCE has bet the farm on HDTV and on the European standard in particular. Thomson has said that having a proprietary European standard 'is indispensable, because it provides a six-month to one-year advance. This is essential for recouping research and development funds.'[7] As TCE senior vice-president Ronald Blunden put it, 'by having to go into a technology they didn't invent, in an environment where they need standards, the Japanese won't be able to test it on their home market. That is the fundamental keystone of our strategy.'[8]

In its HDTV effort, Thomson is counting heavily on the joint venture with Philips. But Philips is financially on shaky ground. Thomson, for its part, has been guaranteed funds from the French government. The French Ministry of Industry announced in April that the French government would recapitalize Thomson with $345 million and provide an HDTV research grant of $103.4 million. The actual amount of aid will be limited by what the EC Commission's Competition Directorate regards as legitimate behavior for government shareholders. The Directorate's mandate is 'to determine whether it contains state aid or represents the normal unaided provision of equity capital by a shareholder acting under normal market conditions.' In determining this, the Directorate will gauge the effects on Thomson's competitors within the EC, and much will depend on how the aid is used.

As a player in the HDTV sweepstakes, Thomson is looking at more than the bottom line. It's a matter of image. Thomson has been highly criticized for being slow in responding to the latest market trends regarding VCRs, CDs, and design tastes, such as flat- and large-screen TVs. Thomson still relies on JVC for building its VCRs through their 50:50 joint ventures in Berlin and Singapore. Until recently, Thomson functioned simply as a distributor for JVC's VCR products in Europe under the Thomson brand name. Thomson's head of planning and strategy has said that it will take until the end of 1995 for the company to 'completely master' VCR technology and that it does not expect to have an HDTV VCR prototype before 1997.[9] Being first on the market with wide-screen receivers is very important to Thomson's image, regardless of price and sales potential.

Even though demand for large-screen TVs has been growing, of the 20 million colour TV sets sold annually in Europe, only 1 percent are of comparable size to the Space System TV, which is priced 25 percent higher. With production currently at 1,000 sets per month, Thomson plans to introduce the Space System TV to the rest of the European market by the end of 1991. One Thomson source has said they expect to sell between 15,000–20,000 sets annually in the initial stages. The price includes installation and a three-year parts and labour warranty. As designed, the receivers are very bulky and would require so much customer support that it would affect profits for several years, according to a Thomson source.[10]

Thomson spent $90 million to retool its Videocolor CRT screen manufacturing plant for the wide aspect ratio of its Space System TV at an annual capacity of 300,000 units. Videocolor plans to produce 10,000 wide-screen units in 1991 and 100,000 in 1992. Traditionally, the plant in Anagni, Italy, has sourced 50 percent of its output to Thomson and the rest to other manufacturers. It might encounter difficulty in servicing more than the European market due to radiation regulations in the US, however. It is not clear whether Thomson's US plant can manufacture in 16:9.

Thomson has set a tentative 'internal' target for US introduction of Space System TVs of 1992, according to Bernard Isautier, CEO of Thomson's US division. However, he stated that the US model probably will not include all the features of the European version. He explained that 'the set is attractive enough by itself that it doesn't require special programs, and its availability should inspire special programming – such as 16:9 programs on videodisc or tape.'[11]

Although Thomson has invested much time and money in the European HDTV standard, it has been involved in other activities that are not necessarily dependent on its adoption. In Europe, for example, Thomson has been involved in R&D of Pal Plus and in digital TV. Thomson has gained significant expertise in digital HDTV through its participation in the US standards-making process. Thomson's US proposal has a limited chance of being selected by the FCC, however, since it was slow in switching to digital and thereby lost time in developing a prototype in time for testing.

Thomson's wide-aspect ratio screens are not necessarily dependent on any particular standard either. Furthermore, Thomson is building a plant to manufacture LCD screens in Grenoble. The joint R&D project with Philips looks likely to focus on LCD technology. The Japanese are far ahead in the field, having honed their expertise in the portable computer market. While Thomson will use its LCD screens initially for defence applications, it will gain valuable experience in what is generally considered the Holy Grail of HDTV components.

Notes

1. 'The Case Against Free Trade', *Fortune* (May 4, 1992): p. 32.
2. 'From National Champion to Global Competitor: An Interview with Thomson's Alain Gomez', *Harvard Business Review* (May–June 1990): p. 127.
3. 'France's High-Tech Warrior: Thomson's Alain Gomez is Targeting Consumer and Defense Electronics', *Business Week* (May 15, 1989): p. 29.
4. The other 7 percent is in white goods. All figures are from Thomson's 1990 Annual Report.
5. 'From National Champion to Global Competitor: An Interview with Thomson's Alain Gomez', *Harvard Business Review* (May–June 1990): p. 129.

6. 'France's High-Tech Warrior: Thomson's Alain Gomez is Targeting Consumer and Defense Electronics', *Business Week* (May 15, 1989): p. 32.
7. Comments of Jean-Philippe Lecat, counsellor to Thomson PDG Alain Gomez, in 'Poker Menteur', *Challenges* (France: July–August, 1991): p. 85.
8. Comments of Robert Blunden, senior vice-president of Thomson Consumer Electronics in 'Power game with too much to lose', *Financial Times* (London: July 17, 1990): p. 12.
9. Comments of Jacques Vannier in 'Power game with too much to lose', *Financial Times* (London: July 17, 1990): p. 12.
10. 'Power game with too much to lose', *Financial Times* (London: July 17, 1990): p. 12.
11. 'Widescreen HDTV Set – Europe now, US in 1992?' *Television Digest* (February 18, 1991): p. 12.

High-definition Television in Europe

British Sky Broadcasting

H. Landis Gabel and Olivier Cadot

British Sky Broadcasting is the second largest pay TV service in Europe, with 1.8 million subscribers. BSkyB is 50 percent held by Rupert Murdoch's News International Corporation. The other major shareholders are Pearson, Chargeurs, Granada, and Reed International. News International is a huge international media conglomerate of newspaper, magazine, and television properties primarily located in the United Kingdom, the US, and Australia.

For the last two years, Murdoch has been struggling to keep News International afloat while burdened with a heavy debt load of $8.39 billion at the end of 1990.[1] Losses from BSkyB have not helped matters. When Sky and British Satellite Broadcasting merged into BSkyB on November 3, 1990, they together were losing $15.6 million each week, $3.9 million of that from Sky.[2] While in the throes of cutting costs, renegotiating debt, and slashing overhead, the new company has been struggling to sign up enough subscribers to cover operating costs. Even before the merger, News International had been negotiating with creditors to reschedule its debt payments. In addition, Murdoch has been selling off media properties in a depressed market. Since the merger, BSkyB has been attempting to renegotiate its movie supply contracts with Hollywood studios in order to cut down programming costs.[3] Back in 1988, when Sky and BSB were aggressively competing for rights to broadcast movies with enough appeal to attract new subscribers, they bid up the price and signed expensive, long-term agreements with the major Hollywood studios. Although it is not certain whether BSkyB will be able to cut down the cost of its current contract obligations, in the future the merged operation will benefit from substantially lower programming costs. Analysts say that it will take at least two years of cost cutting before BSkyB can become profitable.[4]

This case was written by Pamela Denby, Research Associate, under the supervision of H. Landis Gabel, Professor at INSEAD, and Olivier Cadot, Assistant Professor at INSEAD. This is a satellite case to accompany 'High-definition Television in Europe'.
Copyright© 1993 INSEAD, Fontainebleau, France.

BSkyB's options for increasing revenue are dependent on signing up more subscribers. Currently, BSkyB earns 81 percent of its revenue through subscription fees and 19 percent from advertising.[5] The more subscribers the service has, the more revenue – plus the more it can charge to advertisers. Although BSkyB could raise subscription rates in an attempt to increase revenue, this may be counterproductive, since it has had trouble enough signing up subscribers. Its rates are significantly higher than comparable established pay TV services in the US, but they are slightly lower than those of the number one pay TV service in Europe, France's Canal Plus.

Although BSkyB is in a strong position among satellite TV services in the UK, it has had difficulty attracting audience share away from terrestrial broadcasters. The need for an individual satellite dish is a significant barrier for new subscribers, since cable is not prevalent in the UK. At this time, BSkyB has a very small but growing percentage of the British television audience: 4 percent now as compared to 2.3 percent in 1990. Its market penetration is about 10 percent with dish and cable combined. Of satellite homes, BSkyB has 25 percent of the audience. In comparison, the public broadcaster BBC, which is partly funded by user fees, has 45 percent share, while Independent Television (ITV) has the rest. ITV is financed by advertising and receives 97 percent of total television advertising in the UK. A major source of competition in the future may come from the launch of Channel 5, a commercial terrestrial channel expected to begin broadcasting in the mid-1990s.

As a fledgling, loss-making service with a significant debt burden, BSkyB is not in a good position to take on a switch to D2-MAC. What limited programming is available will cost more, although how much more is uncertain. Regarding transmission, the additional cost could be minimal, since BSkyB has the Marco Polo satellite that BSB used for its MAC transmissions. Perhaps fatal costs would be felt in customer confusion, however, since the majority of BSkyB's subscribers would have to switch reception equipment and may cancel in the process. Furthermore, if BSkyB transmitted all of its channels off Marco Polo, Murdoch would be subject to the UK antitrust restrictions that he evades by broadcasting off Astra, a Luxembourg satellite. Moreover, BSkyB would incur the opportunity cost of what it could sell the BSB satellite for after the mandatory simulcast period ends in December 1992.

There are some benefits that HDTV could provide to BSkyB. HDTV in the MAC packet of standards could provide BSkyB with a permanent competitive advantage over its terrestrial broadcast rivals. Since they could not broadcast in high definition if the MAC packet was the *de jure* standard, terrestrial broadcasters would wither away to the benefit of satellite broadcasters like BSkyB. By having a head start, BSkyB might have an advantage over new satellite broadcasting services as well.

With the advantages it provides in the presentation of movies and sports events, HDTV could persuade customers to sign on for BSkyB's services. However, most BSkyB subscribers are moderate-income families with children, who sign on to get the movie channel. For BSkyB's core audience, subscription to satellite TV costs less than taking the family out to the movies. BSkyB's audience would probably not want to pay more to receive movies in high definition, inasmuch as they would have to buy a new wide-screen TV. With most of its subscription fees coming from its movie channel, BSkyB has limited potential for increasing advertising revenue, since viewers subscribe precisely so that movies will not be interrupted. Furthermore, under BSkyB's current contracts for movie rights, it pays more as subscriptions increase. Growth in the non-movie audience will therefore be key to attracting more advertising, but HDTV does not offer much of a competitive edge in showing 'Flipper' reruns. BSkyB's future in presenting sports events is not certain, after its sports channel went off the air recently following an EC ruling in February 1991, that Eurosport no longer had exclusive rights to sports events covered by the European Broadcasting Union.[6]

In BSkyB's present financial situation, any delay in switching to HDTV of any standard will help by postponing the need to make the investment. The European standard is a double-edged sword in that it implies an investment now, in D2-MAC, and again, in digital. Considering the high cost and unreliability of satellites, BSkyB might prefer to use the compression techniques that have been developed in the process of HDTV to increase the number of channels rather than the quality. If BSkyB does switch to high definition, it may benefit from having the same standard as the US by being able to save on programming costs in conjunction with Murdoch's Fox television network. With benefits few and costs many, therefore, BSkyB may never want to switch to HDTV without the help of subsidies.

Notes

1. *Wall Street Journal* (October 22, 1991): Sect. A, p. 17.
2. 'British Sky Broadcasting Gives UK's Satellite TV a Costly Chance of Success', *Wall Street Journal* (January 25, 1991): Sect. B, p. 3F.
3. 'News Corp. Battles over Movie Pact', *Wall Street Journal* (April 10, 1991): Sect. B, p. 1.
4. *Wall Street Journal* (January 25, 1991): op. cit.
5. All figures are from N. Ward, *UK Television: BSkyB & The New Era in TV – Industry report* (UK: Smith New Court Securities PLC, July 1, 1992).
6. 'Eurosport Channel Goes Dark', *Wall Street Journal* (May 7, 1991): Sect. A, p. 19.

CASE 18

Alcatel, France Télécom and the French Government

Douglas Webber

Alcatel is the flagship subsidiary of the Alcatel–Alsthom holding group, France's second biggest company, active in telecommunications, energy and transport equipment (Exhibit 18.1). Until recently Alcatel, formerly the Compagnie Générale d'Electricité (CGE), was primarily a public switching manufacturer heavily dependent on the French market. Since the mid-1980s, however, it has transformed itself – through a number of sizeable international acquisitions – into the world's biggest supplier of digital switching equipment.

France Télécom, which was named the Direction Générale des Télécommunications (DGT) until 1988, is the state-owned monopoly operator of the public

Exhibit 18.1 *Alcatel–Alsthom: sales breakdown by sector, 1991 (percentage of total sales)*

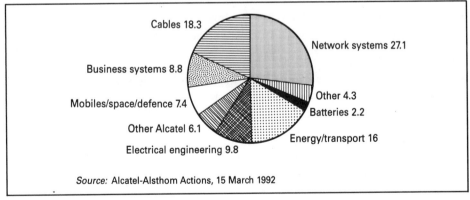

Cables 18.3

Network systems 27.1

Business systems 8.8

Mobiles/space/defence 7.4

Other 4.3

Batteries 2.2

Other Alcatel 6.1

Electrical engineering 9.8

Energy/transport 16

Source: Alcatel-Alsthom Actions, 15 March 1992

This case was written by Razeen Sally, Research Assistant, under the supervision of Douglas Webber, Professor at INSEAD. It is intended to be used as a basis for class discussion rather than to illustrate either effective or ineffective handling of an administrative situation.
Copyright © INSEAD, Fontainebleau, France 1993. Revised 1994.
Financial support from the INSEAD Alumni Fund European Case Programme is gratefully acknowledged.

219

telecommunications network in France. The DGT has had long-standing and intimate relations with Alcatel as a supplier of switching and transmission equipment. Alcatel remains France Télécom's main supplier, just as the latter remains Alcatel's main client.

Successive post-war French governments have had a track record of *dirigiste*, or strong state, intervention in the electronics sector. Alcatel, as the favoured national champion in telecommunications, has been the object of government industrial and technology policy measures in a sector shaped strongly by public procurement and other forms of state involvement.

The case focuses on two periods in order to highlight the evolution of the relationship between Alcatel, on the one hand, and France Télécom and the French government, on the other: first, the agreement, supported by the government, but opposed by the DGT, enabling Alcatel to acquire Thomson Télécommunications in 1983; and, second, the nature of Alcatel–France Télécom links in the late 1980s and early 1990s, in the wake of Alcatel's own internationalization and against a background of moves towards telecommunications deregulation in the European Community (EC).

The 1970s: State Leadership

Up to the 1970s France had one of the most backward telecommunications networks in Europe, with very low levels of telephone density and an appallingly poor quality of service to subscribers. Even during this 'pre-development' era, the DGT, as part of the Postal and Telecommunications (PTT) Ministry, as well as its research arm, the Centre National d'Études des Télécommunications (CNET), consistently favoured the building up of CIT, the precursor of the modern Alcatel, as a viable French-owned equipment supplier. Indeed, the DGT forced the more dominant manufacturers, particularly ITT and Ericsson, to license their technologies to CIT. But the main boost to CIT-Alcatel derived from its intimate cooperation with the CNET in the design and development of the first fully digital switch, the E10, ready for service in 1970, two years ahead of its nearest rival. Until then, CIT-Alcatel had had little research capability; the driving force of the cooperative project was the CNET's technical expertise. Now, with the help of the CNET, CIT–Alcatel had for the first time its own independent product line.

The appointment of Gérard Théry by President Giscard d'Estaing to head the DGT in 1974 ushered in a new era in French telecommunications. From this point, the DGT was much more generously funded, with public credits tripling between 1975–1980, compared with the previous quinquennium. The government's VIIth Plan also designated telecommunications as a priority area. The DGT underwent a major restructuring, strengthening its planning, control and resource allocation mechanisms, and reinforcing its autonomy within the PTT Ministry as well as from other parts of the state apparatus. A new unit, the DAII (Direction des Affaires Industrielles et Internationales), was created to deal with suppliers (Exhibit 18.2).

Exhibit 18.2 *Organization of the DGT (by 1988)*

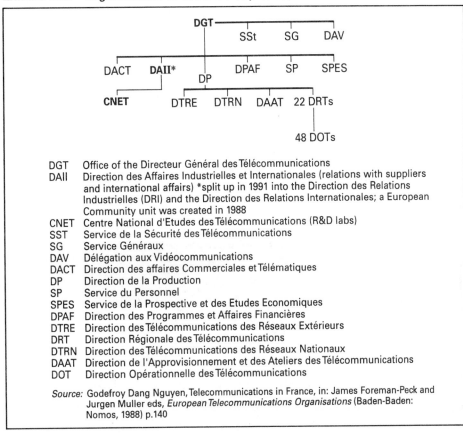

DGT Office of the Directeur Général des Télécommunications
DAII Direction des Affaires Industrielles et Internationales (relations with suppliers and international affairs) *split up in 1991 into the Direction des Relations Industrielles (DRI) and the Direction des Relations Internationales; a European Community unit was created in 1988
CNET Centre National d'Etudes des Télécommunications (R&D labs)
SST Service de la Sécurité des Télécommunications
SG Service Généraux
DAV Délégation aux Vidéocommunications
DACT Direction des affaires Commerciales et Télématiques
DP Direction de la Production
SP Service du Personnel
SPES Service de la Prospective et des Etudes Economiques
DPAF Direction des Programmes et Affaires Financières
DTRE Direction des Télécommunications des Réseaux Extérieurs
DRT Direction Régionale des Télécommunications
DTRN Direction des Télécommunications des Réseaux Nationaux
DAAT Direction de l'Approvisionnement et des Ateliers des Télécommunications
DOT Direction Opérationnelle des Télécommunications

Source: Godefroy Dang Nguyen, Telecommunications in France, in: James Foreman-Peck and Jurgen Muller eds, *European Telecommunications Organisations* (Baden-Baden: Nomos, 1988) p.140

From this base Théry set about reorganizing the supply industry: ITT and Ericsson were pressured to sell the bulk of their French subsidiaries to Thomson, the DGT being keen to introduce the latter as a major force to provide a competitive spur to Alcatel. With Thomson's entry into telecommunications, its share of the equipment market in France literally jumped overnight in 1977 from 0 to 40 percent!

The DGT was now in a position to administer a large-scale expansion of the telephone network, sourcing equipment from the two French-owned national champions. Massive orders were placed for Alcatel's E10 digital switching system as well as for Thomson's MT system, while, in developing both systems, both firms cooperated closely with the CNET.

By the end of this 'catch-up' phase, the French network had been transformed into one of the most modern and digitalized in the world: the number of main lines had trebled in the 1975–85 period and the technological and manufacturing capacities of Thomson and Alcatel had been substantially fortified in the process (Exhibit 18.3).

Exhibit 18.3

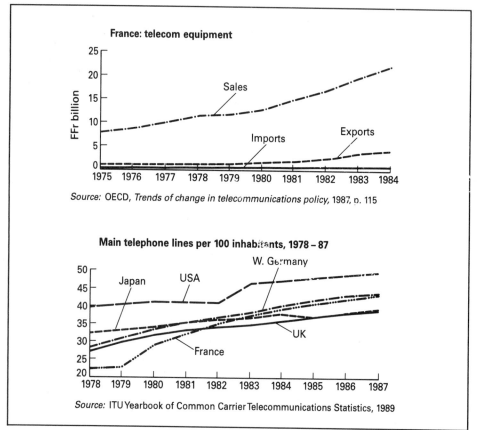

France: telecom equipment

Source: OECD, *Trends of change in telecommunications policy,* 1987, p. 115

Main telephone lines per 100 inhabitants, 1978 – 87

Source: ITU *Yearbook of Common Carrier* Telecommunications Statistics, 1989

The Early 1980s: the Zenith of State Intervention under the Socialists

The election of François Mitterrand as the first Socialist President of the Fifth Republic in 1981, followed soon after by the formation of a Socialist-Communist government with an overwhelming majority in the National Assembly, witnessed a marked change of direction in industrial policy. Six leading industrial concerns were nationalized, including CGE (Alcatel's holding group), Thomson and CGCT, ITT's remaining French subsidiary. State-owned firms now accounted for 30 percent of all industrial sales in France and over half of the electronics industry's production and R&D activities came under the government's wing. The incoming government was determined to pursue a policy of active industrial intervention, particularly in electronics, which was deemed to be 'strategic' for national competitiveness, security and technological independence. The sector was to be restructured in accordance with a *politique des filières* (policy of vertically integrated sectors) aimed at concentrating 'poles of competence' in specialized, vertically integrated state-owned firms. Thomson and Alcatel were to spearhead the national effort in telecommunications. Finally, 3–5 year planning contracts were signed in 1983 between each of the nationalized firms and the Ministry of Industry, committing the firms to reach certain medium-term objectives on investment, profitability, etc., in return for government support of their overall strategies and government financial aid. In fact, initially FFr 70 bn of aid was foreseen for the *filière électronique* programme between 1982 and 1986.

The DGT figured prominently in the new government's plans for the electronics industry. Its remit was broadened to encompass responsibility for the whole *filière électronique* programme, of which telecommunications was only a part. At the same time it was given the green light to launch various new projects that had been part of the *Plan Télématique* formulated in the late 1970s with the aim of taking the modernization of the telecommunications network beyond the digitalization phase to a range of 'telematic' products and infrastructures, such as videotex, an electronic phone directory, teletex, telecopiers, cable television and an Integrated Services Digital Network (ISDN), which combines many types of traffic – voice, data, video and text – on a single digital network. The DGT's revenues were also used to fund broad areas of industrial policy, amounting to nearly FFr 100 billion between 1982 and 1990. Much of this DGT funding was channelled via the Treasury of the Ministry of Finance into the nationalized firms, including Alcatel and Thomson, in the form of equity injections. In contrast to the DGT's direct procurement from and research funding for its suppliers, the DGT could not attach any strings to these funds. The DGT tried in vain to secure a plan from Alcatel on its use of such large-scale resources, at one stage threatening to withhold payment. However, Alcatel got its way by appealing directly to the President.

Despite the trauma of nationalization and the government's having replaced its Président Directeur Général (PDG – chairman and chief executive), Ambroise Roux, with his deputy, Georges Pébereau, Alcatel was in a confident mood: it was the only one of the nationalized groups in profit; its E10 digital switch was a proven success in France and had been ordered by over twenty countries; new markets in telecommunications were being explored; and small acquisitions were being made in the US, a market that Alcatel was keen to break into.

Thomson, on the other hand, was in a completely different situation. Its short experience in telecommunications had been far from happy: there were serious problems in integrating the subsidiaries inherited from ITT and Ericsson; it was widely believed that Thomson Télécommunications was more a creature of the DGT and the CNET than of its own parent company; its MT switching system was not proving to be as successful as Alcatel's digital E10. By 1982 Thomson was losing over $200 million in its telecommunications operations as well as being burdened with substantial excess manufacturing capacity and a cash drain associated with its attempts, inspired by the DGT, to develop a new digital switch. Thomson's difficulties in telecommunications were compounded by its diverse, poorly

Exhibit 18.4 *Companies' net profits (FFr m)*

	1981	1982	1983	1984
CGE	586	638	662	797
Thomson	−167	−2207	−1251	−35
CGCT	−29	−345	−555	−997

Source: Alan Cawson, Kevin Morgan, Douglas Webber, Peter Holmes, Anne Stevens, *Hostile Brothers: Competition and Closure in the European Electronics Industry* (Clarendon Press, Oxford, 1990), p. 132

integrated and loss-making activities in consumer electronics, components and medical electronics, as well as a slowdown in its defence electronics and armaments markets (Exhibit 18.4).

1983: The U-turn and Alcatel's Takeover of Thomson Télécommunications

By late 1982 it was apparent that the Keynesian reflationary experiment begun in 1981 by the Socialist-Communist government was not working. A U-turn in macroeconomic policy followed, emphasizing budgetary stringency. The Ministry of Finance cut back sharply on subsidies to the nationalized firms, with the electronics sector being particularly affected. At the same time, the PDGs of the nationalized companies protested strongly to the President at what they considered to be the unwarranted intervention of the Ministry of Industry in their corporate affairs, leading to the resignation of the minister, Jean-Pierre Chevènement, one of the chief proponents of an interventionist industrial policy. The President and the new Industry Minister, Laurent Fabius, subsequently gave a strong pledge to the PDGs of the state-owned firms that the government would respect their operational autonomy.

During the 1970s, under the powerful influence of its then PDG, Ambroise Roux, CGE had marked out fairly clear lines of strategy for its constituent businesses, with the ultimate aim of catching up with Siemens. Georges Pébereau, then responsible for Alcatel, was convinced that the market for public switching equipment, the core of the telecommunications industry, would become increasingly concentrated, with perhaps only three major suppliers left worldwide by the year 2000. He thought that Siemens and AT&T would be among these three, and began to formulate a long-term strategy to ensure that Alcatel would be up there with them.

Pébereau concluded that Alcatel could survive in its core markets only as an international player with world scale. Being too small at the time, it could gain sufficient critical mass only through acquisitions, both at home and abroad – they represented the sole means of prising open protected national markets. This strategy of international expansion could only succeed, however, if Alcatel safeguarded and consolidated its French base. Alcatel had never been happy with the DGT's introduction of Thomson as a major competitor; so, despite considering other possible acquisition candidates, the company's clear preference by 1981 was to acquire Thomson's telecommunications activities.

Thomson's own view, in contrast to that of Alcatel, was far less clear-cut. There were intra-company divisions on the future of its telecommunications activities. The group's difficulties were compounded by the Socialist government's refusal to allow Alain Gomez, Thomson's newly appointed PDG, to sell the company's medical electronics activities. With financial losses increasing alarmingly and the prospects for Thomson Télécommunications deteriorating, Gomez came around to the view that the company had to withdraw from telecommunications altogether in order to concentrate resources on what he regarded as Thomson's more promising cores in defence electronics, consumer electronics and components.

In late 1982 Gomez and Pébereau started discussions with a view to concluding a deal between their two companies. Detailed and intensive negotiations began and were conducted bilaterally and exclusively between the firms, without the involvement of either the government – the technical side of the Ministry of Industry was not informed at all – or the DGT. There were numerous reports at the time that politicians, civil servants and DGT officials first became aware of the Alcatel–Thomson discussions through the press. Pébereau and Gomez rapidly agreed the broad contours of an eventual deal: Alcatel was to acquire Thomson's wire, cable and telecommunications operations and, in return, to cede to Thomson its (marginal) activities in components and consumer and military electronics. Responsibility for the negotiations was then delegated down to the heads of the operating divisions concerned, who were given wide autonomy to work out the details of an agreement.

Only after a firm deal had been agreed between the two state-owned firms did Pébereau and Gomez involve the government (Exhibit 18.5). At this point, they put their wide contacts in, and intimate knowledge of, the government machine to good use – both were graduates of the civil service *grandes écoles* and leading members of the administrative *grands corps*, with previous senior civil service experience. Taking advantage of the new political climate, emphasizing macroeconomic budgetary stringency and corporate autonomy and profitability, they took their proposals in September 1983 to the Industry Minister, Fabius. As soon as the details of the agreement became known and circulated within the government machine, the DGT started mobilizing its opposition to the Pébereau–Gomez proposals. In effect, the DGT was merely restating a cardinal principle of its policy: to have at least two competing suppliers in each major product area. It had brought Thomson into telecommunications in 1976 precisely to provide effective competition to Alcatel. If the deal went through, the DGT would be confronted with an Alcatel monopoly of supply in switching equipment, given that the only other supplier, CGCT, was moribund after its nationalization and ITT's subsequent withdrawal, and with a near-monopoly of Alcatel in transmission equipment. Within the government, the DGT's opposition to the deal was faithfully articulated by the PTT Minister, Louis Mexandeau.

Exhibit 18.5   *Industrial policy-making in the French government (1985)*

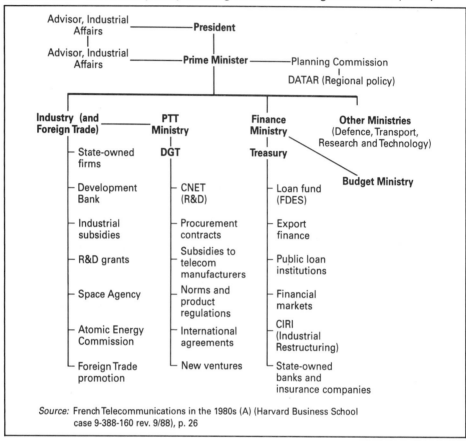

Advisor, Industrial
Affairs ————————President

Advisor, Industrial
Affairs ————————Prime Minister————————Planning Commission

DATAR (Regional policy)

Industry (and Foreign Trade)	PTT Ministry	Finance Ministry	Other Ministries (Defence, Transport, Research and Technology)
State-owned firms	DGT	Treasury	
			Budget Ministry
Development Bank	CNET (R&D)	Loan fund (FDES)	
Industrial subsidies	Procurement contracts	Export finance	
R&D grants	Subsidies to telecom manufacturers	Public loan institutions	
Space Agency	Norms and product regulations	Financial markets	
Atomic Energy Commission	International agreements	CIRI (Industrial Restructuring)	
Foreign Trade promotion	New ventures	State-owned banks and insurance companies	

Source: French Telecommunications in the 1980s (A) (Harvard Business School case 9-388-160 rev. 9/88), p. 26

The DGT, however, found itself isolated. The Finance Ministry shared its reservations concerning the planned deal, fearing, rightly as it turned out, additional claims on the government budget, but it remained on the sidelines of the conflict. A coalition in favour of the Gomez–Pébereau position rapidly formed, comprising the Ministry of Industry, the Prime Minister's Office in the Hôtel Matignon, and the Elysée Palace. The President's own industrial policy advisor, Alain Boublil, was actually one of the most enthusiastic advocates of the deal. Not only did the government give the go-ahead for the deal, with the President's personal blessing, it also restructured the Thomson balance sheet in order not to burden Alcatel with Thomson's losses in telecommunications, provided Alcatel with $300 million of additional funding for 'consolidation' expenses, and committed the DGT to increase the per-line prices for the exchanges which Thomson had previously produced. This outcome was dubbed the 'Second Yalta' of French electronics (the first having been the merger of Thomson and CSF in 1969).

The final agreement stipulated that Thomson Télécommunications would be merged fully with Alcatel by 1987, although, subsequently, this was brought forward to 1985. As a consequence, in 1985 Alcatel's net consolidated sales jumped from FFr 14.5 billion to FFr 21.7 billion, while sales in public switching equipment doubled, giving Alcatel 84 percent of the French market and making it the fourth largest manufacturer worldwide with a 7.2 percent market share (Exhibit 18.6). Nonetheless, the merger involved some problems. Some 7000 jobs – 5000 from Thomson's operations – were lost as a result, causing much industrial unrest and, after two years, the development of the Thomson MT switch was stopped.

From the Mid-1980s Onwards: Alcatel's Privatization and Internationalization

The telecommunications sector has been and still is in the throes of revolutionary

Exhibit 18.6

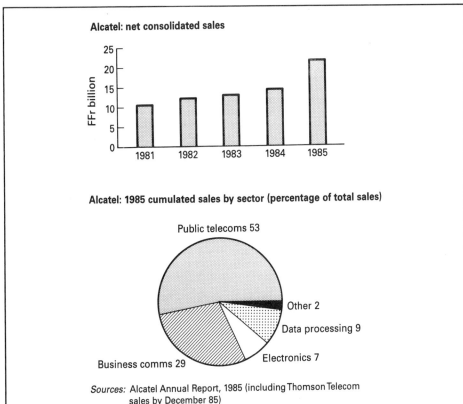

Alcatel: net consolidated sales

Alcatel: 1985 cumulated sales by sector (percentage of total sales)

Sources: Alcatel Annual Report, 1985 (including Thomson Telecom sales by December 85)

technological changes. In particular, the digitalization of switching (i.e. telephone exchanges) and transmission (copper or optical fibre cables, satellites and microwave) networks has facilitated the convergence of telecommunications, consumer electronics and computing technologies into a new telematics sector that has already spawned a wide array of new services far beyond the confines of traditional telephony. This necessitates escalating investments in more expensive R&D, which can be amortized only through more global market coverage. Hence manufacturers have been forced to break out of the thicket of national protection and isolation by internationalizing their activities through mergers, acquisitions and alliances. This has been the recent track record of Alcatel's main competitors, ATT, Northern Telecom, Siemens and Ericsson (Exhibit 18.7).

Alcatel was one of the earliest to formulate an internationalization strategy. Its initial attempts to penetrate the US were abandoned, after it decided that the huge investments needed to adapt to local standards in the newly deregulated American market could not be recovered. Negotiations with AT&T on comprehensive telecommunications cooperation came to no avail: a joint venture to market the E10 in the US, and collaborate in transmissions, collapsed in 1986. Pébereau's

Exhibit 18.7 *Mergers, acquisitions and joint venture activity by Alcatel's competitors, 1984–1990*

1984	AT&T and Philips	Joint venture, APT, renamed ATT NSI after assumption of control by AT&T
1987	*GEC and Plessey	Joint venture, GPT
	*Matra and Ericsson	Acquisition of CGCT, which is renamed MET
	*Autophon and Hasler	Fusion of the two Swiss groups in Ascom
	*Siemens and GTE	Joint venture involving GTE's transmission activities (especially ATEA and GTE Telecommunicazioni) and Siemens Transmission Systems (Siemens 80%, GTE 20%)
1988	*Fujitsu and GTE	Joint venture in private switching equipment, called Fujitsu GTE Business Systems (Fujitsu 80%, GTE 20%)
	*JS Télécom and Bosch	Bosch acquires control of JS Télécom (80%)
1989	*AT&T and GTE	Joint venture in public switching, AG Communications Systems (GTE 51%, AT&T 49%)
	*Siemens and Rolm	Siemens acquires PABX Rolm (in IBM control since 1984)
	*AT&T and Italtel	Cross-holdings to modernize the Italian network
	*GEC/Plessey and Siemens	GEC and Siemens succeed in contested bid for Plessey (Siemens takes 40% of GPT)
1990	Northern Telecom and STC	Northern Telecom bids for STC

Source: France Télécom 76, February 1991, p. 36

attempt to enable AT&T to take over the remaining French equipment supplier, CGCT, also fell through, with CGCT being sold by the French government to a Matra-Ericsson joint venture in 1987.

In keeping with his reputation for negotiating flair in pursuit of a strategic vision, Pébereau commenced talks with ITT, at the time under threat of a takeover bid in the US, even before the breakdown of the deal with AT&T. In July 1986 CGE announced the formation of a new joint venture, Alcatel NV (registered in Holland), in which it would buy 56 percent of ITT's worldwide telecommunications operations, thus gaining substantial access to several new European markets. The jewel in the crown for Alcatel was the Stuttgart-based Standard Elektrik Lorenz (SEL), the second supplier to the Bundespost, after Siemens, with a large share of the West German public switching market. Initially, the project had been intended to be a pan-European one with other minority partners, but, as they withdrew one by one, the deal crystallized into Alcatel assuming management control with ITT retaining a minority 37 percent portfolio stake. The French government, still the owner of Alcatel, was not brought in on the negotiations with ITT and was informed of the deal only after it had been finalized. The acquisition was financed mainly through raising debt, without recourse to government financial aid.

Alcatel–Alsthom announced in early 1992 that it would buy ITT's remaining stake for FFr 18.7 billion. The incorporation of ITT's mainly European operations doubled Alcatel's turnover in 1987/88. Further acquisitions have been made since then: Fiat's telecommunications subsidiary, Telettra, with substantial activities in Italy and Spain, in 1990; the US-based Rockwell International, active in network transmissions, in 1991; and the German AEG Kabel in the same year (Exhibit 18.8). Divestitures have been made in non-core areas, for example by selling SEL's consumer electronics activities to Nokia.

Alcatel has in the last five years become the biggest European telecommunications equipment manufacturer and the world's leading supplier of digital public switching equipment (Exhibit 18.9). Since 1967 its turnover has risen twenty-fold. CIT–Alcatel's E10 switch has been selected in over 60 countries, and SEL–Alcatel's S12 digital equivalent has been chosen in East Germany, Hungary, Poland, Italy, Spain, Taiwan, Australia and China. Sales abroad represent 71 percent of the total, compared to 29 percent in 1981 and 39 percent in 1985. Germany, with 15.5 percent of total sales, is now Alcatel's biggest foreign market by some margin (Exhibit 18.10).

Almost immediately after Georges Pébereau announced his ITT acquisition coup, he was sacked by the new Gaullist–Liberal government, which was irritated at being kept in the dark about Alcatel's dealings with AT&T and ITT. He was replaced by his deputy, Pierre Suard – an appointment which perpetuated the continuity of inhouse senior management that has been the company's hallmark from Roux through Pébereau to the present.

The privatization of CGE in May 1987, long planned by the parties of the Right, went ahead smoothly, with no one group holding a controlling block of shares, although the largest shareholding is held by the privatized French bank, Société

Exhibit 18.8 *Alcatel: path to internationalization*

```
 ──────────────── Major acquisitions ─────────────────▶

            1983            1986            1990            1991
   CIT  ──▶ Thomson  ──▶ ITT Europe  ──▶ Telettra  ──▶ Rockwell
   Alcatel  Télécom       (incl. SEL)      AEG            International
                                           Kabel
```

Overview of main subsidiaries (1990)

	Sales (Ecu m)	Employment
Alcatel FACE	968.0	10495
Alcatel Bell Telephone	793.4	7686
Alcatel Business Systems	1177.4	10517
Alcatel Standard Electrica	1301.6	11742
Alcatel CIT	2500.5	19907
Alcatel SEL	1902.3	20913
Alcatel Cable	3594.4	19939
Others	1208.1	21564
Eliminations	(1051.7)	–
Total Alcatel	**13445.7**	**122763**

Source: Alcatel Annual Report 1991, p. 36

Générale. Suard and his team continued the internationalization strategy put in place by Pébereau, and rationalized and integrated the several and large companies which Alcatel had acquired in a very short space of time. Since 1987 the debt to equity ratio has been halved to 0.23 and the return on sales doubled to 5 percent (1990), figures which compare well with those of other French companies and its competitors in the same industry.

Exhibit 18.9 *Central Office shipments (market shares – worldwide and Europe – for digital local lines)*

Supplier	System	Lines (m)	1992 Share
Alcatel	E10/System 12	11.7	22%
Siemens	EWSD/DCO/GTD5	8.2	15%
AT&T	5ESS/GTD5	9.1	17%
NT	DMS	6.8	13%
Ericsson	AXE	7.1	13%
NEC	NEAX61/D70	3.0	6%
GPT	System X	2.2	4%
Fujitsu	Fetex 150/D70	2.3	4%
Italtel	Linea	1.3	2%
Others	Miscellaneous	2.0	4%
Total		**53.7**	**100%**

Source: Dataquest, April 1993

Exhibit 18.10

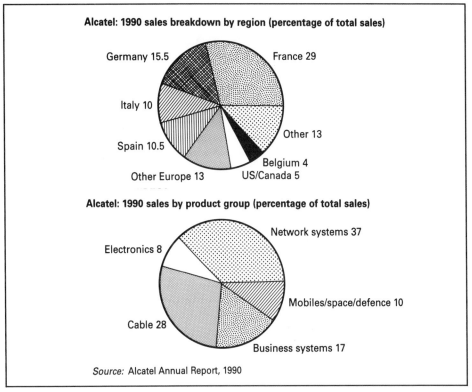

Alcatel: 1990 sales breakdown by region (percentage of total sales)

Germany 15.5

France 29

Italy 10

Other 13

Spain 10.5

Belgium 4

Other Europe 13

US/Canada 5

Alcatel: 1990 sales by product group (percentage of total sales)

Network systems 37

Electronics 8

Mobiles/space/defence 10

Cable 28

Business systems 17

Source: Alcatel Annual Report, 1990

The Late 1980s and Early 1990s: Telecommunications Deregulation and the Reform of France Télécom

Deregulation became the buzz-word in telecommunications policy in the 1980s, starting in the US and the UK. At the EC level, policy action took on a new urgency in light of the Single Market programme, which set 1993 as the date for the creation of a common internal market for telecommunications services and equipment. A moderately radical Green Paper was published by the EC Commission in 1987, followed by the passage of two related EC directives. One required member states to move towards fully open, competitive tendering for public procurement, significantly affecting telecommunications equipment. The other aimed at the full liberalization of the terminal equipment market. Thus far member states have been allowed to preserve the public operator's monopoly of the trunk network in switching and transmission equipment – which account for 70 percent of the total equipment market. Following the liberalization of value added network services (VANS), the telephone service (90 percent of the telecoms services market), however, is to be opened to competition in most EC states in 1998.

The French government initially opposed liberalization, before caving in and joining the evolving consensus in favour of limited deregulation at the end of 1989. France Télécom's recognition of the importance of the European dimension, in common with that of other public network operators, is very recent. Only in 1988 did it establish an EC unit to handle EC regulatory issues, before that having had just two people dealing with these matters. And only with the French Presidency of the EC in 1989 did it become actively involved in the EC policy process. Around the same time, it began to adopt a somewhat more accommodating attitude towards deregulation.

These trends in EC policy were paralleled on the domestic telecommunications scene. After the victory of the Right in the 1986 Parliamentary elections, the DGT was stripped of its supervisory responsibilities for the *filière électronique*, including the telecommunications industry. Attempts by the liberal Minister of Posts and Telecommunications, Gérard Longuet, to push through wide-ranging reforms of the telecommunications regime in France foundered on the rocks of trade union opposition. But this period did engender a fundamental rethinking by the DGT of its own position. It came around to the view that, as a part of the state apparatus, with administrative duties, social tasks and an industrial policy mission, it was constrained and hampered in its ability to serve its own interests and vocation as a network operator in a fast-changing and more competitive environment (Exhibit 18.11). Hence it began to agitate very strongly for a change in its own statute, something which had already been demanded by the Association of the *Ingénieurs des Télécoms* – an administrative *grand corps* in its own right, composed of graduates of the telecommunications *grande école* (*École Nationale Supérieure des Télécommunications*) who dominate the senior management of France Télécom and shape its technically oriented culture.

The new Socialist government, entering office in 1988, took on board France Télécom's preferences, despite initial signals to the contrary. The new minister of

Exhibit 18.11   *The ten leading public telecom operators worldwide (revenues from Telecom Services in $ bn)*

	Country	Revenues in 1989
NTT	Japan	42.2
AT&T	USA	24.6
Deutsche Bundespost	Germany	20.4
British Telecom	UK	18.8
France Télécom	France	16.6
Bell South	USA	14
Nynex	USA	13.2
GTE	USA	12.5
Bell Atlantic	USA	11.4
SIP	Italy	10.8

Source: France Télécom 76, February 1991, p. 37

the PTT, Paul Quilès, finally managed to pass legislation changing France Télécom's statute as of 1991. France Télécom was relieved of its regulatory role, which was transferred to a separate body in the PTT ministry, and transformed into an autonomous (albeit still state-owned) network operator outside the government machine (Exhibit 18.12).

France Télécom signed a three-year planning contract with the government in 1991. The plan contained some outlines of its broad strategy for the longer-term – in particular its intentions to expand operations in Europe and internationally, as well as in new products and services, and to reduce its high level of indebtedness. The annual levy imposed by the government on France Télécom's operations, for long a bone of contention, was to be replaced by a more favourable rate of corporate tax. A new, more decentralized and more marketing-oriented organizational structure was planned to take effect in 1993.

Exhibit 18.12 *Main developments in French telecommunications deregulation*

1986

March: Gérard Longuet is named Secretary of State for the PTT in the Chirac government.

September: Creation of the 'Mission à la réglementation' reporting to M. Longuet on regulation.

September/November: The Leotard law on audiovisual services. The end of the DGT monopoly on the construction of the cable network. The CNCL regulatory authority is given authority for the establishment and utilization of private networks and 'consulted' on the application of the PTT code concerning telecom services.

1987

January: M. Longuet announces the intention to authorize a competitor to the DGT's Radiocom 2000 in mobile communications.

June: In compliance with the Leotard law, the satellite operator TDF is transformed into a private 'Société Anonyme'.

July: M. Longuet authorizes TDF to exploit a radiopaging service in competition with the DGT. He calls for bids to designate the second operator in mobile communications.

August: Notice given of a working text by M. Longuet for a new legal framework for telecommunications.

September: Decree on the regulation of value added networks.

November: M. Longuet (provisionally) abandons his proposals for a new law in the face of trade union opposition.

December: M. Longuet authorizes the Compagnie Générale des Eaux, a private operator, to offer a service of public mobile phones in competition to the DGT's Radiocom 2000.

1988

January: The DGT renames itself France Télécom.

May: Paul Quilès is named the new minister for PTT and for Space.

Autumn: France takes the European Commission to the Court of Justice of the EC on the use of article 90 of the Treaty of Rome to unilaterally push through the directive on the liberalization of the terminal equipment market. France is in principle favourable to the measures, but wishes the right of approval to remain with the Council of Ministers, not the Commission.

Exhibit 18.12 *continued*

December: M. Quilès charges Hubert Prévot with the task of organizing a debate on the nature of the public service in posts and telecommunications.

1989

January: The Dutch PTT administration is transformed into a public company, with the state having a 100% shareholding.

The Lang law creates a new communications regulatory authority, the CSA, devolving the CNCL's powers over the telecommunications sector to it.

Announcement of the preparation of a law, to be put to the National Assembly by the end of March 1990, separating the regulatory and operating responsibilities of public telecommunications.

March: M. Quilès inaugurates the SFR private sector competitor operation to France Télécom's Radiocom 2000, authorized by his predecessor, M. Longuet.

April: The Prévot report on the principal questions concerning the public PTT services is published. M. Quilès uses it to launch a public debate.

May: Creation of a Direction à la Réglementation Générale (DRG) as a regulatory body within the PTT Ministry.

June: The end of the public debate organized by M. Prévot. The Prime Minister, Michel Rocard, declares himself in favour of a PTT reform.

July: The Deutsche Bundespost is split into three autonomous divisions (post, telecommunications and financial services).

1990

July: The Quilès law on the PTT reform is passed by the National Assembly.

1991

January: France Télécom becomes an autonomous public company, fully state-owned, outside the government apparatus.

Source: Télécoms Magazine, no. 27, September 1989, pp. 69–71.

The Future: Alcatel and France Télécom – Partners in the New World of Telecommunications?

For its part, Alcatel played no major role in the public debates on EC deregulation and the change of France Télécom's statute. The leading French participants in these debates have invariably been the French government and France Télécom. Alcatel nevertheless has close and continuous relations on deregulation and other public policy issues with governmental agencies responsible for telecommunications policy and regulation as well as with its main interlocutors in its core national markets, i.e. the public network operators. In an industry still characterized by relations between concentrated, large suppliers and the monopoly operators of the trunk network, in contrast to mass markets for more commodity-based products (e.g. consumer electronics or computers), the network operators remain easily its most important clients.

Away from the glare and controversy of public discussion, in its discreet contacts with the French government and France Télécom, Alcatel has broadly supported liberalization of EC telecommunications and changes in the France Telecom statute. On these issues, the prime concern of the Suard-led management has always been to preserve a strong consensus with France Télécom and its management.

Alcatel remains France Télécom's overwhelming supplier of switching and transmission systems, holding over 80 percent of the French public switching market. Both sides still conceive their relationship as a *partenariat* (partnership). Technological innovations mean that it is becoming increasingly feasible for public operators to choose new additions and modifications to the network from competing suppliers, particularly in transmission systems. Nonetheless, both Alcatel and France Télécom argue that the *partenariat* is more efficient in the maintenance and improvement of network systems, especially in public switching. The initial building of a digital network, so they say, locks the two into a relationship for ten years or more, during which time upgrading, to be compatible with the existing network, can be performed solely by the original supplier. It therefore makes sense to maintain close ties between the two parties, particularly at the technical level. In fact, tight technology-driven links have long existed, especially between CNET and CIT–Alcatel engineers, many of whom belong to the *grand corps* of telecommunications engineers graduating from the same *grande école*.

The Alcatel–France Télécom *partenariat* in network systems is nevertheless affected by a certain dynamic element. Up to 1987 Alcatel was content to leave it to France Télécom to specify exactly what equipment had to be developed and supplied. This reflected Alcatel's organizational weakness in sales and marketing – it had the reputation of being dominated by engineers who did not have much appreciation of the range and depth of clients' requirements. Since 1987, however, the integration of the ITT subsidiaries, particularly SEL, has enabled Alcatel to strengthen not only its R&D and manufacturing capabilities, but also its more downstream functions. More often than not, it is now Alcatel that takes the initiative in developing and determining specifications for products for France Télécom as well as for other public operators.

A central element of the *partenariat* has been the system of sub-contracted research (*marché d'études*), through which the CNET provides funds to outside parties to do specified research on its behalf. This amounted to FFr 2 billion in 1991, 50 percent of France Télécom's total R&D spending. Much of this funding has gone to Alcatel in the past, with the aim of transferring CNET know-how to Alcatel. Following its ITT and later acquisitions, Alcatel has pursued the objective of concentrating poles of research competence in different national sites to achieve a pan-European coverage. Critics of the *marché d'études* argue that it is becoming a CNET subsidy to Alcatel's autonomous research capacity. This highlights a dilemma for France Télécom. It still plays a major role in French industrial life and policy – but is this compatible with its stated objective of being a public network operator, concentrating on choosing the right products and investments at the right price, but leaving product development to its suppliers?

Negotiations between Alcatel and France Télécom on procurement and the *marché d'études* are now somewhat tougher than they used to be. France Télécom is keener to safeguard its intellectual property rights, concerned that they could potentially be used by Alcatel to develop products for other clients, including other public operators with which Alcatel, through its foreign subsidiaries, has procurement relations, notably the Deutsche Telekom (SEL's sales in 1990 were three-quarters of CIT–Alcatel's). France Télécom is also worried because it is much less able to monitor Alcatel's product development when it takes place outside France – for example at SEL in Stuttgart.

Another area in which bilateral negotiations have become more difficult concerns standards. France Télécom, in common with other nationally based public operators, is used to nationally specific standards. Alcatel wants to use new technologies to promote pan-European and international standards such as in the realization of an Integrated Services Digital Network (ISDN) or through its Alcatel 1000 system, which is intended to integrate the E10 and S12 switches into a common broadband network. This concern accounts for Alcatel's heavy involvement in EC-sponsored cooperative R&D projects, especially RACE, the aim of which is to develop ISDN into a broadband network infrastructure accommodating an enlarged range of services.

Beyond their *partenariat* in the core area of network systems, Alcatel and France Télécom are pursuing independent strategies in high-growth areas such as mobile communications, satellites and business systems. France Télécom is in the midst of forging a series of international alliances, with the objective of earning 10 percent of revenues abroad by the year 2000.

Cable television and mobile telecommunications remain relatively weak and underdeveloped in France. France Télécom launched a range of digital mobile telephones on a pan-European standard in 1992. The equipment for this system was to be supplied by consortia headed by Alcatel and Matra. But at the same time Alcatel is also the leading supplier to France Télécom's licensed private sector competitor in mobile phones, SFR, and plans to spread its mobile communications operations in Europe and elsewhere.

One of the growth areas involving the most innovative technologies in telecommunications is in servicing the private communications networks of large corporations. Technological developments and market demand are locating more and more of the 'intelligent' features (i.e. software) of communications technologies in customer premises equipment as opposed to the public network – a trend which has been facilitated by deregulatory measures designed to allow access to the public network by private users. The 'outsourcing' of these corporate private networks is becoming a battlefield, involving increasingly aggressive competition for huge revenue between the public operators, equipment manufacturers and information technology multinationals, such as IBM and DEC. France Télécom is teaming up with the Deutsche Telekom in a joint venture to serve these private networks.

Alcatel reaps nearly a fifth of its worldwide revenues from business systems. It aims to be a leader in supplying equipment to private networks and is already the world's second-largest producer of private office switches (PBXs). The market for private networks, however, is increasingly favouring vertically integrated suppliers-cum-operators, such as AT&T and IBM, which can provide integrated solutions. For a long time, Alcatel deferred from trying to become an operator, for this would bring it into competition and conflict with its chief client in network systems, namely France Télécom. Avoiding competition with France Télécom in areas where the two sides pursue independent strategies was viewed by Alcatel as the price that it had to pay to preserve the *partenariat* in public switching and transmissions. However, in an important change of policy, the company announced in 1993 that it would bid for a licence to provide a third mobile communications network in France.

The right-wing government elected in France in March 1993 announced that it was going to study the possibility of partially privatizing French public utilities, including France Télécom, although it would not make any decisions on the issue before 1995. At the same time, CEO Suard said that Alcatel was thinking seriously about buying a stakeholding in a network operator. Such a move would, he argued, increase planning security for the equipment manufacturer and increase the operator's certainty concerning the long-term delivery of equipment. Alcatel was clearly aiming to emulate the American AT&T in becoming a services and network as well as equipment supplier. Before the end of the century, it could become a part owner of France Télécom.

PART 3

Privatization, Competition Policy and Social Policy

Cases: The Privatization of British Airways, British Airways, British Caledonian Airways

This set of three cases (suited for role playing) addresses the broad issues of (de)regulatory policy, competition policy, and the privatization of nationalized firms. The cases deal specifically with the UK air transport industry, but the conclusions to be drawn from them are more general.

The cases take place at a time when the UK Secretary of State for Transport reluctantly finds himself forced to contemplate, simultaneously, the privatization of British Airways and the regulatory framework for the UK air transport industry post-privatization. In this, as the cases detail, he is caught between the Civil Aviation Authority and British Caledonian on one side and British Airways on the other. As *The Observer* stated at the time:

> Whichever way he [the Secretary] jumps, he now faces political embarrassment. Either he will break up BA – thus delaying its privatisation plans indefinitely – or he will leave BA's route network intact and be seen to have ignored the CAA's most searching policy review for 20 years.

In analyzing the cases, the reader must consider the objectives of and interrelationships between privatization policy, competition policy, and (de)regulatory policy. Is privatization of nationalized firms the means toward some end, or the end itself? Should competition policy be subservient to privatization policy? What is the nexus between the form of ownership of enterprise and economic efficiency? Does economic efficiency come at the expense of other social objectives? How far can free market competition work in the air transport industry?

239

Although the cases focus on UK policy, the reader quickly realizes that policy there cannot be made isolated from the industry changes that have taken place in the US, the state of the Continental air carriers, or the European Commission's plans for gradual liberalization of the European industry.

Case: EC Competition Policy: the Merger and Acquisition Directive (A) and (B)

A central aspect of the internal market programme is EC competition policy. This entails a strengthening of Community's powers, and a challenge to national governments and policy communities. Readers may be reminded of the broader market context which prompted the specific proposal for a directive to strengthen Commission powers on mergers and acquisitions. The first case (A) presents the situation in the EC with regard to competition policy, and mergers and acquisitions, when the Commission proposed a draft directive in November 1988. The second case (B) carries on the story of how, why and by whom modifications were introduced into the final text. Law and legislation lie at the heart of the EC policy process. Readers may consider the relationship in the European Community, and between the varied member states of law, politics and markets.

As in the subsequent case on social policy, the starting point for the reader may be to chart out the relevant national policy communities, as well as the situation facing the Commissioners. Commission and member state positions are far from being homogenous with regard to proposed legislation. What are the protagonists' positions with regard to thresholds? Do they or do they not favour a 'one-stop shop' for competition policy? Do they attach more or less significance to which policy criteria for competition or industrial policy, and why? What positions are taken up by the protagonists with regard to the rights of minority shareholders? How long do they consider that the notification period should be for an impending investigation regarding a merger and acquisition, and should it be ex ante or ex post? What are the varied positions with regard to the scope of eventual Commission powers in this field? In the second case, the reader may reflect on how the Commission and member states mediated a compromise, and what that compromise means for the efficiency and effectiveness of merger and acquisition policy in the future.

Case: The Relaunch of Social Europe

The case, designed either for discussion or for role playing, considers the policy process in the European Community institutions regarding social and labour market policies. The case is set in late 1989 at the end of the French

Presidency, which made considerable progress in furthering legislation on the internal market. Germany is moving fast towards state unity, and the French Presidency with the Commission is determined to complement the internal market with 'accompanying measures' in the form of a Social Charter and European Monetary Union. Over the last thirty years, the Community has made only modest progress in harmonizing social and labour market arrangements. These are deeply entrenched in the laws, institutions, politics, and cultures of the member states. Assumptions, derived in part from economic theories, diverge on the way labour markets operate. Does the demand curve for labour slope downwards or upwards, and what are the implications for policy and institutions?

The reader must sort out the positions of the member states with the regard to the Commission's proposals, and to their own domestic contexts, as well as think about the other policy domains which social policy touches upon. There is also the matter of how these varied policy preferences are defined and promoted by the relevant participants in their own states, and through alliances across, or even outside, the EC. Finally, the reader may make a predictive analysis of the desired and probable outcomes from the perspective of each one of the major protagonists: the Commission President, the French President; the German Chancellor; the British and Spanish Prime Ministers. What are their relevant national policy communities? What are the reasons for their adopting their varied positions on the suggested Social Charter and Action Programme? How have they managed to promote or to defend their preferences? What are the likely outcomes of this Community initiative, from the perspective of December 1989?

The Privatization of British Airways

H. Landis Gabel

In September 1984, Nicholas Ridley, Secretary of State for Transport in the UK government, faced what must have seemed to him an unwinnable situation. In June 1983, Mrs Thatcher's Conservative Party, elected for a second term with a large parliamentary majority, had announced plans for the sale of the nationalized British Airways (BA) to the private sector. Since then, an acrimonious debate both within and outside the Conservative Party had developed and intensified about the future structure of the British airline industry as well as the government's general industrial policies of privatization and competition. (For a summary of the main events of the BA controversy, see Exhibit 19.1.) Mr Ridley had recently been appointed chairman of a Cabinet Committee with the objective of resolving the debate over BA and the airline industry.

Paradoxically, this period of policy uncertainty coincided with the successful turnaround of BA from a loss-making airline into what has since been heralded 'the world's most profitable airline'. Indeed, the prospect of this streamlined, efficient and profitable BA entering the private sector was causing much of the debate. Sir Adam Thomson, Chairman of British Caledonian Airways (BCal), Britain's largest independent airline, expressed the concern he and other relatively small operators felt about the future.

> If I were chairman of a privatized BA, it would be my duty to the shareholders to maximize profits. If I could kick a competitor, however small, out of business and so make more profits for myself and the shareholders, fine – I'd do it. [1]

Sir Adam's fear was, however, mitigated by the opportunity the situation presented to him. If BA shares were to appeal to the private financial community, the regulatory framework within which the UK airline industry operated would have to

---

This case was prepared by Robert Levy, MBA candidate at INSEAD under the supervision of H. Landis Gabel, Associate Professor at INSEAD. It is intended to be used as a basis for class discussion rather than to illustrate either effective or ineffective handling of an administrative situation.

Exhibit 19.1 *Major events in the privatization of British Airways*

Date	Event
May 1979	Conservative Government elected to power under the leadership of Margaret Thatcher, with commitment to sell into private ownership many of Britain's major nationalized industries, including British Airways.
1981	Lord King appointed as Chairman of British Airways, with specific mandate to prepare the airline for privatization. King appoints Colin Marshall as CEO.
1981–1983	Major program of cost reduction and efficiency improvements, involving cutting employment from 59,000 to 37,000.
1983	British Airways announces profit of £180 million.
June 1983	Conservative Government elected for second term with promise to sell British Airways in this Parliament.
1 November 1983	John Moore, Financial Secretary to the Treasury, emphasizes in a major speech that privatization must go 'hand-in-hand' with increased competition.
3 November 1983	British Caledonian Chairman, Sir Adam Thomson, proposes to the Government that his airline should buy British Airways' routes and assets to ensure fair competition in UK aviation.
4 November 1983	British Airways announces half-year profit of £160 million and declares that it will be ready for privatization in eleven months.
16 November 1983	Prime Minister tells Lord King that BA privatization will have to wait until after the massive flotation of British Telecom, i.e. 1985–86.
12 December 1983	Secretary of State for Transport, Nicholas Ridley, announces in the House of Commons that British Airways will be privatized as soon as possible, probably early in 1985. In the same speech, Ridley announces that he has asked John Dent, Chairman of the Civil Aviation Authority, to conduct a major review of the airline industry to determine if changes might be needed in the licensing structure.
1 February 1984	Final submissions to CAA review, including BCal proposals thought to suggest transfer of a third of BA's routes to independent airlines.
3 February 1984	BCal announces that if its proposals for route transfers from BA are accepted, it is likely to offer a share issue for between £100–£150m before the flotation of BA. This would be BCal's first quotation on the stock market.
15 February 1984	CAA announces that it has granted to BCal the right to fly from London to Riyadh, Saudia Arabia, in preference to BA. BA keeps rights to Jeddah and Dhahran.
3 March 1984	BA announces appointment of stockbrokers and merchant bankers to manage its public flotation.

Exhibit 19.1 *continued*

Date	Event
18 April 1984	CAA publishes interim report declaring that airline competition is beneficial, but will remain impossible as long as BA controls 81 percent of its services.
1 May 1984	Sir Adam Thomson proposes that privatization of BA should be delayed to give time for changes in the structure of UK civil aviation.
5 May 1984	Lord King declares that he would regard transfer of routes from BA to BCal as 'a resignation issue'.
6 June 1984	BA publishes its accounts showing bank borrowings of more than £900 million. Full-year profits for BA revealed to be £294 million before interest and tax.
12 June 1984	BA begins a £2 million advertising campaign to counter the claims of the independent airlines.
12 June 1984	Nine independent airlines write to the CAA asking that a legal interpretation of BA's position in the industry be sought from the Monopolies Commission.
16 July 1984	Civil Aviation Authority review of 'Airline Competition Policy' published, proposing significant route transfers from BA, and increasing the strength of independent airlines. BA declares the proposals 'disastrous' and 'unacceptable'.
3 August 1984	A Cabinet Committee, consisting of Norman Tebbitt, Nigel Lawson, Nicholas Ridley, Lord Cockfield and John Wakeham, set up in an attempt to resolve the dispute over British Airways' routes – a decision deferred until 'late Summer'. Deadline set for 13 September.
September 1984	Continued negotiations throughout September between Cabinet Committee, Lord King and Sir Adam Thomson.

be firmly set for the foreseeable future. Thus, Sir Adam had a chance to influence the policymaking bodies of the government to try to challenge the domination of BA – domination which had long been sustained by government policy.

The Background to Privatization

BA was not an isolated example of the sale of public assets to the private sector. By late 1984, eight large formerly nationalized companies had been privatized in the UK, and legislation was enacted to enable the privatization of twelve more (including BA and British Telecom). The policy of privatization reflected a change in mainstream Conservative thinking in the 1970s. The free market, not government intervention, was now to be the preferred medium for achieving the government's economic goals.

As Nigel Lawson, Chancellor of the Exchequer and the man with Cabinet responsibility for the privatization program, said,

> The Conservative Party has never believed that the business of government is the government of business.[2]

The policy was, of course, in sharp contrast to that of the post-Second World War Labour governments which had nationalized many industries with the objective of using them to influence the economy. The post-war nationalizations created some of the biggest organizations in the UK economy – organizations that in 1983 accounted for approximately one-tenth of the UK's gross domestic product, one-seventh of its total investment, and employment of 1.5 million people. Three public enterprises had been established in the airline industry – British Overseas Airways Corporation (BOAC), British European Airways (BEA), and British South American Airways (BSAA). Each was granted a monopoly in a different market. In 1949, BSAA was merged into BOAC, and in 1970, BOAC and BEA were consolidated to form BA.

To Mrs Thatcher's Conservative Party, public enterprise looked inherently less efficient than private enterprise because it was insulated from the discipline of the capital and product markets. BA was taken as a case in point. In 1981, when Mrs Thatcher appointed Lord King Chairman of British Airways, with a mandate to prepare it for privatization, BA was practically bankrupt. Only an immense program of government-guaranteed loans kept BA in the air. (See Exhibits 19.2 to 19.4 for BA's financial reports.)

BA's return to profitability under Lord King was felt to be attributable in good part to the massive cuts 'in overmanning in BA which could not have been achieved if the intention to privatize had not already been expressed.'[3] The Conservative Party's belief seemed to be validated.

A second justification for the planned privatizations was stated in a major policy speech in November 1983 by John Moore, Financial Secretary to the Treasury and guiding hand behind the privatization program.

> The primary objective of the Government's privatization policy is to reduce the power of the monopolist and to encourage competition.[4]

A third justification for the privatizations was that they would permanently remove nationalized firms' future credit demands from the government's public sector borrowing requirement. Despite its recent successful performance, BA in 1984 still owed its creditors 863 million pounds. About half of the estimated 1 billion pound proceeds of BA's sale would be used to reduce the company's outstanding debt – debt which might not otherwise be repaid. (So serious was BA's financial situation that the airline was not considered saleable with its existing debt.)

Finally, the Treasury had an obvious financial motive to sell nationalized companies like BA – and to sell them as dearly as possible.

(Other justifications occasionally referred to include a reduction of state power in order to increase individual freedom, making the civil service more efficient by

Exhibit 19.2 *British Airways financial summary – 1983*

	£m
Airline traffic revenue	2,044
Other earnings	453
Group turnover	2,497
Operating costs	
Airline operating expenditure comprised:	
Staff costs	
Wages and salaries	412
Pension contributions	63
National Insurance	37
Aircraft fuel and oil	531
Landing fees and en route charges	163
Amortization of capital expenditure	105
Commission on traffic revenue	154
Other airline operating expenditure	405
	1,870
Non-airline operating expenditure	437
	2,307
Group operating surplus	190
Associated companies. trade investments and other income	20
Profit before cost of capital borrowings and taxation	210
Interest	(120)
Currency losses on capital borrowings	(28)
Profit before tax	62
Taxation and minority interests	(11)
Profit before extraordinary items	51
Extraordinary items	26
Balance transferred to reserves	77
Internal cash flow	
Profit after extraordinary items	77
Less profit on fixed asset and investment disposals	(36)
Add back non-cash items	
Amortization – airline activity	105
– other	6
	111
Currency losses	28
Other	3

Exhibit 19.2 *continued*

	£m
Cash generated from operations	183
Net proceeds from asset disposals	110
Movement in net current liabilities	(86)
Total cash generated	207
Capital expenditure	(172)
Net cash generated	35
Capital borrowings repaid	(99)
Capital borrowings raised	(64)

Balance sheet

Net assets

Fixed assets	978
Investments	18
Net current liabilities	(164)
	832

Financed by

Shareholders' funds	(221)
Capital borrowings	1,053
	832

Current cost accounts

The change in the result from the historic cost accounts to the current cost accounts is explained below

Current cost operating profit — 133

This is the historic cost result before other income of £196 million, less £63 million additional depreciation resulting from the revaluation of assets in current cost terms

Other income — 12

This is the historic cost amount of other income less an adjustment of £1 million to the historic cost surplus on disposal of fixed assets and investments

Current cost profit before cost of capital borrowings and taxation — 145

Cost of capital borrowings — (100)

This is the historic cost figure of £148 million reduced by the gearing adjustment of £48 million which reflects the burden of inflation borne by lenders who have helped to finance net operating assets

Current cost profit before taxation	45
Taxation and minority interests	(11)
Current cost profit before extraordinary items	34
Extraordinary items	22
Current cost profit attributable to British Airways	56

Exhibit 19.3 *British Airways balance sheet – 1983*

	Note	Group 1983 £m	Group 1982 £m	Board 1983 £m	Board 1982 £m
Net assets					
Fixed assets					
Fleet		**773.7**	751.5	**721.6**	696.2
Property		**123.9**	132.2	**110.1**	112.9
Equipment		**80.0**	88.8	**72.2**	73.3
	10	**977.6**	972.5	**903.9**	882.4
Interests in					
Subsidies	11a			**77.7**	79.0
Associated companies	12a	**15.0**	15.0	**.2**	–
Trade investments	13a	**3.6**	6.2	**.5**	.4
Net current liabilities	15	**(163.8)**	(237.1)	**(211.0)**	(283.3)
		832.4	756.6	**771.3**	678.5
Financed by					
Public Dividend Capital	16	**180.0**	180.0	**180.0**	180.0
Reserves	17	**(325.4)**	(402.0)	**(386.2)**	(472.2)
Exchange equalization account	18bii	**(75.7)**	(34.7)	**(75.7)**	(34.7)
Deficiency of assets over liabilities		**(221.1)**	(256.7)	**(281.9)**	(326.9)
Capital borrowings	18a	**1,053.2**	1,010.6	**1,053.2**	1,005.4
Minority interests		**.3**	2.6		
Deferred taxation	19	**–**	.1		
		832.4	756.6	**771.3**	678.5

streamlining it and eliminating its regulatory mentality, broadening equity markets, and breaking the power of the civil service unions which had long been particularly troublesome in the UK.)[5]

The Civil Aviation Authority Report

It was in the context of the privatization program that Nicholas Ridley first declared in a speech on December 12, 1983 that BA would be privatized with a target date of early 1985. In the same speech he announced that he had ordered the UK air transport regulatory body, the Civil Aviation Authority (CAA), to carry out a major policy review of the airline industry.

The CAA played a role in the UK airline industry that would normally be reserved for the UK Monopolies Commission. The Fair Trading Act of 1973 exempted airlines from the authority of the Monopolies Commission, and a separate act of Parliament assigned its duties to the CAA. Since the CAA had earlier

Exhibit 19.4 *British Airways ten year results and statistics*

Years ended 31 March	1974	1975	1976	1977	1978	1979	1980	1981	1982	1983
Results										
Scheduled services										
Revenue – passenger and baggage (£m)	444.3	526.6.	660.0	898.6	965.1	1,191.4	1,409.9	1,489.5	1,608.7	1,770.9
Revenue – mail (£m)	21.1	22.3	23.6	32.7	33.0	36.2	39.8	41.0	33.7	35.7
Revenue – freight (£m)	68.4	83.8	82.1	105.3	115.3	131.4	152.7	161.7	148.1	151.0
Revenue – total (£m)	533.8	632.7	765.7	1,036.6	1,113.4	1,359.0	1,602.4	1,692.2	1,790.5	1,957.6
Total Airline operations (including Airtours)										
Revenue (£m)	566.1	663.5	801.5	1,073.9	1,156.1	1,403.3	1,654.4	1,749.8	1,861.0	2,043.5
Operating expenditure (£m)	512.9	665.3	798.8	978.1	1,099.3	1,327.3	1,638.4	1,854.0	1,855.1	1,869.5
Operating result (£m)	53.2	(1.8)	2.7	95.8	56.8	76.0	16.0	(104.2)	5.9	174.0
British Airways Group										
Profit before interest and tax (£m)	64.1	5.0	11.6	115.8	79.0	109.8	54.9	(69.9)	10.8*	209.8*
Average net assets (£m)	502.3	511.7	529.7	558.7	639.1	745.3	879.8	1,043.2	938.1	794.5
Return on net assets (%)	12.8	1.0	2.2	20.7	12.4	14.7	6.3	(6.7)	1.2	26.4
Turnover (£m)	647	748	916	1,248	1,355	1,640	1,920	2,061	2,241	2,497
Ratio of turnover of net assets	1.288	1.462	1.729	2.234	1.120	2.200	2.182	1.976	2.389	3.143
Statistics										
Scheduled services										
Revenue passenger km(m)	24,803	24,171	27,280	30,143	29,751	36,366	42,144	40,076	38,521	36,394
Available seat km(m)	41,703	41,126	44,816	48,576	49,637	56,387	62,534	64,043	57,752	54,710
Tonne km – mail(m)	109.4	119.1	128.0	140.2	155.7	165.5	171.5	165.0	150.0	151.8
Tonne km – freight(m)	746.5	721.1	679.4	716.2	818.4	883.2	995.8	995.8	884.9	833.7
Tonne km – total(m)	3,061	2,997	3,249	3,607	3,711	4,417	5,036	4,812	4,503	4,307

* Profit before interest, tax and extraordinary items.

Exhibit 19.4 *continued*

Years ended 31 March	1974	1975	1976	1977	1978	1979	1980	1981	1982	1983
Revenue per passenger km(p)	1.79	2.18	2.42	2.98	3.24	3.28	3.35	3.72	4.17	4.87
Revenue per RTK(p)	17.4	21.1	23.6	28.7	30.0	30.8	31.8	35.2	39.8	45.5
Available tonne km(m)	5,528	5,388	5,856	6,233	6,408	7,164	7,797	7,930	7,147	6,786
Passenger load factor (%)	59.5	58.8	60.9	62.1	59.2	64.5	67.4	62.6	66.7	66.5
Break-even passenger load factor (%)	52.4	59.0	60.6	55.4	56.4	60.3	66.6	67.0	66.6	60.0
Overall load factor (%)	55.4	55.6	55.5	57.9	57.9	61.6	64.6	60.7	63.0	63.5
Break-even overall load factor (%)	49.9	55.8	55.3	52.5	55.0	58.2	64.0	64.5	62.7	57.8
Punctuality (% within 15 mins)	76	81	80	79	64	65	68	81	78	84
Number of passengers carried (000)	14,361	13,349	13,792	14,510	13,370	15,768	17,319	15,918	15,231	14,635
Average distance travelled (km)	1,727	1,811	1,978	2,077	2,225	2,306	2,433	2,518	2,529	2,487
Tonnes of mail carried (000)	31.2	30.5	29.8	33.3	34.9	38.0	39.0	39.0	35.0	38.3
Average distance carried (km)	3,509	3,908	4,304	4,223	4,466	4,355	4,399	4,230	4,288	3,960
Tonnes of freight carried (000)	237.0	219.7	170.1	167.9	192.0	209.9	225.5	203.4	170.2	161.6
Average distance carried (km)	3,150	3,283	3,993	4,265	4,262	4,208	4,415	4,897	5,200	5,176
Total Airline operations (including Airtours)										
Available tonne km(m)	6,077	5,832	6,247	6,555	6,793	7,557	8,153	8,243	7,522	7,208
Revenue hours flown (000)	543.5	490.7	454.8	440.6	431.8	469.0	492.5	447.0	405.5	386.2
ATK per hour	11,181	11,885	13,735	14,876	15,733	16,112	16,553	18,440	18,551	18,664
Revenue aircraft km(m)	321.3	289.4	273.1	267.2	265.7	288.5	307.3	283.1	253.5	244.7

Exhibit 19.4 *continued*

Years ended 31 March	1974	1975	1976	1977	1978	1979	1980	1981	1982	1983
Average speed (km/hr)	591	590	600	606	615	615	625	633	625	634
Revenue stage flights (000)	284.3	267.1	237.3	225.9	212.2	230.4	239.4	211.1	195.6	189.3
Average sector (km)	1,130	1,083	1,151	1,183	1,252	1,252	1,283	1,341	1,296	1,293
Average length of flight (hr)	1.91	1.84	1.92	1.95	2.03	2.04	2.06	2.12	2.07	2.04
Operating expenditure per ATK(p)	8.4	11.4	12.8	14.9	16.2	17.6	20.1	22.5	24.7	25.9
Average staff – Airline activities	54,600	54,861	53,977	54,362	55,438	55,985	56,140	53,616	47,753	39,693
ATK per employee (000)	111.3	106.3	115.7	120.6	122.5	135.0	145.2	153.7	157.5	181.6

Source: British Airways

concluded that BA's dominance brought it under the Fair Trading Act's definition of 'monopoly', it could hardly avoid using this opportunity to try to increase competition in the industry.

After receiving submissions from 105 interested parties, the CAA reported in July 1984. Proclaiming its principal objective to be correcting 'the underlying imbalance of competitive advantage in the airline industry,'[6] the CAA proposed to reduce the relative size of BA for the sake of other airlines. In particular, it recommended:

1.   Replacement of BA by BCal on routes to Saudi Arabia and Zimbabwe.
2.   The transfer of BA's scheduled routes from Gatwick and its European routes originating from provincial airports to independent UK airlines.
3.   Access to Heathrow by other UK trunk airlines, at the expense of BA if necessary.

These proposals were estimated to reduce BA's operating revenues by about 7 percent. No compensation was planned.

The CAA also requested additional powers to promote a more even balance among the competing UK airlines. This request included the power to transfer routes between carriers solely to redress an imbalance and thus to promote competition – a power the CAA did not at the time possess.

> Route licenses are not property . . . Insofar as the State, through the licensing of air services, gives airlines an opportunity to operate profitably, these opportunities remain at the disposal of the State.[7]

BA categorically rejected the CAA's proposals, and amidst intensifying lobbying, a Cabinet Committee chaired by Mr Ridley was set up in August 1984 with a deadline of September 13 to report. This deadline now faced Mr Ridley.

Competition in the UK Airline Industry

The airline industry can be divided into three major market segments. Exhibit 19.5 shows the CAA's estimate of the shares of the segments by carrier in 1983.

1.   The Charter Market

This is the largest sector of the UK market with 42 percent of passenger-trips and is essentially a competitive market. The market is not regulated by bilateral agreements, tariff fixing, or revenue pooling. But since most charter flights are taken as part of package holidays and are subject to schedule restrictions, this market is effectively isolated from the international scheduled market. BA's subsidiary, British Airtours, held a 12.6 percent share of the market.

Exhibit 19.5 *Shares of services (1984)*

Airline shares of United Kingdom charter services

Airline	Passengers
Air Europe	10.4%
Britannia	31.4%
British Airtours	12.6%
Monarch	8.9%
Orion	7.3%

Source: CAA Airline Statistics

Airline shares of United Kingdom domestic scheduled services

Airline	Passengers
British Airways	50.0%
Air Europe	16.4%
British Caledonian	8.6%
Air UK	6.6%
Dan-Air	6.2%
Others*	12.2%

* Sixteen other airlines are involved in domestic
passenger services and a further two in providing
cargo carriage.
Source: CAA Airline Statistics

Airline shares of United Kingdom international scheduled services

Airline	Passengers
British Airways	81.8%
British Caledonian	11.1%
Others	7.1%
	100%

Source: CAA Airline Statistics

2. The Domestic Scheduled Market

BA held a 50 percent share of the domestic scheduled market – a market which
comprised 21 percent of the UK airline industry output. Approximately one-sixth
of BA's revenue came from its domestic routes.

On a formal basis, the domestic market is regulated, but it is relatively
competitive nonetheless. Entry controls exist which give BA monopoly rights to
many routes where its only constraint is the competition from ground transport.
Flight capacity is not controlled on the competitive routes, but fares are set by the
CAA. In general, the situation is similar to that in the US before the period of
deregulation.

The CAA's policy of ad hoc liberalization (such as its grant of Heathrow–Glasgow/Edinburgh routes to British Midland Airlines) has made the domestic market increasingly competitive. BA's heavily discounted 'Super Shuttle' flights to various UK cities are a manifestation of the aggressive competition from the smaller independents.

3.   The International Scheduled Market

This market segment (37 percent of all passenger trips in the UK) was the core of BA's business, and most of the company's routes were international. The Continental routes constituted slightly more than one-quarter and the North American routes slightly less than one-quarter of BA's revenues.

As the traditional UK flag carrier, BA had 82 percent of the British end of this market. It was on the basis of this market share that the CAA reported:

> BA's dominance of the British airline industry in terms of scale brings it firmly within the meaning of a monopoly situation.[8]

Yet regarding the CAA's estimate of BA's market power, Lord King said, 'it is ridiculous to claim that the airline is a monopoly'.[9]

Commenting on the origins of BA's dominant share of the international scheduled market, the CAA said:

> BA has become overwhelmingly dominant in the UK airline industry as a result of historical accident and government policies rather than commercial power.[10]

BA's two overwhelmingly competitive assets – controlled 'as a result of historical accident and government policies' – were its route structure (about which more will be said below) and its exclusive use of Heathrow Airport for international flights.

Heathrow was not only the biggest international scheduled service airport in Britain, it was also the greatest international air service hub in the world. Approximately 80 percent of BA's flights either originated or terminated there. In January 1984, BA served 108 cities in 63 foreign countries from Heathrow. By contrast, in the same month British Caledonian served only 30 cities in 23 countries from its Gatwick base. To quote the CAA:

> Differences of scale and activity between Heathrow and Gatwick . . . have a significant impact on the effectiveness of competition between British carriers.[11]

To illustrate its point, the CAA referred to the case of British Midland Airlines which, when given government permission to fly from Heathrow to Glasgow, gained in a week the same market share it had taken BCal fifteen years to develop flying from Gatwick to Glasgow.

Allocation of capacity at British airports was the responsibility of the British Airports Authority (BAA). It charged a price for landing and takeoff rights, but the price was less than the true market value as evidenced by excessive demand. This was a consequence of the BAA's policy of pricing to cover costs rather than to make a profit or to use pricing as a rationing mechanism. Since rationing was not done by price, the BAA had to use non-price methods of rationing. For example, charters were forbidden to use Heathrow. As recently as 1970, any scheduled carrier could use Heathrow if it wanted. As capacity utilization rose, new carriers were sent to Gatwick and some of the flights previously to or from Heathrow (such as BA's Spanish operations) were moved to Gatwick. (For data on the UK airports, see Exhibits 19.6 and 19.7.)

Heathrow's capacity was 330,000 air traffic movements (ATMs),[12] but a new terminal was soon to open with an annual limit of 275,000 ATMs. Gatwick had only one runway, and the construction of a second would have led to considerable opposition from environmentalists.

Post-war Evolution of the World Airline Industry

The structure of the world airline industry is based on the Chicago Conference of 1944 which stated in Article 1:

> The contracting states recognize that every state has complete and exclusive sovereignty over airspace above its territory.[13]

Exhibit 19.6

United Kingdom airlines' share of international traffic at certain airports (1984)

UK airport	Scheduled	Charter
Heathrow	39.3%	–
Gatwick	60.7%	81.7%
Manchester	35.6%	88.2%
Birmingham	61.2%	84.7%
Glasgow	26.4%	83.4%
Luton	–	89.6%
United Kingdom TOTAL	43.0%	81.9%

Source: CAA Airline Statistics

Percentage of total United Kingdom international traffic served at London area airports (1984)

	Scheduled	Charter
Heathrow	79.1%	0.2%
Gatwick	13.9%	41.5%
Luton		9.2%
Stansted	0.2%	1.7%
Southend		0.2%
	93.2%	52.8%

Source: CAA Airline Statistics

Exhibit 19.7   *Uses and capacities of London airports (1984)*
(thousands of ATMS)

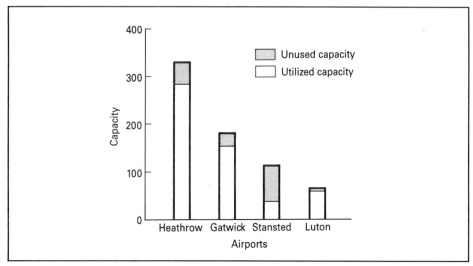

The principal objective of the Conference was to achieve a multilateral system of exchanging air rights. The Conference failed to achieve this, and instead concluded with a system of bilateral international agreements over landing rights,

Exhibit 19.8   *The six freedoms*

1st freedom: the right of a carrier to fly over the territory of another country without landing (e.g. the PanAm airplane can fly over France).

2nd freedom: the right of a carrier to land on the territory of another country for a non-commercial purpose (e.g. the PanAm airplane can make a refueling stop in Paris).

3rd freedom: the right of a carrier to disembark passengers from its home country in another country (e.g. PanAm can leave Americans in Paris).

4th freedom: the right of a carrier to take passengers from another country and to disembark them in its home country (e.g. PanAm can take French travelers to New York).

5th freedom: the right of a carrier to land and take off from a second country and embark and disembark passengers traveling to or from a third country (e.g. the PanAm flight can pick up German travelers in Berlin, land in Paris and disembark a few of them, then continue on to New York).

6th freedom: the right of a carrier to embark and disembark passengers traveling wholly within the boundaries of another country (e.g. the PanAm flight from Berlin can stop in Paris, embark and disembark any passengers, then continue to Marseilles to do the same before leaving for New York).

Source: Paraphrased from Chicago Conference, 1944

gateways, and 'freedoms' (see Exhibit 19.8). Each government designated one of its airlines (its nationalized 'flagship' in most instances) as one of the two airlines (the other being the opposite country's designated airline) entitled to share what was in effect a two-firm cartel on each route. On occasion, a country would designate multiple airlines as joint operators of its half of the cartel. In the case of the UK, the favored airlines were the three nationalized predecessors of BA. By 1985, there were 23,000 bilateral agreements between 200 countries involving 16,000 airports.[14]

In 1945, a further pillar of the post-war aviation industry was established at the Havana Conference where 31 nations approved the articles of a revised International Air Transport Association (IATA). In 1946, the two countries most responsible for the Chicago Agreement, the USA and Britain, signed what was to become the prototype for all other bilateral agreements – the Bermuda Agreement. One of the most important clauses of the agreement delegated the question of whether and how to set fares to the IATA. As one critic of the industry noted:

> As more nations joined the fare-fixing, IATA became both the instrument and the scapegoat for the natural tendencies of the airlines to restrict competition.[15]

IATA also coordinated the growing network of flight routes and timetables. Via its clearing house, IATA created a means whereby travelers could freely transfer from one airline to another using the same ticket (called 'interlining'). It also set up and controlled common safety and navigational standards, engineering cooperation, and pilot training programs.

In Europe, an international agreement in 1967 by the European Civil Aviation Conference (ECAC) set procedures to regulate competition on the Continent. The procedures relied heavily on IATA rules. Under ECAC rules, entry, capacity, route structure, and tariffs were all controlled. An additional method by which the ECAC restricted competition was the 'pooling agreement'. The bilateral negotiations referred to above usually concluded with two designated national airlines flying the same route with equal frequency at a fare above the cost of the high-cost carrier. It was only natural then to establish and share a single pool of revenues. For example, on the Paris–London route, Air France and BA would fly the same number of flights between the two capitals and put their receipts into a pool which would be divided between the two airlines. Fares were fixed by IATA (under the 'double approval' principle by which both governments and both airlines had to agree on the fares), and any service competition (e.g. competition over meals, drinks, movies, etc.) was forbidden. Thus, there was virtually no scope for seeking competitive advantage, and the rewards of any competitive advantage (won, for example, by introducing new aircraft on a shared route) would have to be shared. The only way a carrier could increase its profits relative to its duopoly partner was through relative cost efficiency.

(The situation in Europe contrasted with that in the US where a similar system of fare-fixing by the Civil Aeronautics Board (CAB) prevented price competition, but where there was no revenue pooling and less control of non-price competition.

In particular, there was no control of competition over flight frequency. Thus, US carriers rapidly introduced more and more scheduled flights – and more and more excess capacity – as the principal means of winning customers from other airlines.)

By the early 1980s, very little had changed in Europe. Some international routes had changed hands, but this had only happened when the national flag carriers had declined to exercise their rights to fly these routes.

The US Regulatory Revolution

US airline policy in the late 1970s was an ominous harbinger of change for what Sir Adam Thomson called Europe's 'network of cosy cartels'.[16] President Carter appointed Alfred Kahn, economics professor and ardent deregulator, to head the CAB with a mandate to deregulate the industry and eliminate the agency. This policy was formalized in 1978 with the passage of the Airline Deregulation Act which laid down a six-year timetable (ending in January 1985) for the return of the US domestic airline industry to the discipline of the free market and for the abolition of the CAB.

The 1978 Act phased out entry restrictions and progressively allowed airlines more and more freedom to fly the routes they wished with frequencies and prices they wished. The airlines, previously prohibited from trading routes, began to exchange them to establish efficient networks. Complete freedom to set air fares came on January 1, 1983.

These new freedoms led to the rapid entry of 'instant airlines', principally on local routes where their flexibility was an advantage. By January 1983, 22 wholly new airlines had entered service. This compares to the 28 trunk airlines which existed without increase between the time of the last chartered entrant (1938) and the time of deregulation. Over those forty years of no entry, there was a several thousand percent increase in airline service demand! The new entrants and expanding regional airlines that came with deregulation took 12 percent of the major trunk airlines' market share by 1983.

With relevance to the situation facing the UK in 1984, the new entrants to the US market following deregulation found their expansion hampered by their inability to obtain landing rights at the most popular (and most congested) US airports. Allocation of these rights had been negotiated in scheduling committees made up the older carriers under antitrust immunity. Thus, the established airlines maintained a significant market advantage vis-à-vis the newcomers. But in June 1984, the US Department of Transportation approved an experimental policy of encouraging airlines to buy, sell, or exchange their landing rights at four major US airports (Washington, Chicago, and two in New York City). In approving this experiment with a market for landing slots, the Department of Transportation rejected a proposal to auction the landing slots to start the market. Thus, landing rights now worth millions of dollars were granted for free to their traditional holders. (It was estimated that a 8:00 a.m. departure slot from LaGuardia would be worth hundreds of thousands of dollars in a free market.)

The initial period of US deregulation coincided with record airline profits as the economy boomed and airlines were unable to adjust their capacity. This brief period was followed by the fuel price increase and recession at the end of the decade which resulted in record losses. In 1982, the US industry lost $733 million. But since 1982 the results have been largely positive. Load factors increased, prices fell, price discrimination became less common, and route structures shifted to an efficient 'hub and spoke' system with fewer multistop flights and greater reliance on smaller narrow-bodied jets. As Nicholas Ridley noted:

> Fares are generally lower, the variety of services is enormous . . . There have been extraordinary improvements of air productivity, and the restructuring of air networks more closely reflects what passengers want.[17]

Further studies of the American experience have concluded that 'economies of scale appear to be small or non-existent.'[18] Although most routes in the US continue to be served by only a few carriers (rarely more than two or three), potential entrants make the markets contestable even if their structure is not perfectly competitive.

While it would appear that on the whole the economy benefited from deregulation, there were adverse consequences for some groups including particular consumer groups. Some small communities prevously benefiting from local air service which was cross-subsidized by longer distance flights lost service or faced higher fares. (Traditionally the CAB set fares in direct proportion to distance. Since cost per mile declines with distance, long distance flights earned relatively high margins which supported short low-margin flights.)

Other clear losers have been the employees of some of the older established airlines whose salaries had been much higher than those offered outside the industry or by newer entrants to the market. For example, in 1980, airline typists in America earned forty-one percent more than other typists for the same work.[19]

> Under regulation, airline employees had been able to capture a significant share of the gains of lower-cost technologies by obtaining restrictive work rules and progressively higher wages.[20]

Deregulation changed this dramatically. New airlines were not tied to these historical high-cost wage agreements, and they hired their staff at much lower salaries. For example, they employed pilots at $40,000 per year rather than the typical $80,000 and stewardesses at $15,000 rather than $35,000. Overall, average annual employee compensation in 1983 was $22,000 for the newcomers compared to $42,000 for the older carriers. Labor costs for the former were 18 percent of operating expenses whereas for the latter they were 37 percent. This enabled the 'no frills' airlines to compete very effectively with the established airlines. The latter, in turn, sought to cut their labor costs by renegotiating standing contracts. Some, such as Continental Airlines, filed for bankruptcy to force this renegotiation. In 1983, Continental eliminated two-thirds of its workforce and halved the wages of the remainder.

Further casualties of deregulation were those airlines that did not manage to adjust in terms of cost or route structure to the increasing competition that came with deregulation. At least nine airlines went bankrupt. Furthermore, the charter market virtually disappeared after deregulation since its economic justification rested almost entirely on the regulatory restriction of competition in the scheduled market.

Pressure on the European Cartels

Although the CAB only had unique authority over intra-US flights (where two-fifths of all flights in the world took place), the American experiment constituted a major change in the international environment. The channel through which US policy was transferred to Europe was the North America–Western Europe route network. In 1977, the British and Americans signed a new 'Bermuda 2' agreement to liberalize fares across the Atlantic. When the British tried to maintain some control over price competition, the CAB (with what was to become a familiar tactic) turned to Britain's rival, Holland, and offered the Dutch more American destinations if they accepted the offered agreement. The Dutch agreement was momentous in terms of the precedent it set. There were no restrictions on entry, capacity, or number of designated carriers, and tariffs were to be set unilaterally (with a control only over predatory pricing). No mention was made of IATA. The Dutch agreement forced Britain into a liberal interpretation of 'Bermuda 2' to allow Heathrow and Gatwick (i.e. BA and BCal) to compete with Holland's Schiphol Airport.

In 1982, the US and the members of the ECAC signed the US–ECAC 'Memorandum of Understanding' which led to partial deregulation of all the North Atlantic routes to the US and to dramatic fare reductions. The understanding was reached after the CAB threatened to file an antitrust suit in the US against the airlines for their fare-fixing. The understanding established minimum and maximum fares within which competition would be allowed.

Intensified competition over the North Atlantic led to the entry of low-price 'no frills' airlines such as Sir Freddie Laker's 'Skytrain'. In granting Laker a permit, the CAB hailed Skytrain as 'a golden opportunity to encourage imagination and innovation in the North Atlantic air travel market.' Sir Freddie's innovation was to bring to the scheduled market the low prices of the charter market.

Laker quickly touched off a price war in which the older airlines such as BA and BCal dropped their prices to match or undercut those of Laker. (Sir Adam Thomson described Laker as 'the most disruptive airline on the North Atlantic'.) The price war (or the predatory pricing, as Sir Freddie saw it) and Laker's overexpansion led to the company's bankruptcy in 1982 with a debt of nearly half a billion dollars. In that year, BA set record losses caused in good part by its losses on the Atlantic routes.

Laker's bankruptcy prompted an antitrust investigation by the US Department of Justice which focused on three issues. The first was the allegation that ten major airlines[21] had threatened to end all business with McDonnell Douglas unless the airplane producer pulled out of a reported plan to rescue Laker. The second was the question of whether the companies had used predatory pricing to drive Laker out of business. The final issue was whether Laker had been harmed by a general conspiracy of the ten to fix prices.

In May 1984, the Department of Justice dropped its investigation of the threats to McDonnell Douglas. As of the fall of 1984, it was still investigating the final two issues, but there were rumors that the predatory pricing charge would also be dropped.

The bankruptcy also prompted an antitrust suit in the US by Laker's creditors. The defendants and the charges were the same as those in the US government's investigation. Although this case was civil rather that criminal, the damages for which the defendants could be proven liable were estimated to be about $1.7 billion. In the fall of 1984, the case hung like a pall over BA's privatization. The UK government made no move to offer indemnification to BA's future private-sector owners for any legal obligations, and BA's efforts to negotiate an out-of-court settlement with Laker's creditors had been unsuccessful.

Liberalization Over the Continent?

Deregulation of the North Atlantic routes has left its impact. Over the last ten years, full economy and budget transatlantic fares have fallen by 40 percent in real terms. (By contrast, business fares in Europe doubled in real terms from 1978 to 1984.) The number of passenger-trips has more than doubled from 3 million to 6.4 million annually.

The fervor of deregulation and price competition now seems to be regularly reflected in UK policy statements. To quote Nicholas Ridley:

> The Government stands firmly as the champion of the consumers. We are the flag carriers for lower air fares.[22]

How far price competition can be introduced into Continental markets is unclear, however. In the summer of 1984, the UK and Dutch governments negotiated a 'sixth freedom' agreement between their countries[23] which nearly halved the lowest price round trip fare. The agreement allowed each country to set fares independently of the other, it abolished revenue pooling, and it permitted any carrier from one country to have access to any route to the other with as much capacity as it wanted. An obvious objective was to divert passengers away from routes where the traditional cartel arrangements left uncompetitive prices. Subsequent fare reductions in West Germany, Switzerland, and France can be directly attributed to the agreement. Pressure on Continental European countries to liberalize may thus appear due to the indirect competition of nearby routes. (The process is a repetition of what the US did to induce a liberal UK interpretation of Bermuda 2.) There is a population of 180 million within a radius of 250 miles of Schiphol allowing the airport to siphon traffic from uncompetitive carriers for both UK and inter-continental trips.

(Indirect competition can also originate from fifth freedom carriers such as Singapore Airlines which flies the London–Frankfurt route. But fifth freedom rights apply to only about 1 percent of scheduled inter-ECAC flights.)

Consumer complaints are another source of pressure for liberalization. Again quoting Mr Ridley:

> It will be very difficult to tell the citizens of Paris that the Dutch can have fares lower by two-thirds than they have.[24]

Over the years, IATA has lost influence as the industry price-fixing body as well. In 1960, IATA members carried 90 percent of the world's scheduled passenger traffic. By 1983, that share had fallen to 70 percent as a result of the growth of non-IATA members such as Singapore Airlines, People Express, and Virgin Airlines. And IATA officials admit that only about 60 percent of their official fares are complied with.

Nonetheless, there is considerable resistance to an extension into Europe of the American experience with a free market in airline services. Deregulation US-style would necessitate the agreement of different nations since, in contrast to the US, most intra-European flights are international. (For example, 80 percent of West German air service demand is international, and the country has 11 international airports.) And whereas liberalization obviously looks attractive to a country like Britain with a low-cost carrier and with only ship service to the Continent as an alternative to air service, it looks much less attractive to the large Continental countries with high-cost carriers, relatively large internal markets, and fast international train services.

Change is obviously feared by countries with high-cost carriers. The differences in costs across airlines and countries can be extremely large. According to IATA reports, European operating costs are 67 percent higher than US costs. More costly fuel and landing fees, lower volumes, and shorter average stage lengths account for part of this difference, but salary and other productivity differences are also pronounced. Whereas BA's labor costs are 27 percent of sales, such costs are only 13 percent of sales for all US carriers (post-deregulation) and 5 percent of sales for People Express. Salary costs of Lufthansa and Swissair are three to four times higher than those of BA.[25] Competition would thus have a dramatic impact on the relative fortunes of different employee groups, carriers and countries. (See Exhibit 19.9 for airline cost comparisons.)

Furthermore, all airlines, European and non-European, will need to make heavy investments in the new generation of aircraft now entering service. The 135 airlines which are members of IATA will need $150–$200 billion over the next decade to buy 2,000 new aircraft. (Ironically, much of the demand for new aircraft, especially for a new 150-seater, is due to the changes in route structure and densities caused by the regulatory changes discussed here.) Yet 1984 will be the first year since 1977 in which they will show a combined profit – of only $1.2 billion! Competition, it is claimed, will prevent the necessary profit levels.

The Commission of the European Communities is categorically in favor of liberalizing the European market, but it has not yet had the political power to

Exhibit 19.9   *Airline cost comparisons (1980)**

Carrier	Cost index
British Caledonian	0.91
Pan American	0.94
TWA	0.99
KLM	1.15
Air France	1.18
SAS	1.21
British Airways	1.24
Alitalia	1.25
UTA	1.25
Lufthansa	1.27
Sabena	1.28

* The figures shown are based on an index.
Note that this is prior to BA's cost-cutting.
Source: Findlay and Forsythe, *Competitiveness of
Internationally Traded Services: The Case of
International Airlines*

influence events. In 1974, the European Court of Justice stated that the objectives and rules of the Treaty of Rome (such as non-discrimination and the prohibition of cartels) should apply to the airline industry. Yet it was not until 1984 that the Commission initiated action. Its 'Memorandum No. 2', issued in February 1984, contains proposals for minimum and maximum fares within which airlines would fight it out. (This Memorandum is patterned after that of the US and the ECAC.) The price minimum is intended to prevent 'destructive' price wars detrimental to all carriers but especially small ones. It also recommends ending the revenue-sharing cartels, forcing the 50/50 capacity sharing agreements to vary up to 25/75, and easing entry of small airlines. Yet Memorandum No. 2 has provoked such criticism from European airlines and governments that its future is uncertain. It is estimated to be a couple of years before anything with legal standing comes out of the Commission, and even then the final policy is expected to be weak because it requiries the unanimous approval of the Council of Transport Ministers.

In testifying against Memorandum No. 2 before the Commission, Karl-Heinz Neumeister, Secretary-General of the Association of European Airlines, asked:

> Are antitrust laws applicable to air transport, when governments in Europe already control or own the airlines? Obviously, antitrust laws are a method of protecting the consumer from the potential or real excesses of private enterprise.[26]

The Cabinet Committee's Impending Report

All parties involved directly or indirectly in the Cabinet Committee's decision had reason to fear its outcome.

BA feared that the proposals in the CAA Report would be sustained by the Committee and thus strengthened. Any transfer of routes would be perceived as a betrayal of BA's employees who had suffered so much in the previous few years to improve the company's position. It would also be perceived as a personal betrayal of Lord King whose only fault (apparent to the company) was to have been too successful. And from the purely commercial viewpoint, a loss of routes would reduce the value of BA to the private financial community to whom the airline was soon to be offered.

BCal feared that a privatized BA would be a menace to the rest of the industry and particularly to BCal. Summing up his concern, Sir Adam Thomson said:

> Endowed with profitable routes and public funds, rescued from bankruptcy by a benevolent government, and operating from a virtually impregnable position at Heathrow, the world's busiest international gateway, BA in private hands would be in a position to stifle us.

Perhaps a more subtle fear was that unless the regulatory environment of the industry were changed before the BA sale, it would effectively remain unchangeable for the foreseeable future.

The other independent airlines feared a BA–BCal duopoly. From their point of view, the only thing worse than a BA monopoly was a BA–BCal duopoly implying twice the resistance to the growth of the smaller independents. The fate of Laker and the other 13 independent British airlines to have gone out of business since 1974 was a stark memory.

The CAA feared that rejection of its comprehensive report would destroy its credibility vis-à-vis the airline industry in general and particularly vis-à-vis its biggest regulatory client – BA. And if the CAA's proposals were rejected, BA would constitute an even more obdurate adversary. Although exaggerating to the extent of suggesting that BA was on the verge of monopolizing the British international air transport industry, the CAA specifically cited this problem in its July report.

> If British Airways were to become the sole British operator of international services, it would be the more difficult for this Authority to bring effective pressures to bear upon it.[27]

In terms of the political background to the Cabinet Committee's deliberations, Mrs Thatcher was thought to favor Lord King to whom she had apparently made a promise of an untouched BA for sale to the private market. Lord Whitelaw – the Deputy Prime Minister – was a personal friend of Sir Adam Thomson. The Treasury wanted BA privatized as soon as possible at the highest price. The Trade Secretary, Norman Tebbitt, was a former BOAC pilot whose personal leaning was towards the privatization of BA with no route changes.

Nicholas Ridley's situation as he faced the September 13 deadline was aptly summed up by *The Observer*.

> Whichever way he jumps, he now faces political embarrassment. Either he will break up BA – thus delaying its privatization plans indefinitely – or he will leave BA's route

network intact and be seen to have ignored the CAA's most searching policy review for 20 years.[28]

Notes

1. *Daily Mail,* August 16, 1984.
2. Quoted in D. Heald and D. Steel, 'Privatizing Public Enterprise: An Analysis of the Government's Case', *Political Quarterly*, July 1982, pp. 333–349.
3. M. Beesley and S. Littlechild, 'Privatization: Principles, Problems and Priorities', *Lloyds Bank Review*, July 1983, pp. 1–20.
4. Addressing a conference of stockbrokers, November 1, 1983.
5. Mrs Thatcher was at the time trying to privatize all non-medical services in the National Health Service where unionized cleaners, porters, and catering personnel had led bitter nationwide strikes.
6. CAA, 'Airline Competition Policy', July 1984.
7. Ibid.
8. Ibid.
9. Lord King, in a letter to *The Times*, July 6, 1984.
10. CAA, *op. cit.*
11. Ibid.
12. An ATM is a takeoff or landing of an aircraft engaged in transporting commercial passengers or cargo.
13. Quoted in A. Sampson, *Empire of the Sky*, London, 1984, p. 69.
14. *International Herald Tribune*, May 3, 1985.
15. Sampson, *op. cit.*, p. 74.
16. Sir Adam Thomson, quoted in *The Sunday Telegraph*, August 12, 1984.
17. *Hansard*, May 5, 1984.
18. P. J. Forsyth, 'Airline Regulation in the US: The Lessons for Europe', *Fiscal Studies*, November 1983.
19. Sampson, *op. cit.*
20. D. Graham and D. Kaplan, 'Competition and the Airlines: An evaluation of Deregulation', CAB Staff Report, 1982.
21. The prospective defendants included BA, BCAL, Pan AM, TWA, Lufthansa, Swissair, Sabena, KLM, UTA, and SAS.
22. *Hansard*, June 22, 1984.
23. This means, for example, that a traveler could book a ticket in Glasgow on a KLM flight via Amersterdam to the Far East without going through London. Such a prospect of selling long-haul fares over another airline's home base is clearly advantageous for efficient airlines from small strategically placed countries.
24. *Hansard*, May 5, 1984.
25. *International Herald Tribune*, February 15, 1985.
26. *International Herald Tribune*, November 21, 1984.
27. CAA, *op. cit.* p. 2.
28. *The Observer*, July 22, 1984.

British Airways

H. Landis Gabel

British Airways' market power is a major national asset where the British industry is in competition with foreign operators.[1]

British Airways is in favour of competitive solutions where competitive opportunities are available and where the result of adopting them is the overall strengthening of the UK civil aviation industry and the national interest.[2]

When Lord King (then Sir John King) was appointed Chairman of British Airways (BA) in 1981, there seemed to be little likelihood that BA would be a serious candidate for privatization in the foreseeable future. The company was over-manned, saddled with very heavy debt and losing money (see Exhibits 19.2 to 19.4 of 'The Privatization of British Airways' for BA's financial results). The whole airline industry was in the midst of one of the worst recessions in its history.

The year 1981 saw Lord King and his newly appointed Chief Executive, Colin Marshall, assessing the damaged state of the company and writing off all potential losses to start the next years afresh. The poor operating results for the first few years were exacerbated by huge redundancy payments, but by 1984 BA had reduced its workforce from 59,000 to 37,000, saving £200 million in annual wages. It cut its aircraft fleet by a third to eliminate old high-cost equipment, and it abandoned 62 routes. At the same time, in a demonstration of the government's confidence in BA's new leadership, the airline became one of the first in the industry to place heavy orders for the new generation of fuel-efficient aircraft regarded as essential to long-term profitable operations. BA invested £400 million to acquire 17 Boeing 757s, the most economical aircraft the company ever operated. More recently, it committed a further £200 million to lease 14 smaller Boeing 737s with an option on a further 17.

By 1984, Lord King and Colin Marshall could claim that on the basis of operating results, BA was the world's most profitable airline!

This remarkable reversal in BA's fortunes – at great sacrifice from the existing

---

This case was prepared by Robert Levy, MBA Candidate, INSEAD under the supervision of H. Landis Gabel, Associate Professor at INSEAD. It is intended to be used as a basis for class discussion rather than to illustrate either effective or ineffective handling of an administrative situation.
Copyright © 1985 INSEAD, Fontainebleau, France.

workforce – was accomplished with the specific objective of preparing BA for privatization. And it was reported that Lord King had received assurances from his personal friend, Mrs Thatcher (who had appointed him), and from various ministers that the company would be kept intact in the process of privatization. These implied or explicit assurances were, in turn, communicated to BA's employees.

Now, however, BA was threatened by a proposal from the Civil Aviation Authority (CAA) to transfer routes worth about 7 percent of its operating revenues to its rival, British Caledonian Airways (BCal) (see 'The Privatization of British Airways'). As a BA spokesman put it:

> It would be a poor reward for BA and its staff if the consequence of its efforts were to be the arbitrary removal of a share of its business . . . It would be ironic, not to say unfair, if BA were now to be penalized for its increased efficiency.[3]

Lord King himself echoed the same sentiment:

> The dismemberment of BA would be a breach of faith to the Board which engineered the turnaround in its fortunes and the workforce which made sacrifices enabling the turnaround to become a reality.[4]

> I would regard it as a resignation issue, but whether I would resign, I don't know. My philosophy is that I accept resignations, I don't submit them.[5]

A likely consequence of implementing the CAA's proposals to transfer routes from BA to BCal was suggested in an article in the *Financial Times*:

> If the CAA proposals were approved, the Board would not resign, but would publicly refuse to accept any such transfers . . . That in turn would almost inevitably force Mr Nicholas Ridley . . . to sack the board.[6]

British Airways' Case for Competition

Beyond the political and possibly ethical points noted above, BA argued that to remain competitive in world markets, it could not afford to lose routes to other UK carriers. The company's case was expressed by one of its powerful supporters, Industry Secretary (and former airline pilot) Norman Tebbitt:

> I think that the strongest case for maintaining a large British Airways is that it's existing in competition with a lot of other giants – Pan Am, TWA, Lufthansa, . . . When there is enormous international competition and the competing companies are giants themselves, we need big companies to compete.[7]

Lord King himself also insisted that any transfer of routes from BA to BCal would not enhance competition but would rather 'weaken BA's ability to compete with other international airlines such as Pan Am and TWA'.[8]

The basic argument was that on most international routes, one British airline (BA or BCal) would be competing with a single foreign airline, and any diminution of the market share of the stronger UK airline (presumably BA) would only help the relative position of the foreign carrier. So righting a competitive imbalance between BA and BCal would be no policy success if it created a competitive imbalance between BA and some foreign carriers. In fact, a former BA chief executive, Roy Watts, suggested that a single major British airline be established which would match the power of foreign competitors. The obvious suggestion was that BA should buy BCal after privatization. The suggestion was reportedly made with the knowledge of Lord King.

One specific threat to the UK's national interest, a threat acknowledged by the CAA, was that a transfer of international routes from BA to BCal would also transfer arrivals and departures from Heathrow to Gatwick. Travelers unwilling to accept the move to the less popular Gatwick had the option of flying on a foreign carrier based at Heathrow. Going beyond this, Heathrow competed with overseas airports like Schiphol in the Netherlands which advertised itself as London's third airport. Any weakening of the attractiveness of Heathrow could transfer passengers out of the UK altogether.

BA was willing to accept dual designation on routes where there was sufficient demand (see Exhibits 20.1 and 20.2 for data on route densities), but even the CAA reported that this was not often the case. (Monopoly efficiencies start to become exhausted at about 2,000 passengers daily.)

> It seems fairly clear that only a very limited number of inter-continental markets could support additional competing British services based predominantly on end-to-end traffic.[9]

Since there was so little scope for new route entry, the CAA proposal only amounted to substituting one UK carrier for another with no obvious reason to expect increased competition (see Exhibit 20.3). As a BA spokesman summarized it,

> There is a major fallacy in the argument that to transfer routes from one British airline to another would create more competition.[10]

Exhibit 20.1 *Principal United Kingdom air travel markets*

Market	Passengers (millions)
United Kingdom – Spain	9.6
– USA	5.8
– France	3.3
– Germany	3.2
– Italy	2.5
– Greece	2.0
– Netherlands	1.8
– Ireland	1.6
– Switzerland	1.7
– Canada	1.4
– Portugal	1.1

Source: CAA Airline Statistics

Exhibit 20.2 *London/Europe scheduled passengers (1983) – routes
exceeding 100,000 passengers per annum*

Route	No. of passengers	Route	No. of passengers
Paris*	2,132,000	Stockholm	238,000
Amsterdam*	1,076,000	Munich**	238,000
Dublin*	878,000	Nice	222,000
Frankfurt*	723,000	Malta	203,000
Brussels*	610,000	Malaga	193,000
Zurich*	533,000	Lisbon	184,000
Copenhagen	392,000	Cork*	157,000
Rome	379,000	Rotterdam	147,000
Dusseldorf	371,000	Cologne**	143,000
Athens	366,000	Vienna**	139,000
Milan	353,000	Stuttgart**	127,000
Madrid	336,000	Helsinki**	127,000
Oslo	293,000	Shannon**	124,000
Hamburg**	292,000	Berlin	116,000
Larnaca	258,000	Hanover**	106,000

* Competing Heathrow and Gatwick services operated by British
carriers.
** Competing Heathrow and Gatwick services licensed to British
carriers but not operated from both airports.
Source: CAA Airline Statistics

All of BA's arguments have to be seen in the context of its hopes for privatization. Colin Marshall was explicit about the threat that the policy debate posed for BA's stock flotation.

> From our perspective, any conclusion other than a continuation of the status quo is going to call into question the whole issue of privatization – and certainly the timing of our flotation.[11]

A transfer of some routes to BCal would not only deprive BA of some of its most valuable assets, but it would also set a precedent which could threaten the security of BA's hold on any of its routes. One logical long-term implication of the CAA's proposed policy to 'improve the balance' between BA and BCal was that opportunities for future growth would be directed to the smaller airlines. In addition, a policy of favoring the development of Gatwick would benefit only the smaller airlines since the CAA proposed to move BA out of that airport. The financial market would surely incorporate the implications of any CAA policy changes in its valuation of BA shares.

All these threats risked causing an indefinite postponement of BA's privatization. And this postponement, in turn, could jeopardize the credibility of a government committed to increasing the scope of the private sector.

Exhibit 20.3   *British Airways advertisement*

And may the best airline win.

The Civil Aviation Authority airline proposals recommend handing over 30 major routes that British Airways currently operate to other British airlines on a plate.

This would simply substitute another airline for British Airways on a route, and would give no additional choice at all to the British fare paying passenger.

It does nothing to stimulate better service since there's no extra competition.

And it will greatly damage our airline industry as a whole, and benefit major foreign airlines. First, because the foreigners will no longer have to compete with the strongest national carrier.

And second, because there's no guarantee that passengers who would normally choose British Airways would be happy to switch to other British airlines.

Particularly in overseas markets where they might well be unknown.

Wouldn't a more sensible way of maintaining Britain's share in this fiercely competitive market be to allow other British airlines to fly *in competition* with us on the routes they choose?

Not *instead* of us.

Indeed, with a bit of healthy competition we should build on Britain's share between us.

Let's put it to the test, and may the best airline win.

British airways

The world's favourite airline

Notes

1.   CAA, 'Airline Competition Policy', July 1984.
2.   British Airways' submission to the Civil Aviation Authority, May 11, 1984.
3.   British Airways spokesman quoted in the *Financial Times*, February 2, 1984.
4.   Quoted in *The Observer*, September 19, 1984.
5.   Quoted in *The Times*, May 2, 1984.
6.   *Financial Times*, September 10, 1984.
7.   Quoted in *The Daily Telegraph*, January 9, 1984.
8.   Quoted in *The Observer*, September 23, 1984.
9.   CAA, *op. cit.*, p. 43.
10. BA spokesman, quoted in the *Financial Times*, February 2, 1984.
11. Quoted in *The Times*, March 7, 1984.

British Caledonian Airways

H. Landis Gabel

British Caledonian Airways (BCal) is Europe's largest privately owned scheduled-service airline and operates more than 700 passenger and cargo flights each week. The company was created in 1961 and reached its current form in 1970 following a takeover of British United Airways. BCal has subsequently grown to become Europe's ninth largest airline (larger than some national carriers) and the 28th largest airline in the free world. In 1983 it was designated the 'Business Executives' Airline of the Year'. Of perhaps greater significance, the Caledonian Aviation Group was generally profitable at a time when most airlines lost money (see Exhibits 21.1 and 21.2 for financial data). The Group is very strongly committed to aviation-based activities, and its only non-aviation subsidiaries are in the travel industry (such as travel agencies and hotels).

The success of BCal is a personal tribute to its founder, Sir Adam Thomson. A 58 year old Scotsman, Sir Adam has been described as 'a canny Scot, a very shrewd operator who plays his cards close to his chest'.[1] A British Airways (BA) executive put it differently:

> Give Adam something now and he will be back for more.[2]

He is reputed to be obsessively single-minded and determined when he perceives his airline's interests to be threatened. For example, when Laker Airlines was about to collapse, McDonnell Douglas (the American aircraft manufacturer) was rumored to be planning a rescue by taking a share in the ailing airline. Sir Adam was described as 'incoherent with anger', calling Laker 'the most disruptive airline on the North Atlantic'. He allegedly informed McDonnell Douglas that if the rumor were true, he would cancel all further business dealings with the manufacturer.[3] (This threat became an element of both the US government's antitrust investigation and the antitrust case that Laker's creditors filed in the US against BCal, BA, and eight other large airlines.) This determination characterized Sir Adam's opposition to the

This case was prepared by Robert Levy, MBA Candidate at INSEAD under the supervision of H. Landis Gabel, Associate Professor at INSEAD. It is intended to be used as a basis for class discussion rather than to illustrate either effective or ineffective handling of an administrative situation.

Exhibit 21.1   *British Caledonian consolidated profit and loss account – 1983*

	1983 '000	1982 '000
Turnover	428,484	400,556
Cost of sales	(344,334)	(326,065)
Gross Profit	84,150	74,491
Marketing costs	(31,998)	(27,387)
Administration expenses	(34,965)	(30,260)
Other operating income	513	340
Operating Profit	17,700	17,178
Profits/(losses) on disposal of		
tangible fixed assets and investments	1,851	(178)
Income from shares in related companies	116	94
Income from fixed asset investments	20	19
Net interest payable	(16,350)	(15,577)
Profit on Ordinary Activities before Taxation	3,337	1,542
Tax on profit on ordinary activities	(1,211)	(811)
Profit for the financial year attributable to		
shareholders	2,126	731
Earnings per share	10.7p	3.7p

privatization of British Airways in its current form. Specifically, Sir Adam feared that the UK government would relieve BA of most of its debt and would offer the firm to the private sector with no change in its route structure or airport usage. As *The Sunday Telegraph* put it:

> Competing with an overblown, inefficient, uncanny and unprofitable state-owned airline is one thing. Flying against a slim, motivated, private and – most important of all – decently financed airline, which is what BA could become by this time next year, is another.[4]

This threat and the fact that privatization would necessitate setting and then guaranteeing for the foreseeable future British aviation rules to the satisfaction of the investing public prompted Sir Adam to issue his 'Blue Book' on November 3, 1983. In this report, he outlined his ideas for the future structure of the British aviation industry and offered to buy routes from BA which constituted 20 percent of BA's profits (for details, see Exhibit 21.3).

Tactically, Sir Adam's timing was perfect. Sir John Moore, Financial Secretary to the Treasury, had delivered a major speech only two days earlier stating that the principal objective of privatization was to increase competition in the industry. And in December 1983, the Minister of Transport, Nicholas Ridley, announced that the Civil Aviation Authority (CAA) would carry out a major review of the UK airline industry.

Exhibit 21.2 *British Caledonian consolidated balance sheet – 1983*

	1983 Group '000	1983 Company '000	1982 Group '000	1982 Company '000
Net Assets Employed				
Fixed Assets:				
Intangible assets	1,861	–	2,674	–
Tangible assets	242,782	5,391	227,948	5,216
Investments	3,088	48,036	453	48,836
	247,731	53,427	231,075	54,052
Current Assets				
Stocks	19,168	–	17,725	–
Debtors	85,419	16,926	73,768	12,679
Cash at bank and in hand	69,118	81	56,364	1,457
	173,705	17,007	147,857	14,136
Creditors – Amounts falling due within one year				
Trade and other	(155,937)	(9,417)	(138,871)	(6,978)
Working capital	17,768	7,590	8,986	7,158
Loans and term finance	(34,336)	(413)	(24,278)	(1,000)
Net Current Assets/(Liabilities)	(16,568)	7,177	(15,292)	6,158
Total Assets less Current Liabilities	231,163	60,604	215,783	60,210
Creditors – Amounts falling due after more than one year				
Loans and term finance	(160,297)	(4,372)	(158,773)	(4,785)
Deferred Income	(1,633)	–	(1,585)	–
	69,233	56,232	55,425	55,425
Represented by				
Capital and Reserves				
Called up share capital	19,807	19,807	19,807	19,807
Revaluation reserve	24,381	962	13,798	981
Profit and loss account	25,045	35,463	21,820	34,637
	69,233	56,232	55,425	55,425

BCal's Public Relations Offensive

In a carefully orchestrated and expensive public relations offensive, BCal took its case to the public and, more specifically, to the powerful Conservative backbench MPs.

The core of BCal's argument was that competition in the UK aviation industry only existed to a very limited degree. Over the years, the government had granted BA approximately 80 percent of the UK-originating international scheduled market – a market characterized by cartel pricing and revenue pooling. Furthermore, BA's

Exhibit 21.3 *British Caledonian proposals*

In November 1983, Sir Adam Thomson, Chairman of British Caledonian, made public his bid to secure the transfer of a significant proportion of British Airway's routes and related assets at what he considered a fair market price. His detailed proposals were never published, but knowledgeable sources indicated that they fell into three major categories:

1. British Airways should transfer to British Caledonian licenses to fly routes in the following five categories:
    *   All British Airways routes to Spain, Portugal, Bologna, Naples, Copenhagen, Stockholm originating from Gatwick.
    *   All British Airways flights to eight Caribbean destinations.
    *   The North Pacific routes including Tokyo, Beijing and Seoul.
    *   Low-frequency British Airways flights to Turkey, Cyprus, Greece, Malta, Austria and Finland.
    *   British Airways routes to the Arabian Gulf, including Abu Dhabi and Kuwait.
2. On the transfer of these routes, British Caledonian should reimburse British Airways at their estimated market value of £200–£250 million.
3. In order to serve these routes, British Caledonian would purchase from British Airways seven Boeing 747 jumbo jets and nine Boeing 737 narrow-bodied jets, worth about £300 million.

These proposals formed the basis of British Caledonian's submission to the CAA early in 1984, although it is understood that British Caledonian proposed an even more substantial set of route transfers. As they stood, the November 1983 proposals envisaged the transfer of 20 percent of British Airways' profits, and a significantly higher proportion of its revenues. In addition, Thomson also proposed that British Airways' domestic German routes, its feeder domestic UK traffic, and the charter subsidiary, British Airtours, be sold to other independent airlines. This represented another £20 million in profit. Thomson couched his proposals in the following terms:

> The time has never been more opportune for the Government to take a visionary initiative to create a really strong and highly competitive civil aviation industry in wholly private ownership and to lay down a framework for long-term growth.

He added that:

> Routes have never been sold before, but I'm happy to talk about it to the right people.

Lord King of British Airways, who presumably was one of 'the right people', responded that British Caledonian's proposals were a 'smash and grab raid' and declared:

> The boarding party they have in mind might well have been more successful when we're on our backs.

exclusive right to Heathrow Airport for international departures was a major competitive advantage which, like its international market share, was granted to it by government policy rather than won competitively. From this protected market base, BA would be able to cross-subsidize its operations in the more competitive domestic and charter markets to the detriment of smaller carriers.

The CAA's report was issued in July 1984 and endorsed this argument.

BA is therefore very well placed to use international route profits to support expansion in other markets. Despite regulatory constraints, it could deploy this market power, almost at will, in any particular market where it chose to compete aggressively with other British airlines. It is this potential for exploiting its market power which frightens many respondents . . . It is often difficult to distinguish between normal competitive behavior and behavior that is predatory in character.[5]

As part of its public relations campaign, BCal attempted to refute some of BA's arguments, including BA's claim that it competed 'fiercely' with the other airlines of the world.

It is nonsense for BA to suggest that it competes with hundreds of foreign airlines. Their system is rigged with a network of cosy cartels.[6]

BCal also ridiculed BA's offer to let BCal compete alongside it on any international route BCal chose. As BCal pointed out, the offer sounded fair, but under the current system of bilaterial agreements any entry of BCal onto an international route would require the approval of a foreign government – an unlikely prospect.

Competition cannot exist unless the contestants have equal access to the market place . . . Plainly BA is saying that it is all for competition so long as it can have the High Street supermarket while its competitor must be happy with some corner grocery stores.[7]

BCal's exclusion from most international routes due to the bilateral cartel structure of the route system led to BCal's offer to buy routes from BA. When Lord King, Chairman of BA, called BCal's offer 'a smash and grab raid',[8] Sir Adam replied that at least it would be a golden brick that would come through Lord King's window.

Again, BCal's case had the endorsement of the CAA.

There is a need for an alternative airline, which although relatively smaller than BA, would nonetheless be capable of operating as a world-class airline and could replace BA on a major international route should the need arise. BCal is the only airline which the UK has that is immediately capable of filling that role.[9]

The CAA also sought to encourage indirect competition between BA and BCal. It granted BCal a license to fly to Riyadh in Saudi Arabia in February 1984 while allowing BA to continue scheduled services to Jeddah and Dharan.

The CAA concluded that the interests of users would be better served if more than one British airline operated services to Saudi Arabia . . . Indirect competition is likely to be beneficial and users will gain from the enhanced service and wider choice.[10]

While BCal's campaign emphasized the need for greater competition, stressing that this was the principal declared objective of privatization, it introduced other issues as well. BCal was based at Gatwick Airport while BA was based at Heathrow, Europe's busiest airport. In 1983 Heathrow accounted for nearly 80 percent of total UK scheduled international traffic and Gatwick only 14 percent. Any transfer of routes from BA to BCal would mean a corresponding movement from Heathrow to Gatwick and would further the government's objective of reducing the discrepancy between the two airports. Quoting the CAA:

> Present airports policy . . . has not yet been wholly successful either developing Gatwick's full potential or in providing the infrastructure for a fully competitive British airline industry.[11]

When asked what would happen if BCal were not granted some new routes, Sir Adam replied, 'We would have to apply for a transfer to Heathrow.'[12] It was not clear to observers whether Sir Adam hoped (or threatened) to move all or only some of his flights to Heathrow, but there would be important employment and capacity utilization implications of any significant shift.

BCal emphasized that it did not intend to reduce substantially the size of BA. Even if all the route transfers asked for by BCal were effected, BA would remain the dominant British airline with about 70 percent of international scheduled services. In BCal's view, this would leave BA 'still a most attractive privatization candidate'.[13]

BCal's strongly voiced opinion that the entire industry was threatened by a privatized and unfettered BA monopoly was shared by all the other independent airlines. However, BCal's additional opinion that 'except in special circumstances, there is only room for two international airlines from the UK'[14] led to cynical press commentary.

> Monopolies are like small babies. You may think they are really unattractive – but just wait until you have one of your own![15]

Notes

1. Graham Bright, MP, quoted in *The Times*, August 16, 1984.
2. Ibid.
3. Ibid.
4. *The Sunday Telegraph*, November 13, 1983.
5. CAA, 'Airline Competition Policy,' July 1984, p. 5.
6. Sir Adam Thomson, quoted in *The Sunday Telegraph*, August 12, 1984.
7. BCal, 'The Historic Opportunity'.
8. *The Observer*, November 13, 1983.
9. CAA, *op. cit.*
10. CAA, quoted in the *Financial Times*, February 15, 1984.
11. CAA, *op. cit.*, p. 6.
12. *The Observer*, September 16, 1984.
13. *Financial Times*, September 12, 1984.
14. Sir Adam Thomson, quoted in the *Daily Mail*, February 28, 1984.
15. *Daily Mail, op. cit.*

CASE 22

EC Competition Policy
The Merger and Acquisition Directive

Jonathan Story

Introduction

The European Community's twelve members pledged to create a single market encompassing 320 million consumers by January 1, 1993. Only a home market of that size, they reckoned, would offer EC firms the economies of scale needed to reduce inefficiencies and compete effectively against American and Japanese companies. Various predictions for the expected benefits were floated: the Cecchini report forecast savings of Ecu 200 billion, of which from one-third to one-half would come from rationalization of inefficient firms.

As mergers and acquisitions play a central role in restructuring, Commission oversight of mergers would be key. But here the Commission had a double mandate: competition policy must be flexible enough to allow the sort of concentration needed to achieve the predicted economies and strict enough to prevent the formation of EC-wide or regional oligopolies that impede the entry of new firms and penalize consumers.

Merger Policy: 1957 to 1984

Articles 85 and 86 of the 1957 Treaty of Rome form the legal basis for the Commission's mandate over competition. Article 85 essentially bans cartels, price fixing and other forms of collusion, placing them under the Commission's jurisdiction when they distort competition in the Common Market. Article 86 empowers the Commission to police mergers (Exhibit 22.1).

In the Continental Can case of February, 1973, the European Court of Justice upheld the principle that Article 86 gave the Commission power to police mergers,

This case was written by Ethan Schwartz, Research Assistant, under the supervision of Jonathan Story, Professor at INSEAD. It is intended to be used as a basis for class discussion rather than to illustrate either effective or ineffective handling of an administrative situation.
Copyright © 1991 INSEAD-CEDEP, Fontainebleau, France. Revised 1992.
Financial support from the INSEAD Alumni Fund European Case Programme is gratefully acknowledged.

Exhibit 22.1

Article 85

1. The following shall be prohibited as incompatible with the common market: all agreements between undertakings, decision by associations of undertakings and concerted practices which may affect trade between Member States and which have as their object or effect the prevention, restriction or distortion of competition within the common market, and in particular those which:

(a) directly or indirectly fix purchase or selling prices or any other trading conditions;

(b) limit or control production, markets, technical development, or investment;

(c) share markets or sources of supply;

(d) share dissimilar conditions to equivalent transactions with other trading parties, thereby placing them at a competitive disadvantage;

(e) make the conclusion of contracts subject to acceptance by the other parties of supplementary obligations which, by their nature or according to commercial usage, have no connection with the subject of such contracts.

2. Any agreement or decisions prohibited pursuant to this Article shall be automatically void.

3. The provisions of paragraph 1 may, however, be declared inapplicable in the case of:

– any agreement or category of agreements between undertakings;

– any declaration or category of decisions by associations of undertakings:

– any concerted practice or category of concerted practices;

which contributes to improving the production or distribution of goods or to promoting technical or economic progress, while allowing consumers a fair share of the resulting benefit, and which does not

(a) impose on the undertakings concerned with restrictions which are not indispensable to the attainment of these objectives;

(b) afford such undertakings the possibility of eliminating competition in respect of a substantial part of the products in question.

Article 86

Any abuse by one of more undertakings of dominant position with the common market or in a substantial part of it shall be prohibited as incompatible with the common market in so far as it may affect trade between Member States.

Such abuse may, in particular, consist in:

(a) directly or indirectly imposing unfair purchase or selling prices or other unfair trading conditions;

(b) limiting production, markets or technical development to the prejudice of consumers;

(c) applying dissimilar conditions to equivalent transactions with other trading parties, thereby placing them at a competitive disadvantage;

(d) making the conclusion of contracts subject to acceptance by the other parties of supplementary obligations which, by their nature or according to commercial usage, have no connection with the subject of such contracts.

Source: Treaty of Rome, Annexes 85 and 86

ruling the acquisition of more market share by an already dominant firm could constitute restraint of trade, as defined in the Article. But this only gave the Commission the right to challenge mergers after they occurred – not before. And only acquisitions by an already dominant firm could be challenged. Moreover, the Commission would have to prove abuse had already taken place.[1] Thus, the Court's ruling said Articles 85 and 86 governed only firm behaviour, not structural change to the market like much international anti-trust law. How to interpret dominance and abuse in a 'significant portion of the Community' was left vague.

The first directive draft was presented to the Council of Ministers, in July 1973, but languished for ten years because France, Great Britain and Italy believed it gave the Commission too much power.

In December 1981 the Commission proposed its second draft. Brussels set the threshold for Commission jurisdiction to final turnover of 500 million ECUs. Companies would have to have 20 percent of their sales volume in the whole EC. Mergers involving the acquisition of firms with under 30 million ECU turnover would be exempted. The final say would rest with the Commission, not the states or the Council.[2]

The Commission also affirmed it would block only a concentration that gives a firm the 'power to create an obstacle to effective competition'. So the power to abuse – structural market change – rather than abuse itself, would be enough to ban a merger.

The twelve began forming battle lines.

- France led a group of states demanding the text clearly permit mergers that accomplished national or EC-wide industrial policy aims, or regional and social goals.

- Britain and France still wanted final authority to rest with the member states.

- Italy asked for exemptions for public enterprises. Rome also objected to a proposal that firms notify Brussels of planned mergers before they went through.

- Only Germany and the Benelux countries favoured giving the Commission final authority. And only Denmark sought a 'pure' competition text, with no loopholes for industrial policy.[3]

In February 1984 Brussels drafted a new version, raising the threshold to 750 million ECU turnover. Below that number, fusions would be considered only if they produced companies with 50 percent EC market share. Again, firms with less than 20 percent total volume in the EC could merge as they wished, and purchases of firms with less than 30 million ECU turnover would be legal. Some wordage was thrown in to pledge greater consultation between the Commission and Council. But the Commission would keep final authority to approve or reject.[4]

Council, however, still showed little determination to overcome its differences and adopt Community-level merger control.

Germany

Government

The federal system means the governing coalition must strive for consensus with the Länder and private interests. The Ministry of Finance controls finance, taxation, and the industrial subsidies, while the Ministry for Economic Affairs manages broader issues including medium-term economic policy, regional and structural policies, and competition.[5] The need to win over the regional governments encourages high public subsidies.

The Bundesbank and the Bundeskartellamt both influence mergers and acquisitions. The latter is considered to be among the strongest anti-trust bodies in Europe.[6] It investigates, holds inquests, and makes the initial rulings on mergers, company agreements, and other threats to competition, and can impose fines and sanctions. Still, final authority rests with the Minister of Economics, who may overturn the Bundeskartellamt rulings on 'national interest' grounds such as technology, defence and energy policy, or regional and social policy.

Nationalized Industries

The German government owns a small proportion of national business. Federal and Länder governments run railroads, mail, telecommunications and 'essential industries'. Federal and state banks with 1988 assets of DM 170 billion, excluding the Bundesbank, play some role in carrying out industrial and regional policies.

Germany pursued some privatization in the late 1980s, cutting the number of firms with federal participation from 808 in 1985 to 239 in 1988.[7] But regional pressures limited the impact of the exercise.

Private Industry

Concentration was the trend in the 1970s and 1980s, with a handful of 'elephants' emerging. By the early 1980s eight large industrial groups – VEBA, VW, Daimler-Benz, Siemens, Hoechst, BASF, Bayer, and Thyssen – were taking 42 percent of Germany's turnover.[8]

The Banks

The link between Germany's universal banks, particularly the big three – Deutsche Bank, Dresdner Bank and Commerzbank – and major industrial groups forms the 'structural bedrock' of Germany's economy.[9] A 1978 Monopolies Commission inquiry found 22 out of 26 major bank holdings in the top 100 firms amounted to more than the 25 percent required by law to block shareholder approval. The Commission concluded the banks 'substantially influence a good portion of the overall decision-making of the large firms'. By 1988 the ten largest financial institutions held 37.3 percent of all financial institution assets.[10]

Labour

Organized labour wields a unique clout in Germany. A 1976 regulation requires that half of all supervisory board members in firms with over 2,000 employees must be chosen by workers. Workers' councils give labour additional influence. German unions, unlike those in other countries, are organized around pan-industrial bodies rather than at the shop or local level. Union chiefs can thus thrash out major settlements with industry and government and have sufficient authority to ensure that their own clientele implement them. Labour has the power to help steer industrial policy.

Merger Policy

The Bundeskartellamt has control over mergers between companies with aggregate turnover of at least DM 500 million; or aggregate employment of more than 10,000 people; or aggregate sales of at least DM 1 billion; or firms that would give the participants 20 percent of a market.

   Still, with final authority resting with the Ministry of Economics, competition authorities banned only four of 582 mergers which came under their purview between 1973 and 1975.[11]

   Otto von Lambsdorff, as Economics Minister, approved several major mergers over Bundeskartellamt opposition.[12] The Bundeskartellamt and the Social Democrats also called for stricter anti-trust enforcement against the 'elephants'[13] and there were similar calls from small and mid-size firms for protection,[14] with some support from the Liberal Party (FDP). A September 1980 amendment gave the Bundeskartellamt control over smaller mergers, but again left final authority with the minister.

   The Daimler-Benz's takeover of AEG illustrates the disputes over concentration law and the role of Germany's big three banks.

The Daimler-Benz MBB Merger

While the Liberal Party called for new bank limits, Liberal Minister Bangemann became the mastermind of the most controversial merger proposal in post-war Germany, Daimler-Benz's acquisition of MBB aeronautics and defence. Bangemann launched the suggestion in late 1987, claiming he wanted to get Airbus, in which MBB owned a 37.9 percent stake, out of the public trough by hooking MBB up with a cash-rich firm.[15] He painted the deal in liberal colours, claiming it marked a 'major advance towards denationalization' of German industries.[16]

The Bundeskartellamt, however, believed Bangemann, with backing from the big banks and industry, favoured a pro-active industrial policy to form national giants over competition concerns. The deal moved forward in spring, 1987, when Deutschebank's chief, Alfred Herrhausen, used the bank's influence – it held a 28 percent share in Daimler – to force out its president and install Edzard Reuter in his place. The two businessmen made no secret that they wanted to pursue Bangemann's suggestion to bid for MBB. But they demanded government guarantees against possible currency losses in Airbus.[17]

Critics began to howl over such an 'elephant marriage'. The new firm would receive 40 percent of Germany's defence spending, so the Defence Ministry balked.[18] Daimler already had a lead into the Christian Democrats; Kohl rarely left the country without a Daimler official by his side.[19]

The mammoth metal workers union was struggling with Daimler over work schedules and pay, and feared any strengthening of Daimler's industrial clout.[20] The governments of Bavaria, Hamburg and Bremen together owned the majority stake in MBB and would have to vet any deal. Social Democrats lambasted the proposed strengthening of the 'military–industrial complex'.[21] The Liberal Party's Von Lambsdorff raised doubts about Bangemann's plans, under pressure from Kartte, the head of the Bundeskartellamt, who called the proposed fusion 'idiotic'.[22] The Christian Democrats were divided, the Christian Democratic Union's Mittelstand-vereinigung – the association of mid-size enterprises – criticized the move as a threat to smaller firms. Monopoly Commission director Ulrich Immenga attacked the proposal.[23] And overseas, US Trade Representative Clayton Yeutter called the planned fusion 'unacceptable', saying Bonn's promises to guarantee Daimler losses would violate GATT rules and worsen US-German trade tensions.[24]

Bangemann went to Brussels with the new Commission in winter of 1988–89, only deepening the Bundeskartellamt's fear of industrial policy leanings in the EC.

Barriers to Takeover

Most foreigners see Germany as a difficult market for acquisitions. Its stock markets are tiny relative to Britain's (Exhibit 22.2). The high ratio of bank assets to capitalization suggests far greater reliance on banks than stock issues for finance. The two-tier board system makes it difficult to change management, and labour can block unwanted bids. Poor access to shareholders, ability to restrict voting rights, and the voting of proxy shares by banks means there is little tradition of a 'shareholders' democracy'.

France

French industry has depended traditionally on the government for direction, finance and support.

Exhibit 22.2

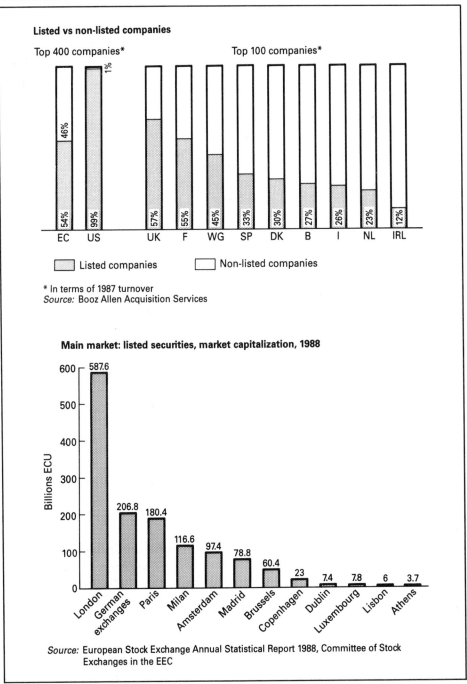

Listed vs non-listed companies

Top 400 companies*   Top 100 companies*

1%

46%

54%   99%   57%   55%   45%   33%   30%   27%   26%   23%   12%

EC   US   UK   F   WG   SP   DK   B   I   NL   IRL

☐ Listed companies   ☐ Non-listed companies

* In terms of 1987 turnover
Source: Booz Allen Acquisition Services

Main market: listed securities, market capitalization, 1988

587.6

206.8 180.4
                116.6 97.4 78.8 60.4 23 7.4 7.8 6 3.7

London German Paris Milan Amsterdam Madrid Brussels Copenhagen Dublin Luxembourg Lisbon Athens
       exchanges

Billions ECU

Source: European Stock Exchange Annual Statistical Report 1988, Committee of Stock
Exchanges in the EEC

Government

The Ministry of Finance and Economics keeps discretionary powers over merger activity. No clear criteria exist for evaluating proposed fusions; they are considered under general competition standards.[25]

Nationalized Industries

François Mitterrand came to power in 1981, and his first two years in office saw extensive nationalizations. All told, the government nationalized 36 banks, two financial companies, and eleven industrial concerns from 1981 to 1986. By 1986 the state managed 24 percent of France's employees, controlled 32 percent of France's sales, 30 percent of its exports and 60 percent of its annual investment in industry and energy.[26]

. . . and Chirac's Privatizations

Jacques Chirac's centre-right coalition came to power in 1986 advocating industrial restructuring and a massive privatization program involving 66 nationally owned firms worth 300 billion French francs and employing 900,000 workers, pledging to make France a nation of shareholders and property owners.

The 1987 stockmarket crash halted the sell-off in mid-stream, and only eight big corporations, three smaller banks and three small firms, all profitable, were sold. Twenty-five percent of the holdings in most firms were sold to a 'noyau stable' or stable nucleus of approximately ten investors. Almost all these big buyers came from an old-boys network with close ties to French industry and political leaders.[27] Both the public share offerings and 'noyau stable' offerings were over-subscribed, suggesting heavy discounting of corporate value.

The government also slapped on new restrictions against foreign share purchases and erected several new barriers to outside takeovers. Foreigners were initially allowed to purchase only 20 percent of the new privatized firms; if they attempted to buy more on the market, the Minister of Finance could create 'preference shares' to dilute foreign control.

Purchase of 20 percent of any firm's capital by foreigners would henceforth require notification of the ministry, and non-EC purchasers would need approval from the Committee for the Establishment of Credit. Purchasers of minority stakes would now be required to notify the ministry when their holdings passed thresholds of 5, 10, 20, 33 and 50 percent, allowing ample time for defensive measures. And many firms enacted measures to publicize any purchase of more than 1 percent of their stock.

Mitterrand halted the privatization plan when 1988 elections returned him to power. Then began the era of the 'ni-ni', neither-nor, when the Socialists said they would neither renew nationalization nor hold further equity sales of nationalized corporations.

Finance

From 1961 to 1982 the Bourse remained neutered, as France pursued a state-guided credit-based financial system. In 1972 one government loan amounted to three times the total for all Bourse issues of the year.[28] State funding crowded out both stock and private banks as sources for credit, and nearly three-quarters of all banks belonged to the state.

Slowly reforms started to take hold. In the 1970s and 80s, new financial instruments were permitted, both long- and short-term, and negotiable bank certificates of deposit were created. In 1986 the Paris financial futures market was opened, and it became competitive with the London International Financial Futures Exchange. Fixed commissions for financial services were cut back. The 'Commission des Opérations de la Bourse', the main regulatory body, was given greater oversight powers, with new transparency regulations enacted. Finally, the financial markets were invigorated by a surge of international competition.

On the banking side, the government cut back on state credit-control. In 1979, state or para-state institutions provided 75 percent of all loans to businesses. By 1986 only one of six original types of state subsidized loans was left. Exchange controls were all but lifted in 1985.[29] The money supply and interest rates became market regulated.

By the end of the 1980s France was preaching market-based restructuring of her industries. Still, tremendous domestic and social pressure for pro-active industrial and economic solutions continued to exist.

Barriers to Acquisitions

Financial markets were less developed in France than in the United States or Great Britain; the Bourse's market capitalization stood at 20.3 percent of GDP in 1988.[30] The relative economic weight of listed companies; and the market value of domestically listed companies were all low (Exhibit 22.2); the ratio of bank assets to stock capitalization stood at $250 billion in France in 1987.[31]

A 1989 study written for the European Commission concluded France, along with West Germany, was one of the most restrictive markets for takeovers.[32] Continued state ownership of many firms; the ways in which privatization was undertaken – including the 'noyau dur' and new prior clearance regulations for foreigners – presented hurdles for foreign buyers.

The government had shown willingness to use anti-trust rules as a protection against foreign buyers. The audit profession was underdeveloped and reliable information was hard to come by. Bank, family, and cross-shareholdings between subsidiaries and parent companies were all considered barriers to unwanted bids – companies could issue warrants to 'protectors clubs' to be used in case of danger.[33]

Other barriers include a 5 percent notification threshold, which corporations can lower to 0.5 percent of capital; boards' abilities to vote blank votes; and the fact that share trading may be suspended at the time of any offer. Offerors must aim to acquire at least two-thirds of voting rights.

A cultural block against foreign purchases also existed. One French banker said 'Paris is a small community – everyone knows everyone else. The establishment really does exist. The French raiders – Benedetti and Goldsmith – are in fact members of the Parisian financial establishment. There are unwritten rules and codes of behaviour... It would be dangerous to be excluded from the establishment. A highly speculative profession does not exist in France.'[34]

Great Britain

For most of the post-war period, Britain's *laissez-faire* faith was tempered by a dominant policy of Keynesian economic manipulation, as successive governments looked to macro-economic demand management in an attempt to seek full employment, greater growth, and avoid the pitfalls of the market cycle.[35]

Government

The British government's economic policy revolves around two institutions, the Bank of England and the Treasury. Both have shown little concern for industry. Britain's civil service takes decisions in great secrecy and policy incrementalism is the rule.

The Labour Party has, since its inception, been clearly suspicious of industrial capital,[36] as have elements of the Conservative Party. Both views mitigated against a heavily interventionist industrial policy. Conservative capitalism evolved to show more concern for banking and 'city' interests rather than industrial benefit.[37] British manufacturing came to rely on the stock market and issues of equity for capital.

Unions in Great Britain have traditionally had a far wider reach than their French counterparts, with one-half of the workforce enrolled in 1975. But internally unions are weak, as they are structured along trade and shop lines. Union leadership could never impose industrial reform on its rank and file.

Industrial Policy and Public Enterprises

The post-war Labour government's nationalization of some key sectors such as electricity, gas, mail services, telecommunications and water gave Britain one of Europe's largest public enterprise sectors through to 1979.[38]

In the 1960s, Britain's manufacturing sector was rocked by a dwindling share of world trade, productivity growth that lagged behind Japan and continental Europe, and low investment rates. This led to greater concentration among companies: the share of the top 100 manufacturers in the islands' net output rose from 16 percent in 1909 to 41 percent in 1970.[39]

Government industrial subsidies also rose. Between 1971 and 1979 the government spent £920 million on private sector subsidies, the same portion of domestic GNP as that spent by France and Germany.[40] The Department of Industry became the lead ministry for industrial policy. In 1975 the National Enterprise Board was upgraded to acquire firms, but it soon became burdened by the acquisitions of beleaguered companies like Ferranti, British Leyland, Alfred Herbert, and Rolls-Royce.

Margaret Thatcher took over the reins of British government in 1979 promising a market-led revolution for Britain's economy. The government cut back on the rescue missions of ailing firms, but subsidies continued as the government awaited the end of the recession. With the economic upturn, the government began privatizations, and by the end of 1985 at least one-half of government shares in a dozen companies under state ownership were sold.[41] More than 400,000 jobs went private, and £7 billion was raised through the sales.

Britain's privatization was far more directed towards individual shareholders than was France's. But the goal of a shareholders' democracy remained elusive, as many buyers sold out quickly to institutions for quick capital gains. It was also unclear to what extent the Thatcher government sought to place these firms under competitive market pressures. 'When the crunch came, private ownership was much higher on the government's priorities than competition.'[42]

Competition Policy

Britain's competition policy is non-statutory, and therefore highly discretionary. Authorities examine whether mergers are in the 'public interest', rather than just anti-competitive.

A 1973 bill placed all acquisitions worth more than £5 million, or all fusions involving a combined market share of 25 percent or more under government control. The threshold was raised to £15 million in 1980, and £30 million in 1984 – reflecting a Thatcherite belief firms should be given leeway to restructure. Criticism of the government's concentration policies have stressed inconsistent goals, influenced by 'behind the scenes lobbying', with the 'more noise opponents of a merger make, the more likely it will be referred' to the Monopoly Commission (which makes recommendations on mergers to the Minister of Industry).[43]

Under Thatcher, a record number of mergers were sent to the Monopoly Commission for evaluation. The government took a particularly hard view of conglomerate mergers even if the fusions did not increase market share, but simply gave the new conglomerate greater resources with which to fight off potential entrants.[44]

Still, the Monopoly Commission's criteria for evaluating fusions remained fuzzy. Several mergers saw the Ministry overrule either the Monopoly Commission or the Office of Fair Trade to protect national firms, or the Commission hand down judgements based on assessment of the new management team's competence.[45] The vagueness of the Monopoly Commission's mandate and evaluation procedures came under fire from investment bankers. 'The biggest risk is the uncertainty of monopoly laws and their uneven application', said one New York arbitrager.[46]

Tebbit Pledges Competition

In July, 1984, Norman Tebbit, the new Secretary of State for Trade and Industry, pledged competition would be the main criteria for evaluation. But the discretionary procedure was still retained. A director of Morgan Grenfell said 'companies and their buyers can never be absolutely sure what the ground rules are'.[47]

There were several controversial cases.

The government's decision to heed the Monopoly Commission's blocking of GEC's bid for Plessey capped a major political battle. GEC's chief Lord Weinstock had argued in favour of the purchase on the grounds it would help GEC face international competition. The Ministry of Trade and Industry, as well as the city's bankers, supported him. But the Minister of Defence opposed the fusion on the grounds it would give too much power to British defence contractors, who are protected by political pressure to 'buy domestic' from international competition.[48] The Commission rejected Weinstock's argument about the need for electronic giants to compete worldwide. Thus, the bid was blocked more because it could not be proven to be 'in the public interest', than because it would harm competition.

- As the merger boom continued, critics became more vociferous. The Labour Party railed against the financial casino. Among the Conservatives, Michael Heseltine sought to use merger policy for broader industrial aims. In Spring 1988 he led a group of Conservatives who wanted the Swiss Nestlé's bid for Rowntree referred on national interest grounds. The government refused, declaring that on competition grounds the bid posed no danger, and any attempt to block it might draw retaliation against British bidders for foreign firms.

- Fears of foreign takeovers of British firms, and complaints about barriers in other countries, became a major issue. In 1988–89 Rowntree, Jaguar, Intercontinental Hotels, Pearl Group, and Metal Box were among the many that fell to overseas owners.

There were cries in British industry either to 'level the playing field' and eliminate barriers to acquisitions overseas, or erect barriers at home. These could be discriminatory – just against countries deemed protectionist, or non-discretionary – designed to make British firms as safe as those in continental countries and Japan. But banks, eager to continue their business, lobbied against any protectionist measures.

Barriers to Acquisitions

Aside from the non-statutory nature of British anti-trust procedures, the market resembles that in the United States for openness and transparency. Market capitalization is high, equalling 98.1 percent of GDP in 1988 (Exhibit 22.2). In 1987, the ratio of bank assets to stock capitalization stood at one to one. Information is regulated and consistent.[49] A 1989 study commissioned by the European Commission and authored by Booz Allen ranked Britain as one of the most liberal markets for acquisition.

Italy

Italian politics, economics, public and private life are enmeshed in a system of warring power groups that depend on regional, social, and political allegiances.

Government

In Italy, the political parties rule. The dominant Christian Democratic Party is really a conglomeration of clannish factions. All party factions use state positions to aid their own clientele. They make appointments at all levels of the administration, in the mammoth state industries and banks, and in a host of government agencies. Federal spending sends money to regional clientele, and plays an essential role in unifying the fractured nation. One-half of Italy's gross domestic product is spent by the government, compared to about one-third in the United States.

Nationalized Industry

Italian public enterprises are of a scale that has 'no parallel in any other country',[50] with only Austria's government owning more in developed states. The IRI, a government holding company created in 1933 to support key sectors of the economy, controls 100 percent of shipbuilding and airlines, four-fifths of the nation's steel and metal works, almost all telecommunications, and a heavy chunk of auto-related industries. ENI, another holding company, does about 20 billion Lire business a year in the energy sector.

The 1970s saw more than 50 nationalizations of private companies, but policy changed in the 1980s, thanks to a growing government deficit. Although a dozen companies were sold off in the early 80s, Italy's privatization was only one-fifth the size of either Great Britain's or France's. The companies themselves decided what pieces to sell, making the process subject to Italian political and social pressures.[51] The Minister of State-Financed Enterprises' authority was debated on a case by case basis.

The sell-offs did little to create a shareholders' democracy in Italy, as shares were largely shifted to large private groups.[52] Thus, Agnelli's Fiat was allowed to buy Alfa Romeo, though Ford made a better offer. A ferocious union–industrial–regional battle preceded the decision, but ultimately 'national' interest in keeping Alfa fully Italian was proclaimed.

Private Sector

The Italian government's industrial clout, fractured as it is among political parties, is matched by the power of a few private sector groups. Chief among these is Fiat's Agnelli family, the Pirelli group, and Montedison.

The Agnelli family itself controls nearly one-quarter of the Italian stock exchange, or $25 billion worth of quoted companies.[53] Fiat has been nicknamed the EC's '13th member state' for its continental-wide influence, often opposed to the Italian government. Through Mediobanca, several captains of industry pool minority stakes to give them control over a satellite of companies orbiting around Fiat, Pirelli, Olivetti, Montedison, Mondadori, Zanussi and Generalli. Their 1988 holdings tallied about $2.5 billion, but they were believed to control far more. In the late 1980s these industrialists' ability to takeover a nominally public bank sparked a national outcry. The lack of information and strict accounting standards made tracing the web of power difficult.

One private sector specialty was to sell off to government ailing private firms – usually portrayed as an act of generosity by the seller – or force government to sell off public holdings for bargain-basement prices. The major buyers and sellers in Italy's markets for corporate assets were thus the government and private sector groups.

Trade unions, with eight million private sector members, represent labour in the power mix. They are in continual negotiations with employers and the government, and all have political affiliations.

Barriers to Acquisitions

Financial markets were extremely weak in Italy; the market capitalization of the main market of Milan stood at only 16.4 percent of GDP in 1988.[54] The relative economic weight of listed companies as well as the value of domestically listed companies were all very low (see Exhibit 22.2).

The ratio of bank assets to stock capitalization in 1987 stood at near $17 billion, suggesting strong reliance on banks as a source of financing.

In Italy, legal and technical barriers to acquisition were hard to pinpoint, perhaps because Italian industry is so protected by its strong cultural allergy to foreign acquisitions, and the intricacy of its internal allegiances and political–industrial links. Information about most corporations is exceptionally limited, and of over 200 listed companies, only seven have more than half of their shares in public hands. Two-thirds of the market value of the Milan Exchange is controlled by five groups: Generali, Fiat, IRI, Ferruzzi, and De Benedetti, who take 18, 17, 16, 7, and 6 percent of the exchange respectively. High debt/equity ratios on the market made financing difficult. The partnership form of quoted companies is another barrier, as are non-voting shares and notification requirements after 2 percent ownership is taken.[55]

The prospect of a competitive threat from a borderless Europe, and the political parties' perpetual efforts to wrest control from the industrial magnates led to some efforts in 1987 to draft stricter merger-control laws. Cesare Romiti, the Fiat chief, denounced the efforts in Summer 1987 as 'anti-capitalist vomit'.[56]

Spain

Spanish industrial policy under General Franco centred on twin goals: protectionism against foreign goods, and domestic intervention to ensure self-sufficiency and economic stability.[57]

For most of the post-war period, therefore, Spanish companies faced almost no external and very little internal competition. Self-sufficiency in key sectors was obtained through subsidies and nationalization of industries by the State holding company, INI, founded in 1941. In the 1970s INI supported weak sectors and absorbed firms too ill to remain in the private sector. INI subsidies rose from 3.5 billion francs in 1975 to 39 billion in 1983. That same year INI was 11 billion Francs in the red.

The Socialists came to power in 1982, and set out to reform the industrial landscape. Selling off loss-makers, particularly to foreign firms, was a major component of that project. So, the automobile producer Seat went to Volkswagen in 1986, Secoinsa Informatica was sold to Fujitsu, and Ateinsa and la Maquinista, two transport firms, became part of Alsthom as part of a Spanish deal to purchase trains from the French firm. All told, 30 INI enterprises out of 180 were privatized between 1985 and 1988, bringing it a 1.5 billion franc profit in 1988.[58]

The presence of multinationals in the Spanish economy increased, and by the late 1980s foreign based firms accounted for roughly 47 percent of all turnover in major industries and 43 percent of employment.[59]

Barriers to Acquisitions

The lack of reliable corporate information, non-disclosure of shareholdings, and links between banks and families presented strong barriers to takeover in Spain. Cross-shareholdings between corporations and subsidiaries could also be used to block unwanted bids. Nonetheless, the Madrid stockmarket was one of the most buoyant in the late 1980s.

The Smaller Countries

As a rule, financial markets in the 1980s were far less developed in the smaller EC states – as in France and West Germany – than in Great Britain. Far fewer firms were listed publicly, holdings were more concentrated, and acquisitions were more difficult to finance through public offerings (Exhibit 22.2).

Most of the smaller states were deemed highly hostile to foreign takeovers, with structural, technical, and cultural barriers in place.

Cross-ownership presented a barrier in Belgium, as did the use of non-voting shares. Belgium's business community has also been described as close-knit and secretive.[60]

The Netherlands also had a close-knit and secretive business community. But here the technical barriers to taking control of management presented the most formidable obstacles. These included the two-tier board structure which makes it difficult to change management; the use of priority shares and foundations to control companies; the employees works council, which can delay acquisitions for at least one month, or longer if it appeals to the courts to block a bid; the lack of access to shareholders; and various barriers which prevent small shareholders from responding to attractive bids.[61]

Danish companies were well protected by widespread family ownership. Foundations were used to avoid inheritance taxes while retaining family control. Corporations could raise capital through issuance of special 'B' shares that carry reduced voting rights. Also, the use of partnerships as a form of ownership for quoted companies reduces the risks of takeovers. Finally, issuance of non-voting shares also presented a barrier.

Overall, a 1989 study commissioned by the European Commission and authored by the consulting firm Booz Allen ranked Belgium and Britain as the most liberal markets for acquisitions; Denmark, Spain and Italy as moderately restrictive, and the Netherlands, West Germany and France as highly restrictive for takeovers. Contested takeovers were very rare outside of the UK; in 1988 there were 44 there, 6 in France, 3 in Belgium, 2 in Spain, 1 in the Netherlands, 1 in Denmark, and none anywhere else, including West Germany.

Rebirth of Commission Merger Control

The merger mania that swept Europe in the mid 1980s highlighted the need for a Community text on mergers and acquisitions. The value of takeovers tripled from 1985 to 1988 in the UK to 57 billion ECUs, and increased sevenfold in France to 26.5 billion ECUs.[62] Cross border mergers within the EC, particularly acquisitions by French and Italian firms, soared (Exhibit 22.3). Corporate restructuring became a political buzzword in France, Spain, and other countries which felt their industries too small to compete on a global scale.

Commissioner Peter Sutherland, responsible for DG IV, dealing with competition, pushed for a tough anti-concentration line, and greater power for the

Exhibit 22.3 *Cross-border acquisitions*

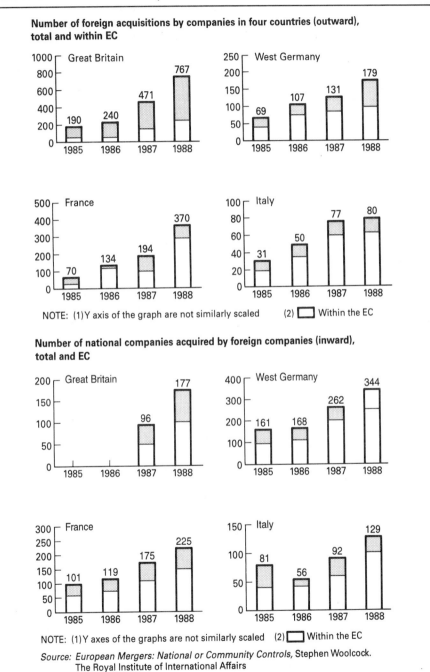

Number of foreign acquisitions by companies in four countries (outward), total and within EC

NOTE: (1) Y axis of the graph are not similarly scaled   (2) ☐ Within the EC

Number of national companies acquired by foreign companies (inward), total and EC

NOTE: (1) Y axes of the graphs are not similarly scaled   (2) ☐ Within the EC

Source: European Mergers: National or Community Controls, Stephen Woolcock. The Royal Institute of International Affairs

Commission. He pledged the Commission would take a soft line on mergers needed to fight US and Japanese competition. But he also threatened the Commission would use its court-granted powers to fight mergers with Articles 85 and 86 if no new text was adopted.

Several court rulings bolstered his threat. In the 1987 Philip Morris ruling, the Court upheld the Commission's right to ban the taking of minority stakes – a move which typically precedes acquisitions – under Article 85. Industry feared Article 85 because of its breadth and automatic nullification of illegal moves. And the decision raised questions about how joint ventures would be defined.

Sutherland scored another major victory in early 1988, when British Airways and British Caledonian agreed to his demand to change the terms of their merger and cede key landing rights, even though British merger authorities had approved the deal. Finally that year the Commission blocked the takeover of Irish Distillers Group by GC&C, a holding company formed by a British consortium of three drink-firms, after complaints the holding company had been formed specifically to prevent more competitive bids. Industry screamed for a clarification of EC merger controls. The Commission also preferred a merger regulation as a way to augment its 'federal' powers.

In spring 1988 Sutherland presented yet another draft regulation for Council consideration. This one would ban any creation or reinforcement of a dominant position. It would only cover mergers leading to creation of a firm with more than one billion ECUs turnover worldwide. The acquired firm would have to have a turnover of 50 million ECUs. Also, if the new firm were to have more than three-quarters of sales in one state, it could be judged by national authorities – an important plum. Finally, if its market share were under 20 percent in the whole EC or a substantial part, it would be legal.

There were other important caveats. The text said the Commission must consider factors 'other' than mere dominance, such as 'the amelioration of production and distribution, promotion of technical or economic progress, and amelioration of the competitive structure in the interior of the common market', though these criteria would be considered only in so far as the merger did not block competition.

The Commission also would promise to take account of 'international competition', i.e. the United States and Japan, 'as well as the interests of the consumers.'

In another important point, the draft spoke of firms acquiring 'control' of other companies. Thus, the 25 percent acquisition allowing for blockage of corporate action in Germany, or the 33.3 percent allowing such action in France, might often fall under the EC's purview.[63] Finally, the Commission would 'liaise with the Council'. But still, final say would rest with the Commission.

Sutherland estimated the regulation would have given the Commission control of about 150 mergers over 1986–87; numbers furnished by the member states placed that figure closer to 200 (Exhibit 22.4). Germany might see 112 mergers involving a German firm going to the Commission, Great Britain 81, and France.

In July 1988 Sutherland amended the draft further to woo more Council members, adding dominance itself would not be the sin. Rather, the Commission would have to prove the new structure 'harms the market'.[64]

The Member States React

Germany

Germany's decision to back Sutherland's efforts to draft a Community-level merger control marked a crucial impetus in his campaign in 1987.[65] German officials involved in the issue took the stance, at least publicly, that any European text should evaluate mergers on competition grounds alone, and not be muddied by industrial policy issues as demanded by other member states.[66]

However, German officials' motives for supporting a pure competition document differed. Clearly, the Bundeskartellamt favoured a strict text for competition reasons. But Commission and Bundeskartellamt officials believed the Ministry of Economics – with Bangemann at the helm – favoured such a text because German industrialists complained that their continental competitors in member states without strong anti-trust rules had an advantage because they could restructure and merge domestically without facing Bundeskartellamt-like restrictions. So, elements in German industry and in the ministry had a somewhat less than pure motive for supporting a text: a means of 'levelling the playing field' by forcing Bundeskartellamt-like structures on other European firms, or, if the text was weak, a means of escaping the Bundeskartellamt back home.

> 'The German firms always claimed they were handicapped, because of the strong competition system in Germany,' one Bundeskartellamt official said. 'Volkswagen could never buy BMW, but Fiat could buy Alfa Romeo, or French and Italian firms could merge. So German industries wished either to weaken the German position, or strengthen the Commission's.'

The Bundeskartellamt, thus, never trusted Brussels to enforce a competition policy clean of any politicking – particularly after Bangemann arrived.[67]

Under pressure from Kartte, Germany floated proposals for a two-step process under which an independent body similar to the Bundeskartellamt would evaluate the proposed fusion on pure competition grounds, and the Commission would then accept or reject the decision. This, it was thought, would force the Commission to either defend its decision publicly or admit to political considerations.[68] National authorities would retain powers to veto Commission approval on competition grounds. German federal authorities favoured a text that would have the Commission 'tolerating', rather than 'authorizing' mergers.[69]

Kartte's distrust of Brussels, particularly after Bangemann took over as Commissioner of Internal Market and Industrial Affairs, made him all the more keen to keep powers in Berlin, officials at the Bundeskartellamt said. And after the MBB-Daimler merger, Bonn had to appease him, at least symbolically.[70]

Exhibit 22.4 *Distribution of national, community and international mergers (including acquisitions of majority holdings) in the industrial sector by country in 1986/87 (combined turnover >1, >2, >5, >10 billion ECU)*

Countries (EEC)	National (1)				Community (2)				International (3)				Total			
	>1	>2	>5	>10	>1	>2	>5	>10	>1	>2	>5	>10	>1	>2	>5	>10
1. Belgium	1				1	1							2	1		
2. Denmark					1								1			
3. FRG	24	19	11	4	12	10	5	1	1	1			37	30	16	5
4. Greece																
5. France	28	21	12	6	9	5	3	3	4	2	2		41	28	17	10
6. Ireland					1	1							1	1		
7. Italy	10	6	6	3	10	10	6	2	1				21	16	12	4
8. Luxembourg					1	1							1	1		
9. Netherlands	5	4	3	1	1	2	2						6	6	4	1
10. UK	40	22	9	3	8	7	3	3					50	29	12	6
11. Spain	3	1	1	1	8	5	5	4	2				11	6	6	5
12. Portugal																
Total	111	73	42	18	52	42	24	13	8	3	2		171	118	67	31

(1) Mergers of firms from the same member country
(2) Mergers of firms from different member countries
(3) Mergers of firms from member countries and third countries with effects on the Community markets

Exhibit 22.4 *continued*

Countries (EEC)	National (1)				Community (2)				International (3)				Total			
	>1	>2	>5	>10	>1	>2	>5	>10	>1	>2	>5	>10	>1	>2	>5	>10
1. Belgium																
2. Denmark																
3. FRG	5	4	3	1									5	4	3	1
4. Greece																
5. France	4	3	1	0									4	3	1	0
6. Ireland																
7. Italy																
8. Luxembourg																
9. Netherlands	2	1			1	1	1						3	2	1	0
10. UK	8	4	2	0									8	4	2	0
11. Spain					1	1	1						1	1	1	0
12. Portugal																
Total	19	12	6	1	2	2	2						21	14	8	1

(1) Mergers of firms from the same member country
(2) Mergers of firms from different member countries
(3) Mergers of firms from member countries and third countries with effects on the Community markets
Source: Internal French memo based on Commission statistics

Great Britain

The Office of Fair Trading, too, wanted British negotiators to make the achievement of a pure competition text their foremost goal. It fought to have the proposed text exclude all non-competitive criteria for merger consideration, and formed an alliance with the Bundeskartellamt on the question.

Free-market faith also led the British to back wording that would block only dominant positions that would act as barriers to competition – not dominant positions *per se*.

Some in the Ministry of Trade and Industry wanted to have the Commission vet almost all Community mergers, thereby superseding continental national authorities who were perceived as using anti-trust law to block foreign takeovers. This paralleled the wish by many British industrialists, as well as in investment banking, to seek a one-stop shop that would clarify the anti-trust hurdles to mergers. Many in banking saw British anti-trust policy as one of the few domestic hurdles to mergers, and hoped transferring some powers to Brussels might lower the barrier.

Underlying OFT's unwillingness to consider these other goals was a deep mistrust of Brussels, particularly of Directorate General III. Officials in OFT, and those who supported the office in the ministry, were convinced Brussels would use any anti-trust regulation to impose a European industrial policy, rather than rely on the market.

'The moment the full horror of it struck was when it became apparent the Commission was seeking a one-stop shop. That meant whatever objections national authorities had, they would be powerless to oppose the Commission,' a British official in the Department of Trade and Industry said. But that horror may have been less of a concern in quarters of the Department of Trade and Industry where the goal was to clarify the jurisdictional situation and eliminate barriers in other member states. These officials were not sympathetic to Germany's wish to retain national authority, and suspected the Bundeskartellamt's proposed two-step approach might be manipulated by others in Germany and elsewhere for industrial policy aims.

'We told the Germans if one benefit is to eliminate barriers to entry, then it really is in our interest to rely on the Commission and not allow loopholes,' another DTI official said.

The same British negotiators, however, sought to insert a clause that would allow a loophole giving national authorities the right to take measures to protect 'national public interest'. There was fear of other states' public firms buying private British ones, as well as a general wish to see British authorities retain the 'public interest' discretion enshrined in their own anti-trust laws. At the same time, the British suspected any attempts by Germany, France, or others to retain controls for their national authorities, fearing non-competition criteria might creep in. Like the French, they wanted some discretion at home, but none abroad.

France

The French debate involved the Ministry of Industry, the Ministry of Economics and Finance, and Foreign Affairs and other industries seeking a symbolic victory in France's push for a strengthened EC. A desire to circumvent anti-trust authorities in foreign states, the wish for juridical clarity to aid French acquisitions in Europe and the need to be seen as supporting the EC all pointed to giving maximum authority to the Commission. But the need to retain national control to protect against foreign investment, and the wish to place as few restrictions as possible on French firms seeking to restructure – both domestically and abroad – called for restricting Commission powers as much as possible. To that end, the French claimed they supported a loose text that would allow firms to merge for industrial and technological reasons, even if competition was weakened. But at the same time, many in the Ministry of Finance feared giving Brussels such discretionary powers to determine France's own industrial policy.

In the summer of 1988, after Mitterrand had been returned to power, the Ministry of Industry sided with giving the Commission more power. The Ministry of Finance still had its doubts. For one, the Commission might become involved in local markets such as cement or distribution, where acquisitions might surpass the proposed thresholds but the effects would be felt only regionally. Also, the Commission might take decisions without looking at inflationary effects. And finally, that any draft would reverse EC legal precedents that gave member states strong rights to control cartels and other competitive practices. France had just lifted price controls, and was planning to take a strong tack against restraint of trade, informed sources said.

Foreign investment and takeovers were another worry. An internal Ministry study showed that the benefits of using an EC merger regulation to overcome the Bundeskartellamt would be vastly outweighed by the prospect of unrestrained German acquisitions in France. French investment in West Germany amounted to F647 million in 1987, it cited, while West German investment in France was three times that level. The Bundeskartellamt, it argued, had only blocked one or two French acquisitions, with no sign of discriminatory practices against foreigners.

The Finance Ministry argued that any European text would not incorporate French concerns over non-EC competition. Nor would it consider the need for mergers to be judged by broad economic, rather than pure competition criteria, to allow restructuring by smaller European industries.

Support of industrial policy criteria in the text was also confused. Minister of Finance Pierre Bérégovoy lobbied to have a 'bilan économique global,' the total economic effect, stated as a criteria in any text. At the same time, he expressed fears of the Commission making industrial policy decisions for France. He did call, however, for strong rules that would consider international competition, as well as third country's attitudes towards EC firms. France could already do that domestically, but feared non-EC firms could enter through loose regimes elsewhere in the EC.

British and German firms were larger than France's, wrote Bérégovoy in a memo to Edith Cresson on the merger draft. 'French industry is in a period of full restructuring' and restraints must not be placed in their way.

Italy and Spain

Italy, like France, took the view throughout the negotiations that industrial policy considerations should be among the criteria used by the Commission to judge mergers. Rome also opposed automatic suspension of mergers pending Commission decisions, and remained suspicious of any limitations on publicly owned industries.

Some, but not all, in Italian government were worried about the unrestrained power of the Italian captains of industry, and wanted to use Brussels law to circumvent them. One Italian official suggested to the French that individual member state 'offices', as well as the government itself, should have the right to request Commission rulings below thresholds specified in any final regulation. Italian industries' domestic allies obviously felt differently. Publicly, the Italians told French and other officials their goal was to bring anti-trust controls in from Brussels, as well as eliminate barriers to acquisitions posed by cartel authorities in other countries. But Italy, they knew, had high structural and cultural barriers to acquisition. Also, officials in Italy who did seek anti-trust control for its own merit may have seen the construction of a Brussels regime as a means of circumventing domestic opposition from the big Italian industrialists.

Spain, like France, wanted as few barriers as possible placed in front of its smaller national firms seeking to restructure. Prestige was also important for the Spaniards. During the Spanish presidency of first half 1989, Spain wanted to be seen as closely allied with the big three of West Germany, Great Britain and France. Finally Spain, like many smaller countries, wanted the criteria in any text to reflect the poorer countries' need for accelerated economic growth and development.

The Smaller States

Many of the smaller countries did not have domestic anti-trust regimes. Yet, like the Italians, it was precisely these states which claimed Brussels authority should be wide-ranging, so as to eliminate anti-trust barriers to trade in other countries, as well as control their own domestic industries. Perhaps there was a creeping fear that their domestic barriers to acquisition would not slow down the tide of takeovers by larger European firms.

On other points, Ireland, Belgium and Denmark all favoured automatic suspension of deals pending Commission approval. The Spanish, Portuguese and other poorer states all backed inclusion of industrial policy criteria in the text. Finally, the Latin states and Greece threw in last minute demands for Commission recognition of the need to encourage 'cohesion', or development in the poorer countries.

Industry and Trade Associations

The clout shown by the Commission in the Philip Morris case, the British Caledonian case and others led to a dramatic reaction by European industrialists, who realized they faced a confused legal environment in which both the Commission and national authorities might rule on proposed mergers.

So in 1987, industrial groups began to back the Commission's efforts. Their greatest priority was for a 'one stop shop', a regulation that clearly delineated where national authorities' powers ended and the Commission's began. UNICE's president declared in 1988 'we have the worst of all possible worlds at the moment – narrow national controls supported by a Commission control where nobody knows the criteria'.[71]

The European Round Table of industrialists echoed UNICE's demands. The Fédération de l'Industrie Chimique made clear any new regulation should supplant any other competing EC regulations or powers afforded by the Commission under Articles 85 and 86 of the Treaty of Rome, demanding these two articles somehow be declared inapplicable.

The US Chamber of Commerce also backed the formation of a clear 'one-stop shop'. The Americans favoured higher thresholds for Commission jurisdiction and consideration of only European, not worldwide turnover. The US group also favoured *a posteriori* notification of the Commission following the completion of a merger, not *a posteriori* notification and consideration. But industrialists were divided on whether the Commission should adopt a pure competition stance or one that left more room for industrial policy. Many industrialists appeared to fear the powers given to the 'little sheriff' Sutherland under court interpretations of the Treaty of Rome – particularly Article 85 – even more than a merger regulation.

- UNICE and other groups asserted the regulation should not be too restrictive, and should not restrain European industries' abilities to restructure in the face of foreign competition. UNICE asked for a text that would force the Commission to prove both market dominance and a serious possibility for restraint of trade, before ruling a proposed merger illegal. Twelve hi-tech companies warned too tight a regulation might impede their ability to do battle with American and Japanese giants.

- The general industrial sentiment in favour of a clear 'one stop shop' put German groups such as the Federation of German Industries (BDI) at odds with the Bundeskartellamt, which was lobbying for a retention of powers that might let it overturn Commission rulings.

The Confederation of British Industry similarly opposed the government view that national authorities should be allowed to overrule the Commission for public interest reasons, as did the French industrial groups, with support from their Ministry. British officials said much of the merchant banking community again supported a clear delineation of powers to clarify European merger procedures. These bankers, as well as British industrialists who felt Britain's own rules were too vague or too strict, were at odds with those in the Office of Fair Trading and elsewhere, who felt one-stop decision making in Brussels was a 'horror' which might allow the Commission to use merger control as an instrument of industrial policy, unopposed by national competition authorities. 'At a certain time British industry supported the Community initiative more than the government, probably to escape their own national control', said one UNICE official.

According to the Department of Trade and Industry, there were other divisions among European industrialists. Some British industrialists lobbied for further Commission regulations to dismantle barriers to acquisition on the Continent. According to officials, other British industrial groups came to support the retention of a national public interest clause or other recourse to national authorities, and therefore oppose one-stop shopping, if it would allow the government to overrule takeovers by foreign firms in EC or non-EC states which retain barriers to mergers.

Concurrent to the debate on an EC regulation, some British industrial representatives backed the erection of non-discriminatory hurdles that might bring their protection in Britain up to the level enjoyed in most continental states. That, however, was opposed by many in the British financial community, and shareholders' groups.

Faced with this chorus of competing demands, the Commission put forward a new draft in November, 1988 (Exhibit 22.5).

Question

The Directive submitted by the Commission is grinding its way through the EC process. You represent one of the players listed below. You have to think through your own objectives and interests, as well as those of the other players; you have to read through the proposed text, pulling out the paragraphs which are concessions to you, and forming positions for or against on other sections.

There are some key issues which you must bear in mind: thresholds – where do you think that the line on Commission jurisdiction be drawn? The one-stop shop: do you go for juridical clarity, or try to retain some national control. Criteria – are you for pure competition, or do you accept an opening for industrial policy? Public companies – should they be covered by the text? Minority shareholding: should it be covered by the text? Commission notification: how do you wish to proceed on this? Commission powers: should the Commission be able to suspend deals? National industrial goals: what are they with respect to restructuring and mergers and acquisitions?

1. Great Britain.
2. West Germany.
3. France.
4. Italy.
5. UNICE.
6. Commissioner Sutherland.

Exhibit 22.5 *Abridged version of Official Journal of the European Communities No. C 22/14, 28.1.89*

II
Preparatory Acts

COMMISSION

Amended proposal for a Council Regulation (EEC) on the control of concentrations between undertakings

COM(88) 734 final – revised version

(Submitted by the Commission pursuant to Article 149(3) of the EEC Treaty on 30 November 1988)
(89/C 22/6)

The Council of the European Communities,

(1) Whereas, for the achievements of the aims of the Treaty establishing the European Economic Community, Article 3(f) requires the Community to institute 'a system ensuring that competition in the common market is not distorted';

(2) Whereas this system is essential for the achievement of the internal market by 1992;

(3) Whereas the dismantling of internal frontiers can be expected to result in major corporate reorganizations in the Community, particularly in the form of concentrations;

(4) Whereas such a development must be welcomed as being in line with the requirements of dynamic competition and liable to strengthen the competitiveness of European industry;

(5) Whereas, however, it must be ensured that the process of reorganization does not give rise to lasting damage to competition;

(9) Whereas the scope of application of this Regulation should therefore be defined according to the territory of operations of the undertakings concerned and be limited by quantitative thresholds in order to include only those operations of concentration which have a Community dimension;

(10) Whereas this is the case where the aggregate turnover of all the undertakings concerned exceeds a given level and where at least two of the undertakings concerned have their sole or principal field of activities in a different Member State or where, although the undertakings in question act mainly in one and the same Member State, at least one of them has substantial operations in at least one other Member State through subsidiaries or direct sales; whereas this is also the case where the concentrations effected by undertakings which do not have their principal field of activities in the Community are such as to have an effect within the common market;

(12) Whereas it is necessary, however, to create a legal framework which makes it possible to treat in a comprehensive way all concentrations having the same impact on the competitive structure of the common market or a substantial part thereof;

(14) Whereas the Regulation should establish the principle that concentrations which create or strengthen a position as a result of which the maintenance or development of effective competition is impeded in the common market or in a substantial part thereof are to be declared incompatible with the common market;

Exhibit 22.5 *continued*

(15) Whereas concentrations which, by reason of the limited market share of the undertakings concerned, are not liable to impede effective competition may be presumed to be compatible with the common market; whereas, in particular, this may be presumed where the market share of the undertakings concerned does not exceed 25 percent either in the common market or in a substantial part thereof;

(16) Whereas authorization should be available in respect of concentrations which, although they impede effective competition, contribute to the attainment of the basic objectives of the Treaty in such a way that, on balance, their economic benefits prevail over the damage they cause to competition;

(18) Whereas the Commission should have the task of taking all the decisions necessary to establish whether or not concentrations which fall within the scope of application of the Regulation are compatible with the common market;

(19) Whereas, to ensure effective supervision, prior notification and the suspension of concentrations should be made obligatory;

(22) Whereas the Commission should act in close and constant liaison with the competent authorities of the Member States and should obtain the views of those most directly concerned by a concentration;

(25) Whereas it is appropriate to define the concept of concentration in such a manner as to cover operations bringing about a change in the structure of the undertakings concerned; whereas it is therefore necessary to exclude from the scope of application of this Regulation those operations which have as their object or effect the coordination of the competitive behaviour of independent undertakings, since such operations fall to be examined under the provisions of other regulations implementing Articles 85 or 86;

(26) Whereas the Commission should be given exclusive competence to apply this Regulation, subject to review by the Court of Justice; whereas it should also be stipulated that the provisions of this Regulation apply to all concentrations with a Community dimension, whether or not they fall within the scope of Article 85 or 86;

(27) Whereas the Member States may not apply their national legislation on competition to concentrations having a Community dimension, unless expressly empowered to do so by the Commission;

(28) Whereas, however, this principle does not prevent Member States from taking appropriate measures in so far as is necessary to protect legitimate interests provided that such interests are sufficiently defined and protected by domestic law and that such measures are compatible with the other provisions of Community law;

Has adopted this Regulation:

Article 1
Scope of Application

1. This Regulation shall apply to all concentrations having a Community dimension as defined in paragraph 2, whether or not they fall within the scope of Article 85 or 86.
2. For the purposes of this Regulation, a concentration has a Community dimension where:

(a) the aggregate worldwide turnover of all the undertakings concerned is more than ECU 1,000 million, and

Exhibit 22.5 *continued*

(b) the aggregate Community-wide turnover of each of at least two of the undertakings concerned is more than ECU 100 million,

unless each of the undertakings concerned achieves more than three-quarters of its aggregate Community-wide turnover within one and the same Member State.

Article 2
Appraisal of Concentration

1. Concentrations falling within the scope of this Regulation shall be appraised with a view to establishing whether or not they are compatible with the common market, by reference in particular to the market position of the undertakings concerned and to their economic and financial power, to opportunities of choice available to suppliers and users, to their access to supplies or markets, to the structure of the markets affected taking account of international competition, to legal and factual barriers to entry, and to supply and demand trends for the relevant goods or services.

2. Concentrations which do not create or strengthen a position as a result of which the maintenance or development of effective competition would be impeded in the common market or in a substantial part thereof shall be declared compatible with the common market.

3. Concentrations which create or strengthen a position as a result of which the maintenance or development of effective competition is impeded in the common market or in a substantial part thereof shall be declared incompatible with the common market unless authorized on the ground that their contribution to improving production and distribution, to promoting technical or economic progress or to improving the competitive structure within the common market outweighs the damage to competition. In this respect, the competitiveness of the sectors concerned with regard to international competition and the interests of consumers shall be taken into account.

Concentrations shall be authorized on account of their compatibility with the common market only in so far as they do not:

(a) impose on the undertakings concerned restrictions which are not indispensable to the implementation of the concentration, and

(b) afford the undertakings concerned the possibility of eliminating competition in respect of a substantial part of the goods or services concerned.

Article 3
Definition of Concentration

1. A concentration shall be deemed to occur where:

(a) two or more undertakings merge; or

(b) – one or more persons already controlling at least one undertaking, or
 – one or more undertakings
 acquire, whether by purchase of shares or assets, by contract or by any other means, direct or indirect control of the whole or parts of one or more undertakings.

2. Operations which have as their objects or effect the coordination of the competitive behaviour of independent undertakings shall be deemed not to give rise to a concentration within the meaning of paragraph 1(b).

Exhibit 22.5 *continued*

3. The creation of a joint venture performing on a lasting basis all the functions of an autonomous economic entity, which does not have as its objects or effect the coordination of the competitive behaviour of the undertakings concerned, shall be deemed to be a concentration within the meaning of paragraph 1(b).

4. Control is acquired by persons, undertakings or groups of persons or undertakings which:

(a) are holders of the rights or entitled to rights under the contracts concerned;

(b) while not being holders of such rights or entitled to rights under such contracts, have power to exercise the rights deriving therefrom;

(c) in a fiduciary capacity derived from a private law contract, hold assets of an undertaking or shares in an undertaking, and have power to exercise the rights attaching thereto, unless that power may be revoked at any time or unless they are bound by special instructions from their principals.

Article 4

Prior Notification of Concentrations

1. Concentrations as referred to by this Regulation, whether or not they form the subject-matter of an agreement, shall be notified to the Commission before they are put into effect.

Article 6

As regards notified concentrations decisions pursuant to paragraphs 1 and 2 shall be undertaken within a period not exceeding one month, unless the undertaking concerned agreed to extend that period.

Article 7

Suspension of the Concentration

1. Undertakings shall suspend the implementation of a concentration which falls within the scope of application of this Regulation until the Commission has decided on initiation of a proceeding pursuant to Article 6.

2. In order to ensure conditions of effective competition, the Commission may decide, when it initiates a proceeding pursuant to Article 6(1), that the suspension of the implementation of a concentration should be extended until it takes a final decision pursuant to Article 8.

3. The provisions of paragraphs 1 and 2 shall not impede the implementation of a public takeover or exhange bid which has been notified to the Commission by the date of its announcement, provided that the acquirer does not exercise the voting rights attached to the shares in question.

4. The Commission may, on request, waive the provisions of paragraphs 1 and 2 or the proviso contained in paragraph 3.

Article 8

Powers of Decision of the Commission

2. Whereas the Commission finds that a notified concentration fulfils the conditions of compatibility laid down in Article 2(2), it shall issue a decision declaring the concentration compatible with the common market; conditions and obligations may be attached thereto

Exhibit 22.5 *continued*

in order to ensure conditions of effective competition. In such a case, the Commission may also empower Member States which are directly concerned by the concentration to apply their national legislation on competition in order to ensure conditions of effective competition in local markets within their respective territories.

3. Where the Commission finds that a notified concentration fulfils all the conditions laid down in Article 2(3), it shall issue a decision authorizing the concentration as being compatible with the common market; conditions and obligations may be attached thereto in order to ensure conditions of effective competition. The decision granting the authorization shall also cover additional restrictions reasonably ancillary to the implementation of the concentration.

4. Where the Commission finds that a concentration fulfils the conditions of incompatibility laid down in Article 2(3) but does not fulfil the conditions for an authorization laid down therein, it shall issue a decision refusing the authorization and declaring the concentration incompatible with the common market.

7. Authorizations of concentrations by the Commission shall in no way alter collective workers' rights in force in the undertakings concerned.

Article 9
Time Limits for Decisions

1. Decisions pursuant to Article 8(2) concerning notified concentrations shall be taken within one month following the date of initiation of the proceeding.

2. Decisions pursuant to Article 8(3) and (4) concerned notified concentration shall be taken within four months following the close of initiation of the proceeding.

Article 10
Requests for Information

1. In carrying out the duties assigned to it by this Regulation, the Commission may obtain all necessary information from the governments and competent authorities of the Member States and from persons, undertakings and associations of undertakings.

Article 11
Investigations by the Authorities of the Member States

1. At the request of the Commission, the competent authorities of the Member States shall undertake the investigations which the Commission considers to be necessary under Article 12(1), or which it has ordered by decision pursuant to Article 12(3). The officials of the competent authorities of the Member States responsible for conducting these investigations shall exercise their powers upon production of an authorization in writing issued by the competent authority of the Member State in whose territory the investigation is to be made. Such authorization shall specify the subject matter and purpose of the investigation.

2. If so requested by the Commission or by the competent authority of the Member State in whose territory the investigation is to be made, officials of the Commission may assist the officials of such authority in carrying out their duties.

Exhibit 22.5   *continued*

Article 12
Investigating Powers of the Commission

1. In carrying out the duties assigned to it by this Regulation, the Commission may undertake all necessary investigations into undertakings and associations of undertakings.

To this end the officials authorized by the Commission are empowered:

6. Where an undertaking opposes an investigation ordered pursuant to this Article, the Member State concerned shall afford the necessary assistance to the officials authorized by the Commission to enable them to make their investigation.

Article 13
Fines

1. The Commission may by decision impose on persons, undertakings or associations of undertakings fines of from ECU 1,000 to ECU 100,000

(a) to examine the books and other business records;

(b) to take or demand copies of or extracts from the books and business records;

(c) to ask for oral explanation on the spot;

(d) to enter any premises, land and means of transport of undertakings.

Article 14
Periodic Penalty Payments

1. The Commission may by decision impose on persons, undertakings or associations of undertakings periodic penalty payments of up to ECU 50,000 for each day of the delay.

Article 15
Review by the Court of Justice

The Court of Justice shall have unlimited jurisdiction within the meaning of Article 172 of the Treaty to review decisions whereby the Commission has fixed a fine or periodic penalty payment; it may cancel, reduce or increase the fine or periodic penalty payment imposed.

Article 16
Professional Secrecy

1. Information acquired as a result of the application of Articles 10, 11 and 12 shall be used only for the purposes of the relevant request or investigation.

2. Without prejudice ot the provisions of Article 19, the Commission and the competent authorities of the Member States, their officials and other servants shall not disclose information acquired by them as a result of the application of this Regulation and of the kind covered by the obligation of professional secrecy.

Article 18
Liaison with the Authorities of the Member States

1. The Commission shall transmit forthwith to the competent authorities of the Member States copies of notifications and of the most important documents lodged with or issued by the Commission pursuant to this Regulation.

2. The Commission shall carry out the procedures set out in this Regulation in close and constant liaison with the competent authorities of the Member States, which may express their views upon those procedures. It shall obtain the views of the competent authorities

Exhibit 22.5 *continued*

of the Member States which show that they are directly concerned by the concentration, in particular with a view to the application of Article 8(2).

5. Consultation shall take place at a joint meeting convened at the invitation of and chaired by the Commission. A summary of the facts, together with the most important documents and a preliminary draft of the decision to be taken, shall be sent with the invitation. The meeting shall take place no earlier than fourteen days after the invitation has been sent. The Commission may, however, shorten this period in order to avoid serious harm to one or more of the undertakings concerned by a concentration.

6. The Advisory Committee shall deliver an opinion on the Commission's draft decision, if necessary by taking a vote. The Advisory Committee may deliver an opinion even if some members are absent and unrepresented. The opinion shall be delivered in writing and appended to the draft decision. It shall not be made public.

7. The Commission shall take the utmost account of the opinion delivered by the Committee. It shall inform the Committee of the manner in which its opinion has been taken into account.

Article 20
Jurisdiction

1. Subject to review by the Court of Justice, the Commission shall have sole competence to take the decisions provided for in this Regulation.

2. Member States shall not apply their national legislation on competition to concentrations having a Community dimension, unless expressly empowered to do so by the Commission in accordance with the provisions of the last sentence of Article 8(2).

3. Notwithstanding the provisions of paragraphs (1) and (2), Member States may take appropriate measures where necessary to protect legitimate interests other than those pursued by this Regulation, provided that such interests are sufficiently defined and protected in domestic law and that such measures are compatible with other provisions of Community law.

Source: Official Journal of the European Communities

You are a lawyer in the Brussels office of the Wall Street-based firm, Not so Free, Not so Frank, Shriver and Harass. You meet Sutherland at a cocktail party. He has some problems in bridging the various requirements of the players. Suggest some legal solutions on: the criteria; the one-stop shop; the thresholds.

Notes

1. Sophie Gérondeau, Antoine Winckler, 'Étude Critique du Règlement CEE sur le Contrôle des Concentrations d'Entreprises' in *Revue du Marché Commun*, No. 339, August–September 1990, p. 552; also *Revue du Marché Commun*, No. 339, August 1989.
2. Com(81) 773 final.

3. Ibid., also ECOSOC opinion of July 2, 1982.
4. COM(84) 59 Final; *Europolitique*, 20 September 1986.
5. A. P. Black, 'Industrial Policy in West Germany. Policy in Search of a Goal', in *European Industrial Policy*, pp. 88–89.
6. *Financial Times*, 9 January, 1989.
7. OECD Annual Report, West Germany, July 1989.
8. *Allemagne d'Aujourd'hui*, July 1983.
9. Kenneth Dyson, 'Economic Policy', in *Developments in West German Politics*, ed. Gordon Smith, William Paterson, Peter H. Merkl, Macmillan, London, 1989.
10. Biennial Report 1988–89, Monopolies Commission.
11. *Financial Times*, 29 November, 1977.
12. French embassy press release, 6 March, 1979.
13. *Wall Street Journal*, 21 August, 1979.
14. *Financial Times*, 29 November, 1977.
15. *The Economist*, 16 September, 1989.
16. Document Economique #5, 1988.
17. *Financial Times*, 19 July, 1988.
18. Ibid.
19. *Le Point*, 11 April, 1988.
20. *Le Figaro*, 25 July, 1988.
21. *La Tribune d'Allemagne*, 21 August, 1988.
22. *Financial Times*, 28 October, 1987.
23. *Financial Times*, 9 September, 1989.
24. *La Tribune de L'Expansion*, 9 November, 1988.
25. *Revue de la Direction Générale du Conseil de la Concurrence*, October, 1989.
26. Peter Hall, *The Mitterand Experiment: Continuity and Change in Modern France*, ed. Stanley Hoffman *et al.*, Polity Press, 1987, p. 59.
27. Michael Bauer, *The Politics of State-Directed Privatisation*, pp. 49–60.
28. *Financial Times*, 26 January, 1973.
29. Philip G. Cerny, 'The Little Big Bang in Paris: financial market deregulation in a dirigiste system', *European Journal of Political Research*, 17, 1989, pp. 169–192.
30. *Barriers to Takeovers in the European Community*, Coopers and Lybrand, Her Majesty's Stationery Office, London, 1989, p. 10.
31. *Barriers to Takeovers*, Coopers and Lybrand, p. 15.
32. *Study on Obstacles*, Booz Allen, p. 52.
33. *Les Acquisitions en France Depuis 10 Ans, Revue de Droit des Affaires Internationales*, No. 3, 1988.
34. Ibid.
35. Trevor Smith, 'Industrial Planning in Britain', in *Planning, Politics and Public Policy: the British, French and Italian Experiences*, ed. Jack Hayward, Cambridge University Press, London, 1975. Also Peter Hall, *Governing the Economy*.
36. Peter Hall, *Governing the Economy*, pp. 65–68.
37. Ibid.
38. David Heald, 'The United Kingdom: Privatisation and its Political Context', in West European Politics, Volume 11, No. 4, October, 1988, p. 36.
39. *Financial Times*, 24 March, 1977.
40. Peter Hall, *Governing the Economy*, p. 52.
41. Ibid., p. 110.

42. David Heald, *Privatisation and its Political Context*, p. 43.
43. *Financial Times*, 18 May, 1982.
44. *Financial Times*, 23 November, 1981.
45. In one noted controversy, the Commission rejected the flamboyant 'Tiny' Rowland's 1981 bid for Harrod's Department Store, officially because it did not think his executive team competent, though perhaps because it did not like Rowland's 'style', *Financial Times*, 10 December, 1981.
46. *Wall Street Journal*, 16 March, 1984.
47. *Wall Street Journal*, 16 December, 1985.
48. *La Tribune de L'Economie*, 7 August, 1986.
49. *Barriers to Takeovers*, Coopers and Lybrand.
50. Patrizio Bianchi, Sabino Cassese, Vincent Della Sala, 'Privatization in Italy: Aims and Constraints', in *West European Politics*, Volume ii, No. 4, October 1988, pp. 87–100.
51. Ibid.
52. Ibid.
53. Friedman, *Agnelli and the Network of Italian Power*, p. 5.
54. *Study on Obstacles*, Booz Allen.
55. Ibid.
56. Friedman, *Agnelli and the Network of Italian Power*, pp. 136–8.
57. Thierry Maliniak, *Les Espagnols – de la Movida à l'Europe*, Centurion, Paris, 1990, p. 51–86.
58. Ibid., p. 76.
59. Peter Buckley and Patrick Artesien, 'Policy Issues of intra-EC Investment: Britain, France, and German Multinationals in Greece, Portugal, and Spain, with Specific Reference to Employment Effects', *Journal of Common Market Studies*, December, 1987, p. 218.
60. *Barriers to Takeovers*, Coopers and Lybrand.
61. Ibid.
62. Ibid.
63. Internal French negotiating documents made available to the author.
64. *Europolitique*, No. 1429, 10 September, 1988.
65. Stephen–Woolcock, *European Mergers: National or Community Controls?*, Royal Institute for International Affairs, London, 1989.
66. Agence Europe, No. 4845, 5 September, 1988. German Secretary of State Otto Schlecht declared in September 1988 the EC's new regulation should lead to the banning of anti-competitive mergers, even if they assisted in the efficient restructuring of European industry. Similarly, Bundeskartellamt director Katrre repeatedly fought French and other efforts to insert industrial policy considerations in the text.
67. Officials in Berlin told the author.
68. According to Bundeskartellamt officials interviewed by the author.
69. *Financial Times*, 20 December, 1988.
70. Officials in Brussels, London and the Bundeskartellamt told the author.
71. *Financial Times*, 20 December, 1988.

CASE 23

Strategy, Ideology and Politics
The Relaunch of Social Europe, 1987–1989

Jonathan Story

Introduction

It was late into the evening on December 8, 1989. Leaders of the twelve European Community members were arrayed around a table in the elegant Palais des Congrès in Strasbourg. President Mitterrand had suggested a ten-minute break after an arduous session on monetary union. Suddenly, the power failed, leaving the twelve most powerful European figures in darkness.

A moment of silence ensued. Then came British Prime Minister Margaret Thatcher's voice from the gloom:

Shall we talk about the social charter now?[1]

The Community Charter of Worker's Fundamental Social Rights (see Exhibit 23.1) came to be one of the most contentious instruments approved by the European Council as a prelude to 1993. In an highly unusual move, it was adopted as a 'solemn declaration' by 11 of the 12 EC leaders – Great Britain excluded – at the Strasbourg Summit. France, West Germany and most other EC member states viewed it as one of the 'plinths' on which the internal market of 1993 would be built, a means of ensuring 'the benefits [of the single market] be distributed and the final results improve the life and working conditions of all community citizens'.[2]

More prosaically, it amounted to a non-binding declaration favouring the right to a 'decent' wage, 'adequate' employment, and worker health and safety. It also endorsed the principles of transferable unemployment benefits and mutual recognition of job qualifications, moves that would ensure a more mobile EC labour market. Most contentiously, it affirmed the right of all employees to some form of participation in management, but left the specifics vague. The declaration was to be followed by an 'Action Programme' containing a list of measures for the Commission to propose to the Council of Ministers (see Exhibit 23.1).

This case was prepared by Jonathan Story, Professor at INSEAD and Ethan Schwartz, Research Assistant at INSEAD. It is intended to be used as a basis for class discussion rather than to illustrate either effective or ineffective handling of an administrative situation.
Copyright © 1990 INSEAD-CEDEP, Fontainebleau, France.
Financial support from the INSEAD Alumni Fund European Case Programme and la Centrale des Cas et de Médias Pédagogiques (Paris) is gratefully acknowledged.

Exhibit 23.1

COMMISSION
OF THE EUROPEAN
COMMUNITIES

Jean Monnet House
8 Storey's Gate London SW1P 3AT
Telephone: 01-222 8122
Fax: 01-222 0900

ISEC/B18/90
6 April 1990

BACKGROUND REPORT

SOCIAL DIMENSION 1992: THE COMMUNITY WORKERS' CHARTER

AND SUPPLEMENTARY ACTION PROGRAMME

SUMMARY

In adopting the Community Workers' Charter last December, the European Council of Strasbourg set out to highlight the importance of the social dimension in the process of completing the internal market. In November 1989 the Commission for its part adopted an action programme intended to implement the general principles contained in the Charter.

These Commission initiatives are inspired by increasingly marked awareness of the role of social factors in the strengthening of economic and social cohesion and by the danger of social dumping possibly accelerating the trend towards a two-speed Community as well as by the calls made by various institutions such as the European Parliament, the Economic and Social Committee and, on behalf of the workers, the European Trade Union Confederation.

The first reaction to these preoccupations came from the President of the Commission, Jacques Delors, who in May 1988 made a commitment to the Congress of the European Trade Union Confederation to begin work on the drafting of a charter containing a minimum platform of social rights. The successive European Councils (Hanover and Rhodes in 1988) confirmed the commitment of the Commission, which decided to carry out consultations with the Economic and Social Committee.

The Commission then drew up a preliminary draft Social Charter in May 1989, arriving at a final draft in September of the same year. This final draft was discussed again at ministerial level and on 9 December 1989, culminated in a solemn declaration of the Charter by eleven Heads of State and Government meeting at the European Council in Strasbourg.

This declaration has not ceased to give rise to controversy and criticism from the European Parliament, which takes the view that its content is excessively vague. Parliament deplores the fact that the Charter now only refers to workers' rights whereas initially it covered all citizens. The Charter contains the fundamental principles relating to 12 main themes:

1.   Free movement of workers based on the principles of equal treatment in access to employment and social protection.

Exhibit 23.1 *continued*

---

2.   Employment and remuneration based on the principle of fair remuneration.

3.   Improvement of living and working conditions.

4.   Social protection based on the rules and practices proper to each country.

5.   Freedom of association and collective bargaining.

6.   Vocational training.

7.   Equal treatment of both men and women.

8.   Information, consultation and participation of workers.

9.   Protection of health and safety at the workplace.

10.   Protection of children and adolescents.

11.   The elderly.

12.   The disabled.

Having made this declaration, the Council stated that the burden of responsibility for implementing the provisions of the Charter lay mainly with Member States. However, the Council then invited the Commission to present those initiatives which fall within its terms of reference. Thus, on 29 November 1989, the Commission drew up a social action programme. This programme has 47 new initiatives contained in it. The proposals for action at Community level relate mainly to: the social security of migrant workers; freedom of movement; employment and working conditions; vocational training and the improvement of the working environment.

THE CHARTER AND THE ACTION PROGRAMME

INTRODUCTION

On 27 September 1989 the Commission presented a draft Community Charter of fundamental social rights in which reference is made to an action programme. In its report to the European Council of 8 and 9 December 1989, the Presidency, at the end of the Social Affairs Council of 30 October 1989, has taken note of the Commission's intention to present an action programme relating to the concrete implementation of the rights defined in the Charter. The result was a document[1] called "Communication from the Community Charter of basic social rights for Workers" which appeared on 29 November 1989. In it the measures proposed are grouped under thirteen short chapters, each covering an area relating to the development of the social dimension of the internal market and which, apart from the chapter on employment and the labour market, correspond to the various sections of the Charter in the context of completing the internal market and more generally, implementing the Treaty as amended by the Single European Act.

Each of the thirteen chapters also reviews measures already adopted by the Community with regard to the area concerned. Reference is also made to work that will be continued

---

[1] COM (89) 568 Final

Exhibit 23.1 *continued*

ISEC/B18/90

in each of these areas to adapt existing instruments to social change or change in the Community (for example, adaptation of certain directives concerning the safety and health of workers).

In accordance with the principle of subsidiarity whereby the Community acts when the set objectives can be reached more effectively at its level than at that of the Member States, the Commission's proposals relate to only part of the issues raised in certain articles of the draft Charter. The Commission takes the view that responsibility for the initiatives to be taken as regards the implementation of social rights lies with the Member States, their constituent parts or the two sides of industry as well as, within the limits of its powers, with the European Community.

The Commission has therefore limited its proposals for directives or regulations to those areas where Community legislation seems necessary to achieve the social dimension of the internal market and more generally, to contribute to the economic and social cohesion of the Community.

In some cases, the Commission is not proposing any initiative. This applies in the case of that section of the draft Charter which is devoted to the right to freedom of association and collection bargaining. By seeking to make a distinction between the measures to be taken by the Community and those to be taken by the Member States or the two sides of industry, the Commission believes it is acting fully in consonance with the request made by the Heads of State and of Government at the European Council in Madrid which emphasised that "the role to be played by Community standards, national legislation and contractual relations must be clearly established".

The Commission believes that an Action Programme should include components concerning employment, training and workers' living and working conditions. In most cases, the Commission has indicated the nature of the proposals to be presented: proposals for directive, regulation, decision, recommendation or communications, or again opinions within the meaning of Article 118 of the Treaty. With respect to the implementation of this Action Programme, the Commission will present all the proposals set out in the second part of the Action Programme. The first set of proposals, representing the most urgent priorities, will be put forward in the Commission's 1990 work programme. A second set will be included in the 1991 work programme. Any further proposals will be presented in 1992. The Commission also expects the Governments of the Member States to transmit an initial report by the end of 1990 stating how they have applied the principles of the Charter.

THE ACTION PROGRAMME

In brief, the main initiatives announced by the Commission are as follows:

In the field of free movement, the Commission intends to submit a proposal for a Community instrument in the field of public contracts and sub-contracting in order to afford Community workers equal treatment as regards access to employment, working conditions and social protection in the host country. As regards employment and working conditions, four draft directives will emerge. There will be one on the organisation of working time;

Exhibit 23.1 *continued*

ISEC/B18/90

two on employment contracts; one proposal on contracts and employment relationships other than those of a full-time nature and indeterminate duration (re-updating of two draft directives of 1982 which have never been adopted), another on the introduction of a form proving the existence of an employment contract or employment relationship; and a fourth comprising the revision of the 1975 directive on collective redundancies. The Commission also plans to propose appropriate instruments to promote the information, consultation and participation of workers in companies with a European dimension. On this subject, the Commission submitted in August 1989 a double proposal with two inseparable components: a regulation on the European company statute and a directive on the place of workers in the European company.

Three directives will be proposed relating to pregnant women at work, the protection of young people and measures to improve the situation of those with reduced mobility.

Lastly, the Commission will continue the action which it has embarked upon in the fields of health protection and safety at the workplace (ten directives are to be drawn up) and vocational training (comparability of qualifications, exchange programmes etc).

Certain aspects of the action programme will be given their first concrete expression in 1990. Four directives: organisation of working time, a typical employment, introduction of a form to be used as proof of a typical employment, protection of pregnant women. The Commission will also continue the activities begun in 1988 in the field of health and safety at the workplace. In this connection directives are expected on: medical assistance on board ships, temporary and mobile worksites, industrial exploration, information on dangerous industrial substances and safety signs at the workplace.

In the field of vocational training, the Commission will amplify the current Community activities with emphasis on the priority sectors, the FORCE programme will help to provide every worker in the Community with vocational training opportunities and access to vocational training throughout working life. The implementation of the EUROTECNET programme II will serve to adapt training to technological change. Lastly, the Commission will step up its efforts to develop the Community social dialogue which has recently made important progress with the adoption of new joint opinions between the two sides of industry at European level.

THE ACTION PROGRAMME – NEW INITIATIVES

Section One – the Labour Market:

- "Employment in Europe" report;

- "Observatory" and documentation system on employment;

- Action programmes on employment creation for specific target groups;

- Revision of Part II of Regulation 1612/68 on the clearance of vacancies and applications for employment and the related procedural decisions (SEDOC);

- Monitoring and evaluation of the activities of the Social Fund.

Exhibit 23.1 *continued*

Section Two – Employment and Remuneration:

–   Opinion on the introduction of an equitable wage by the Member States;

–   Directive on contracts and employment relationships other than full-time open-ended contracts;

Section Three – Improvement of Living and working conditions:

–   Directive for the adaptation of working time;

–   Council directive on the introduction of a form to serve as proof of an employment contract or relationship;

–   Revision of the Council Directive of 17 February 1975 (75/129/EEC) on the approximation of the laws of the Member States pertaining to collective redundancies;

–   Memorandum on the social integration of migrants from non-member countries.

Section Four – Freedom of Movement:

–   Revision of Commission Regulation (EEC) 1251/70 of 29 June 1970 on the right of workers to remain on the territory of a Member State after having been employed in the State;

–   Proposal for a regulation extending Council Regulation (EEC) 1408/71 on the application of social security schemes to employed persons, to self-employed persons and to members of their families moving within the Community and Council Regulation (EEC) 574/72 (laying down the procedure for implementing Regulation 1408/71) to all insured persons;

–   Proposal for a Community instrument on working conditions applicable to workers from another State performing work in the host country in the framework of the freedom to provide services, especially on behalf of a sub-contracting undertaking;

–   Proposal for a Community instrument on the introduction of a labour clause into public contracts;

–   Communication on supplementary social security schemes;

–   Communication from the Commission to the Council on the living and working conditions of Community citizens residing in frontier regions and of frontier workers in particular.

Section Five – Social Protection:

–   Recommendation on social protection: convergence of objectives;

–   Recommendation on common criteria concerning sufficient resources and social assistance in the social protection systems.

Exhibit 23.1 *continued*

Section Six – Freedom of association and collective bargaining:

–   Communication on the role of the social partners in collective bargaining;

Section Seven – Information, consultation and participation:

–   Community instrument on the procedures for the information, consultation and participation of the workers of European-scale undertakings;

–   Commission instrument on equity-sharing and financial participation by workers;

Section Eight – equal treatment for men and women:

–   Third Community programme on equal opportunities for women;

–   Directive on the protection of pregnant women at work;

–   Recommendation concerning child care;

–   Recommendation concerning a code of good conduct on the protection of pregnancy and maternity.

Section Nine – Vocational Training:

–   Proposal for a Community instrument on access to vocational training;

–   Updating of the 1963 proposal for a Council decision on the general principles for implementing a common vocational training policy;

–   Communication on the rationalisation and coordination of Community action programmes in the field of initial and continuing vocational training policy;

–   Proposal concerning the joint programme for the exchange of young workers and youth exchanges;

–   Comparability of qualifications.

Section Ten – Health Protection and Safety at the workplace:

–   Proposal for a Council Directive on the minimum health and safety requirements to encourage improved medical assistance on board vessels;

–   Proposal for a Council Directive on the minimum health and safety requirements for work at temporary or mobile work sites;

–   Proposal for a Council Directive on the minimum requirements to be applied in improving the safety and health of workers in the drilling industries;

–   Proposal for a Council Directive on the minimum requirements to be applied in improving the safety and health of workers in the quarrying and open-case mining industries;

–   Proposal for a Council Directive on the minimum safety and health requirements for fishing vessels;

Exhibit 23.1 *continued*

ISEC/B18/90

–   Recommendation to the Member States on the adoption of a European schedule for industrial diseases;

–   Proposal for a Council Directive on the minimum requirements for safety and health signs at the workplace;

–   Proposal for a Council Directive defining a system of specific information for workers exposed to certain dangerous industrial agents;

–   Proposal for a Council Directive on the minimum safety and health requirements regarding the exposure of workers to the risks caused by physical agents;

–   Proposal for a Council Directive amending Directive 83/447/EEC on the protection of workers from the risks related to exposure to asbestos at work;

–   Proposal for a Council Directive on the minimum safety and health requirements for activities in the transport sector;

–   Proposal for the establishment of a safety, hygiene health agency.

Section Eleven – Protection of children and adolescents:

–   Council Directive on the approximation of the laws of the Member States on the protection of young people.

Section Twelve – The Elderly:

–   Community initiative for the elderly (communication and proposal for a decision).

Section Thirteen – The disabled:

–   Proposal for a Council Decision establishing a third Community action programme for disabled people (helios) for the period 1992–96;

–   Proposal for a Council Directive on the introduction of measures aimed at promoting an improvement in the travel conditions of workers with motor disabilities.

History of Social Europe

The history of Social Europe can be divided into two phases – an initial 'minimalist' phase from 1957 to 1972, and a more interventionist phase from 1972 to the mid-1980s. They produced some important steps towards raising labour mobility in Europe, though neither produced any startling initiatives or major changes in the social benefit aspects of European labour markets. Rather, concrete action remained stalled due to national differences and competing concerns.[3]

Phase I: The Minimalist Phase: Social Policy 1958–1972

The minimalist philosophy guiding the first phase can be seen in an ILO report issued in 1956. It argued intervention should be tried only when national wages are so low as to present an artificial competitive edge, rather than productivity differentials.[4] The report also argued against any rigid, trans-border wage structure, and urged the length of the work-week and overtime be left largely to national discretion.

On the positive side, the paper said health and safety regulations could be standardized, and a fund created to aid disadvantaged European nations. This approach was reflected in the 1957 Treaty of Rome, setting up the European Community (EC). In Article 3, only one sub-clause deals with social policy. Articles 117–128 oblige states to work towards the harmonization of their social systems, but the matter is left vague. Article 119 urges men and women receive equal pay, but it was only in 1970 that the European Court of Justice interpreted this as applying to individuals. Article 120 urges member states to work towards equivalent holiday schemes, while articles 121 and 122 ask the Commission to produce a report on social developments. Articles 123 to 128 deal with creation of a Social Fund to train and otherwise improve opportunities for workers.

The next decade saw some directives issued by the Community, mainly with a view to facilitating migration from southern Italy. Community Regulation No. 15 of 1961 authorized – but did not grant workers the automatic right – to hold salaried jobs in other member states.[5] It also laid down limits, specifying aliens could come in immediately only where job shortages existed. Where they did not, national applicants would have a three-week priority in applying for jobs. Article 6 gave alien workers the right to renew work permits after one year in a host country, and to move to a new profession after three years. After four years foreigners would get the same salary as national workers. Other articles allowed spouses and children to immigrate, and specified children would receive vocational training.

The next few years saw haggling over aliens' rights to participate in work councils – opposed by West Germany, and an end to the preference for citizens – opposed by Italy. In a compromise, aliens were allowed to join councils after three years, and granted the right to change jobs after two.[6] A 1964 regulation, No. 38, allowed parents and grandparents of workers to immigrate with them, and stated public order, safety and health excuses could not be used to exclude EC member aliens.[7]

Council resolution 16/2/66 and directive 68/360 EEC went further. They stated any EC citizen could apply, or live in another state in order to apply for the right to settle there and be joined by families. Aliens would also enjoy the same rights as nationals vis-à-vis working conditions and the terms of employment. This directive was widely interpreted as removing the lion's share of legal barriers to the free movement of labour.[8]

The European Social Fund was constituted in 1962 as a means of training workers and easing labour dislocations. By 1968, one million people had been trained. About 340,000 trained Italians had settled in France and Germany.[9] Still,

EC labour market disequilibriums persisted. In 1968, an average 423,000 skilled jobs stayed unfilled each month, though unemployment was near one million. Six of every ten foreign workers were non-EC members.[10]

Some criticized the Fund, saying it exacerbated a 'brain drain' of skilled workers from poorer countries. So in 1969, the European Parliament passed a resolution urging adoption of a 'common social policy'. It called on the Council to reform the Fund, saying it should 'become a genuine common tool for a policy of full employment and for raising living standards in the Community'.[11]

The EC took other small measures during the decade. The Council authorized the Commission to begin collecting data on uniform wage definitions and labour costs in 1960. In 1962, the Commission established its Industrial Health and Safety Division. It pushed for the adoption of some directives in the 1960s on dangerous substances, minimum health and safety standards for child workers, industrial medicine, and payment for industrial diseases. In 1963, Council watered down a Commission proposal to study national training systems, saying it did not want to create a 'uniform system'. A handful of youth exchange programmes were established.[12]

Social security remained a complicated, though essential issue. From 1945 to 1958 the six original member states signed nearly 80 bilateral agreements. Article 51 of the Treaty of Rome called for social security reforms to ensure a free labour market.

Regulations No. 3 and No. 4 of 1958 called for equal treatment of aliens while in another country; the accumulation of aggregate benefits by migrant workers in more than one EC country; and the exportation of benefits. But the rules left many issues cloudy, failing to define social security adequately, or discuss benefits used in one country – such as French payments to large families – that were contested in densely populated EC member states.[13]

In sum, the 60s saw some attempt to deal with outstanding social issues, mostly directed towards ensuring a free labour market. There was little move towards harmonizing member states' vastly different social and labour systems.

Phase II: The Social Action Programme: 1974–1985

By the late 1960s, political momentum was building for a more interventionist approach, going beyond the limited measures alluded to in the Rome Treaty.[14] At the Hague Summit of 1969 the then West German Chancellor Willi Brandt called for greater progress on social matters.[15] The 1972 Paris Summit 'attached as much importance to vigorous action in the social field as to the achievement of economic union'. The Summit concluded it was 'essential to ensure the increasing involvement of labour and management in the economic and social decisions of the Community.'[16]

The Council adopted a Social Action Programme in 1974. It pledged to seek full and better employment, improved living and work conditions, and greater worker participation in economic and social decisions. Worker consultation, migrant worker needs, vocational training, equality for men and women, worker health and safety, needs of the handicapped and laws on collective dismissals were all to be addressed by the programme.[17] An assessment ten years on indicated some successes, but the overall verdict was one of failure.[18]

Equality

In addressing perceived pay discrimination against women, a 1975 directive obliged states to remove legal and administrative barriers to equal pay. A 1976 directive forced states to establish appeal mechanisms for cases of alleged discrimination.

A 1978 directive eliminated discrimination in social security benefits and contributions. A 1986 directive extended anti-discrimination rules into private sector social security benefits. But there were disagreements. A 1983 draft directive would have entitled parents to take three months' leave in addition to standard maternity leave, with more time for parents of handicapped children or single parents. Great Britain opposed it, as well as another directive allowing leaves in the case of ill family members.[19]

Health and Safety

Some progress was also made on health and safety issues. Various directives harmonized safety signs and dealt with toxic substances such as vinyl chloride and asbestos. In 1986 the Council passed a directive to protect workers from noise. A 1987 action programme dealt with safety and ergonomics at work, with pledges for more directives on biological agents, carcinogens, calcium compounds and lead, as well as safety needs in small businesses.[20]

Aid to Poorer Regions

The Social Fund over the period moved increasingly from efforts to aid worker mobility to schemes to help depressed member states and regions. It grew from 170 million ECU in 1973 to 2,188,350 million in 1985 – only 6.8 percent of the EC's total budget.[21]

Against these successes lie important failures in key policy areas such as employee consultation and participation, social security, irregular work, and harmonization of degrees and qualifications.

Worker Consultation

In 1972 the Fifth Directive was put to the Council. Originally intended for companies with more than 500 workers, the directive, based on West German models for worker participation, proposed firms establish two-tier boards – one supervisory, for overall policy, and one handling day to day activities. The supervisory board would feature a near-even split of labour and management representatives, with management having a slim majority through weighted voting accorded the chairman. Even West Germany, where employee participation is strong, opposed the draft as ill-conceived and overly ambitious.[22]

A new proposal was offered in October 1983, covering companies with over 1,000 workers. It would have offered companies a choice between two-tier and single-tier boards, and four forms of worker participation. It too languished in disagreement.[23]

The idea for a European Company statute, to include worker participation provisions, would be picked up again by Delors during his second presidency.

Even more controversial was the so-called Vredeling Directive of 1980, named after the Dutch Social Affairs Commissioner. It would have required employers to consult and inform employees in varying degrees and with varying regularity. The proposal laid out different rules for companies of varying size, and, in its original form, would have been binding only on multinationals. Great Britain vetoed it in 1983, Ireland raised it again in a less obligatory form during its EC presidency, but the UK knocked it down again in 1986.[24]

Even when Council members were able to agree on worker consultation, they failed to back up their decrees with enforcement. A February 17, 1975 directive required employers about to implement collective layoffs to consult workers and public powers. But when Michelin closed a Belgian plant in 1986 without following the directive, the Council could not agree on sanctions.[25]

Irregular Work and Contracts

Definition of rights for part-time and other irregular workers was another contentious area of Commission concern. In a 1979 report, Community Measures on Work Sharing, the Commission called on the EC to agree on the maximum number of work hours, limits on overtime, and directives concerning shift work, part time and temporary work.[26]

In 1981 the Commission offered a draft directive on part time work. It would have set equal rights for part time and full time workers, proportional pay, and rules on holidays, redundancy and retirement. It would also have given part time workers the priority when full time vacancies exist. Given to the Council in 1982, the draft was dropped over UK and other Council members' doubts.[27]

In 1984 the French EC presidency and the UK clashed when Great Britain vetoed a proposed recommendation to reduce working time. France, under strong domestic pressure, had been behind the move.[28] Other proposals that would cover temporary workers and grant them rights similar to normal labourers, as well as proposals to cover fixed-contract employees, languished in the Council. Again, Great Britain led the opposition.

Job Qualifications

Still more disagreements impeded efforts to harmonize degree requirements. In 1980 the Council adopted a resolution calling for improved labour market knowledge, coordinated placement services, and 'forward-looking management of labour markets'.[29] But the Council did not move beyond these vague pledges and steps.

Social Security

Efforts to harmonize social security regulations – a key factor in labour costs and worker mobility – advanced only slightly. Regulations 1408/71 and 574/72 laid down the rights of migrant workers within existing domestic social security schemes.[30] Diversity across the Community impeded a move to any uniformity.

In sum, while the Commission attempted a more activist approach through the mid-80s, its successes were slim. Health and safety regulations remained a favourite topic for action by consensus, as did equal opportunity for men and women – explicitly mentioned in the Treaty of Rome. But issues touching on complex domestic and social legislation – such as company law, worker participation and social security – failed to find consensus. In short, EC social policy was at an impasse when Jacques Delors assumed the Commission Presidency in January, 1985.

European Labour Markets

A look at labour markets, legal systems and social protection outlays in EC member states showed different traditions and philosophical motivations for policy. These differences could not be ascribed simply to wealth or per capita income. Moreover, competing domestic trends – such as rising xenophobia and anti-immigrant politics – worked against competing calls for socialization or mobile labour.[31]

The diverging shape of European labour came out clearly in employment/population ratios (Exhibit 23.2). In most member states the ratio declined over the 1980s, leading to a widening, rather than a narrowing of the gaps between the twelve. The twelve's economies too, depended in vastly different degrees on part time and temporary labour (see Exhibit 23.3 and Exhibit 23.4).

Most EC states adopted national legislation restricting fixed-term contracts in the 1970s, though rules were loosened again over the next decade. A mixed bag of rules were left regarding temporary workers. Italy had the most restrictive regime – while Germany, France, Belgium, the Netherlands and Denmark closely regulated temporary work.[32] Great Britain regulated, but did not restrict, temporary work agencies (see Exhibit 23.5).

The link between part time work and self employment varied greatly across the twelve. In the UK many part time workers were also self employed, so the proportions of both types of labourers rose in tandem.[33] But one-quarter of Italians worked for themselves, though only 5 percent of the total workforce worked part-time. In the Netherlands those ratios were reversed.[34]

On wages, working hours, paid leave, and worker participation, the differences among the twelve appeared still greater.

Hourly labour costs varied enormously, from a low of $2.96 in Portugal to a high of $18.17 for West Germany in 1987 (see Exhibit 23.6). Methods for fixing wages also diverged sharply, from Denmark's method of concluding national agreements to the highly diverse British system of negotiating contracts at the sectoral and company level (see Exhibit 23.7). These differences hampered Commission efforts to devise common rules mandating employee participation and union representation.

Exhibit 23.2 *Employment/population ratio in 1986**

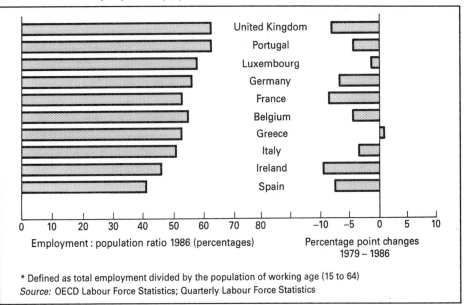

Employment : population ratio 1986 (percentages)

Percentage point changes
1979 – 1986

* Defined as total employment divided by the population of working age (15 to 64)
Source: OECD Labour Force Statistics; Quarterly Labour Force Statistics

Exhibit 23.3 *Size and composition of part time employment, 1979–1986*

Part time employment as a percentage of

	Total employment			Male employment			Female employment			Women's share in part time employment		
	1979	1983	1986	1979	1983	1986	1979	1983	1986	1979	1983	1986
France	8.2	9.7	11.7	2.5	2.6	3.5	17.0	20.1	23.1	82.0	84.6	83.0
Germany	11.2	12.6	12.3	1.5	1.7	2.1	27.6	30.0	28.4	91.6	91.9	89.8
Greece	–	6.5	–	–	3.7	–	–	12.1	–	–	61.2	–
Ireland	5.1	6.7	6.5	2.1	2.7	2.4	13.1	15.7	15.5	71.2	72.0	74.3
Italy	5.3	4.6	5.3	3.0	2.4	3.0	10.6	9.4	10.1	61.4	64.8	61.6
Luxembourg	5.8	6.7	7.3	1.0	1.0	2.6	17.1	18.8	16.3	87.5	90.0	76.6
Netherlands	11.1	22.0	24.0	2.8	7.8	8.7	31.7	50.5	54.2	82.5	76.2	76.1
UK	16.4	19.1	21.2	1.9	3.3	4.2	39.0	42.4	44.9	92.8	89.6	88.5

Source: OECD Employment Outlook 1987

The twelve also had varying means for fixing minimum wages and indexing salaries (see Exhibit 23.7), as well as informing workers about changes in technology (see Exhibit 23.8). German and Irish rules dated back to the first half of the century, while in France a law defining a statutory work week was defined only in 1982, by the Socialist government.[35]

Exhibit 23.4 *Demographic composition of wage and salary workers with temporary jobs (1985)*

Percentages (percentages of permanent jobs are given in brackets)				
	Age 15 to 24	Age 25 to 54	Age 55 and over	Men	Women
Belgium	47.4	50.5	2.1	44.8	55.2
	(15.5)	(77.5)	(7.0)	(65.2)	(34.8)
Denmark	62.8	33.3	3.9	50.2	49.8
	(23.1)	(66.6)	(10.3)	(53.2)	(46.8)
France	62.9	35.5	1.6	58.7	41.3
	(15.6)	(77.5)	(6.9)	(57.5)	(42.5)
Ireland	58.3	37.8	3.9	48.9	51.1
	(30.0)	(61.6)	(8.4)	(64.6)	(35.4)
Italy	30.8	57.6	11.6	50.9	49.1
	(15.3)	(75.4)	(9.3)	(66.5)	(33.5)
Luxembourg	65.6	34.4	0.0	49.2	50.8
	(23.0)	(61.5)	(5.5)	(66.0)	(34.0)
United Kingdom	51.1	41.3	8.6	45.3	54.7
	(22.1)	(64.8)	(13.1)	(56.2)	(43.8)

Source: OECD Employment Outlook 1987

Exhibit 23.5 *Regulation of private sector temporary wage agencies*

France	Limited under licensing system
Germany	Limited under licensing system
Italy	Illegal; law strongly prefers permanent employment contracts
United Kingdom	Controlled under licensing system
Belgium	Limited under licensing system
Netherlands	Limited under licensing system
Denmark	Limited under licensing system (only permitted in business and office branches
Norway	Limited under licensing system (only permitted in business and office branches)
Sweden	Illegal; direct temporary employment severely restricted since 1974
Switzerland	No legislation
Ireland	Controlled under licensing system
Greece	Limited to specific activities

Source: Emerson, 1987

Working time and laws regulating it also varied among the twelve (see Exhibit 23.9). Britain and Denmark had no legislation fixing a maximum normal work week, France set it at 39 hours, while West Germany, Ireland, Italy, the Netherlands and Portugal set the maximum at 48 hours, though wage agreements often bargained that number down. Overtime systems varied as well. There were nationally set rules

Exhibit 23.6 *European workers: big gaps in pay and benefits*

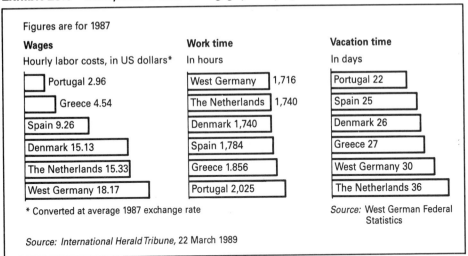

Figures are for 1987

Wages	Work time	Vacation time
Hourly labor costs, in US dollars*	In hours	In days
Portugal 2.96	West Germany 1,716	Portugal 22
Greece 4.54	The Netherlands 1,740	Spain 25
Spain 9.26	Denmark 1,740	Denmark 26
Denmark 15.13	Spain 1,784	Greece 27
The Netherlands 15.33	Greece 1.856	West Germany 30
West Germany 18.17	Portugal 2,025	The Netherlands 36

* Converted at average 1987 exchange rate   *Source:* West German Federal Statistics

Source: International Herald Tribune, 22 March 1989

in Italy and Great Britain, while Luxembourg set a maximum of two hours, Denmark decided the rules through collective bargaining and other states chose a range of requirements.

Annual paid leave was another area of divergence (see Exhibit 23.10). Britain again took the least regulated route, with no rules governing paid public holidays or statutory paid leave. Spain mandated 14 paid holidays and 30 days off a year. The Netherlands required six days paid holiday and four weeks off, with collective agreements bumping the annual paid leave up to five or six weeks a year. West Germany, Ireland and the Netherlands mandated minimum levels of vacation time which were then raised through collective and case-specific bargaining. Denmark, France, Greece and Luxembourg legislated more days off, added to only slightly through collective bargaining.

As to social security provisions, widely divergent policies among the twelve made agreement difficult. French and British systems of family benefits, for example, differed tremendously in rules governing the payments for additional children and the overall French support for large families.[36]

Pension philosophies differed, with Britain and Ireland providing occupational pensions that covered only basic life-necessities, while Spain, Italy and Portugal tied pension payments to earnings.[37] Other states' policies lay between these two poles.

Efforts to deal with growing problems – such as the ageing of the population, the rise in single parent families and other unforeseen trends would further complicate efforts at harmonization. Nonetheless, there were some areas of broad agreement. The twelve shared similar goals and philosophies on health and safety at work. But here too one found sharply differing systems for ensuring worker protection. Only Britain and Denmark – the two states most opposed to EC

Exhibit 23.7 *Wage-fixing systems in the member states of the EC*

Country	Pay increases of employed persons 1986		Negotiating level	Minimum age	Indexation
	Trend National	Real			
Belgium	3.0	1.8	Interprofessional agreements (2 years) taking account of wage moderation and competitiveness	Statutory minimum wage since 1975	Indexation reduced since Royal decree 178 of 30/3/86 – 2 percent
Denmark	3.1	0.6	National agreements taking account of government recommendations	Agreed minimum wage in very few agreements	Indexation suspended since March 1983
Spain	8.6	0.6	Local and sectoral collective agreements (1–2 years), major state involvement	Statutory minimum wage	No official indexation mechanism but safeguard clauses
France	4.3	1.9	Sectoral agreements and agreements at company level (1 year), major state involvement	Statutory minimum wage (SMIC) (Law of 2 January 1970)	No official indexation but safeguard clauses which are tending to disappear
Greece	15.2	–5.9	Central agreement for private sector and sectoral agreements in a number of branches	Statutory wage since 1982	*A priori* indexation since May 1983

Exhibit 23.7 *continued*

Country	Pay increases of employed persons 1986		Negotiating level	Minimum age	Indexation
	Trend				
	National	Real			
Ireland	6.6	3.6	Sectoral agreements and agreements at company level (12–18 months)	Minimum wage rates fixed by joint labour committees*	No wage indexation mechanism
Italy	7.6	1.8	Three year sectoral agreements taking account of 1983 protocol	Agreed minimum wage in each industry	Automatic indexation since 1957, in low year since 1983
Luxembourg	4.2	3.3	Sectoral negotiations, major state involvement	Statutory minimum social wage since 1944. Statutory minimum income since July 1986	Return to automatic wage indexation in January 1986
Netherlands	2.2	2.2	Sectoral agreements and agreements at company level (1 or 2 years). Considerable state intervention limited, however, by law of April '86	Statutory minimum wage since 1986	Automatic indexation tending to disappear from agreements and be replaced by a single payment
Portugal	17.2	4.6	Sectoral agreements (1 year)	Statutory minimum wage	No indexation mechanism
West Germany	4.0	4.0	Sectoral agreements (1 year)	No statutory minimum wage	Prohibition of sliding scale
UK	7.7	3.6	Negotiations at sector and company level	Minimum rates fixed by Wages Councils*	No indexation mechanism

* Wage committees statutorily authorized to fix minimum rates for workers not covered by collective agreements.
Source: EC Internal and External Adaption of Firms, 1987

Exhibit 23.8   *Procedures on informing and consulting workers in relation to technological changes*

Country	Law	Multisector agreements	Sectoral agreements	Company agreements
Belgium	Works Council informed AS 27.11.1973	Works Council informed cc. No. 9, 9.9.1972 Information, consultation and deliberation with representative bodies cc. No. 39, 13.12.1983	Printing, textiles, banking and insurance, distribution	Agreements, national agreements
Denmark	Information and consultation of technological committee 1981 Agreement for private sector 1981 Agreement for public sector and administrative bodies	Banks and saving banks, consumer cooperatives, breweries	Agreements to implement national agreements	
Germany	Information and consultation of Works Council Law of 15.1.1972		Metalworking, footwear, leather, paper	More than a hundred collective agreements
France	Information and consultation of Works Committee Auroux Laws of 1982	Banking and insurance	Undertakings in the following sectors: chemicals, oil, cement, banking and insurance	
Spain	Information and consultation of staff representatives or Works Committee. Workers' Statute. Law 8 1980 of 10.3.1980			

Exhibit 23.8 *continued*

Country	Law	Multisector agreements	Sectoral agreements	Company agreements
Greece	Information for trade union representatives Law No. 1264 of 1.1.1982 Information and consultation of health and safety committee Law 1568 1985		Agreement of July 1980 for the press and printing industry	
Ireland			Press, printing, graphic arts, banking	Joint Committees
Italy		Public sector IRI-Agreement, 18.12.1984 EFIM Agreement, July 1986	Employee's rights to information	Numerous agreements
Luxembourg	Information and consultation of Works Committee Law of 6.5.1974		Iron and steel industry	
Netherlands	Information and consultation of Works Council Laws of 1971, 1979 and 1982		Metal working Building Printing	
United Kingdom			Public services	
Portugal	Information and consultation of workers committees Law 46 79 of 1979			Several hundred agreements

Source: EC Internal and External Adaption of Firms, 1987

Exhibit 23.9   *Statutory regulation of working time in EC*

Country	Working week	Overtime max
Belgium	40 hours	65 hours per 3 months
Denmark	No legislation	Governed by collective agreement
West Germany	48 hours	2 hours a day for up to 30 days a year on the basis of 48-hour week
Greece	5-day week 40 hours in private sector	3 hours a day, 18 hours a week, 150 hours a year
Spain	40 hours	80 hours a year
France	39 hours	9 hours a week, 130 a year plus more when authorised
Ireland	48 hours	2 hours a day, 12 hours a week, 240 hours a year
Italy	48 hours	No legislation
Luxembourg	40 hours	2 hours a day
Netherlands	48 hours	Between ½ and 3½ hours a day
Portugal	48 hours	2 hours a day, 160 a year
UK	No general legislation	No legislation

Source: Financial Times, 12 June 1989

Exhibit 23.10   *Statutory public holiday and paid annual leave in EC*

Country	Public holidays	Paid annual leave	
		Statutory	Collective agreements
Belgium	10	24 days	
Denmark	No legislation	30 days	
West Germany	10–14	18 days	5 to 6 weeks
Greece	13	24 days	
Spain	14	30 days	
France	11	30 days	
Ireland	8	3 weeks	6 weeks
Italy	4 national+11 others	No specific number	5 to 6 weeks
Luxembourg	10	25 days	26 to 28 days
Netherlands	6 plus one every 5 years	4 weeks	5 to 6 weeks
Portugal	12	21 to 30	
UK	No legislation	No legislation	20 to 27 days

Source: Financial Times, June 12, 1989

federalism – had a central government agency charged with enforcing all safety codes.[38] France divided the responsibility among several agencies, while Germany has a dual inspection system with a health and safety inspectorate in each of the Länder, and a network of 95 mutual insurance bodies covering specific industries and financed by employers' contributions.

The twelve also agreed on the need to upgrade training. Competition in product markets placed a premium on skilled workforces. But national systems varied too. The Federal Republic trained 600 to 700 thousand apprentices between the ages of 16 and 19, laying the basis for excellence that characterizes German workmanship. Financing came from government and trade associations. In France, training fell under the aegis of national education. Neglect of training in Britain in the 1970s and 1980s posed a major problem for British-based corporations, requiring skilled labour (see Exhibit 23.11).

Revival of Social Europe: 1985–90

The Commission's Contribution

For each of the major players in the Social Europe debate a range of domestic and international imperatives coalesced to forge support or opposition to the Social Charter. Commission President Delors played a central part in the effort to revive the activist EC social policy of 1974.[39] Delors' personal history as a Catholic trade unionist presented a varied path, from experience in the Bank of France; an activist role in Prime Minister Chaban-Delmas' efforts to introduce a 'New Society' programme from 1969 to 1972; to membership in the French Socialist Party delegation to the first directly elected European Parliament. Finally, he served as Mitterrand's first Minister of Finance from 1981–1984, with the change in government that July. Delors had been the central figure in the March 1983 negotiations with the Bundesbank, leading to the decision to keep the franc in the exchange rate mechanism and stabilize the French economy, ending the hope of reducing the nation's unemployment rates through the gentle expansionary policies of the preceding two years.[40] The premise of the Delors stabilization plan was to claw the country back to trade surplus, through domestic adjustments – a policy that won him acclaim in the prevailing conservative climate of the time. This led to the accord in July 1984 for his nomination as Commission President.

Delors' experience confirmed his conviction that the only answer to stagnation in France lay in a relaunch of the Community, and of the EC's social policy.[41] He spelt out his position in his January 1985 speech to the European Parliament, calling for a strengthening of Commission powers; the elimination of all remaining internal barriers to trade by 1993; the furtherance of the European Monetary System (EMS), expansionary economic policies and the promotion by the Community of joint research and industrial undertakings. But efficiency had to be complemented by considerations of equity, as the cornerstone of 'our common democratic and European inheritance'. The single market had to be followed by creation of a 'single European social space'. 'Social dumping', understood as the competitive bidding down of acquired social rights as employers took advantage of cheap labour regions among the twelve, had to be avoided.[42]

Delors took a three-part tack in reviving EC social policy. First, he resurrected the 'social dialogue', with talks between employers, represented by the Union of Industries of the European Community (UNICE), and workers, represented by the

Exhibit 23.11   *Productivity: better but not best*

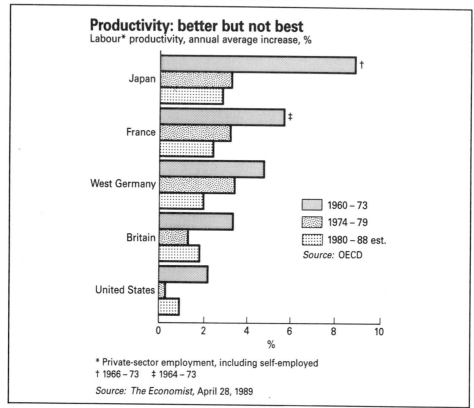

Productivity: better but not best
Labour* productivity, annual average increase, %

Legend:
- 1960 – 73
- 1974 – 79
- 1980 – 88 est.

Source: OECD

Countries (top to bottom): Japan †, France ‡, West Germany, Britain, United States

x-axis: 0, 2, 4, 6, 8, 10 — %

* Private-sector employment, including self-employed
† 1966 – 73   ‡ 1964 – 73

Source: The Economist, April 28, 1989

European Trade Union Congress (ETUC), begun in Belgium in November 1985. The main result was an improvement in the political climate, and a 1986 proposal for an expansionary EC economic policy.[43] A vague agreement was reached on the advisability of worker consultation in relation to the introduction of new technologies.[44]

Second, the Commission attempted to revive the proposals for worker participation. But the July 1986 Council of Ministers under the British Presidency postponed the issue until 1989.[45]

Third, the Commission found allies in the ETUC and the Belgian EC Presidency of early 1987 to fend off the deregulatory action programme advanced by the British government in December 1986 (see below). The Belgian Presidency proposed a 'plinth' of fundamental social rights to accompany the move to the internal market. The Commission's July 1986 Marin memorandum – named after the newly appointed Spanish Social Affairs Commissioner – suggested that the member states seek to avoid competitive advantage through any reduction of social security coverage.[46] The matter then moved to the back of the Community agenda, pending ratification of the Single European Act (SEA) and settlement of the budgetary problem at the Brussels special European Council of February 1988, during the German EC Presidency. Chancellor Kohl agreed in February 1988 during the German EC Presidency to increase German budget contributions by nearly 50 percent, involving a doubling of the EC's regional funds by 1993. The deal freed the EC agenda for focus on the internal market programme.

The SEA had come into effect in July 1987, extending the Commission's powers in Social Policy. Article 118A allows the Council to adopt regulations on health and safety by a qualified majority of members. Article 118B instructs the Commission 'to develop the dialogue of the social partners at Community level.' But Britain inserted a phrase under Article 100A – governing qualified majority votes on the internal market – specifying the Council can only deal with the 'rights and interests of salaried workers' by unanimous vote.

The Commission announced its guiding principles in February 1988, directly after the resolution of the EC's budgetary problems.[47] Chancellor Kohl had agreed at a special European Council meeting in Brussels to increase budget contributions by nearly 50 percent, involving a doubling of EC regional funds by 1993. The deal freed the EC agenda for focus on the internal market programme. The promise of free markets, directed to business,[48] was spelt out in the Commission's study on 'the costs of non-Europe'.[49] Pressure would be felt on social standards. Delors launched his crusade for the Community's 'social dimension' at the ETUC's meeting in Stockholm in May, 1988.[50] The 'plinth', or 'European Charter of Social Rights', went through three main versions, advanced by the Commission on September 14, 1988;[51] in April, 1989[52] and a final version on September 27.[53] The matter then passed into the hands of the French Presidency, providing a prime example of 'cooperative federalism' at work between Commission and the EC Presidency.[54]

Delors outlined his main ideas in May 1988 at the ETUC meeting in Stockholm. He proposed a three part package: a 'plinth' of guaranteed social rights; a social dialogue, notably about the rights of workers to permanent education; and the revival of a European Company statute that would enshrine worker participation.[55] The Congress adopted resolutions demanding the 'establishment of rights to information, consultation and negotiations, in companies or groups operating on 'a European and transnational scale'.[56] Delors floated proposals for the EC company statute in June just before the European Council Summit at Hanover.[57] A carefully crafted document it would, unlike the Vredeling proposal, serve as an option which member states companies could choose on top of national law, rather than a compulsory regulation. It proposed trans-European businesses choose to incorporate under European rather than national law, allowing them to write off foreign subsidiary losses and garner other legal and tax benefits. The draft also proposed that companies be allowed to choose one of three models for worker participation: a West German model, where workers elect between a third and a half of the members of a supervisory board; a model used in Belgium, France and Italy, through which employee councils – separate from the main management board – monitor the firm; and a loose collective bargaining system.[58]

The Hanover Summit of June 1988 in effect laid out agreement for the coming three presidencies – Greek, Spanish and French. The basis of this was a pact between France and Germany to press ahead with a broad community programme: liberalizing trade in the internal market, starting discussions on monetary union, and pushing ahead with the construction of some form of social space.

The summer months saw the Commission turn up the pitch in debates over social Europe and EC federalism. In July, Delors declared he foresaw centralization of decision-making in Brussels within the next decade.[59] Questioned about the need for EC legislation to advance Social Europe, he stated 'The common patrimony of European societies, that which distinguishes them from other countries, is their attachment to generalized systems of social protection and employee–union relations, of which the philosophy runs deeper than negotiations on wages alone'.[60] Yet 'the diversity in Europe is such that we cannot envision in the short term legislation to harmonize' social conditions.[61]

The Social Charter's passage through the EC institutions was not easy. On September 7, 1988, Social Affairs Commissioner Marin of Spain presented a report to the Commission on the Social Dimension of the Internal Market. It comprised a 15 page list of proposed areas for action. These included setting up conditions for free worker circulation and settlement. It also emphasized the need to eliminate special treatment of the public sector, a clear nod towards poorer countries such as Spain and Portugal.[62] It also called for the coordination of rules on social security applied to immigrant workers, the unemployed, and the early retired, so they might transfer benefits abroad while searching for work – another free labour-market idea. 'All social politics must have as its priority the contribution to the resolution of the grave problem of unemployment,' the report declared. Marin added that 'the fear of social dumping' was 'unfounded'. Labour costs alone would not govern companies' choice of production sites.[63]

Marin failed to satisfy either unions or employers. At an October meeting in Madrid, the ETUC criticized his plan as 'inadequate', demanding legislation on education leave, security, health, hygiene, worker participation, and irregular work contracts.[64] UNICE Secretary General Zygmunt Tyszkiewicz, on the other hand, criticized what he called some Commission members' 'temptation to swim in the warm seas of social policy, rather than enter the icy, turbulent waters of removal of barriers.'[65] Marin himself was shipped to another job in Delors' new Commission of 1989 and replaced by London University educated – though hardly more specific – Vasso Papandreou of Greece.

Meanwhile, Delors had the package submitted to the Economic and Social Council (ECOSOC) in February 1989. The Council approved it by an overwhelming majority of 135 votes in favour, 22 against, and 8 abstentions. The no votes came from British employer representatives and Confederation Generale du Travail (CGT) officials.[66]

The Commission hit a further snag in January, when the European Court of Justice ruled France would have to pay family benefits to an Italian worker's children even though they lived in Italy.[67] France, along with Germany and Belgium, began to seek new rules to define how family benefits should be treated, a move resisted by Greece, Italy and other labour exporting countries.

The new Commissioner, Vasso Papandreou, meanwhile had taken over the Social Affairs dossier. In a February 28 appearance before the European Parliament Committee on Social Affairs, she pledged social protection would not trail economic efficiency in the move towards '92.[68] On 15 March the Committee's Portuguese inspired report was overwhelmingly adopted by the whole parliament, as a clarification of Marin's September document. A sheaf of declarations proposed the EC fix minimum wages relative to every country's average revenue, as well as rules on information, consultation and participation, union protection, work duration, and irregular work. Irregular work would become a prime focus of Papandreou's efforts.

On March 7, 1989, a meeting of EC labour ministers in Seville agreed eleven to one – the one being Great Britain – to take up ECOSOC's call for a social charter to elaborate rights in the EC. But it soon became apparent the twelve would not agree on the Charter's juridical status, and would settle instead for a 'solemn declaration' rather than a legally binding statement or declaration.[69] This was incorporated into the Commission's April version of the Social Charter, to which an action programme would later be appended outlining proposals on workers rights to be offered by the Commission by mid-1990. The new Charter text contained a list of undefined references to 'decent' wages; health and security rights; transferable unemployment benefits; and mutual recognition of degrees and qualifications. It also stated nations would determine appropriate wage structures for themselves. With British opposition unrelenting, the Spanish Presidency, at the European Council of June 27–28, 1989, scripted an ambiguous communiqué that placed social policy within the purview of national governments. In clear reference to the principle of subsidiarity, the summit communiqué stated that 'the role to be played by Community standards, national legislation and contractual relations must be clearly established'.

The French Contribution: France and Social Europe

French President François Mitterrand had embraced the notion of a 'European Space for Workers' since his first term in office. He first advanced the concept of a European 'social space' in June 1981, incorporating it that October in a paper on a Community relaunch.[70] It was politely ignored. In March 1983 Mitterrand opted to keep the franc in the EMS. In November of that year France proposed to the Council an EC-wide industrial policy that would be coupled with protectionist measures to shelter its economy. Council members rejected the French position, another move that would stoke French eagerness for social Europe as a means of preserving France's social structure.

Mitterrand floated the social theme again in two key speeches during his tenure as EC President in early 1984, at The Hague and Strasbourg. He affirmed it was 'more than desirable that the representatives of workers should get organized at the [Community] level, as do firms and governments.'[71] The Social Affairs Council of June 1984 supported the 'political will to progress in the construction of a European social space'.[72] Delors was nominated to lead the Commission following that month's Fontainebleau Summit, signifying the close link between the EC relaunch of 1985 and the preferences of President Mitterrand.

Domestically, political motives pushed France further towards a European social space as the limits to a liberal market policy became evident during Prime Minister Chirac's administration from 1986–1988. The Chirac government emphasized its commitment to preserving social policy arrangements, in view of the electorate's sensitivity to any cutbacks.[73] The initial enthusiasm in France for 'Europe 1992' turned to a wider concern about its possible effects.[74] By February 1989, 58 percent of the French people interviewed declared themselves worried about the internal market.[75] Only 28 percent considered the economic difficulties it would cause would be limited.[76] It was the Chirac government which commissioned the Aubry report on Social Europe, a text later adopted by the Socialists when it was presented to Rocard's Social Affairs Minister, Jean-Pierre Soisson, in September 1988. It was to serve as a basis for policy during the French Presidency, and was similar to the proposals of the Commission.[77]

Mitterrand ran again for the French presidency in May 1988 as the champion of a 'social democratic, humanist future for Europe', a Europe of liberal economic principles coupled with generous social policies. He won by 54 percent to 46 percent of the vote, and approved Michel Rocard as his Prime Minister. His centre-left government included a near even balance of Socialists, centrist and non-partisan ministers. In a June speech to the National Assembly, Rocard pledged 'France will make progress in the European (social) space a condition of progress registered in other areas'.[78] The Tenth Plan of February 1989 placed priority on the erection of minimum social standards that would prevent 'social dumping' and downward pressure on wages,[79] again signifying the synchronicity between the Commission and Paris. Competition would come through upstream moves to value added production.

The re-election of Mitterrand and a Socialist government opened prospects for a deal between France and Germany. France would support German goals of reducing Europe's dependence on nuclear deterrence, plus German Ostpolitik made possible by a 'kinder, gentler' Soviet Union. Germany would line up behind the EC relaunch with measures to ensure both monetary union, freeing of the internal market, and a Community social policy.

The groundwork was laid for a Franco-German alliance at a May 25, 1988 meeting between the new French Foreign Minister Roland Dumas and his free democrat colleague Genscher, a staunch supporter of the EMS, in Bonn. One report saw Germany lining up with France for the EC relaunch as a means of 'taking advantage of Gorbachev, while resting firmly in Europe'.[80] Mitterrand met Kohl at Evian in early June. 'One more time, one sees from this meeting that it is France and the RFA who are setting the pace for the construction of Europe,' commented

Le Monde. [81] The stage was set for the Hanover Summit of June 1988, where the twelve stressed 'social aspects of progress towards the objectives of 1992'.

The German Presidency

By the latter part of the 1980s Germany saw movement towards Social Europe as a key element of a 1993 package. The package would include German leadership of an integrated European economy, some binding of the Deutschmark in a European Monetary Union, and support for German Ostpolitik.

The reasons for Germany's push for an EEC relaunch are clear. About three-quarters of Germany's exports went to Western Europe throughout the decade, while European trade made up 95 percent of the nation's trade surplus. Germany would lead a unified European economy, as it accounted for 11.5 percent of world trade as against France or Italy's 5 to 6 percent. Its investment was twice that of Great Britain's in 1987, but 2.5 times less than Japan's.[82] The Federal Republic had a strong interest in liberalizing the European market further if it was to have the large internal market from which to sustain a competitive position against Japan. But Germany's highly paid and well-treated workers feared the loss of jobs to poorer EC member states in a liberalized market. German unions therefore led the cries against social dumping and, with their considerable prestige, promoted pan-European union efforts to erect a social 'plinth' in the 1993 programme.

Domestically, the Social Europe flag allowed Kohl's Christian Democrats to restore the corporatist consensus between labour and management that has long been a hallmark of German society. Cooperation with labour and business in opposition to the dual 'materialisms' of Capitalism and Communism is a dearly held tenet of the Christian Democratic faith. As *Suddeutsche Zeitung* foreign editor Josef Joffe said in an August 1988 interview: 'Thatcher revived the class struggle when she said "I'm going to take on the miners – I'm going to break them." But that is as alien to German thinking as Catholics questioning the immaculate conception.'[83]

In the face of concern over Japanese inroads, there was some flickering of liberal economic policy in Germany in the early part of the decade. Count Lambsdorff enunciated principles in a September 1982 memo, calling for cuts in social spending, taxes and subsidies. The memo marked the end of the Free Democrats' alliance with the Social Democrats, a union that had lasted since 1969. The new Christian-Democratic–Free Democrat coalition pledged some reforms, but did not change much.[84] Rather, regional subsidies rose, as did support for new technologies.

The government offered some slight cuts in welfare benefits and legislation to promote part time work. But it did not change the fabric of the German economy.

Meanwhile, government–union strife was on the rise, as employers resisted union calls for cuts in working hours and protection against irregular work schedules.[85] The Kohl government pushed through an amended strike law limiting unemployment benefits for workers on sympathy strikes.[86] At the January 1987 general elections the Christian Democrats won only 44.3 percent of the vote, down four points from 1983.[87]

The domestic situation would grow still more tense. A late 1987 economic slowdown brought rising cries for a budget stimulus, plus industrialist complaints over high labour costs.[88] By Spring 1988 unions were protesting the 'démontage social',[89] as well as the closing of a Krupp steel mill. The same season saw CD regional losses to the SPD in Schleswig Holstein. More worries came in June, when it appeared the state pension system would collapse, meaning Germans might have to work longer before retirement.[90]

The tense domestic situation was beginning to affect Germans' attitudes toward the EC. A July poll[91] showed only 49 percent of the populace held favourable attitudes towards the EC, down a stunning 13 points in 6 months. *Le Monde* of June 17 wrote that Germans were accusing Kohl of 'sacrificing national interests to the European idea'.

For a politically beleaguered Kohl, Social Europe was one means of reforging a domestic consensus while lining up support for Europe '93. Social Europe might also prevent Japanese internal investment, increasingly feared by Bonn, by raising worker costs around Europe and depriving Japan of cheap labour in countries to which German manufacturers could not transfer operations, without severe political consequences.[92]

In March 1988 Kohl appealed to German business to actively sustain the social market economy.[93] At the National Europa Conferences of December 1988 and August 1989 – shaped by Kohl to win corporate and union backing for '1992' – the Chancellor hammered home his message: The Federal Republic's social market economy had won widespread acceptance in the EC; Germany's main advantage in international competition was its record of stability; he would resist any trend in the EC policy that promoted social dumping; not least, he advised German employers to aggressively promote Germany's participation practices in the Community.

Trade unions became Kohl's pivotal domestic ally in promoting EC social policy. The shift from a public stance of confrontation on domestic economic policy to widespread agreement between government and unions on EC affairs came in April 1988, at a meeting between Kohl, Labour Minister Blum and DGB President Ernst Breit. The three agreed social standards were to be preserved, and social policy would be treated on an equal footing with economic objectives in the EC relaunch and domestically. The unions attended the Europa conferences, while extending their European alliances. In this they were sustained by the prestige of Germany's social market economy; the leading positions occupied by German trade unionists in the ETUC, the abundant resources of such unions as IG-Chemie or IG-Metall, relative to the hard-pressed unions in France, Italy, Spain or Britain; and not least by the agreement between the DGB and the employer organizations of June 1989 in favour of a Social Charter.[94] The government, employers and unions subsequently agreed on a nine-point plan for minimum social rights, to be incorporated into the Commission's action programme.[95] The German unions led the campaign during the French presidency for binding legislation, and sought to promote worker rights for consultation and collective bargaining, notably with respect to the debates on the European Company Statute.

Germany's leading role in the EC burst on the world's attention at Hanover.[96] The heads of government endorsed their Finance Ministers' accord to liberalize capital movements in the EC by July 1, 1990.[97] This decision signified a political commitment to the internal market's success and provided a timetable for enactment. Britain won commitment to a financial services regime; Chancellor Kohl acquiesced in the appointment of a committee to study a possible move to monetary union. All heads of government agreed to a statement to the effect that '93 must benefit all citizens.

The Hanover communiqué itself was a model of diplomatic tact. It noted 'the achievement of a grand single market offers the surest means . . . to promote employment and the growth of general prosperity for all the community, to the benefit of all citizens'. But the Council decided 'the internal market must be considered in such a way as to benefit all citizens of the Community. To this end, it is necessary not only to ameliorate the conditions of work and the levels of the quality of life, but also to assure better protection of health and work security in places of work'.[98]

Kohl acknowledged the communiqué included the Social emphasis to reflect his countrymen's fears about having their high wages and labour standards undercut in the coming single market.[99]

A *Financial Times* editorial of July 18 1988 praised the West German presidency for forwarding 'more internal market liberalization measures, even than Britain'. But the seeds for a liberal–federalist clash had already been sown.

Great Britain and the Liberal Camp

As the Social Charter debate progressed Thatcherite Britain became the lone vocal critic. Powerful ideological, domestic and international imperatives underlay this stance.

At the most basic level, Social Europe flew in the face of Thatcher's basic vision of the EC and everything she had attempted to achieve domestically during her terms in office. Simply put, the Thatcher vision saw deregulation of factor markets and liberalization of trade as the surest means of ensuring economic growth, fighting unemployment, and building a mobile and dynamic domestic and European economy. The Economic Community would be 'open for business', with the Rome Treaty interpreted as a 'charter for economic liberty'.[100] On the domestic labour front this would mean weakening unions, while reforming health, education and other costly social programmes to concentrate on the long-term unemployed.

At home Thatcher's third term, following her June 1987 victory, had as its centre-piece the dismantlement of 'municipal socialism' including major revisions of basic social programmes. Unions, too, had been weakened by legislative measures and economic growth in non-unionized industries, as non-unionism doubled over four years from 1980 to 1984[101] and union membership fell 20.7 percent, 10.5 million, from 1979 to 1986.[102] A June 1988 law protected non-strikers' right to work. The act also allowed employees to leave unions and barred employers from deducting non-members' union dues from wages.[103]

For Thatcher, freer labour markets were an essential component of efforts to revive the UK's economy. The Tory government boasted in a March 1989 paper that 'since March 1983, 2.8 million jobs and training places have been created, with 1.6 million new jobs of which 863 million are full time . . . trade unions create an artificial barrier to the operation of an efficient labour market, and it makes sense to reduce their freedom of action'.[104]

Prime Minister Thatcher was a notable proponent of the liberal, internal market principles advocated in Lord Cockfield's White Book, presented to the Council in 1985. Here was a chance for positive British EC diplomacy after the bitter debates on the organization's budget of the early 1980s.[105] Domestic and foreign trade impera-tives would mesh with what Thatcher thought was in the EC's own best interest. High unemployment relative to the US and Japan, thought to stem from the high cost of welfare systems,[106] would be cured with labour mobility and a freer labour market, as Thatcher was attempting to do in Britain. Dual labour markets consisting of highly compensated workers and the unemployed would be eliminated.[107]

Liberalization would also eliminate Continental mercantilist barriers, particu-larly in West Germany, which accounted for roughly 40 percent of Great Britain's trade deficit.

The liberal offensive in the Community gathered momentum during the 1986 British Presidency. London's 'Big Bang' of October stimulated emulation in the major EC financial markets; an Action Programme for Employment and Growth[108] through the freeing of EC labour markets was presented. But it was scotched by an alliance between the Commission and the early 1987 Belgian Presidency.

As calls for Social Europe progressed, they clashed head on with Thatcher's liberal ideals. Social Europe marked, in Thatcher's eyes, an attempt to re-constitute through Brussels all the socialist scaffolding she was struggling against back home. Thatcher came out against Social Europe in her Bruges and Brighton speeches of September 20, 1988 and October 14, 1988 respectively. At the Brighton party conference, she declared to the Tory faithful 'we have not worked all these years to free Britain from the paralysis of socialism only to see it creep in through the back door of central control and bureaucracy from Brussels'.

She also enunciated a number of key themes at the Collège d'Europe, at Bruges.[109] Social policy was a prime area for the application of the principle of subsidiarity, allowing for the diversity of labour market conditions and customs across the Community.[110] Priority in social policy was to go to labour flexibility and hence to job creation, with government efforts going to help the long-term unemployed.[111]

The Labour party, on the other hand, came to embrace the EC precisely for the 'creeping socialism' it offered. Labour's 1987 manifesto removed references to leaving the European Community, and in February 1988 the party signed onto a

European Socialist manifesto based largely on support for the 'social dimension' of 1992.[112]

In the words of one unionist at the Bournemouth September 8, 1988 meeting of the Trade Union Congress (TUC), which Delors addressed: 'for nine years we have been imprisoned . . . the light at the end of the tunnel is the EC's social rights'.[113] Said Ron Todd of the Transport and General Workers' Union 'In the short term we have not a cat in hell's chance of achieving that [the EC Social Charter] in Westminster'.[114]

The Thatcher vision had much in common with the ideas advanced by President Reagan on the other side of the Atlantic during his term in office. Thus, the Social Europe debate – for Thatcher and her EC adversaries – became a part of the broader debate over Britain's 'special relationship' with the United States as well as what role Washington would play in a continent changing economically and politically. This too was enunciated in Thatcher's Bruges speech, as she called on the Community to preserve 'that Atlantic Community – that Europe on both sides of the Atlantic which is our greatest inheritance and our greatest strength'. But this too would place her on a collision course with rising continental calls for disarmament in the face of *perestroika*, German efforts to bind Moscow in some pan-European security system and the overall need to re-think NATO, following the collapse of the Warsaw Pact.

One major weakness of the free market crusade was the fragility of the British economy. The freeing of foreign exchange controls had led to a massive build-up in Britain's overseas corporate assets.[115] Free wage bargaining allowed union monopolies and management to push up real wages faster than overseas competitors. Free exchange rates led first to an overvaluation of sterling, and then to its weakening as oil prices fell in 1986. The manufacturing sector of 20 percent GNP – the smallest among the leading industrial countries – proved inadequate to claw the country back to current account surplus. So the government engineered a boom, facilitating the Tory victory of June 1987. But the trade deficit widened, while interest rates and inflation rose again. Britain was advertised[116] as a choice location for investment inside the EC, with a low strike record; low labour costs; and low corporate tax rates.[117] Thatcher's arguments against the Social Charter were therefore that it would raise labour costs, create unemployment, and scare away United States and Japanese investment. Its thrust was incompatible with the Tory government's domestic labour market policies.[118] The main difference lay in the argument on labour market 'rigidities': for Thatcher, they had to be removed. For Germany, they were built in to the social market economy: the competition in the Community between regional authorities or national governments to attract multinational investments[119] would be over access to high technologies, requiring high cost but trained manpower.[120]

The Mediterranean Presidencies

The Greek and Spanish Presidencies from July 1988 through July 1989 were essentially a socialist bridge between the German leadership of early 1988 through the French Presidency that would follow Spain. Nevertheless, the Spanish Socialists in particular presented some complications, as they sought to join the Continental consensus for Social Europe while advancing their goals of encouraging rapid economic growth and investment in underdeveloped Spain.

Spain's socialist trade union, the Union General de Trabajadores (UGT), launched a nationwide strike on December 14, 1988, only weeks before Spain was to lead the EC. The strike marked the culmination of several years' tension between the once tightly bound Socialist party and labour organization.[121] The Gonzalez government had largely abandoned its traditional socialist views and blue collar support by doggedly pursuing austerity measures throughout the mid 1980s. Government priorities remained reducing inflation and the nation's budget deficit, while using Spain's attractive low-wage economy to draw European, Japanese and American investment. By late 1980s hard-line union leaders were accusing Gonzalez of being a 'trendy neo-liberal' or closet 'Thatcherite'.[122]

Indeed, much of the government's domestic tack appeared to fly in the face of 'Social Europe'. As a proportion of GNP, social spending in Spain was lower than in any other EC nation except Portugal,[123] and had declined in relative terms since 1983. Company profits had quadrupled from 1987 to 1988. Also, the government encouraged the use of temporary and part-time work to cut unemployment, with these contracts rising from 5 percent of all new agreements in 1987 to 20 percent of all labour contracts by 1989.[124] By 1988, 73 percent of the unemployed were officially without benefits.

Internationally, one might expect this domestic thriftiness to lead Spain to oppose an activist EC social programme, particularly as a low labour cost country attempting to attract investment. But Spain could only gain from unanimity with the EC consensus. Moreover, Gonzalez owed a major debt to Kohl for his championing of Spain's application for EC membership, and Madrid's request for a major portion of EC funding. Cooperation with the other eleven was Spain's only option if it was to continue to earn political and economic support.

Moreover, Spanish union membership – while declining – still made up between 15 and 20 percent of Gonzalez' electoral support.[125] As a closet monetarist, Gonzalez could, like Mitterrand, use the Social Europe flag as a means of retaining his Socialist label. As one editorial described the Madrid Summit: 'The Socialist credentials of Mr Mitterrand and Mr Gonzalez have in recent years come under fire from their own trade unions; that very questioning probably makes both men all the more inclined towards a socialist gesture on the European stage.'[126]

Some problems did arise during the Greek and Spanish presidencies. Commissioner Marin downplayed the risks of social dumping, a reflection of Madrid's views. In late February 1989 his replacement, Papandreou, helped rally the European Parliament's Committee for Social Affairs to support a Portuguese-inspired report advocating tough social legislation out of Brussels. The plenary adopted it overwhelmingly in mid-March as a decided attempt to correct Marin's text.[127]

The main accomplishment of the Greek Presidency was agreement at the Rhodes European Council on the Commission's proposal for a yearly report on employment. The Spanish presidency in April 1989 had the Council adopt three work rules on minimal health and safety standards at the workplace; machinery standards; and rules for protective clothing.[128] There were some disagreements on social matters under both presidencies. Greece, as noted above, and Italy opposed French and West German attempts to tighten regulations on family benefits for aliens. The Mediterranean states and France did not join the German, Benelux consensus demanding juridical social instruments, advanced at the Madrid Summit.[129]

Preparations for the French Presidency: 1988–89

Mitterrand's France took the Social Charter under its wing from the Hanover Summit onwards; it was to become the centrepiece of France's achievement as EC leader the next year. Mitterrand presented Social Europe as an indispensable element of social cohesion along the path to European Union. President and government formed a united front to have the Social Charter on the agenda at the Strasbourg European Council. Preparation had started in September, 1988, when Edith Cresson, the Minister for European Affairs, created a study group in September with noted 'personalities' from French 'economic and social life' to study the EC. There would be three emphases: the market, monetary systems, and social Europe.[130] In a February interview she affirmed 'the young people of Europe will not be swayed by talk of capital movements and the free flow of goods. What is needed is the cultural dimension – a humanistic message'.[131]

In February 1989 the French Government published its Tenth Plan, calling for the establishment of minimum standards to prevent downward wage competition.[132] Echoing the German view, the plan affirmed competitiveness would be assured by a move upstream to value added production.

Over the spring, French Labour Minister Soisson took a pragmatic view of the Charter, saying it could be adopted as a solemn declaration that would not be binding and would respect subsidiarity. French Prime Minister Rocard echoed that view, saying 'it would be, at this stage, illusory, absurd to search to harmonize all the social statutes of Europe'.[133] The French Council of State advised the government that the Commission be held to staying within Treaty provisions.[134]

Nonetheless, the French government edged towards having the Charter adopted by a majority Council vote. Spring saw Thatcher grow increasingly isolated, as Thatcher and Kohl did battle over NATO nuclear policy, and Bush aligned with Germany. In a June tour of the continent the US President called for further moves to European integration. The *Independent* commented: 'It was evident during Mr Bush's week-long European tour that if there is a special relationship being nurtured by the United States with a European country, that country is West Germany, not Britain.'[135] The Tories were trounced in the June European Parliament elections. On 12 June, Britain stood alone among the twelve labour ministers in opposition to the Charter. The British minister, Norman Fowler, said: 'We are being asked to sign a blank cheque before anyone has defined what the rights would be, and what they would cost.'[136]

Prime Minister Gonzalez, however, was eager to avoid a confrontation with Thatcher at the Madrid Summit. The communiqué placed social policy within national governments' prerogatives.[137] The Social Charter thus passed into the hands of the French Presidency.

There were three key elements to the politicking that led up to the Strasbourg European Council 'solemn declaration' and action programme: the Commission proposal for a European Company Statute; The Commission's powers under the SEA; and French policy to get the Social Charter confirmed.

The Company Statute

The Commission proposed a new version of the EC Company Statute in July 1989. Bowing towards Germany, the new version proposed that member states could require companies to obey national laws on their own territories.[138] Delors also proposed the statute be considered by majority vote.[139]

Reaction to the proposals was mixed. Britain favoured aids to transcontinental mergers and restructuring, but opposed any precedent for action out of Brussels on worker participation. Thatcher's government also opposed taking action by majority vote.[140]

Germany, followed by the Dutch and to some extent the Irish, matched the British objections for opposing reasons. Germany opposed the majority vote for fear the Council would use it to legislate social standards downward. Also, German unions believed the statute might open the door for companies to avoid strict German law, putting pressure on them to give back social gains.

Finally, German corporations, anxious to avoid hostile takeovers, realized the presence of union members on their boards helped protect them. This meshed with Ministry of Economics' fear that Mittelstand firms might become prey to European predators.[141] So, Great Britain's open market approach and Germany's protectionist corporate networks conspired to keep this key element of social policy firmly within the domain of state prerogatives.

The Commission Powers

Delors told the European Parliament on September 13, 1989 the Commission would not seek to stretch the meaning of Article 118A to cover more than it implied.[142] But if the legal framework proved too narrow, the Commission would suggest to the heads of government an enlargement of the Treaty basis for social policy in the intergovernmental conference, planned for end 1990.

French Policy

In the build-up to Strasbourg – and in the face of German and Benelux demands for concrete action on nine points – France offered its own proposals in late September. But they were all on relatively minor and non-controversial issues. Paris called for coordination of social security benefits for students; coordination of regimes for 'retraite complémentaire'; and a resolution to cover the exclusion of the handicapped.[143]

The Commission's final version of the Social Charter was completed on September 27, 1989. The text amounted to a package recognizing employees' rights to minimum health and security standards; greater facilities for trans-frontier job mobility, notably for skilled personnel; a 'fair wage', whatever that might mean; rights to social protection and the freedom of association; the prospect for life-long training; equality of treatment between men and women; a right to consultation and information, especially for workers in multinational companies; the harmonization of work conditions throughout the Community and provisions for old age, children and the handicapped. Papandreou emphasized wage agreements and definitions would be left to national governments and groups to decide.[144]

The French Presidency of late 1989, and the Social Charter

With the Social Charter too controversial for the Commission to handle, the French Presidency took charge. Matters had come to a head with Great Britain in June 1989, when the Christian Democrat Social Affairs Ministers from Germany and the Benelux countries had strongly endorsed the Commission's April 1989 draft Social Charter; the Tories had been trounced in the European parliamentary elections of June; and the German unions and employers had signed an accord to preserve social peace in 'Standort Deutschland'. There was to be no internal market without a social programme. Both Bonn and Paris favoured a Social Charter for workers, rather than for citizens.[145] The French made no secret of their determination to have the charter adopted by majority.

The French Presidency had its text for the Charter adopted at the Social Affairs Council of October 30, with Britain withholding its support, as it would again at Strasbourg. There were some problems. Portugal, allied with Spain, opposed requirements for host states to give citizens and aliens equal benefits – a possible impediment to labour imports from low-wage countries.[146] Soisson bent over backwards to woo the trade unions in France, Germany, Italy and the Benelux countries, while seeking to accommodate Spanish and Portuguese demands for access of their workers and firms to public works' contracts.[147] He managed to bring Eire and Denmark around to support for the Charter, by reference to the Commission staying within its Treaty powers.

On the other side of the coin, West Germany, Belgium, Italy, the Netherlands and Luxembourg requested a nine point action plan be attached to the package. The plan would specify four weeks of holiday yearly plus paid public holidays; 14 weeks' paid maternity leave; free government job placement and minimum acceptable standards for protection in the workplace. The nine points were turned down, but served as an input to the Commission's Action Programme.[148]

Faced with rising ETUC attacks on the non-binding Charter, Soisson adopted a hard posture in October against Thatcher, saying he would oppose any text that was watered down. In any event the Charter was assured of support, though the controversial content and juridical status was to be passed onto the Action Programme. Moreover, he affirmed for Ireland and Denmark that the Commission would stay within its treaty powers.

In November, the Commission adopted its action programme, comprising 45 measures contained in 26 articles.[149] The most controversial matters covered wage competition in subcontracting and procurement; consultation; and worker participation. Numerous measures on health and safety were promised under Article 118A. The Commission tempered its respect for the principle of subsidiarity – whereby the states would remain primarily responsible for areas such as collective bargaining, non-discrimination, and minimum wages – with reference to the desirability of achieving 'convergence' in national policy. The Commission recommended the states not allow their social security systems to prevent the free movement of employees, and pledged to elaborate criteria with respect to minimum wage policy. The Commission's first proposals were offered in January 1990, covering such topics as 'atypical work' with a view to limiting labour market competition; working hours; work contracts; and an EC instrument for information, consultation and participation.

Social policy, for France, was one 'plinth' in the construction of Europe, including monetary policy and other 'accompanying measures'. At Strasbourg, Mitterrand secured the German government's support for an intergovernmental conference to be opened under the Italian EC Presidency during the second half of 1990. In response to the breaching of the Berlin Wall on November 8, 1989, the heads of state and government also pledged support for the German people to 'refined unity through free self-determination'.

Question

You are in the situations room of your key policy committee preparing for the post-Strasbourg Summit of December 8–9, 1989. The doors are barred. The room has been swept for bugs. No newspaper reporters are in earshot. The drinks have just been served. The air is heavy with cigar smoke. This is no place for pompous pontificating. It is a no-holds-barred debate on the Social Charter, and its significance to you. Assuming the following roles, explain your policy position on it with a view to the substance, process and linkages of policy.

1. The Commission President
2. The French President
3. The German Chancellor

4. The British Prime Minister
5. The Spanish Prime Minister
6. M. Bezzler and Bain of Existence Consultancy Company. Your clients are frantically faxing to find out what this Social Charter is about. Is it serious? How did it get to where it is?

Notes

1. Reuters.
2. Marin report, September 7, 1988.
3. For a superb overview of EC social policy and labour markets see Chris Brewster and Paul Teague, *European Community Social Policy*, Institute of Personnel Management, London, 1989.
4. Ibid.
5. Ibid. A regulation is an EC statute which is immediately binding in all twelve member countries. A directive is a statute which states a goal to be achieved, but leaves it up to member states to decide how to accomplish it through national legislation. In principle, however, it is often as narrowly worded and binding as a regulation.
6. Ibid.
7. Ibid.
8. Ibid.
9. Ibid.
10. Ibid.
11. Ibid.
12. Ibid.
13. Ibid.
14. Michael Shanks, *European Social Policy, Today and Tomorrow*, Pergamon Press, Oxford, 1977.
15. Brewster and Teague.
16. Ibid.
17. Ibid.
18. Extracts from 'La politique sociale de la Communauté', *Observatoire Social Européen*, August, 1986. Also Ivor Richards, 'Le réexamen de la dimension communautaire de la politique sociale à moyen terme s'impose', *Bulletin d'Informations sociales*, ILO, No. 1/85, pp. 11–18. Commissioner Richards responded that unemployment rates and part time work had risen to double digits. Of the fifteen directives adopted by the Council since the launching of the June 1974 Social Action Programme, eight related to work conditions. The Commission's directives on participation had been stalled. The dialogue between 'social partners' had engendered acrimony.
19. Brewster and Teague.
20. Ibid.
21. Ibid.
22. Ibid.
23. Ibid.
24. Ibid.
25. Ibid.

26. Ibid.
27. Ibid.
28. Ibid.
29. Ibid.
30. Anthony M. Messina, 'Political Impediments to the Resumption of Labour Migration to Western Europe', *West European Politics*, January 1990.
31. Brewster and Teague.
32. Ibid.
33. *Financial Times*, April 24, 1989.
34. Ibid.
35. Brewster and Teague.
36. Ibid.
37. Ibid.
38. *Financial Times*, April 24, 1989.
39. Shanks.
40. *L'Année Politique, Economique et Sociale en France*, 1983, Paris, Editions du Moniteur, 1984, pp. 35–6.
41. *Pour Une Nouvelle Politique Sociale en Europe*. Avant-propos de M. Jacques Delors. Paris, *Economica*, 1984. This is the compendium of a conference at the French Senate, held October 6–8, 1983. It was part of the wider definition of French Community policy, going on at that time. In September 1983 the French government had presented to the other member states a document. 'Une Nouvelle Etape pour l'Europe: un espace commun de l'industrie et de la recherche', *Europe Documents*, No. 1274. Agence Europe, September 16, 1983.
42. 'Les orientations de la Commission des Communautés Européennes', *Futuribles*, March, 1985, pp. 3–18.
43. Brewster and Teague.
44. Commission des CE, Patrick Venturini, *Un Espace Social Européen a l'Horizon 1992*, Luxembourg, Office des publications officielles, 1988, Exhibit 4, pp. 93–96.
45. Ibid.
46. *Observatoire Social Européen*, 'La politique social de la Communauté', August, 1986, pp. 21–23.
47. 'La Commission européene fixe les lignes directrices de la politique sociale communautaire pour les années à venir.' *Information*, Commission of the European Communities, February 24, 1988.
48. Economie Européenne, Commission des Communautés Européennes, *1992: La Nouvelle Economie Européenne*, No. 35, March 1988, p. 21.
49. Commission Européenne, 1992, *Le Défi*. Preface by Jacques Delors, Flammarion, 1988. Growth would accompany the measures, along with the creation of between 1.8 to 5 million jobs. Inevitably, though, greater emphasis on market forces would lead to an initial loss of jobs inherent to a process of corporate rationalization and restructuring.
50. *Financial Times*, May 9, 1988; *Le Monde*, May 8–9, 1988.
51. *Europolitique*, No. 1475, February 25, 1989.
52. *Europolitique*, No. 1486, April 8, 1989.
53. This amounts to a package, giving employees minimum health and security standards; greater facilities for trans-frontier job mobility, notably for skilled personnel; a 'fair wage'; rights to social protection and the freedom of association; the prospect of life-long training; equality of treatment between men and women; a right to consultation

and information, especially for workers in multinational companies; the harmonization of work conditions throughout the Community and provisions for old age, children and the handicapped.

54. On cooperative federalism, see Simon Bulmer and Wolfgang Wessels, *The European Council, Decision-Making in European Politics*, London, Macmillan, 1987. The German Presidency had the Hanover European Council insert an initial reference to social policy; the Greek Presidency had the Rhodes European council support the Commission's demands for a yearly report on employment in the Community; the Spanish Presidency managed British susceptibilities in an ambiguous communiqué that placed social policy within the purview of national governments.

55. *Le Monde*, May 8, 9, 14, 1988; *Financial Times*, May 9, 1988.

56. *Le Monde*, May 14, 1988.

57. *Financial Times*, June 11, 1988.

58. *Financial Times*, October 17, 1988.

59. *Financial Times*, July 7, 1988.

60. *Liberation*, August 29, 1988.

61. Ibid.

62. *Marché Communautaire*, No. 1428.

63. *Le Monde*, September 7, 1988.

64. *Le Monde*, October 12, 1988 and *Financial Times*, November 9, 1988.

65. *Financial Times*, November 9, 1988.

66. *La Tribune de L'Expansion*, February 24, 1989.

67. *Le Monde*, March 25, 1989.

68. *Europolitique*, No. 1478, March 8, 1989.

69. *International Herald Tribune*, March 22, 1989.

70. 'Le gouvernement français souhaite relancer la politique sociale Européenne', *Le Monde*, June 12, 1981; Memorandum sur la relance de la Communauté Européenne, Bulletin des CE, No. 11, 1981; Roland Dumas, 'Espace social européen', *Le Monde*, March 20, 1982.

71. 'Une victoire de la Communauté sur elle-même', May 24, 1984. In François Mitterrand, *Réflexions sur la Politique extérieure de la France*, Paris, Fayard, 1986, p. 288.

72. *Journal Officiel des Communautés Européennes*, No. C. 175/1 Conclusions du Conseil du 22 juin, 1984.

73. On June 18, 1987, Social Affairs Minister Philippe Seguin, in his speech to the National Assembly on the financing of the social security regime, stated that 'the cathedral' constructed in 1945 had to be preserved. Quoted in *L'Année politique*, 1987. Paris, Editions du Moniteur, 1988, p. 305.

74. By February 1989, 58 percent of French people interviewed declared themselves worried about the internal market. *Le Monde*, SOFRES, March 3, 1989.

75. *Le Monde*, March 3, 1989.

76. Ibid.

77. Martine Aubry, *Pour une Europe sociale*, September, 1989, Paris, La Documentation Française.

78. La déclaration de politique générale du premier ministre au Parlement. 'Construire un nouvel espoir', *Le Monde*, July 1, 1988.

79. Un entretien avec Lionel Stoleru, 'L'Europe sociale doit orienter les mutations industrielles vers la valeur ajoutée', *La Tribune de l'Expansion*, February 27, 1989.

80. *Le Monde*, May 25, 1988.

81. *Le Monde*, June 4, 1988.
82. OECD Economic Surveys, Germany, 1988/89.
83. *Financial Times*, August 15, 1988.
84. Josef Esser, State, Business and Trade Unions in West Germany after the 'Political Wende', *West European Politics*, Vol. 9, April 1986, No. 2, pp. 198–214.
85. *Financial Times*, December 15, 1986.
86. *Financial Times*, April 8, 1986.
87. Elizabeth Noelle–Neumann, 'Europa-das unbekannte, ungeliebte Wesen?' *Frankfurter Allgemeine Zeitung*, December 19, 1988; 'Europe: la grande prudence des Allemands face à 1992', *Les Echos*, March 6, 1989.
88. *Financial Times*, December 1, 1987.
89. *Stuttgarter Nachrichten*, March 6, 1988.
90. *Financial Times*, June 7, 1988.
91. *Financial Times*, July 25, 1988.
92. *Financial Times*, May 24, 1988.
93. Presse und Informationsamt der Bundesregierung, nr. 40/S 333, Bonn, March 22, 1988. Ansprache des Bundeskanzlers, '*Europas Zukunft-Vollendung des Binnenmarktes 1992*'. Nr. 172/S 1525. Bonn. December 9, 1988. Erklärung des Bundeskanzlers zur Eröffnung. Nationale Europe-Konferenz in Bonn. Also Handelsblatt, August 31, 1989, '*Europakonferenz: Kohl will Mitbestimmungsmodell offensiv vertreten*'.
94. Arbeitgeber, *Bundesvereinigung der Deutschen Arbeitgeberverbande*, Jahresbericht, 1989, pp. 135–137.
95. *Financial Times*, October 31, 1989.
96. Peter Hort, 'Ein Bilanz der deutschen EC-Präsidentschaft', *Europa-Archiv* 15, 1988, pp. 421–428. François Puaux, *La politique internationale des années quatre-vingt*, Paris, Presses Universitaires de France, 1989, pp. 159–177.
97. France and Italy agreed provisional on EC success in approximating indirect and withholding tax regimes. Exemptions were granted for the weaker currency new comers of Spain, Portugal and Greece.
98. Conseil Européen de Hanovre. 27–28/6/88. Conclusions de la Présidence sur le 'Volet Social'.
99. *Financial Times*, June 12, 1988.
100. Mrs Thatcher's Bruges Speech. Also, 'The Conservatives at Brighton: PM warns on Brussels "socialism"'. *Financial Times*, October 15, 1988.
101. *Financial Times*, May 3, 1988.
102. *The Economist*, May 7, 1988.
103. *Le Monde*, August 5, 1988.
104. *Removing Barriers to Employment, Proposals for the further reform of industrial relations and trade union law*, March 1989, Cm. 655, London, Her Majesty's Stationery Office.
105. Christopher Tugenhat and William Wallace, *Options for British Foreign Policy in the 1990s*, London, Routledge, 1988; Angelika Volle, *Grossbritannien und der europäischen Einigungsprozess*, Bonn, 1988. (*Arbeitspapiere zur Internationalen Politik des Forschunginstituts der Deutschen Gesellschaft für Auswartige Politik*, Vol. 51.)
106. Murray Seeger, Europe Social Programs: endangered species, *International Herald Tribune*, March 12, 1981. Also *Le Monde*, May 29, 1982. Assessment of the early 1980s by the then Social Affairs Commissioner Ivor Richards, 'Le réexamen de la dimension communautaire de la politique social à moyen terme s'impos', *Bulletin d'Informations*

sociales. ILO. No. 1/85 pp. 11–18; 'Devant les prélèvements communautaires', *Revue du Marché Commun*, juin 1985. No. 288, pp. 301–306.

107. Office des Publications Officielles de la Communauté. *La Politique Sociale de la Communauté*, 8/87, pp. 12–13; 23–24, 60. Parlement Européen, *Documents de Séance*, Strasbourg, August 16, 1988. Serie A. Doc. A2-177/88.

108. Brewster and Teague, pp. 94–99. Résolution du Conseil du 22 décembre 1986 concernant un programme d'action pour la croissance de l'emploi (86/C 340/02).

109. Mrs Thatcher's Bruges Speech, *Financial Times*, September 21, 1988.

110. Francis Maude, Grossbritannien kan dem Entwurf nicht zustimmen, *Handelsblatt*, December 7, 1989.

111. *Services de Presse de l'Ambassade de Grande-Bretagne*, Paris, Textes et Déclaration, January 9, 1989. Lynda Chalker, Le Dimension sociale de l'Europe: les dangers à éviter, Speech at Brussels, November 23, 1988.

112. *Financial Times*, February 9, 1988.

113. *Libération*, September 9, 1988.

114. *The Guardian*, September 9, 1988.

115. From 1985–88, the outflow of foreign direct investment from Britain was over 18 percent of gross fixed capital formation, compared to 4.5 percent and 4.1 percent in Germany and France. OECD Economic Surveys. Germany. 1988/1989. Exhibit, p. 122.

116. 'They use us', Thatcher declared, 'as a springboard in Europe. They come here because of our traditions and because we are British.' *Service de Presse de l'Ambassade de Grande-Bretagne*, Paris, Textes et Declarations, July 29, 1988. Extracts from BBC interview with Prime Minister Thatcher, July 27, 1988.

117. Corporate tax rates lowered from 52 to 35 percent in the March 1988 budget, Michael Prowse, Lawson's cultural revolution, *Financial Times*, March 19, 1988.

118. *Removing Barriers to Employment, Proposals for the further reform of industrial relations and trade union law*, March 1989, Cm. 655, London, Her Majesty's Stationery Office.

119. 'Les Etats membres ont rivalisé pour attirer les capitaux internationaux, par exemple les usines de production automobile.' Quoted from the first Commission report on Employment in the EC. *Le Monde*, July 21, 1989.

120. David Hart, Helping the Poor Get Richer, *International Management*, June 1989, pp. 41–43.

121. Richard Gillespie, The Break-up of the 'Socialist Family': Party–Union Relations in Spain, 1982–89, *West European Politics*, Vol. 13, No. 1, January 1990.

122. Ibid.

123. Ibid.

124. Ibid.

125. Ibid.

126. *Financial Times*, June 12, 1989.

127. *Europolitique*, March 15, 1989.

128. *Europolitique*, April 8, 1989.

129. *Le Monde*, June 14, 1989.

130. *Le Monde*, September 3, 1988.

131. *International Management*, February 1989.

132. Une entretien avec Lionel Stoleru, 'L'Europe sociale doit orienter les mutations industrielles vers la valeur ajoutée,' *La Tribune de l'Expansion*, February 27, 1989.

133. *Le Monde*, April 17, 1989.

134. Un rapport du Conseil d'Etat à M. Rocard, *Le Monde*, June 10, 1989.
135. *The Independent*, June 2, 1989.
136. *Financial Times*, June 13, 1989.
137. Extracts from the summit communiqué, *Financial Times*, June 28, 1989.
138. *Financial Times*, July 13, 1989.
139. Ibid.
140. Brewster and Teague, pp. 91–4; 141; 225–227.
141. *Frankfurter Allgemeine Zeitung*, January 20, 1989.
142. Président Delors, La cohésion économique et sociale est au coeur de notre projet, Extracts from speech of September 13, to the European Parliament. *La Semaine Européenne*. No. 25, 22 September 1989. Also Charte Sociale: vers un élargissement des bases en matière sociale? *Europolitique*, September 16, 1989. No. 1523. Nonetheless, Article 118A has been interpreted as giving the Commission a right of initiative in fostering collective negotiations between the social partners.
143. *Europolitique*, No. 1526, September 27, 1989.
144. Assemblée Consultative Economique et Sociale, Communiqué de Presse, *M. Jean-Pierre Soisson au CES Européen*, October 19, 1989.
145. *The Wall Street Journal*, September 21, 1989; *Financial Times*, September 29, 1989.
146. *Financial Times*, October 30, 1989.
147. Communautés Européennes, Comité Economique et Social, Bruxelles, October 19, 1989, *M. Jean-Pierre Soisson au CES Européen*.
148. *Le Monde*, November 1, 1989.
149. Commission des Communautés Européennes. Information. *La Commission présente un programme d'action dans le domaine de l'emploi, des relations industrielles, des affaires sociales et de la formation*, Bruxelles, November 20, 1989, *Europolitique*, No. 1542, November 22, 1989, Charte Sociale: La Commission présente son programme d'action.